Dynamic Modeling and Simulation for Control Systems

Dynamic Modeling and Simulation for Control Systems

Editor

Adrian Olaru

MDPI • Basel • Beijing • Wuhan • Barcelona • Belgrade • Manchester • Tokyo • Cluj • Tianjin

Editor
Adrian Olaru
University Politehnica
of Bucharest
Bucharest
Romania

Editorial Office
MDPI
St. Alban-Anlage 66
4052 Basel, Switzerland

This is a reprint of articles from the Special Issue published online in the open access journal *Mathematics* (ISSN 2227-7390) (available at: https://www.mdpi.com/si/mathematics/Dynamic_Modeling_Simulation_Control_Systems).

For citation purposes, cite each article independently as indicated on the article page online and as indicated below:

LastName, A.A.; LastName, B.B.; LastName, C.C. Article Title. *Journal Name* **Year**, *Volume Number*, Page Range.

ISBN 978-3-0365-7104-1 (Hbk)
ISBN 978-3-0365-7105-8 (PDF)

© 2023 by the authors. Articles in this book are Open Access and distributed under the Creative Commons Attribution (CC BY) license, which allows users to download, copy and build upon published articles, as long as the author and publisher are properly credited, which ensures maximum dissemination and a wider impact of our publications.

The book as a whole is distributed by MDPI under the terms and conditions of the Creative Commons license CC BY-NC-ND.

Contents

About the Editor vii

You Li and Haizhao Liang
Robust Finite-Time Control Algorithm Based on Dynamic Sliding Mode for Satellite Attitude Maneuver
Reprinted from: *Mathematics* **2022**, *10*, 111, doi:10.3390/math10010111 1

CH. Naga Sai Kalyan, B. Srikanth Goud, Mohit Bajaj, Malligunta Kiran Kumar, Emad M. Ahmed and Salah Kamel
Water-Cycle-Algorithm-Tuned Intelligent Fuzzy Controller for Stability of Multi-Area Multi-Fuel Power System with Time Delays
Reprinted from: *Mathematics* **2022**, *10*, 508, doi:10.3390/math10030508 27

Roxana Motorga, Vlad Mureșan, Mihaela-Ligia Unguresan, Mihail Abrudean, Honoriu Vălean and Iulia Clitan
Artificial Intelligence in Fractional-Order Systems Approximation with High Performances: Application in Modelling of an Isotopic Separation Process
Reprinted from: *Mathematics* **2022**, *10*, 1459, doi:10.3390/math10091459 43

Kinjal Prajapati, Ratheesh Ramakrishnan, Madhuri Bhavsar, Alka Mahajan, Zunnun Narmawala, Archana Bhavsar, et al.
Log Transformed Coherency Matrix for Differentiating Scattering Behaviour of Oil Spill Emulsions Using SAR Images
Reprinted from: *Mathematics* **2022**, *10*, 1697, doi:10.3390/math10101697 75

Akram M. Abdurraqeeb, Abdullrahman A. Al-Shamma'a, Abdulaziz Alkuhayli, Abdullah M. Noman and Khaled E. Addoweesh
RST Digital Robust Control for DC/DC Buck Converter Feeding Constant Power Load
Reprinted from: *Mathematics* **2022**, *10*, 1782, doi:10.3390/math10101782 97

Yong Nie, Jiajia Liu, Gang Liu, Litong Lyu, Jie Li and Zheng Chen
Force Tracking Impedance Control of Hydraulic Series Elastic Actuators Interacting with Unknown Environment
Reprinted from: *Mathematics* **2022**, *10*, 3383, doi:10.3390/math10183383 113

Zengwei Li, Lin Zhu, Zhenling Wang and Weiwei Che
Data-Driven Event-Triggered Platoon Control under Denial-of-Service Attacks
Reprinted from: *Mathematics* **2022**, *10*, 3985, doi:10.3390/math10213985 129

Liping Yin, Jianguo Liu, Hongquan Qu and Tao Li
Two-Step Neural-Network-Based Fault Isolation for Stochastic Systems
Reprinted from: *Mathematics* **2022**, *10*, 4261, doi:10.3390/math10224261 143

Syed Wajahat Ali, Anant Kumar Verma, Yacine Terriche, Muhammad Sadiq, Chun-Lien Su, Chung-Hong Lee and Mahmoud Elsisi
Finite-Control-Set Model Predictive Control for Low-Voltage-Ride-Through Enhancement of PMSG Based Wind Energy Grid Connection Systems
Reprinted from: *Mathematics* **2022**, *10*, 4266, doi:10.3390/math10224266 155

Hao Chen, Mingde Gong, Dingxuan Zhao, Wei Zhang, Wenbin Liu and Yue Zhang
Design and Motion Characteristics of Active–Passive Composite Suspension Actuator
Reprinted from: *Mathematics* **2022**, *10*, 4303, doi:10.3390/math10224303 177

Walter Gil-González, Oscar Danilo Montoya, Sebastián Riffo, Carlos Restrepo and Javier Muñoz
Adaptive Sensorless PI+Passivity-Based Control of a Boost Converter Supplying an Unknown CPL
Reprinted from: *Mathematics* **2022**, *10*, 4321, doi:10.3390/math10224321 . . . . **199**

Viorel Chihaia, Mihalache Ghinea, Stefan Chihaia and Andreea Neacsu
Mathematical Chemistry Approaches for Computer-Aid Design of Free-Shaped Structures in Architecture and Construction Engineering
Reprinted from: *Mathematics* **2022**, *10*, 4415, doi:10.3390/math10234415 . . . . **215**

About the Editor

Adrian Olaru

Adrian Olaru, Ph.D., is a Full Professor at the University Politehnica of Bucharest, Romania. He graduated from the Faculty of Machines and Manufacturing Systems, Politehnica University of Bucharest, Romania, in 1974. From 1974 to 1990, he worked as a design engineer at the "Optica Romana" Enterprise and was also an associate assistant at the Faculty of Machine-Building Technology of the Polytechnic Institute of Bucharest. In 1990, Prof. Adrian became an appointed lecturer at the Faculty of Technological Systems Engineering and Management, the Machine-Tools Department. Prof. Adrian Olaru has published over 160 national and international papers concerning the modeling and simulation of control systems, including hydraulic power systems, transport systems, electrical and hydraulic servo systems, and the dynamic behavior of industrial robots. He also has substantial contributions to over ten technical books. Prof. Adrian Olaru has been an invited professor at several universities around the world and invited speaker at different international conferences. He was coopted each year in more than 20 International Technical Committees and as general co-chair at different international conferences around the world.

Article

Robust Finite-Time Control Algorithm Based on Dynamic Sliding Mode for Satellite Attitude Maneuver

You Li [1] and Haizhao Liang [2,*]

[1] School of Aerospace Science and Technology, Xidian University, Xi'an 710126, China; liyouhahaha@163.com
[2] School of Aeronautics and Astronautics, Sun Yat-sen University, Guangzhou 510275, China
* Correspondence: lianghch5@mail.sysu.edu.cn

Abstract: Robust finite-time control algorithms for satellite attitude maneuvers are proposed in this paper. The standard sliding mode is modified, hence the inherent robustness could be maintained, and this fixed sliding mode is modified to dynamic, therefore the finite-time stability could be achieved. First, the finite-time sliding mode based on attitude quaternion is proposed and the loose finite-time stability is achieved by enlarging the sliding mode parameter. In order to get the strict finite-time stability, a sliding mode based on the Euler axis is then given. The fixed norm property of the Euler axis is used, and a sliding mode parameter without singularity issue is achieved. System performance near the equilibrium point is largely improved by the proposed sliding modes. The singularity issue of finite-time control is solved by the property of rotation around a fixed axis. System finite-time stability and robustness are analyzed by the Lyapunov method. The superiority of proposed controllers and system robustness to some typical perturbations such as disturbance torque, model uncertainty and actuator error are demonstrated by simulation results.

Keywords: finite-time control; robust control; dynamic sliding mode; satellite attitude maneuver

Citation: Li, Y.; Liang, H. Robust Finite-Time Control Algorithm Based on Dynamic Sliding Mode for Satellite Attitude Maneuver. *Mathematics* **2022**, *10*, 111. https://doi.org/10.3390/math10010111

Academic Editor: António M. Lopes

Received: 13 November 2021
Accepted: 24 December 2021
Published: 30 December 2021

Publisher's Note: MDPI stays neutral with regard to jurisdictional claims in published maps and institutional affiliations.

Copyright: © 2021 by the authors. Licensee MDPI, Basel, Switzerland. This article is an open access article distributed under the terms and conditions of the Creative Commons Attribution (CC BY) license (https://creativecommons.org/licenses/by/4.0/).

1. Introduction

With regard to the matter of satellite attitude control, the standard sliding mode is a mature and widely used control algorithm. The structure of the standard sliding mode for satellite attitude control is simple and has definite physical meaning. Moreover, the physical meaning brings strong robustness to some typical perturbations such as unknown disturbance, inertia matrix uncertainty and control actuator error. Some work [1–3] has been done on the design of sliding mode controllers and has demonstrated the superiority of the standard sliding mode. However, the system on this sliding mode has an exponential convergence rate, which means that with infinite time, the system could reach its equilibrium point strictly. However, some current space missions such as push-broom imaging and staring imaging demand the fast attitude maneuver capability. In order to improve system convergence rates, some researches focus on the field fast attitude maneuver. Li, Ye and so on [4–7] have done some work to improve the convergence rate of standard controllers. They pointed out that the key to improve the system convergence rate is to design angular velocity properly. The maneuver stage with constant angular velocity is designed and the convergence rate could be maintained during the stage. However, most of the work did not solve the exponential convergence issue, and the terminal convergence rate could still be improved. Zhang [8], Verbin [9] and Rojsiraphisal [10] designed the "braking curve" of angular velocity for satellite attitude control. The trajectory of angular velocity is optimized and the trajectory of the slowing down process is designed. The focus of their work was improving the system convergence rate, but the exponential convergence rate issue still exists.

In order to get finite-time stability near the system equilibrium point, researchers have done a lot of work. Ye and Xiao and so on [11,12] designed finite-time controllers for satellite control. The focus of their work is the control torque allocation algorithm and the fault tolerant algorithm. Wu [13,14] presented some methods to analyze finite time stability, such as the Lyapunov method and the terminal sliding mode method. The focus of his work is the structure of finite-time controllers for classic nonlinear systems and the standard structure of the terminal sliding mode. Liang, Wang and so on [15–17] designed finite-time controllers for satellite attitude control and the finite-time stability is analyzed by the Lyapunov method. Some typical Lyapunov functions are proposed in their works. Nguyen [18] designed a robust finite-time guidance law for maneuverable targets with unpredictable evasive strategies. Khelil [19] proposed a fast finite-time convergent guidance law with a nonlinear disturbance observer for unmanned aerial vehicle collision avoidance. Guo [20] designed a new continuous adaptive finite time guidance law against highly maneuvering targets. Generally, in order to get finite-time stability, the design of the controller needs some special modifications and the system loses the inherent strong robustness to perturbations. The design of robust finite-time controllers is another major concern of current research.

As discussed above, model uncertainty, unknown disturbance and actuator error are some typical perturbations in the satellite attitude system. In order to deal with perturbation issues, researchers have done some work. Xiao [21–23] designed fault tolerant controllers, and system model uncertainty and actuator error are estimated by the fault diagnosis function. However, the method is suitable for several typical uncertainty models but not suitable for the random noise model. Hu [24–26] designed some robust controllers to system uncertainty. The sign function terms are added in the controllers and the system uncertainty is treated as Gauss white noise with an upper bounded norm. However, the sign function terms would bring high frequency vibrations, which is harmful to the actuator and physical system. In order to deal with the uncertainty issue without bringing high frequency vibration, adaptive control was developed by some researchers. Qiao [27] and Gui [28] designed finite-tine attitude maneuver controllers considering the disturbance torque with Gauss white noise character and sine function character. Wang [29] and Ai [30] designed finite-time sliding modes for satellite attitude control, and the convergence time is estimated by the proposed methods and disturbance torque with consideration of the upper bounded norm. Some researchers [31–34] also designed finite time controllers for robot manipulator and vehicle systems. Generally, the finite-time controller considering overall perturbations still needs developing, and in order to deal with perturbations, the structure of finite-time controllers is relatively complex.

In this paper, the standard sliding mode will be modified to achieve finite-time stability. The strong robustness could be maintained by the similar structure with standard sliding mode and robust controllers with relatively simple structures would be given, considering some typical perturbations. Compared with existing methods, a finite time controller based on a dynamic sliding mode will be proposed based on a standard sliding mode surface; the advantage of a fast convergence rate and strong robustness would be combined in this proposed method.

The structure of this paper is constructed as follows: 1. Section 1 describes the background and innovation of this paper; 2. Section 2 gives the math models used in this paper; 3. Section 3 describes the issue needs to be solved in this paper; 4. Section 4 presents a finite-time controller based on attitude quaternion and proves some properties of this controller; 5. Section 5 presents a finite-time controller based on the Euler axis and system performance is improved comparing with that in Section 4; 6. Section 6 demonstrates the controller performance by simulation results; 7. Section 7 concludes the paper.

2. Dynamics and Models

The dynamic model of rigid satellite could be modeled as follows [4–7]:

$$J\dot{\omega} + \omega^{\times} J\omega = u + d \tag{1}$$

where ω is angular velocity which is a 3×1 vector, J is inertia matrix of satellite which is a 3×3 positive definite symmetric matrix, d is 3×1 unknown disturbance torque with norm upper bound $\|d\| < \bar{d}$. Product matrix $r^\times$ of vector r is defined as

$$r^\times = \begin{bmatrix} 0 & -r_3 & r_2 \\ r_3 & 0 & -r_1 \\ -r_2 & r_1 & 0 \end{bmatrix} \quad (2)$$

generally inertia matrix J could not be accurate known and it is assumed that

$$J = \hat{J} + \tilde{J} \quad (3)$$

where $\hat{J}$ is the inertia matrix estimation and $\tilde{J}$ is the error matrix. In this paper, the error matrix $\tilde{J}$ could be treated as a disturbance in control system and one of the main goals is to design adaptive law to suppress this disturbance.

The kinetic model based on Euler axis/Angle could be written as follows [4–7]

$$\begin{cases} \dot{e} = \frac{1}{2} e^\times \left(I_3 - \cot \frac{\varphi}{2} e^\times \right) \omega \\ \dot{\varphi} = \frac{1}{2} e^T \omega \end{cases} \quad (4)$$

where e is Euler axis and φ is rotate angle. Based on (4) it could be found that kinetic model (4) has singularity issue when $\varphi \to 0$ i.e., the Euler axis e is not continuous near the system equilibrium point.

The kinetic model based on attitude quaternion could be written as follows [4–7]

$$\begin{cases} \dot{q}_0 = -\frac{1}{2} q_v^T \omega \\ \dot{q}_v = \frac{1}{2}(q_0 I_3 + q_v^\times) \omega = \frac{1}{2} F \omega \end{cases} \quad (5)$$

Considering that q and $-q$ describes the same attitude, the scalar part of attitude quaternion is assumed to be non-negative in this paper i.e., $q_0 \geq 0$.

3. Problem Formulation

In satellite attitude control issue, standard sliding mode could written as follows

$$s = \omega + k q_v, (k > 0) \quad (6)$$

when system converges along the sliding mode (11) it could be found that

$$\omega = -k q_v$$
$$\dot{q}_v = \frac{1}{2}(q_0 I_3 + q_v^\times) \omega = -\frac{1}{2} k q_0 q_v \quad (7)$$

when system maneuvers along (6), angular velocity vector is reversed to attitude quaternion vector and lot of work have been done based on this sliding mode. The model uncertainty and unknown disturbance issue could be effectively solved using sliding mode (6) and it could be concluded that the reverse property could improve system robustness. However, based on equation (6) it could be easily found that the convergence rate of q_v is exponential which means system would reach the equilibrium point with infinite time and the convergence rate needs to be improved.

In order to improve system convergence rate, finite-time controller is an effective method. Generally in order to achieve the finite-time stability, fraction order feedback is used as follows to construct the sliding mode.

$$\dot{x} = -k sign(x) |x|^r, 0 < r < 1 \quad (8)$$

where $sign(x)$ is the sign function of vector x.

Sliding mode (8) would bring another issue i.e., the singularity issue. Since the control torque is always related to $\ddot{x}$ i.e., the 2nd derivative of x, the singularity term x^{r-1} would be brought into the controller. In order to deal with the singularity issue some typical finite-time controllers are designed [4,11,13]. However, system robustness issue is not taken into consideration and the reverse property does not hold in these works. System robustness needs to be improved to suppress the perturbations such as inertia matrix uncertainty and unknown disturbance. In summary, the robustness issue and singularity issue should be both taken into consideration to design the robust finite-time controller.

Based on the discussion above, the goal of this paper could be as: design finite time controller for satellite stabilization issue and following properties should be satisfied:

1. Comparing with standard sliding mode, system convergence rate near the equilibrium point should be largely improved;
2. Finite-time stability should be satisfied i.e., there exist positive scalar ε and T to satisfy $\|q_v\| \leq \varepsilon$ for $\forall t \geq T$;
3. The singularity issue should be solved i.e., $q_v, \dot{q}_v, \omega, \dot{\omega}$ are all bounded during the whole control process;
4. The controller should be robust to inertia matrix uncertainty and unknown disturbance torque.

4. Finite-Time Controller Based on Attitude Quaternion

In paper [5], the author pointed out that the fixed sliding mode caused the low convergence rate and a dynamic sliding mode is constructed in this paper. The maneuver stage with constant angular velocity and converge stage with a constant angular acceleration is designed based on the update law of sliding mode parameter k, and the system convergence rate is largely improved when compared with the standard sliding mode. Inspired by the method in [5], the finite-time sliding mode proposed in this paper could written as follows:

$$s = \omega + kq_v$$

$$\dot{k} = \begin{cases} 0 & \|s\| > \varepsilon_1 \\ \frac{k}{2}(1-\alpha)\beta q_0 \|q_v\|^{\alpha-1} & \|s\| \leq \varepsilon_1 \end{cases} \quad (9)$$

$$1/2 < \alpha < 1, \beta = k(t_0)/\|q_v(t_0)\|^{\alpha-1} \quad (10)$$

where the initial value of k and satisfies $k(t_0) > 0$, ε_1 is a small positive scalar, α, β are all positive scalars.

Sliding mode (9) has the same structure as standard sliding mode hence the reversed property could be maintained. Moreover, the same structure could make it possible to design a robust finite-time controller based on standard sliding mode methods. Based on (9) it could be found that the maneuver process is constructed as two stages: in the first stage i.e., $\|s\| > \varepsilon_1$, system performance is totally same as that of standard sliding mode, and sliding mode parameter k is fixed; in the second stage i.e., $\|s\| \leq \varepsilon_1$, it could be treated that system has reached the sliding mode and angular velocity vector has been reversed to attitude quaternion vector. In this stage, sliding mode parameter k begins to update. Moreover, based on the update law of k it could be found that k is monotonically increasing to effect the exponential convergence rate. The key work of this paper is the update law of sliding mode parameter k and when system convergences along (9) i.e., $s = 0$, system (5) would converges to its equilibrium point within finite time, and during this process ω and $\dot{\omega}$ are all norm upper bounded.

First the finite-time stability on sliding mode (9) is discussed. When system reaches sliding mode (9), define as follows and calculate its derivative it could be got that

$$V_q = \boldsymbol{q}_v^T \boldsymbol{q}_v = \|\boldsymbol{q}_v\|^2 \tag{11}$$

$$\dot{V}_q = 2\boldsymbol{q}_v^T \dot{\boldsymbol{q}}_v = -kq_0 \boldsymbol{q}_v^T \boldsymbol{q}_v = -kq_0 \|\boldsymbol{q}_v\|^2 \tag{12}$$

In order to achieve the goal of finite-time stability, the derivative of Lyapunov function should satisfy following inequality

$$\dot{V}_q \leq -\gamma q_0 \|\boldsymbol{q}_v\|^{\alpha+1}, \ with \ \alpha \in (0,1), \gamma > 0 \tag{13}$$

Comparing with (12) and (13) it could be got that if there exist positive scalar γ to satisfy following inequality, the finite-time stability could be ensured.

$$k = \gamma \|\boldsymbol{q}_v\|^{\alpha-1} \tag{14}$$

In order to satisfy finite-time condition (14), fixed parameter k is not feasible since the right part of (14) tends to infinite, and a very large k would cause the control torque an angular velocity exceed system upper bound drastically. Hence it is necessary to design a time-variable parameter k and its update law to satisfy (14) and that is how the dynamic sliding mode (9) is got. In fact, select parameters as follows, it could be got that

$$\gamma = k(t_0)/\|\boldsymbol{q}_v(t_0)\|^{\alpha-1}, \beta = \gamma \tag{15}$$

Noticing that the structure of sliding mode parameter update law in (9), it could be got that

$$k(t_0) = \gamma \|\boldsymbol{q}_v(t_0)\|^{\alpha-1}$$
$$\dot{k} = \tfrac{1}{2}k(1-\alpha)\beta q_0 \|\boldsymbol{q}_v\|^{\alpha-1} = \tfrac{1}{2}k(1-\alpha_0)\gamma q_0 \|\boldsymbol{q}_v\|^{\alpha-1} = \tfrac{d\gamma \|\boldsymbol{q}_v\|^{\alpha-1}}{dt} \tag{16}$$

Based on (15) and (16) it could be found that finite-time condition (14) is satisfied, and (12) could be transformed to

$$\dot{V}_q = 2\boldsymbol{q}_v^T \dot{\boldsymbol{q}}_v = -kq_0 \boldsymbol{q}_v^T \boldsymbol{q}_v = -kq_0 \|\boldsymbol{q}_v\|^2 \leq -\beta q_0 \|\boldsymbol{q}_v\|^{\alpha+1} = -\beta q_0 V_q^{\alpha+1/2} \tag{17}$$

System converge time satisfies

$$t_f \leq \frac{2V^{\frac{1-\alpha}{2}}(t_0)}{\beta q_0(t_0)(1-\alpha)} \tag{18}$$

The next step is to prove on sliding mode (9), $\boldsymbol{\omega}, \dot{\boldsymbol{\omega}}$ are all norm upper bounded. It is obviously that angular velocity $\boldsymbol{\omega}$ satisfies following property and is norm upper bounded.

$$\|\boldsymbol{\omega}\| = \|-k\boldsymbol{q}_v\| = \|\boldsymbol{q}_v\|^{\alpha} \tag{19}$$

Calculate the derivative of angular velocity $\boldsymbol{\omega}$ it could be got that

$$\begin{aligned}
\dot{\boldsymbol{\omega}} &= -k\dot{\boldsymbol{q}}_v - \dot{k}\boldsymbol{q}_v \\
&= -k(q_0 I_3 + \boldsymbol{q}_v^{\times})(-k\boldsymbol{q}_v) - \tfrac{k}{2}(1-\alpha)\beta q_0 \|\boldsymbol{q}_v\|^{\alpha-1}\boldsymbol{q}_v \\
&= q_0 k^2 \boldsymbol{q}_v - \tfrac{k}{2}(1-\alpha)\beta q_0 \|\boldsymbol{q}_v\|^{\alpha-1}\boldsymbol{q}_v \\
&= q_0 \beta^2 \|\boldsymbol{q}_v\|^{2\alpha-1}e - \tfrac{1}{2}(1-\alpha)\beta^2 q_0 \|\boldsymbol{q}_v\|^{2\alpha-1}e
\end{aligned} \tag{20}$$

Consider that $1/2 < \alpha < 1$, hence $\omega, \dot{\omega}$ are all norm upper bounded during the whole maneuver process, and the demand control torque is also norm upper bounded i.e., the singularity issue is solved.

Based on the discussion above it could be found that the system state on the sliding mode (9) is norm upper bounded, however according to the update law of k it could be found that sliding mode parameter k tends to infinity as the system convergence. Although the system state and control actuator would not be influenced by this divergence, the computation system would break down under sliding mode (9). Hence for engineering practice, finite-time sliding mode (9) could be re-written as follows

$$s = \omega + kq_v$$

$$\dot{k} = \begin{cases} 0 & \|s\| > \varepsilon_1 \\ \frac{k}{2}(1-\alpha)\beta q_0 \|q_v\|^{\alpha-1} & \|s\| \leq \varepsilon_1, \|q_v\| > \varepsilon_2 \\ 0 & \|s\| \leq \varepsilon_1, \|q_v\| \leq \varepsilon_2 \end{cases} \quad (21)$$

where ε_1 and ε_2 are all small positive scalars. It could be found that the basic structure of (21) is the same as (9), hence the system's finite-time stability and bounded state property could be maintained, and the only difference is that when the system approaches the equilibrium point, the sliding mode parameter stops updating to avoid the parameter singularity issue.

The closed control loop scheme block diagram is shown as follows.

Shown as Figure 1, the control system is constructed as a sliding mode surface, controller and update law. The latest one is the main contribution of this paper and it will be described in the text.

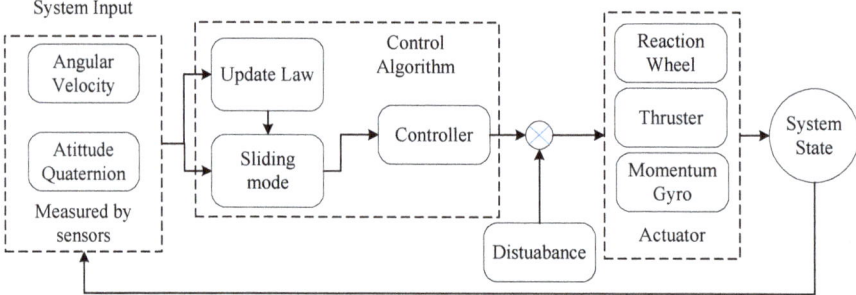

Figure 1. Control block diagram.

The next step is to propose the attitude controller after giving the sliding mode (21). The robust finite-time controller proposed in this paper based on (21) could be written as follows

$$u = \begin{cases} -k_s \text{sig}^r(s) + \omega^\times \hat{J}\omega - \frac{1}{2}k\hat{J}F\omega - l_1 \text{sign}(s) & \|s\| > \varepsilon_1 \\ -k_s \text{sig}^r(s) + \omega^\times \hat{J}\omega - \frac{1}{2}k\hat{J}F\omega - l_2 \text{sign}(s) \\ \quad - \frac{k}{2}(1-\alpha)\beta q_0 \|q_v\|^{\alpha-1}\hat{J}q_v & \|s\| \leq \varepsilon_1, \|q_v\| > \varepsilon_2 \\ -k_s \text{sig}^r(s) + \omega^\times \hat{J}\omega - \frac{1}{2}k\hat{J}F\omega - l_3 \text{sign}(s) & \|s\| \leq \varepsilon_1, \|q_v\| \leq \varepsilon_2 \end{cases} \quad (22)$$

where k_s is a positive scalar, r is a positive scalar which satisfies $0 < r < 1$, vector function $sig^r(x)$ and l_i are defined as follows

$$sig^r(x) = x/\|x\|^r$$

$$\begin{cases} l_1 = \overline{d} + \lambda\|\omega\|^2 + \frac{k}{2}\lambda\|\omega\| \\ l_2 = \overline{d} + \lambda\|\omega\|^2 + \frac{k}{2}\lambda\|\omega\| + \frac{k}{2}\lambda(1-\alpha)\beta q_0\|q_v\|^\alpha \\ l_3 = \overline{d} + \lambda\|\omega\|^2 + \frac{k}{2}\lambda\|\omega\| \end{cases} \quad (23)$$

where λ is a positive scalar which satisfies $\lambda \geq \lambda_M(\widetilde{J})$ with $\lambda_M(\widetilde{J})$ is the maximum eigenvalue value of error inertia matrix $\widetilde{J}$.

Controller (22) has the three following properties: (1) there is no negative power term of system state in controller (22) hence the control torque are norm upper-bounded during the whole control process; (2) as the system state converges, most sign function terms in l_i tends to zero hence at the steady stage the actual sign function term is $\overline{d}$ to suppress the disturbance torque; and (3) the system inertia matrix uncertainty is treated as king of disturbance related to system state with norm upper bound and suppressed by sign function terms, hence controller (23) is robust to model uncertainty.

The next step is to prove that governed by controller (22), system could reach sliding mode (21) within finite-time. Select Lyapunov function as follows

$$V_s = \frac{1}{2} s^T J s \quad (24)$$

The V function satisfies following property

$$V \geq \frac{1}{2}\lambda_m(J)\|s\|^2 \quad (25)$$

where $\lambda_m(J)$ is the minimum eigenvalue value of matrix J.

When $\|s\| > \varepsilon_1$ and $\|s\| \leq \varepsilon_1, \|q_v\| \leq \varepsilon_2$, calculate the derivative of V function and noticing (25) it could be got that

$$\begin{aligned} \dot{V}_s &= s^T J \dot{s} = s^T J \dot{\omega} + k s^T J \dot{q}_v \\ &= s^T u - s^T \omega^\times J \omega + s^T d + \frac{k}{2} s^T J F \omega \\ &= k_s s^T sig^r(s) - s^T \omega^\times \widetilde{J} \omega + s^T d + \frac{k}{2} s^T \widetilde{J} F \omega \\ &\quad - \left(\overline{d} + \lambda\|\omega\|^2 + \frac{k}{2}\lambda\|\omega\|\right) s^T sign(s) \\ &\leq -k_s\|s\|^{r+1} + \overline{d}\|s\| + \lambda_M(\widetilde{J})\|s\|\|\omega\|^2 + \frac{k}{2}\lambda_M(\widetilde{J})\|s\|\|\omega\| \\ &\quad - \left(\overline{d} + \lambda\|\omega\|^2 + \frac{k}{2}\lambda\|\omega\|\right)\|s\| - \overline{d}\|s\| \\ &\leq -k_s\|s\|^{r+1} \leq -\mu V^{\frac{r+1}{2}} \end{aligned} \quad (26)$$

When $\|s\| \leq \varepsilon_1, \|q_v\| > \varepsilon_2$ calculate the derivative of V function and noticing (25) it could be got that

$$\begin{aligned}
\dot{V}_s &= s^T J \dot{s} = s^T J \dot{\omega} + k s^T J \dot{q}_v + \dot{k} s^T J q_v \\
&= s^T u - s^T \omega^\times J \omega + s^T d + \tfrac{k}{2} s^T J F \omega + \dot{k} s^T J q_v \\
&= k_s s^T sig^r(s) - s^T \omega^\times \tilde{J} \omega + s^T d + \tfrac{k}{2} s^T \tilde{J} F \omega + \dot{k} s^T \tilde{J} q_v \\
&\quad - \left(\bar{d} + \lambda \|\omega\|^2 + \tfrac{k}{2} \lambda \|\omega\| + \dot{k} \lambda \|q_v\| \right) s^T sign(s) \\
&\leq -k_s \|s\|^{r+1} + \bar{d}\|s\| + \lambda_M(\tilde{J}) \|s\| \|\omega\|^2 + \tfrac{k}{2} \lambda_M(\tilde{J}) \|s\| \|\omega\| + \dot{k} \lambda_M(\tilde{J}) \|s\| \|q_v\| \\
&\quad - \left(\bar{d} + \lambda \|\omega\|^2 + \tfrac{k}{2} \lambda \|\omega\| + \dot{k} \lambda \|q_v\| \right) \|s\| - \bar{d}\|s\| \\
&\leq -k_s \|s\|^{r+1} \leq -\mu V^{\frac{r+1}{2}}
\end{aligned} \quad (27)$$

In (26) and (27), parameter μ is defined as follows

$$\mu = k_s (2/\lambda_m(J))^{\frac{r+1}{2}} \quad (28)$$

Based on (26) and (27) it could be found that system (1), (5) governed by controller (22) could reach finite-time sliding mode (21) within finite-time, and along this sliding mode system would converge to $\|q_v\| \leq \varepsilon_2$ within finite-time.

In this section, a finite-time sliding mode based on standard sliding mode is proposed. The basic structure, physical meaning and inherent robustness of the standard sliding mode could be maintained, and the fixed parameter is modified to time-varying with the typical update law. The strict finite-time time stability could be achieved by updating the sliding mode parameter to infinite without causing the singularity issue of the system state, however the computation system would break down by this method. Hence the finite-time stability is loosed and when system state approaches to its equilibrium point close enough, the parameter stops updating.

5. Finite-Time Controller Based on Euler Axis

In the last section, in order to avoid the singularity issue of the sliding mode parameter, the system lost its strict finite-time stability. Hence, this section will discuss another finite-time sliding mode based on the standard sliding mode to achieve strict finite-time stability without causing any singularity issues.

According to the description in Section 2, the Euler axis could also be used to describe attitude information, and is related to attitude quaternion tightly. However, this description has its own singularity issue i.e., when $\varphi \to 0$, $\dot{e} \to \infty$. The Euler axis is a unit vector and describes the direction of the attitude quaternion; a small change in attitude quaternion would cause a huge change in its direction when the system approaches its equilibrium point. This would explain why, when the Euler angle tends to zero, the kinetic model of the Euler axis is not continuous, and this property causes a huge challenge to design controllers based on the Euler axis/angle. However, noticing that when angular velocity vector is reversed to attitude quaternion vector i.e.,

$$\omega = -k_1 q_v = -k_2 e \quad (29)$$

The kinetic model of Euler axis could be transformed to

$$\dot{e} = \tfrac{1}{2} e^\times \left(I_3 - \cot \tfrac{\varphi}{2} e^\times \right) \omega = -\tfrac{1}{2} k_2 e^\times \left(I_3 - \cot \tfrac{\varphi}{2} e^\times \right) e = 0 \quad (30)$$

It could be found that the singularity issue does not exist in this condition. In essence, when angular velocity vector parallels to attitude quaternion vector, the direction of the

Euler axis is constant. Based on this property, the sliding mode based on the Euler axis could be constructed as two stages: (1) the system angular velocity vector should be reversed to attitude quaternion vector; and (2) maintain the reverse property and adjust the norm of angular velocity to achieve strict finite-time stability. Hence the finite-time sliding mode proposed in this section could be written as follows

$$s = \omega + ke$$

$$\dot{k} = \begin{cases} 0 & \|s\| > \varepsilon_1 \\ -\frac{1}{2}q_0\alpha\beta k\|q_v\|^{\alpha-1} - \gamma_1 g - \gamma_2 sign(g)|g|^{\alpha_0} & \|s\| \leq \varepsilon_1 \end{cases} \quad (31)$$

where ε_1 is a small positive scalar, $k(t_0)$ is the initial value of k and is a positive scalar, β is a positive scalar, α satisfies $1/2 < \alpha < 1$, α_0 satisfies $0 < \alpha < 1$, γ_1 and γ_2 are all positive scalars, and parameter g is defined as follows

$$g = k - \beta\|q_v\|^{\alpha} \quad (32)$$

It could be found that the structure of sliding mode (31) is similar as (9) in the previous section; the first step is also to achieve the reverse of angular velocity and attitude quaternion, and during this process the sliding mode parameter is fixed. When the reverse property has been satisfied, the sliding mode parameter begins to update to achieve strict finite-time stability.

It is worth noting that when maneuvering along the sliding mode (31), the update law, $k \to \beta\|q_v\|^{\alpha}$ could be achieved within finite-time. In fact, select the Lyapunov function as follows and calculate its derivative

$$V_g = \frac{1}{2}g^2 \quad (33)$$

$$\begin{aligned}
\dot{V}_g &= g\dot{g} \\
&= g\left(\dot{k} - \beta\frac{d\|q_v\|}{dt}\right) \\
&= g\left(-\frac{1}{2}q_0\alpha\beta k\|q_v\|^{\alpha-1} - \gamma_1 g - \gamma_2 sign(g)|g|^{\alpha_0} + \frac{1}{2}q_0\alpha\beta k\|q_v\|^{\alpha-1}\right) \\
&= -\gamma_1 g^2 - \gamma_2 g^{\alpha_0+1} \\
&\leq -\gamma_2 g^{\alpha_0+1} = -\gamma_2(2V_g)^{\alpha_0+1/2}
\end{aligned} \quad (34)$$

Considering the range of α_0 it could be found that the error state system is finite-time stable i.e., $g \to 0$ could be achieved within finite-time, hence $k \to \beta\|q_v\|^{\alpha}$ could be achieved within finite-time.

The next step is to discuss system stability on sliding mode (31). Define Lyapunov function as follows

$$V_q = q_v^T q_v = \|q_v\|^2 \quad (35)$$

Calculate its derivative and noticing the relationship between k and $\|q_v\|$, it could be got that when near the equilibrium point

$$\begin{aligned}
\dot{V}_q &= 2q_v^T \dot{q}_v = q_v^T(q_0 I_3 + q_v^{\times})(-ke) = -kq_0\|q_v\| \\
&= -q_0\beta\|q_v\|^{\alpha+1} \leq q_0\beta V_q^{\alpha+1/2}
\end{aligned} \quad (36)$$

Hence system has strict finite-time stability on sliding mode (31). Moreover, noticing that

$$k = \beta\|q_v\|^{\alpha}, \dot{k} = -q_0\alpha\beta^2\|q_v\|^{2\alpha-1} \quad (37)$$

Noticing that $1/2 < \alpha < 1$, hence

$$k = \beta \|q_v\|^\alpha \to 0$$

$$\|\omega\| = \|-ke\| = \beta \|q_v\|^\alpha \to 0 \tag{38}$$

$$\|\dot{\omega}\| = \|-k\dot{e} - \dot{k}e\| = q_0 \alpha \beta^2 \|q_v\|^{2\alpha-1} \to 0$$

This means that on sliding mode (31) system state and sliding mode parameter has no singularity issue during the whole convergence process. Compared to the finite-time sliding mode in the previous section, the sliding mode (31) maintains the strict finite-time stability and solves the parameter singularity issue. Since the norm of the Euler axis is bounded to 1, a convergent parameter k could achieve the finite-time goal without causing the singularity issue, and this is a main contribution of this paper. Moreover, the basic structure of standard sliding mode is maintained in this section, and the physical meaning and inherent robustness could be maintained in (31).

As discussed above, in order to avoid the inherent kinetic model singularity of Euler axis, an important assumption should be made: when approaching the equilibrium point, angular velocity vector has been reversed to attitude quaternion vector, i.e., for a small positive scalar ε_2, when $\|q_v\| \le \varepsilon_2$ is satisfied, $\omega = -ke$ has been satisfied. It is worth noticing that except for some small angle maneuver, this assumption could be achieved since the initial Euler angle is relatively large, hence this assumption is reasonable.

The finite-time controller based on sliding mode (31) could be written as follows

$$u = \begin{cases} -k_s \mathbf{sig}^r(s) + \omega^\times \hat{J}\omega - \frac{1}{2}k\hat{J}G\omega - l_1 \mathbf{sign}(s) & \|s\| > \varepsilon_1 \\ -k_s \mathbf{sig}^r(s) + \omega^\times \hat{J}\omega - \dot{k}\hat{J}e - l_2 \mathbf{sign}(s) & \|s\| \le \varepsilon_1 \end{cases} \tag{39}$$

where the definition of vector function $\mathbf{sig}^r(\cdot)$ and sign function $\mathbf{sign}(\cdot)$ are totally same as previous section, r is a positive scalar which satisfies $0 < r < 1$, k_s is a positive scalar, the definition of $\dot{k}$ is given in (33), matrix G and scalars l_i are defined as follows

$$G = e^\times \left(I_3 - \cot \frac{\varphi}{2} e^\times \right)$$

$$\begin{cases} l_1 = \bar{d} + \lambda \|\omega\|^2 + \frac{k}{2}\lambda \left(1 + \cot \frac{\varphi}{2}\right) \|\omega\| \\ l_2 = \bar{d} + \lambda \|\omega\|^2 + \|\dot{k}\| \end{cases} \tag{40}$$

where λ is a positive scalar which satisfies $\lambda \ge \lambda_M(\tilde{J})$ with $\lambda_M(\tilde{J})$ is the maximum eigenvalue value of error inertia matrix $\tilde{J}$.

As discussed in previous section, controller (38) also has three properties: control torque norm upper bounded, most sign function terms tend to zero and robust to inertia matrix uncertainty.

Next step is to prove system (1) and (5) governed by controller (38) could reach the sliding mode (31) within finite-time. Select Lyapunov function as follows

$$V_s = \frac{1}{2} s^T J s \tag{41}$$

The V function i.e., Lyapunov function satisfies

$$V \ge \frac{1}{2} \lambda_m(J) \|s\|^2 \tag{42}$$

When $\|s\| > \varepsilon_1$, calculate the derivative of (43)

$$\begin{aligned}
\dot{V}_s &= s^T J \dot{s} = s^T J \dot{\omega} + k s^T J \dot{e} + \dot{k} s^T J e \\
&= s^T u - s^T \omega^\times J \omega + s^T d + \tfrac{k}{2} s^T J G \omega \\
&= k_s s^T sig^r(s) - s^T \omega^\times \tilde{J} \omega + s^T d + \tfrac{k_2}{2} s^T \tilde{J} G \omega \\
&\quad - \left(\bar{d} + \lambda \|\omega\|^2 + \tfrac{k}{2} \lambda \left(1 + \cot \tfrac{\varphi}{2}\right) \|\omega\| \right) s^T sign(s) \\
&\leq -k_s \|s\|^{r+1} + \bar{d} \|s\| + \lambda_M(\tilde{J}) \|s\| \|\omega\|^2 + \tfrac{k}{2} \lambda_M(\tilde{J}) \left(1 + \cot \tfrac{\varphi}{2}\right) \|s\| \|\omega\| \\
&\quad - \left(\bar{d} + \lambda \|\omega\|^2 + \tfrac{k_2}{2} \lambda \left(1 + \cot \tfrac{\varphi}{2}\right) \|\omega\| \right) \|s\| - \bar{d} \|s\| \\
&\leq -k \|s\|^{r+1} \leq -\mu V^{\frac{r+1}{2}}
\end{aligned} \quad (43)$$

When $\|s\| \leq \varepsilon_1$, calculate the derivative of (41) and noticing that angular velocity vector has been reversed to attitude quaternion vector i.e., $\dot{e} = 0$

$$\begin{aligned}
\dot{V}_s &= s^T J \dot{s} = s^T J \dot{\omega} + k s^T J \dot{e} + \dot{k} s^T J e \\
&= s^T u - s^T \omega^\times J \omega + s^T d + \dot{k} s^T J e \\
&= k_s s^T sig^r(s) - s^T \omega^\times \tilde{J} \omega + s^T d - q_0 \alpha \beta^2 \|q_v\|^{2\alpha - 1} s^T \tilde{J} e \\
&\quad - \left(\bar{d} + \lambda \|\omega\|^2 + \lambda q_0 \alpha \beta^2 \|q_v\|^{2\alpha - 1} \right) s^T sign(s) \\
&\leq -k_s \|s\|^{r+1} + \bar{d} \|s\| + \lambda_M(\tilde{J}) \|s\| \|\omega\|^2 + q_0 \alpha \beta^2 \lambda_M(\tilde{J}) \|q_v\|^{2\alpha - 1} \|s\| \\
&\quad - \left(\bar{d} + \lambda \|\omega\|^2 + \lambda q_0 \alpha \beta^2 \|q_v\|^{2\alpha - 1} \right) \|s\| - \bar{d} \|s\| \\
&\leq -k \|s\|^{r+1} \leq -\mu V^{\frac{r+1}{2}}
\end{aligned} \quad (44)$$

In (42) and (43), parameter μ is defined as follows

$$\mu = k(2/\lambda_m(J))^{\frac{r+1}{2}} \quad (45)$$

Based on (43) and (44), it could be found that system (1) and (5) governed by controller (39) could reach finite-time sliding mode (31) within finite-time, and along this sliding mode the system would converge to the equilibrium point within finite-time; strict system finite-time stability has been proven.

In this section, the standard sliding mode is modified to have strict finite-time stability based on the Euler axis description. The property that norm of Euler axis is bounded is used to design the update law of sliding mode parameter, hence the system state and sliding mode parameter could be ensured norm upper bounded during the whole control process. Compared with the controller proposed in last section, the controller (39) has better convergence performance and robustness. However it is worth noticing that differs from last section, the control method in this section needs high attitude determination, since when approaching the system equilibrium point, a small error in attitude quaternion would cause a huge error in the Euler axis, thus the control accuracy would be influenced. In essence, finite-time attitude control issue is transformed to a high accuracy attitude determination issue.

6. Simulation

In order to demonstrate the superiority of the adaptive finite-time controller (22) and (39) presented in this paper, the standard sliding mode controller (46) without the inertia matrix uncertainty constructed is compared as follows:

$$u = -ks + \omega^\times J\omega - \frac{k_1}{2}(q_0 I_3 + q_v^\times)\omega - \bar{d}sgn(s)$$

$$s = \omega + k_1 q_v$$
(46)

Set the simulation parameters as follows

$$J = diag(30, 25, 20) \text{kg} \cdot \text{m}^2, k = 0.1, k_s = 10$$

$$\omega(0) = [-0.03 \ -0.04 \ 0.05]^T \text{rad/s}, q(0) = [\ 0 \ \sqrt{6}/6 \ \sqrt{3}/3 \ \sqrt{2}/2\ ]^T$$
(47)

Assume the disturbance torque consists of Gauss white noise and sinusoidal signal written as follows

$$d_i = 5 \times 10^{-4} randn(-1,1) + 5 \times 10^{-4} \sin t + 5 \times 10^{-4} \|\omega_i\| randn(-1,1)$$
(48)

Hence the norm upper bound of disturbance torque satisfies

$$\bar{d} = 10^{-3}$$
(49)

The simulation results of standard sliding mode controller (48) are given as follows.

Based on Figures 2–4 it could be found that system converges to the equilibrium point more than 120 s, and the steady accuracy at 150 s is about 1×10^{-4} rad/s of angular velocity and 1×10^{-3} of attitude quaternion. Based on the simulation parameters it could be found that the total rotate angle is 180deg and the maneuver time is longer than 120 s, hence the average angular velocity is about 1.5deg/s. The low convergence rate is caused by the drop of angular velocity and this could be found in Figure 1. Moreover, based on Figure 3 it could be found that the initial control torque is about 1.5 Nm and drops to zero drastically, hence it could concluded that the efficiency on control torque of standard sliding mode controller is relatively low.

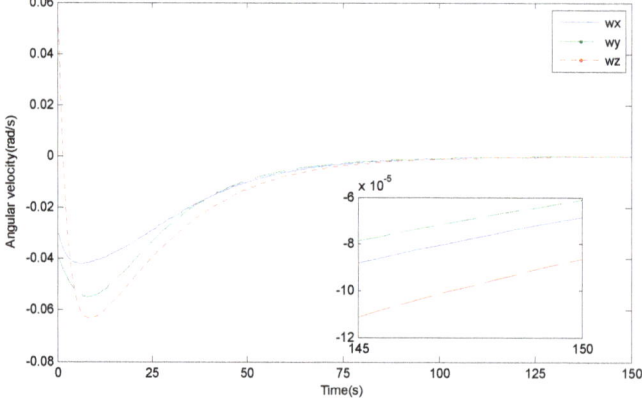

Figure 2. Curve of angular velocity.

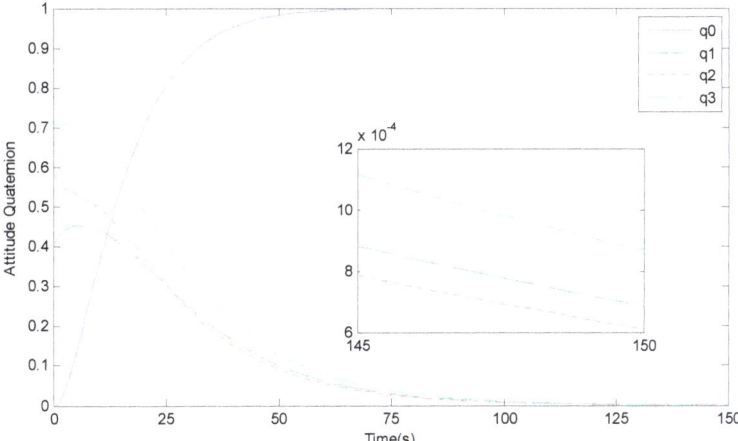

Figure 3. Curve of attitude quaternion.

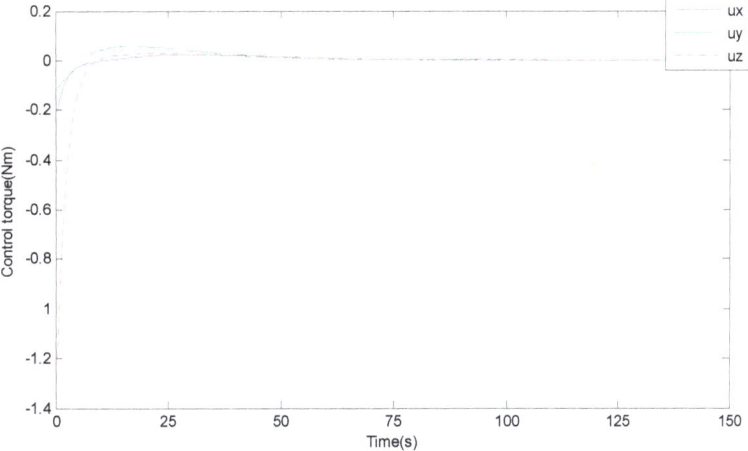

Figure 4. Curve of control torque.

6.1. Simulation for Controller Based on Attitude Quaternion

In this section, simulation results for finite-time controller (22) in Section 4 a given. Set system parameters as follows.

$$\hat{J} = diag(28, 24, 21) \text{kg·m}^2, \lambda = 3, \bar{d} = 10^{-3} \tag{50}$$

Generally, larger r and $k(t_0)$ brings faster convergence rate, but the demanded control torque is also enlarged, and smaller r makes sliding mode (9) degenerates to standard sliding mode. Also larger k_s makes system could reach the finite-time sliding mode faster, moreover, smaller α and larger β bring better convergence rate along the sliding mode. Considering that system performance under exponential convergence rate when away from the equilibrium point, the superiority of finite-time property mainly reflects on the performance near system equilibrium point. Above all, control parameters for controller (22) are selected as follows

$$\varepsilon_1 = 10^{-3}, \varepsilon_2 = 10^{-4}, r = 1/3, k_s = 2$$
$$k(t_0) = 0.1, \alpha = 2/3, \beta = 2 \tag{51}$$

Based on the discussion in previous section, system convergence time from initial condition to the field of $\|q_v\| \leq 10^{-4}$ could be got as follows

$$T_s \leq 2\frac{\left(V_s(t_0)/\varepsilon_1^2\right)^{1-r/2}}{k_s(2/\lambda_m(J))^{r+1/2}(1-r)} \approx 14 \text{ s}, T_q \leq 2\frac{\left(1/\varepsilon_2^2\right)^{1-\alpha/2}}{\beta(1-\alpha)} \approx 44 \text{ s}$$
$$T_0 \leq T_s + T_q = 58 \text{ s} \tag{52}$$

where T_s is the time form initial state to the sliding mode, and T_q is the convergence time along sliding mode (21).

The simulation results are shown as follows

Based on Figures 5 and 6 it could be found that system convergence time is about 30 s, which is much larger than that of the standard sliding mode, also the finite-time stability calculated in (54) has been proved. The hsystem steady accuracy at 40 s is about 2×10^{-6} rad/s of angular velocity and 4×10^{-8} of attitude quaternion. System performance including convergence rate and steady accuracy is largely improved compared with that of standard sliding mode, and the superiority of the proposed controller in this paper is illustrated by simulation results. Based on Figures 5, 7 and 8 it could be found that the norm of angular velocity and control torque are upper bounded during the whole maneuver process, hence the singularity issue of finite-time control does not occur in the proposed controller. Based on Figure 7, it could be found that the updating sliding mode parameter k is the key to improve the system convergence rate. From the initial value to its terminal value, parameter k has enlarged more than 3000 times (from 0.1 to more than 30), and this property could offset the drawback brought by the exponential convergence rate. However, it is obvious that the curve of k is very cliffy when the system state approaches the equilibrium point, and if the system continues to update parameter k, it would tend to infinity and cause the breakdown of the computing system. Moreover, noting the disturbance torque and model uncertainty in the simulation configuration, it could be concluded that controller (24) is robust to disturbance and model uncertainty. Above all, a finite-time controller (24) based on attitude quaternion proposed in this paper could achieve the goal of finite-time stability without causing the singularity issue, but the cost is that the finite-time stability is not strict (the system state could only reach the neighborhood of equilibrium point but not the actual equilibrium point within finite-time) to avoid the breakdown of computing system.

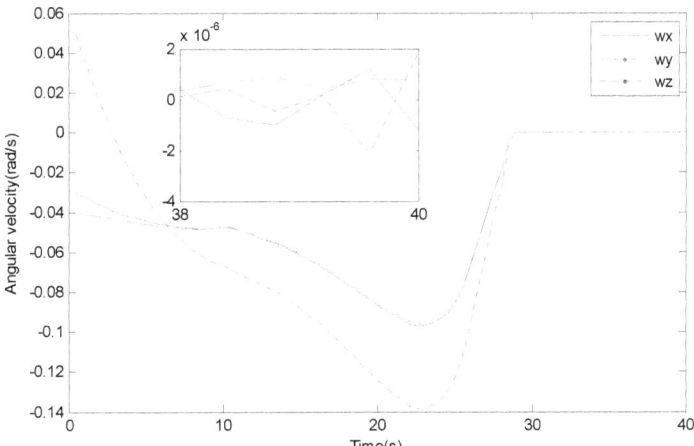

Figure 5. Curve of angular velocity.

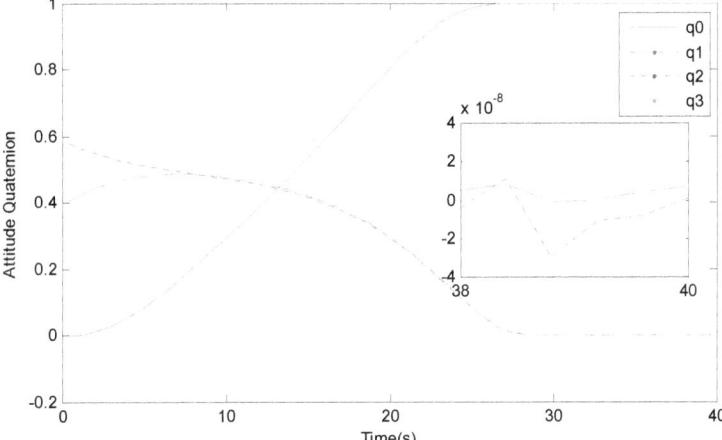

Figure 6. Curve of attitude quaternion.

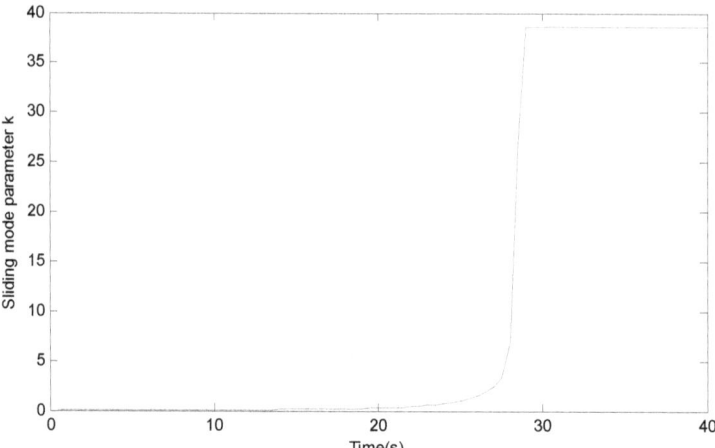

Figure 7. Curve of sliding mode parameter.

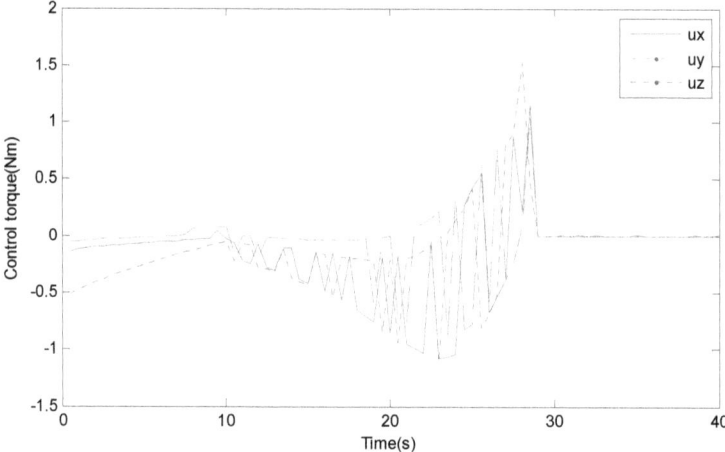

Figure 8. Curve of control torque.

Considering that the proposed sliding mode is modified based on standard sliding mode, hence some advantages such as the inherent robustness could be maintained. In order to demonstrate this property, set system configurations under controller (22) as follows

$$d = 1 \times 10^{-2} \times rand(3 \times 1) \text{Nm}$$

$$\overline{d} = 0, \lambda = 0, u' = diag(0.9, 0.8, 0.7)u \tag{53}$$

$$J = diag(30, 25, 20) \text{kg} \cdot \text{m}^2, \hat{J} = diag(22, 18, 15) \text{kg} \cdot \text{m}^2$$

Based on (53) it could be found that the unknown disturbance torque is enlarged to the 10^{-2}Nm level, and the term $\overline{d}$ to suppress disturbance in controller is set to be zero. Moreover, inertia matrix estimation has larger than 25% error comparing with actual inertia matrix, and the term λ to suppress this perturbation is also set to be zero. The actual control output has constant bias from desired control torque. Above all, under this configuration system has three perturbation aspects: (1) larger disturbance and no offset term in controller; (2) larger model uncertainty and no offset term in controller; and (3) control output error in actuator.

Simulation results under condition (53) are show as follows.

Based on Figures 9 and 10 it could be found that the system could still converge to the equilibrium point under such perturbations. Comparing this group of simulation with Figures 5–8 it could be found that the main difference is the convergence time. Based on Figures 9–11 it could be found that system converge time is about 43 s and the convergence time of controller (22) is about 30 s, and the steady accuracy could approximately be treated as the same level with controller (22). Moreover, Figures 11 and 12 demonstrate that finite-time sliding mode based on the standard sliding mode could resist some typical perturbations such as unknown disturbance, inertia matrix uncertainty and actuator error. Also, it is worth noting that although the demand control torque is discontinuous in Figure 12, it could be achieved by a reaction wheel, the function of which is to produce controlled torque by accelerating and decelerating its rotation speed, and this acceleration could be discontinuous. This proves that by designing the sliding mode properly, the finite-time stability and strong robustness could both be maintained.

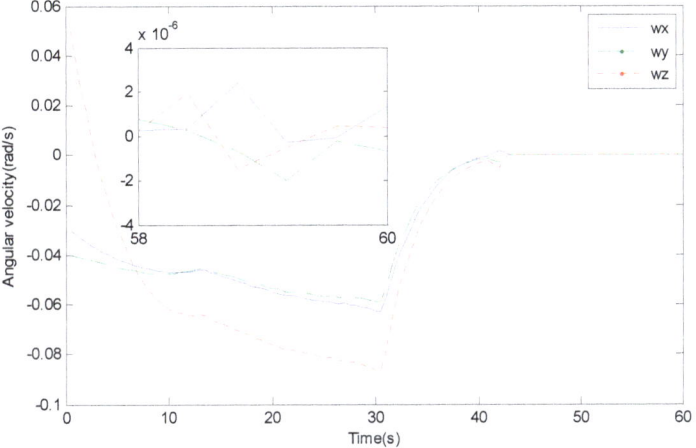

Figure 9. Curve of angular velocity.

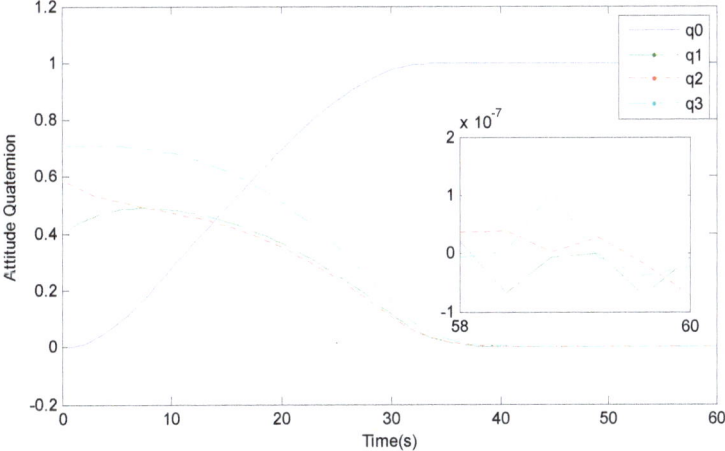

Figure 10. Curve of attitude quaternion.

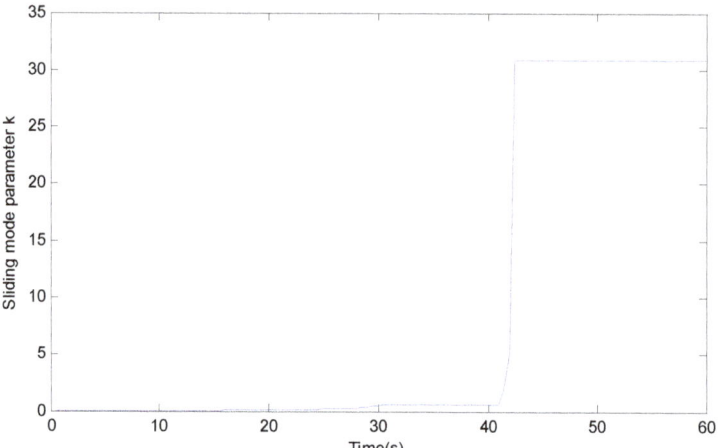

Figure 11. Curve of sliding mode parameter.

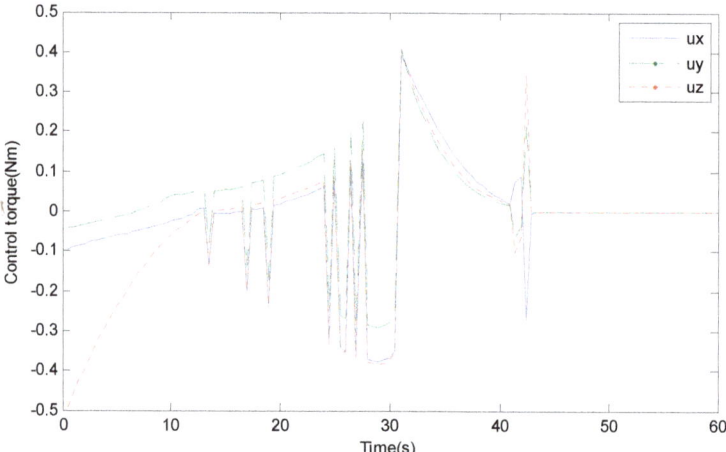

Figure 12. Curve of control torque.

In this section, simulation results for finite-time controller based on attitude quaternion are given. By the update law of sliding mode parameter, the finite-time stability could be ensured and the inherent robustness of the standard sliding mode could both be maintained. This is one of the main contributions of this paper and offers a new method to achieve finite-time stability. Also, it could be found that the parameter would tend to infinity and cause the breakdown of the computing system if the controller is not designed properly, hence the controller in Section 4 has some risk of the breakdown of the control system.

6.2. Simulation for Controller Based on Euler Axis

In this section, the simulation results of controller in Section 5 are given. Set system parameters as follows.

$$\hat{J} = diag(28, 24, 21) \text{kg·m}^2, \lambda = 3, \bar{d} = 10^{-3} \tag{54}$$

similar as discussed in Section 6.1, larger r and $k(t_0)$ brings faster convergence rate, but the demanded control torque is also enlarged, and smaller r makes sliding mode (9) degenerates to standard sliding mode. Also larger k_s makes system could reach the finite-time sliding mode faster, moreover, smaller α and larger β bring better convergence rate along the sliding mode. Larger γ_1 and γ_2 could ensure sliding mode parameter k reach the desired trajectory. Considering the selection of control parameters in references [4–7], some control parameters could be selected similarly. Generally, larger sliding mode parameters could bring better convergence rates but the demanded control torque is also larger. Above all, control parameters for controller (39) are selected as follows

$$\varepsilon_1 = 10^{-4}, r = 1/3, k_s = 2, \gamma_1 = \gamma_2 = 2$$
$$k(t_0) = 0.1, \alpha = 2/3, \beta = 1$$
(55)

Assume that when $\|q_v\| \leq \varepsilon_2 = 10^{-4}$ is satisfied the system could be treated as converged to the equilibrium point, and the system convergence time could be calculated as follows:

$$T_s \leq 2\frac{(V_s(t_0)/\varepsilon^2)^{1-r/2}}{k_s(2/\lambda_m(J))^{r+1/2}(1-r)} \approx 12 \text{ s}, T_k \leq 2\frac{(\beta/k(t_0))^{1-\alpha/2}}{\beta(1-\alpha)} \approx 9 \text{ s}$$

$$T_q \leq 2\frac{(1/\varepsilon_2^2)^{1-\alpha/2}}{\beta(1-\alpha)} \approx 31 \text{ s}, T_0 \leq T_s + T_k + T_q = 52 \text{ s}$$
(56)

where T_s is the time form initial state to the sliding mode, T_k is the time of k chasing the desired trajectory, and T_q is the convergence time along the proposed sliding mode.

The simulation results of controller (39) proposed in Section 5 is given as follows.

Based on Figures 13 and 14, it could be found that the system converges to the equilibrium point within 30 s, and this proves the system finite-time stability calculated in Equation (56). Moreover, the system steady accuracy at 50 s is about 2×10^{-5} rad/s of angular velocity and 6×10^{-7} of attitude quaternion, which satisfy the converge condition claimed previously. Based on Figures 15 and 16, it could be found that control torque and sliding mode parameter are all norm upper bounded and the singularity issue does not occur in this condition. Comparing simulation results in this section with those in Section 6.1 it could be found that system convergence time is faster in this section, and the major improvement is the curve of sliding mode parameter k. In this section the sliding mode parameter tends to zero, hence it is not necessary to stop the update law of the sliding mode parameter. The robustness of the control system is strengthened by this property compared with the controller in Section 4. It is worth noting that when maneuvering along the proposed trajectory, the sliding mode parameter k should be strictly monotonic decreasing. However, based on Figure 15, it could found that the parameter is not strictly monotonic decreasing and has some wave characters. This is caused by the discontinuous property of the Euler axis, since when approaching the equilibrium point, the Euler axis e changes fast and is easily interfered with by random disturbance torque. Consider that under this situation, the changing rate of e tends to infinite and the controller could not offset this perturbation, hence the system state deviates from the desired trajectory until the control torque overwhelms the discontinuous perturbation torque.

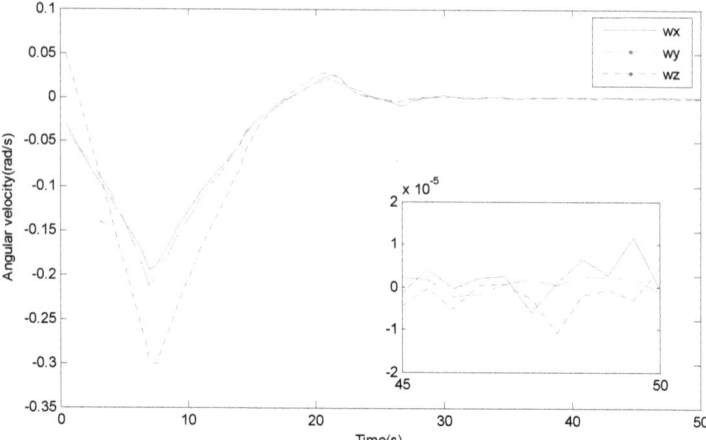

Figure 13. Curve of angular velocity.

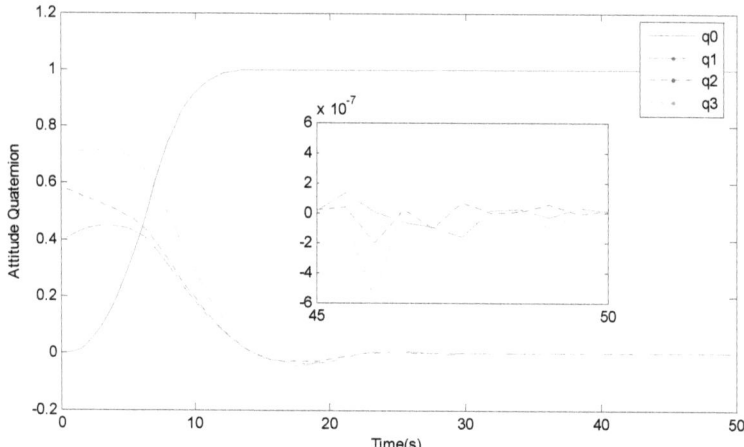

Figure 14. Curve of attitude quaternion.

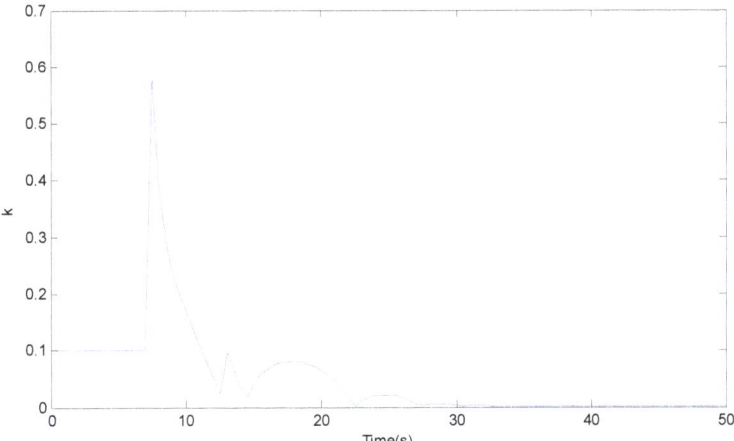

Figure 15. Curve of sliding mode parameter.

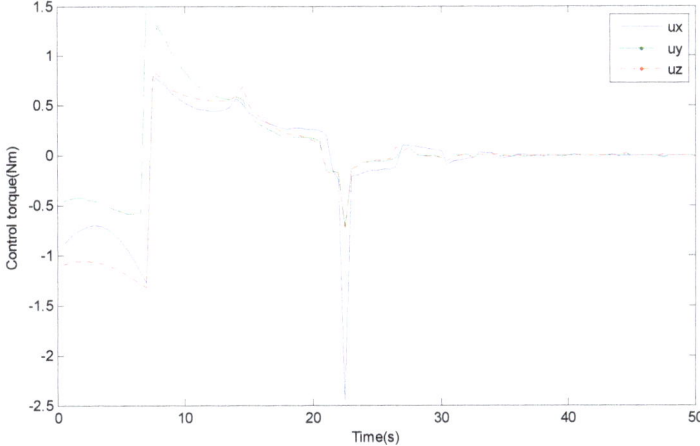

Figure 16. Curve of control torque.

Similar to the discussion in the previous section, in order to demonstrate this property, set system configurations under controller (39) are as follows:

$$d = 1 \times 10^{-2} \times rand(3 \times 1)\text{Nm} + 1 \times 10^{-3} \times \|\omega\| rand(3 \times 1)\text{Nm}$$

$$\bar{d} = 0, \lambda = 0, u' = diag(0.9, 0.8, 0.7)u \qquad (57)$$

$$J = diag(30, 25, 20)\text{kg} \cdot \text{m}^2, \hat{J} = diag(22, 18, 15)\text{kg} \cdot \text{m}^2$$

It could be found that under this configuration system has three aspect perturbations: (1) larger disturbance and no offset term in controller; (2) larger model uncertainty and no offset term in the controller; and (3) control output error in the actuator. The simulation results under strong perturbations are given as follows.

Based on Figures 17–20, it could be found that the system could still converge to the equilibrium point under such perturbations. Comparing this group of simulations with Figures 13–16, it could be found that the main difference is the convergence time. In this group of simulations, the system converges to the equilibrium point about 30 s slower compared with that in the controller (39). Figures 17 and 18 demonstrate that the finite-time sliding mode (31) could achieve a high steady accuracy and resist some typical perturbations such as unknown disturbance, inertia matrix uncertainty and actuator error. This proves that by designing the sliding mode properly, the finite-time stability and strong robustness could both be maintained. Generally, disturbance torque would influence the system steady performance (a larger disturbance would bring a larger sign function term and the system chattering issue would be aggravated), and system steady accuracy would drop.

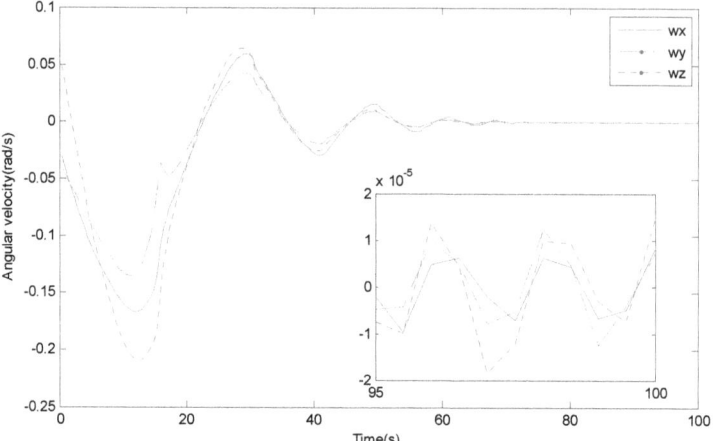

Figure 17. Curve of angular velocity.

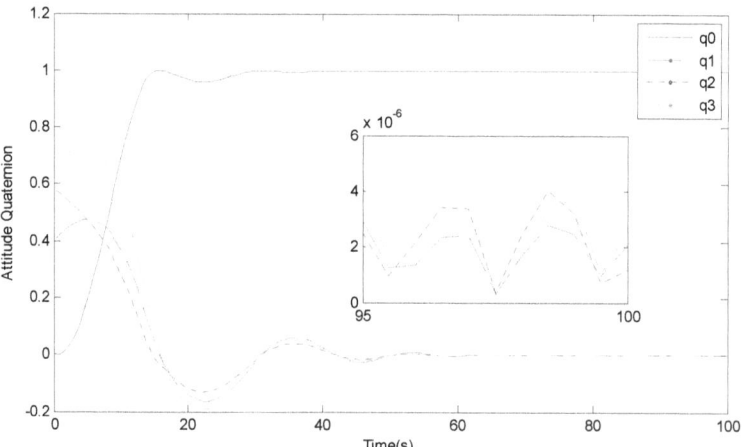

Figure 18. Curve of attitude quaternion.

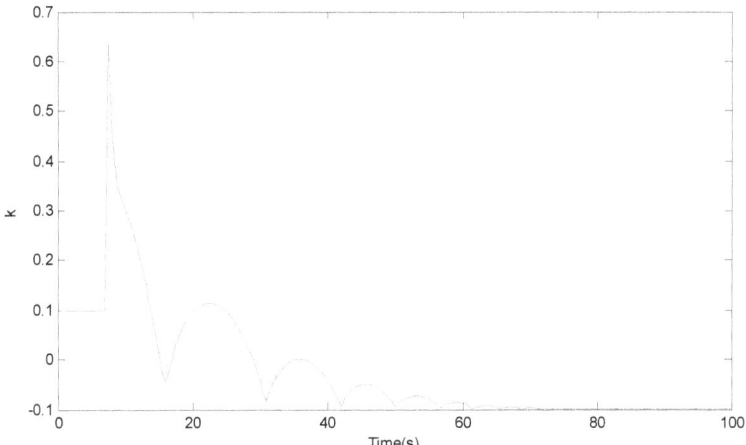

Figure 19. Curve of sliding mode parameter.

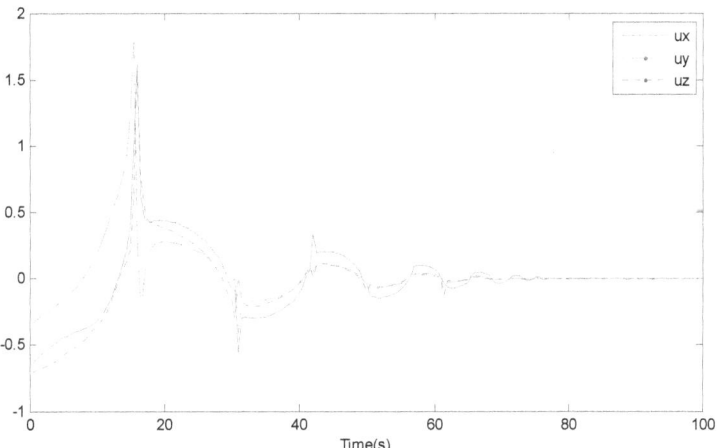

Figure 20. Curve of control torque.

Based on Table 1 it could be found that the proposed controller in this paper mostly maintained the advantage of the standard sliding mode controller, and the system convergence rate is largely improved. Also, the steady accuracy is also largely improved.

Table 1. Simulation results comparison.

	Standard Sliding Mode	Finite Time Based on Attitude Quaternion	Finite Time Based on Euler Axis
Convergence time	Low	Medium	High
Steady accuracy	Low	Medium	High
Robustness	Strong	Medium	Medium
Singularity Issue	None	None	Weak
Controller Structure	Simple	Complex	Complex

In this section, performance of the finite-time controller proposed in Section 5 is demonstrated. Compared with the controller in Section 4, the controller (39) could maintain the strong inherent robustness of the standard sliding mode and finite-time stability and the singularity issue of the sliding mode parameter is solved in this situation. The fixed norm of the Euler axis beings this property and this also brings some by-effect to the system, in fact, the control issue is transformed to an attitude determination issue since the small error of the Euler axis could bring large perturbation to system near the system equilibrium point.

7. Conclusions

In this paper, finite-time sliding modes are proposed based on standard sliding ones. A novel structure of finite time sliding mode surface is proposed based on a standard sliding mode surface. A system finite time stability is achieved by implementing the update law of sliding mode parameters and the singularity issue is avoided by using the property when angular velocity is reversed to the attitude quaternion.

Generally, by enlarging the sliding mode parameter, the system convergence rate could be improved significantly, and when the update law is designed properly, the desired system performance could be achieved. Also, it could be found that when using attitude quaternion to design the finite-time sliding mode, the sliding mode parameter tends to infinity as the system state converges to zero and the singularity issue of control torque is transformed to the singularity issue of the sliding mode parameter. In order to avoid the breakdown of the computer system caused by this singularity issue, it is necessary to stop updating the parameter when approaching the system equilibrium point. In order to get the strictly finite-time stability, the Euler axis parameter could be used to design a finite time sliding mode. The norm of the Euler axis is fixed, and this property brings some convenience to the design of the finite-time sliding mode. The singularity issue is solved and the system state, control torque and sliding mode parameters are all norm upper bounded. However, the control issue is transformed to a measurement issue since a small error could bring a large perturbation under some typical conditions.

Above all, two kinds of finite time sliding modes are proposed in this paper and each has its advantages and disadvantages. When selecting the sliding mode properly based on the onboard condition and space mission requirement, desired system performance can be achieved.

Author Contributions: Conceptualization, Y.L. and H.L.; methodology, formal analysis and software Y.L.; investigation, H.L.; writing—original draft preparation, Y.L.; writing—review and editing, Y.L. and H.L. All authors have read and agreed to the published version of the manuscript.

Funding: This work was supported partially by the National Natural Science Foundation of China (Project Nos. 61903289, 62003375 and 62103452). The authors greatly appreciate the above financial support. The authors would also like to thank the associate editor and reviewers for their valuable comments and constructive suggestions that helped to improve the paper significantly.

Institutional Review Board Statement: This paper does not have any issues involved with human or animal research.

Informed Consent Statement: This paper does not have any issues involved with human or animal research.

Data Availability Statement: If anyone wants to get the original data of this paper, please contact with You Li by liyou@xidian.edu.cn.

Acknowledgments: This work was supported by National Science Foundation of China (Project Nos.61903289 62003375 and 62103452) and the authors greatly appreciate the above financial support. The authors greatly appreciate the above financial support. The authors would also like to thank the associate editor and reviewers for their valuable comments and constructive suggestions that helped to improve the paper significantly.

Conflicts of Interest: We declare that we have no financial and personal relationships with other people or organizations that can inappropriately influence our work, there is no professional or other personal interest of any nature or kind in any product, service and/or company that could be construed as influencing the position presented in, or the review of, the manuscript entitled.

References

1. Gao, S.; Li, Y.; Yao, S.Y. Robust PD plus Control Algorithm for Satellite Attitude Tracking for Dynamic Targets. *Math. Probl. Eng.* **2021**, 6680994. [CrossRef]
2. Zhang, T.; Zhang, A. Robust Finite-Time Tracking Control for Robotic Manipulators with Time Delay Estimation. *Mathematics* **2020**, *8*, 165. [CrossRef]
3. Song, C.; Fei, S.; Cao, J.; Huang, C. Robust Synchronization of Fractional-Order Uncertain Chaotic Systems Based on Output Feedback Sliding Mode Control. *Mathematics* **2019**, *7*, 599. [CrossRef]
4. Li, Y.; Ye, D.; Sun, Z.W. Robust finite time control algorithm for satellite attitude control. *Aerosp. Sci. Technol.* **2017**, *68*, 46–57. [CrossRef]
5. Li, Y.; Ye, D. Time efficient sliding mode controller based on Bang-Bang logic for satellite attitude control. *Aerosp. Sci. Technol.* **2018**, *75*, 342–352. [CrossRef]
6. Li, Y.; Ye, D. Near time-optimal controller based on analytical trajectory planning algorithm for satellite attitude maneuver. *Aerosp. Sci. Technol.* **2019**, *84*, 497–509.
7. Ye, D.; Li, Y.; Xiao, B.; Li, W.E. Robust finite-time adaptive control algorithm for satellite fast attitude maneuver. *J. Frankl. Inst. -Eng. Appl. Math.* **2020**, *357*, 11558–11583. [CrossRef]
8. Zhang, Y.; Nie, Y.; Chen, L. Adaptive Fuzzy Fault-Tolerant Control against Time-Varying Faults via a New Sliding Mode Observer Method. *Symmetry* **2021**, *13*, 1615. [CrossRef]
9. Verbin, D.; Lappas, V.J.; Joseph, Z.B. Time efficient angular steering laws for rigid satellites. *J. Guid. Control. Dyn.* **2011**, *34*, 878–892. [CrossRef]
10. Rojsiraphisal, T.; Mobayen, S.; Asad, J.H.; Vu, M.T.; Chang, A.; Puangmalai, J. Fast Terminal Sliding Control of Underactuated Robotic Systems Based on Disturbance Observer with Experimental Validation. *Mathematics* **2021**, *9*, 1935. [CrossRef]
11. Ye, D.; Zhang, H.Z.; Tian, Y.X.; Zhao, Y.; Sun, Z.W. Fuzzy Sliding Mode Control of Nonparallel-ground-track Imaging Satellite with High Precision. *Int. J. Control. Autom. Syst.* **2020**, *18*, 1617–1628. [CrossRef]
12. Ye, D.; Zou, A.M.; Sun, Z.W. Predefined-Time Predefined-Bounded Attitude Tracking Control for Rigid Spacecraft. *IEEE Trans. Aerosp. Electron. Syst.* **2021**. [CrossRef]
13. Wu, S.N.; Radice, G.; Gao, Y.S.; Sun, Z.W. Quaternion-based finite time control for spacecraft attitude tracking. *Acta Astronaut.* **2011**, *69*, 48–58. [CrossRef]
14. Wu, S.N.; Radice, G.; Gao, Y.S.; Sun, Z.W. Robust finite-time control for flexible spacecraft attitude maneuver. *J. Aerosp. Eng.* **2014**, *27*, 185–190. [CrossRef]
15. Liang, H.Z.; Sun, Z.W.; Wang, J.Y. Finite-time attitude synchronization controllers design for spacecraft formations via behavior-based approach. *Part G J. Aerosp. Eng.* **2013**, *227*, 1737–1753. [CrossRef]
16. Wang, J.Y.; Liang, H.Z.; Sun, Z.W. Dual-quaternion-based finite-time control for spacecraft tracking in six degrees of freedom. *Part G J. Aerosp. Eng.* **2013**, *227*, 528–545. [CrossRef]
17. Wang, J.Y.; Liang, H.Z.; Sun, Z.W.; Zhang, S.J.; Liu, M. Finite-time control for spacecraft formation with dual-number-based description. *J. Guid. Control. Dyn.* **2012**, *35*, 950–962. [CrossRef]
18. Nguyen, N.P.; Mung, N.X.; Thanh Ha, L.N.N.; Huynh, T.T.; Hong, S.K. Finite-Time Attitude Fault Tolerant Control of Quadcopter System via Neural Networks. *Mathematics* **2020**, *8*, 1541. [CrossRef]
19. Khelil, N.; Otis, M.J.D. Finite-Time Stabilization of Homogeneous Non-Lipschitz Systems. *Mathematics* **2016**, *4*, 58. [CrossRef]
20. Guo, J.G.; Li, Y.F.; Zhou, J. A new continuous adaptive finite time guidance law against highly maneuvering targets. *Aerosp. Sci. Technol.* **2019**, *85*, 40–47. [CrossRef]
21. Xiao, B.; Yin, S.; Wu, L.G. A structure simple controller for satellite attitude tracking maneuver. *IEEE Trans. Ind. Electron.* **2017**, *64*, 1436–1446. [CrossRef]
22. Xiao, B.; Yin, S.; Gao, H.J. Tracking control of robotic manipulators with uncertain kinematics and dynamics. *IEEE Trans. Ind. Electron.* **2016**, *63*, 6439–6449. [CrossRef]
23. Xiao, B.; Yin, S. Velocity-free Fault tolerant and uncertainty attenuation control for a class of nonlinear systems. *IEEE Trans. Ind. Electron.* **2016**, *63*, 4400–4411. [CrossRef]
24. Hu, Q.L.; Zhang, X.X.; Niu, G.L. Observer-based fault tolerant control and experimental verification for rigid spacecraft. *Aerosp. Sci. Technol.* **2019**, *92*, 373–386. [CrossRef]
25. Hu, Q.L.; Xie, J.J.; Wang, C.L. Trajectory optimization for accompanying satellite obstacle avoidance. *Aerosp. Sci. Technol.* **2018**, *82–83*, 220–233. [CrossRef]
26. Hu, Q.L.; Zhang, J.; Zhang, Y.M. Velocity-free attitude coordinated tracking control for spacecraft formation flying. *ISA Trans.* **2018**, *73*, 54–65. [CrossRef] [PubMed]
27. Qiao, J.Z.; Zhang, D.F.; Zhu, Y.K.; Zhang, P.X. Disturbance observer-based finite-time attitude maneuver control for micro satellite under actuator deviation fault. *Aerosp. Sci. Technol.* **2018**, *82–83*, 262–271. [CrossRef]
28. Gui, H.C.; Geogre, V. Distributed almost global finite-time attitude consensus of multiple spacecraft without velocity measurements. *Aerosp. Sci. Technol.* **2018**, *75*, 284–296. [CrossRef]

29. Wang, Y.; Ji, H.B. Integrated relative position and attitude control for spacecraft rendezvous with ISS and finite-time convergence. *Aerosp. Sci. Technol.* **2019**, *85*, 234–245. [CrossRef]
30. Ai, X.L.; Yu, J.Q. Fixed-time trajectory tracking for a quadrotor with external disturbances: A flatness-based sliding mode control approach. *Aerosp. Sci. Technol.* **2019**, *89*, 58–76. [CrossRef]
31. Roman, R.C.; Precup, R.E.; Petriu, E.M. Hybrid data-driven fuzzy active disturbance rejection control for tower crane systems. *Eur. J. Control* **2021**, *58*, 373–387. [CrossRef]
32. Hou, Z.S.; Xiong, S.S. On Model-Free Adaptive Control and Its Stability Analysis. *IEEE Trans. Autom. Control.* **2019**, *64*, 4555–4569. [CrossRef]
33. Li, K.L.; Boonto, S.; Nuchkrua, T. On-line Self Tuning of Contouring Control for High Accuracy Robot Manipulators under Various Operations. *Int. J. Control. Autom. Syst.* **2020**, *18*, 1818–1828. [CrossRef]
34. Li, K.L.; Nuchkrua, T.; Zhao, H.; Yuan, Y.; Boonto, S. Learning-based Adaptive Robust Control of Manipulated Pneumatic Artificial Muscle Driven by H2-based Metal Hydride. In Proceedings of the 2018 IEEE 14th International Conference on Automation Science and Engineering (CASE), Munich, Germany, 20–24 August 2018; pp. 1284–1289.

Article

Water-Cycle-Algorithm-Tuned Intelligent Fuzzy Controller for Stability of Multi-Area Multi-Fuel Power System with Time Delays

CH. Naga Sai Kalyan [1], B. Srikanth Goud [2], Mohit Bajaj [3], Malligunta Kiran Kumar [4], Emad M. Ahmed [5,*] and Salah Kamel [6]

[1] Department of Electrical and Electronics Engineering, Vasireddy Venkatadri Institute of Technology, Guntur 522508, India; kalyanchallapalli@gmail.com
[2] Department of Electrical and Electronics Engineering, Anurag College of Engineering, Ghatkesar 501301, India; srikanth.b@anuraghyd.ac.in
[3] Department of Electrical and Electronics Engineering, National Institute of Technology, New Delhi 110040, India; mohitbajaj@nitdelhi.ac.in
[4] Department of Electrical and Electronics Engineering, Koneru Lakshmaiah Education Foundation, Guntur 522502, India; kiran.malligunta@gmail.com
[5] Department of Electrical Engineering, College of Engineering, Jouf University, Sakaka 72388, Saudi Arabia
[6] Electrical Engineering Department, Faculty of Engineering, Aswan University, Aswan 81542, Egypt; skamel@aswu.edu.eg
* Correspondence: emamahmoud@ju.edu.sa

Abstract: In this paper, a fuzzy (F) proportional (P)–integral (I)–derivative (D) (PID) (FPID) controller optimized with a water cycle algorithm is proposed for load frequency control of a multi-area multi-fuel (MAMF) power system. The MAMF system has the realistic feature of communication time delays (CTDs), in order to conduct an analysis nearer to realistic practice. Initially, the MAMF system is analyzed when subjected to a step load disturbance (SLD) of 10% on area 1. The superiority of the fuzzy PID controller is revealed upon comparing it with PID plus double derivative (DD) (PIDD) and PID controllers. The MAMF system is investigated with and without CTDs, to demonstrate their impact on system performance. Later, an additional HVDC line is incorporated in parallel with the existing AC line for further enhancement of the system performance. Finally, the MAMF system is targeted with random loading to validate the robustness of the presented control scheme.

Keywords: FPID controller; stability analysis; frequency regulation; MAMF power system; CTDs

1. Introduction

In modern times, frequency regulation is the most indispensable task in power systems, due to the rapid growth in load demand, integration of several renewable conversion units, formation of microgrids, the emergence of unintentional time delays and power system intricacy. Frequency fluctuations arise because of the real power gap between demand and generation. Necessary steps must be taken to minimize the real power mismatch, in order to hold the power system frequency within the specified range. This action is governed by the load frequency controller (LFC), which plays a vital role in the automatic generation control (AGC) of the interconnected power system (IPS). The IPS comprises several areas with different generation units representing diverse generation sources that are running in synchronism and are connected through transmission lines in the form of tie lines. These lines facilitate the real power exchange between deficit and surplus generation areas. Power interchange between the control areas via tie lines should be done without violating the limits. Otherwise, the lines reach the maximum feasible thermal limit, leading to line outages and hence affecting the stability of the IPS.

The LFC safeguards the IPS stability by regulating the system frequency and power exchange via tie lines, to prevent violation of the specified range by varying generation unit operating points. The concept of the LFC was proposed by Cohen [1] using tie-line bias control in the year 1957. Later, Elgerd and Fosha [2] introduced classical controllers as frequency regulators for the multi-area thermal system, in the year 1970. Since then, researchers have concentrated more on designing frequency regulators for the IPS, to maintain stability. A literature survey discloses the usage of different power system models comprised of thermal–thermal units, hydrothermal units and a combination of conventional and renewable-energy-based systems with and without considering the constraints of non-linearity such as the governor dead band (GDB) and the generation rate constraint (GRC), etc. These are consolidated in [3]. Irrespective of the power system model, different classical control strategies such as PI fine-tuned using a simulated annealing (SA)/genetic algorithm (GA) [4], PI/PID [5] based on the grey wolf optimizer (GWO), PID [6] with a harmony search algorithm (HSA), PI/PID [7] using a backtracking search algorithm (BSA), imperialist competitive approach (ICA)-based [8] PI/PID, ant lion optimizer (ALO)-based [9] PID with double derivative (DD) gain PIDD, PID tuned with differential evolution (DE) [10], PID using an elephant herd optimizer (EHO) [11], PID optimized with a cuckoo search algorithm (CSA) [12], firefly algorithm (FA)-based PI [13], whale optimizer (WO)-based [14] PID, falcon optimization algorithm (FOA)-tuned PID/PIDD [15], PID [16] based on a grasshopper optimization approach (GOA) and other hybrid (H) algorithms such as the artificial field (HAEFA) approach [17], HFA–pattern search (PS) method [18], DE–AEFA [19] etc., are reported in the literature. However, classical regulators are not sufficient to handle power system models with the non-linearity features of GRC, GDB and time delays. Some modified classical controllers such as PID with filter (N) PIDN [20] and other fractional order (FO) FOPI–FOPD controllers [21] have been proposed by researchers using some of the newest optimization algorithms to overcome the problem stated above, but only to a certain extent.

Fuzzy logic controllers (FLCs) are proven to be more efficacious in handling IPS models, especially with non-linearity constraints. However, selecting the shape of the membership functions (MFs) and the framing of the rule-based interface engine require the utmost care; otherwise, the FLC may worsen the IPS performance. In general, selection of MFs is based on pragmatic rules, which are never optimal. Thus, various optimization methods have been implemented to select the most suitable parameters for FLCs. Hence, fuzzy-aided classical controllers are gaining momentum, especially in the power system optimization domain, compared to classical controllers alone. Different fuzzy (F)-aided classical controllers that have been reported in the recent literature, such as bacteria foraging optimization (BFO) [22]/ICA [23]/tuned FPI, DEPS-tuned [24] FPI/FPID, Type-II FPID [25] based on the GWO sine cosine approach, modified DE-approach-based FPID [26], FA-tuned FPID [27], symbiotic organism search (SOS)-based FPID [28], SOA-optimized FOFPID [29], etc., are available.

WCA is a recent meta-heuristic and population-based search method which mimics the movement of the water cycle on the Earth's surface. WCA is more efficient for solving constrained optimization problems and is more efficient compared to the other population- and stochastic-based methods explained briefly in [30]. In [25], it was observed that WCA-tuned controller parameters are more robust for handling IPSs with parametric uncertainty and that they show better stability. Implementation of WCA in LFCs has not been much studied in the recent literature; moreover, its robustness and ability to maintain a balance between the phases of exploitation and exploration motivated the researchers in this study to adopt WCA for the optimal tuning of FPID for the stability of an IPS. Moreover, the MAMF system is considered with the realistic constraints of GRC and CTDs. The literature survey disclosed the articles that are available with test system models considering the non-linearity of GRC and GDB. Researchers have concentrated much less on considering CTDs with a power system model for analysis purposes. Few papers have considered and demonstrated the impact of CTDs on IPS performance, and their analysis is confined to regulation by traditional PID [31] controllers only. Hence, the power system model studied in this paper is considered with CTDs, and the effect of CTDs on system performance in combination with a GRC is presented under the regulation of a WCA-tuned FPID controller.

Further, an HVDC line is laid in parallel with the existing AC tie line as a territorial control strategy to enhance the dynamical behaviour of the MAMF IPS. The designed secondary regulators can withstand the fluctuations that arise in the system only to a certain extent. During large load disturbances, secondary regulators alone would not be able to restore system stability. Thus, territorial control schemes are necessary to prevent system instability during time-intensive load variations. The presented AC/DC lines of the territory strategy facilitate the bulk power transfer capability among control areas whenever required; therefore, the demand in the deficit generation control area is met quickly from surplus generation areas.

Considering the above discussion, this work makes the following contributions:

a. An LFC for a MAMF IPS depicted in Figure 1 is developed in MATLAB/Simulink version R2016a.
b. A WCA-based FPID is presented as a frequency regulator whose efficacy is revealed compared to conventional PIDD/PID controllers.
c. System non-linearity constraints of GRC and CTDs are considered, to conduct research that is close to realistic practice.
d. The effect of CTDs on the MAMF IPS performance is visualized and justified.
e. The territorial control strategy of AC/DC lines is employed to further enhance the MAMF system dynamical behaviour.
f. The robustness of the presented control schemes is validated by subjecting the MAMF system to a wide range of load fluctuations in both areas.

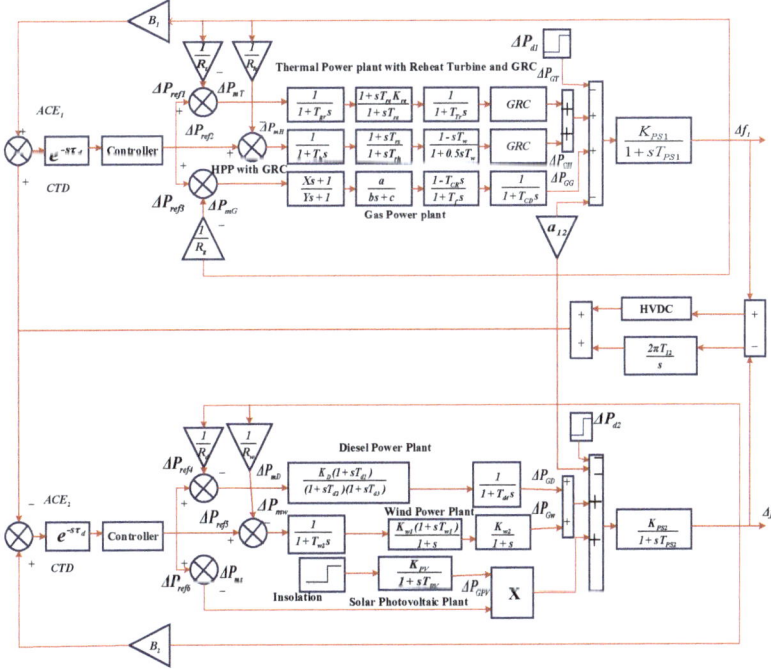

Figure 1. Transfer function model of multi-area multi-fuel power system.

2. Power System Model

The power system model under investigation comprises two areas with a 2:1 ratio of generation capacities. Area 1 is integrated with conventional hydrothermal–gas power generation plants and area 2 is integrated with diesel–solar photovoltaic–wind units. The non-linearity feature of the generation rate constraint (GRC) is considered with the hydrothermal units, to conduct an analysis close to realistic practice. For the thermal plant, a 3%/min GRC is considered, whereas for the hydro units 360%/min and 270%/min constraints are considered for valve lowering and raising. The model of the power system depicted in Figure 1 was developed using the MATLAB/Simulink version R2016a platform, and the required parameters were taken from [31]. Individual generation units are approximated by transfer functions as follows:

$$\frac{\Delta P_{GT}(S)}{\Delta P_{mT}(S)} = \frac{(1 + ST_{re}K_{re})}{(1 + T_{gr}S)(1 + ST_{re})(1 + T_{Tr}S)} \quad (1)$$

Hydro unit:

$$\frac{\Delta P_{GH}(S)}{\Delta P_{mH}(S)} = \frac{(1 + ST_{rs})(1 - ST_W)}{(1 + T_h S)(1 + T_{rh} S)(1 + 0.5T_W S)} \quad (2)$$

Gas unit:

$$\frac{\Delta P_{GG}(S)}{\Delta P_{mG}(S)} = \frac{(1 + XS)(1 - T_{CR}S)a}{(1 + YS)(c + bS)(1 + T_F S)(1 + T_{CD}S)} \quad (3)$$

Diesel unit:

$$\frac{\Delta P_{GD}(S)}{\Delta P_{mD}(S)} = \frac{K_D(1 + ST_{d1})}{(1 + T_{d4}S)(1 + T_{d2}S)(1 + T_{d3}S)} \quad (4)$$

Wind unit:

$$\frac{\Delta P_{GW}(S)}{\Delta P_{mW}(S)} = \frac{K_{W1}K_{W2}(1 + ST_{W1})}{(1 + T_{W2}S)(1 + 2S + S^2)} \quad (5)$$

Solar photovoltaic unit:

$$\frac{\Delta P_{GPV}(S)}{\varphi} = \frac{K_{PV}}{1 + T_{PV}S} \quad (6)$$

The power generated by the individual units in area 1 and area 2 is modeled as

$$P_{G1} = P_{GT} + P_{GH} + P_{GG} \quad (7)$$

$$P_{G2} = P_{GD} + P_{GW} + P_{GPV} \quad (8)$$

During perturbed conditions, the variation in power generated by the units in area 1 and area 2 is modeled as

$$\Delta P_{G1} = \Delta P_{GT} + \Delta P_{GH} + \Delta P_{GG} \quad (9)$$

$$\Delta P_{G2} = \Delta P_{GD} + \Delta P_{GW} + \Delta P_{GPV} \quad (10)$$

The exchange of power between the areas with only an AC tie line is given as

$$P_{tieAC} = P_{12}\sin(\delta_1 - \delta_2) \quad (11)$$

During perturbed conditions, Equation (11) can be redefined as

$$\begin{aligned}\Delta P_{tieAC} &= T_{12}(\Delta \delta_1 - \Delta \delta_2) \\ &= T_{12}(\Delta f_1 - \Delta f_2)\end{aligned} \quad (12)$$

With the incorporation of the HVDC link in parallel with the existing AC line, power flow deviations can be controlled up to a certain level. The HVDC link cannot be designed without considering the model of the power system. The gain (K_{DC}) and time (T_{DC}) parameters of the HVDC line are optimized using the optimization technique. Power flow in the AC/DC tie line is defined as in Equation (13), and the single-line representation of the MAMF system with AC/DC lines is shown in Figure 2.

$$P_{tie12} = P_{tieAC} + P_{tieDC} \tag{13}$$

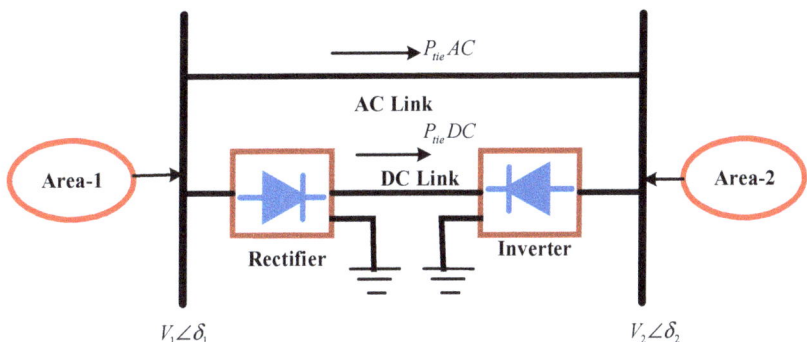

Figure 2. Single-line diagram of interconnected power system with AC/DC lines.

The change in power flow via the DC line under perturbing conditions is modeled as

$$\Delta P_{tieDC} = \frac{K_{DC}}{(1 + T_{DC}S)}(\Delta f_1 - \Delta f_2) \tag{14}$$

Modeling of the area control error (ACE) with AC/DC tie-lines is given by

$$ACE_1 = B_1 \Delta f_1 + (\Delta P_{tieAC} + \Delta P_{tieDC}) \tag{15}$$

$$ACE_2 = B_2 \Delta f_2 + (\Delta P_{tieAC} + \Delta P_{tieDC}) \tag{16}$$

3. Communication Time Delays

The modern-day IPS has become very complex with the penetration of different distributed generation (DG) sources. Usually, the power system network is situated in a vast area and has more sensing and phase-measuring devices in remote terminal locations. The measured data from devices located in remote terminals are transmitted to the command control center. Control signals, generated from the command control center based on the data received from remote devices, are transmitted to the secondary regulator in the plant location to alter the operating point of the system with respect to the varying load demand. The transmission and reception of signals among various devices located at large distances are achieved via communication channels. Communication channels are characterized by certain time delays, as data communication cannot take place instantly. Due to these CTDs, the delay in altering the power plant operating point leads to an increase in the real power mismatch between load and generation. These real power mismatches lead to fluctuations in system frequency, thereby affecting the power system stability. Moreover, in the case of severe CTDs, the designed secondary regulator may not handle the fluctuations and may become unstable. To overcome the instability issues due to the emergence of unintentional time delays within the system, the power system model must be considered with CTDs, and the secondary regulator must be designed in the presence of CTDs. The modeling of the CTDs considered in this paper is as follows [31]:

$$e^{-s\tau_d} = \frac{1 - \frac{\tau_d}{2}s}{1 + \frac{\tau_d}{2}s} \tag{17}$$

4. Controller and Objective Function

Usually, traditional controllers such as I/PI/PID controllers are extensively adopted by researchers to regulate the power system frequency, due to their easy implementation and design simplicity. However, these classical controllers are not competent enough during uncertainties or for power system models with non-linear features. Fuzzy logic controllers (FLC) are the most efficient for handling non-linear systems [32]. However, the design of the FLC interface and the selection of the membership functions (MFs) requires the utmost care. Otherwise, the FLC may degrade the power system performance. Triangular MFs, as shown in Figure 3, were chosen for the FLC in this study, because of their simplicity and low memory utilization. Moreover, these triangular MFs with an overlap of 50% yield satisfactory results. Triangular MFs with linguistic variables such as (LP) large positive, (SP) small positive, (Z) zero, (SN) small negative and (LN) large negative [33] were considered. The area control error (ACE) and the derivative of the ACE were given as input to the FLC unit, and then the output of the FLC was fed to the PID to generate the final output to shift the operating point subjected to load fluctuations. The fuzzy PID structure utilized in this work is depicted in Figure 4 [34].

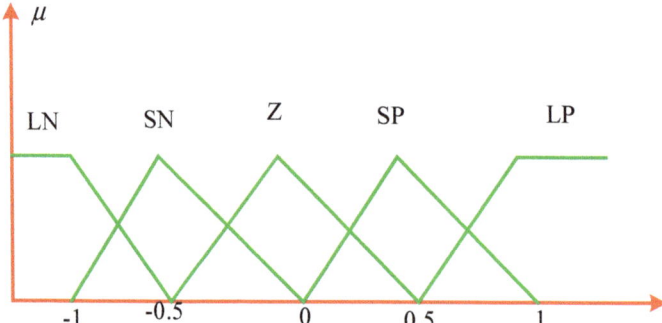

Figure 3. Fuzzy membership functions.

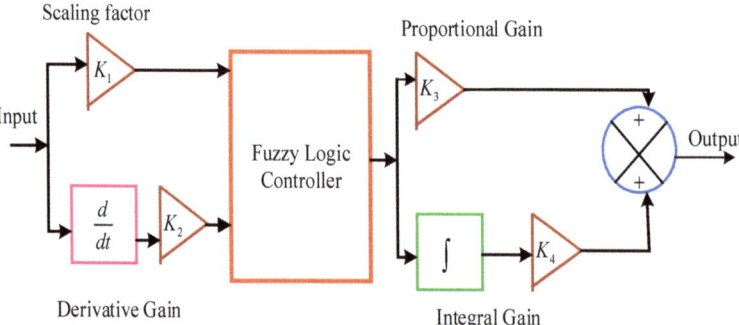

Figure 4. Structure of fuzzy-aided PID controller [34].

A Mamdani-type FLC system was designed in this work, with the center of gravity method [35,36] of defuzzification. The fuzzy output was calculated based on the rules shown in Table 1. The gains of the fuzzy-aided PID were optimized using the meta-heuristic optimization approach of a WCA subjected to the minimization of the ISE objective function. Compared to other time-domain-based objective functions, ISE is more effective in dampening peak deviations by maintaining the average balance with settling time. Therefore, we adopted ISE in this work, as shown in Equation (18).

$$J_{ISE} = \int_0^{T_{Sim}} (\Delta f_1^2 + \Delta P_{tie12}^2 + \Delta f_2^2) \tag{18}$$

Table 1. FLC system input and output rules.

ACE	ΔACE				
	LN	SN	Z	SP	LP
LN	LN	LN	LN	SN	Z
SN	LN	LN	SN	Z	SP
Z	LN	SN	Z	SP	LP
SP	SN	Z	SP	LP	LP
LP	LP	Z	SP	LP	LP

5. Water Cycle Algorithm

The water cycle algorithm (WCA) is one of the newest population-based meta-heuristic optimization techniques that many researchers are focusing on, especially for constrained engineering optimization problems. The evolution of this algorithm, introduced by Eskander et al. [37] in 2012, was inspired by the phenomena of the water cycle on the Earth's surface. Since then, this approach has found applications in many research fields. However, the implementation of the WCA approach in power system regulation has not been significant to date. This motivated the researchers in this study to implement this searching algorithm to find the optimal parameters of the secondary regulator to regulate the frequency and maintain the stability of interconnected power system models.

The searching strategy of the WCA starts with an initial population of raindrops or snowflakes that accumulate on hills or mountains and later collectively move downwards to form streams and rivers. Finally, these streams and rivers are assumed to be joined at the sea, treated as the global best solution.

For a solution with variables $1 \times N_{var}$, the vector of rain drops (RD) is formulated as

$$RD_i = Y_i = [y_1, y_2 \ldots \ldots \ldots y_{Nvar}] \tag{19}$$

$$RD\ Population = \begin{bmatrix} RD_1 \\ --- \\ RD_i \\ --- \\ RD_{N_{POP}} \end{bmatrix} \tag{20}$$

After defining the initial population, the cost of an individual RD is evaluated considering the time-domain objective index of ISE, as formulated in Equation (18).

Subsequently, the positions (P) of rivers/streams are updated, as shown in Equations (21) and (22), based on the assumption that these join at the sea eventually.

$$P_{stream}^{new} = P_{stream} + rand() * C * (P_{river} - P_{stream}) \tag{21}$$

$$P_{river}^{new} = P_{river} + rand() * C * (P_{sea} - P_{river}) \tag{22}$$

The parameter C is constant and is generated randomly, taking a value lying between 0 and 2, whereas rand () takes a value between 0 and 1. If the evaluated cost index value of the stream happens to be less than that of the river, then the positions of the stream and river will be exchanged. A similar process is applied for rivers and the sea.

To facilitate space for rainwater in the sea, the optimization algorithm is operated with an evaporation phase for seawater. Further, this loop will avoid rapid convergence and impart excellent capability to the searching mechanism. The phase of evaporation terminates if

$$|P_{sea} - P_{river}| < d_{max} \qquad (23)$$

where d_{max} is a number close to zero, which decreases automatically as

$$d_{max}^{new} = d_{max} - (d_{max}/max.iteration) \qquad (24)$$

The phase of rain starts immediately after the termination of the evaporation process. During rain, new streams will be formed at different locations, and their positions are found using

$$P_{stream}^{new} = P_{sea} + \sqrt{U} \times rand(1, N_{var}) \qquad (25)$$

where U indicates the rate of search close to the sea. The algorithm displays the global best solution when it reaches the maximum iteration count. The parametric values implemented while designing the WCA algorithm for power system optimization in this study are given in Table 2, and the flowchart is depicted in Figure 5.

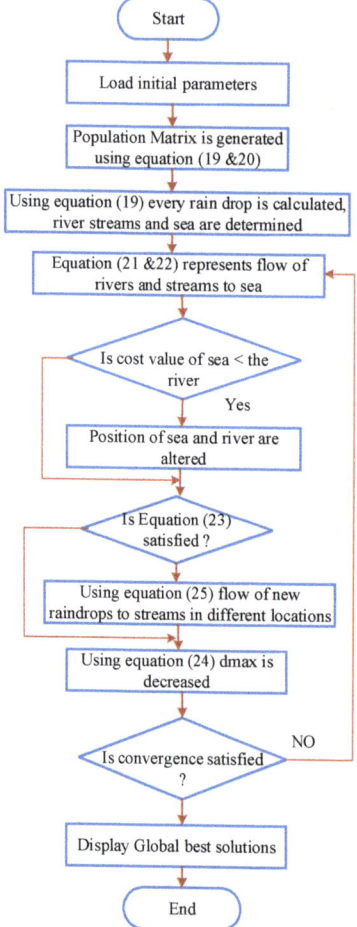

Figure 5. WCA flowchart.

Table 2. WCA parameters.

Parameter	Value
N_{Var}	21
N_{POP}	100
C	2
U	0.04
d_{max}	0.001
Max.iteration	50

6. Simulation Results

6.1. Case 1: Analysis of MAMF System without Considering CTDs

The performance of the MAMF system was assessed without taking the feature of CTDs into account. Various controllers such as PID/PIDD/fuzzy PID were implemented as secondary regulators one after the other in both the areas, and were optimized using the WCA algorithm. To obtain the most comparative analysis, responses under different controllers are compared in Figure 6 in terms of frequency deviation in area 1 (Δf_1) and area 2 (Δf_2), and tie-line power flow deviations (ΔP_{tie12}). Moreover, the responses shown in Figure 6 are numerically interpolated with regard to the settling time (T_s) provided in Table 3, and the controller's optimum gains are noted in Table 4. Further, the peak undershoot (U_S) values obtained with the presented FPID were lower (Δf_1 = 0.0098 Hz, ΔP_{tie12} = 0.00541 Pu.MW, Δf_2 = 0.000303 Hz) than those using PIDD (Δf_1 = 0.01311 Hz, ΔP_{tie12} = 0.00868 Pu.MW, Δf_2 = 0.00068 Hz) and PID (Δf_1 = 0.01659 Hz, ΔP_{tie12} = 0.01315 Pu.MW, Δf_2 = 0.001021 Hz). From Figure 6 and Table 3, it can be primarily concluded that the fuzzy PID completely outperforms the PID/PIDD in diminishing the peak undershoots/overshoots as well as in damping out the oscillations. Further, with the fuzzy PID, the objective index is very slightly minimized, whereas it is enhanced by 60.94% with PIDD and 78.63% with PID.

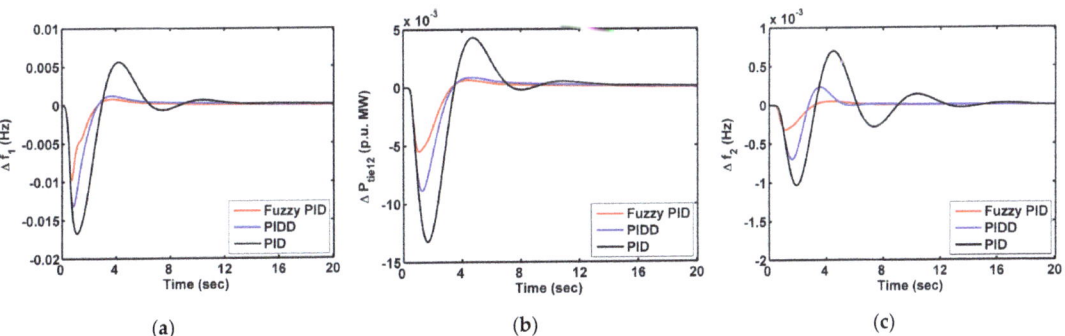

Figure 6. MAMF system responses for case 1: (a) Δf_1; (b) ΔP_{tie12}; (c) Δf_2.

Table 3. MAMF system response settling time (in sec) for various cases.

Settling Time (in sec)	Case 1			Case 2		
	FPID	PIDD	PID	FPID	PIDD	PID
Δf_1	7.56	8.95	12.69	9.721	11.88	15.97
ΔP_{tie12}	10.160	11.46	13.21	11.23	12.40	14.26
Δf_2	8.322	11.80	14.89	9.834	13.16	16.39
ISE $\times 10^{-3}$	7.769	19.893	36.355	29.275	52.283	85.098

Table 4. MAMF system response settling time (in sec) for various cases.

Controller	Area 1			Area 2		
	FPID	PIDD	PID	FPID	PIDD	PID
Case 1	$K_1 = 0.5757$ $K_2 = 0.7573$ $K_3 = 0.8315$ $K_4 = 0.3394$	$K_P = 2.0755$ $K_I = 1.1281$ $K_D = 0.7329$ $K_{DD} = 0.1430$	$K_P = 3.1388$ $K_I = 2.0944$ $K_D = 1.4939$	$K_1 = 0.8861$ $K_2 = 0.6994$ $K_3 = 0.8606$ $K_4 = 0.3766$	$K_P = 1.9575$ $K_I = 1.6113$ $K_D = 0.5889$ $K_{DD} = 0.1495$	$K_P = 2.9936$ $K_I = 1.8112$ $K_D = 0.8632$
Case 2	$K_1 = 0.5014$ $K_2 = 0.7113$ $K_3 = 0.6592$ $K_4 = 0.4588$	$K_P = 1.8098$ $K_I = 1.2760$ $K_D = 0.9630$ $K_{DD} = 0.0607$	$K_P = 2.9861$ $K_I = 1.9060$ $K_D = 1.1464$	$K_1 = 0.8130$ $K_2 = 0.8248$ $K_3 = 0.6416$ $K_4 = 0.4268$	$K_P = 1.9623$ $K_I = 1.2260$ $K_D = 0.6232$ $K_{DD} = 0.4939$	$K_P = 3.0283$ $K_I = 2.0519$ $K_D = 0.8964$

6.2. Case 2: Analysis of MAMF System with CTDs Considered

The MAMF system performance was assessed taking the feature of CTDs into account. A realistic time delay of 0.25 sec was considered in this work, to analyze its impact on system performance. The WCA-optimized controllers such as PID/PIDD/fuzzy PID were implemented in the MAMF system one after another in both the areas for the same disturbance loading on area 1 of 10% SLD. The responses for this case are shown in Figure 7, and the corresponding numerical results are given in Table 3. From the responses depicted in Figure 7, it can be concluded that the fuzzy PID showed superior performance in handling the system behaviour, even when considering CTDs. Moreover, the peak U_S values are greatly diminished with FPID ($\Delta f_1 = 0.0187$ Hz, $\Delta P_{tie12} = 0.01074$ Pu.MW, $\Delta f_2 = 0.00064$ Hz) compared with using PIDD ($\Delta f_1 = 0.02033$ Hz, $\Delta P_{tie12} = 0.01293$ Pu.MW, $\Delta f_2 = 0.00086$ Hz) and PID ($\Delta f_1 = 0.02569$ Hz, $\Delta P_{tie12} = 0.01813$ Pu.MW, $\Delta f_2 = 0.001359$ Hz). The ISE index is greatly minimized by the fuzzy PID but is improved by 44.06% with PIDD and 65.59% with PID.

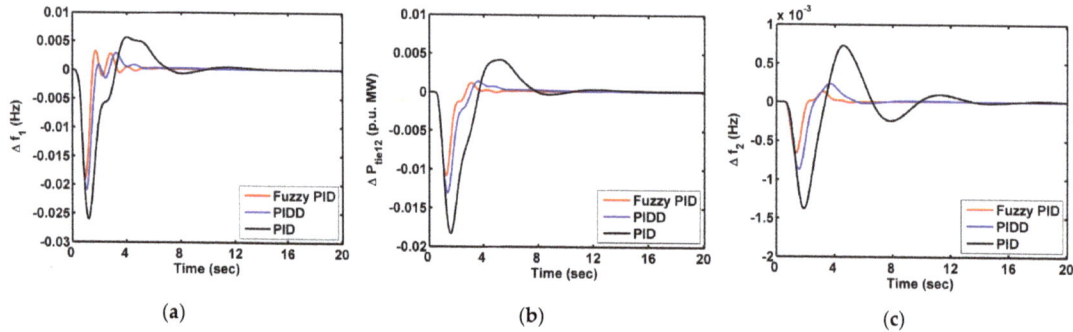

Figure 7. MAMF system responses for case 2: (**a**) Δf_1; (**b**) ΔP_{tie12}; (**c**) Δf_2.

6.3. Case 3: Comparative Analysis of MAMF System Responses without and with Consideration of CTDs

To demonstrate the predominance of CTDs in the MAMF system performance, responses with and without considering CTDs under the supervision of the WCA-based fuzzy PID controller are compared in Figure 8. As the fuzzy PID exhibits more dominance in regulating the deviations in responses compared to the PID/PIDD, the responses under fuzzy PID only are compared in Figure 8. From the MAMF system responses compared in Figure 8, it can be concluded that the responses with CTDs have more deviations and take slightly more time for the oscillations to settle down. Moreover, the responses of the MAMF system with CTDs take more time to reach a steady condition. This is because of the time delay between transmission and reception of the measured data signals and control signals among different devices situated in various locations. With these time delays, the data from sensors installed at distant locations will be transmitted to the command control center with some delay. Based on these data, the control signal will be generated and fed as input to the regulator in the plant location to alter the real power generation subjected to a fluctuating load demand. Hence, the delay in generating the control signal and the delay in transmitting the control signal to the regulator in the plant location leads to a more real power mismatch between generation and demand and hence to deviations in the system dynamical behaviour. Thus, we strongly endorse considering the CTDs within the power system when designing the regulator, to avoid stability issues. A regulator designed without taking CTDs into account will no longer maintain system stability in the event of unintentional time delays emerging within the power system.

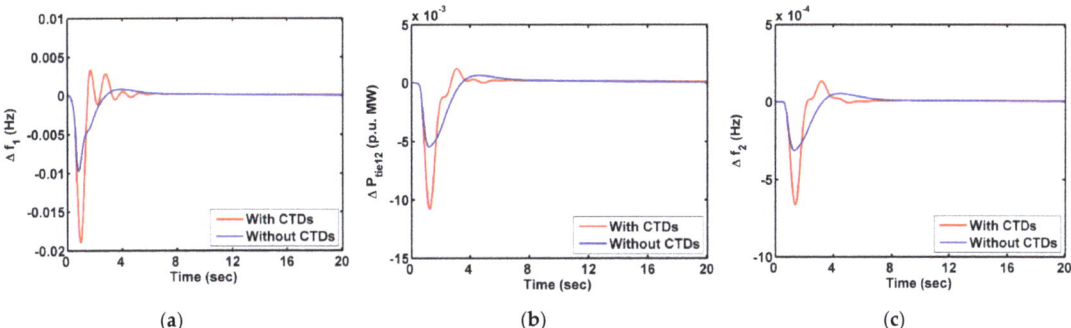

Figure 8. MAMF system responses for case 3: (**a**) Δf_1; (**b**) ΔP_{tie12}; (**c**) Δf_2.

6.4. Case 4: Analysis of MAMF System with AC/DC Lines

To substantiate the oscillations that occur in the system dynamical behaviour because of CTDs and the deviations in peak undershoot/overshoot, an additional HVDC tie line was incorporated in the MAMF system in parallel with the existing AC line. The system responses with the AC line and AC/DC lines are compared in Figure 9, to visualize the efficacy of adopting the additional HVDC tie line in the system and numerical results are provided in Table 5. The deviations were greatly mitigated, and the responses settled down more quickly when employing AC/DC lines than when employing only AC lines. Thus, it is concluded that the territorial control strategy of employing AC/DC lines in the interconnected power system enhances the system dynamical behaviour.

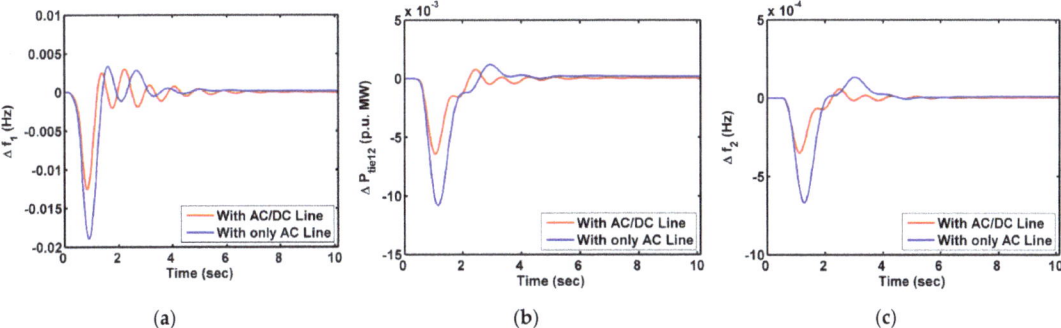

Figure 9. MAMF system responses for case 4: (**a**) Δf_1; (**b**) ΔP_{tie12}; (**c**) Δf_2.

Table 5. MAMF system response settling time (in sec) for AC/DC lines.

Parameter	Δf_1	ΔP_{tie12}	Δf_2	ISE $\times 10^{-3}$
With AC line only	9.721	11.23	9.834	29.275
With AC/DC lines	7.758	6.746	7.112	17.362

6.5. Case 5: Robustness Analysis

To show the robustness of the presented control mechanism, the MAMF system with CTDs was subjected to loadings of 10% SLD on area 1 only, and 10% SLD and 20% SLD on both areas. Even though the system was subjected to different loadings, the deviations in system dynamical behaviour, as shown in Figure 10, are not marked. Thus, the presented control strategy of the fuzzy PID and the territorial control strategy of AC/DC lines were considered robust. Further, to validate the presented control scheme, the MAMF system was targeted with random loadings, as shown in Figure 11.

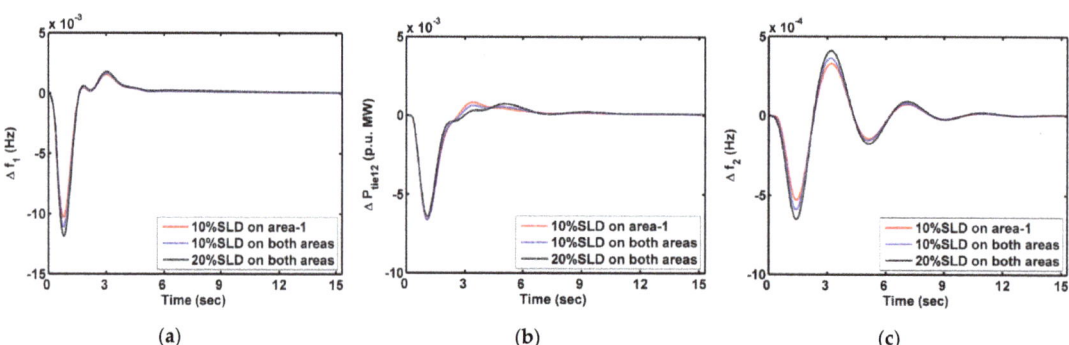

Figure 10. MAMF system responses for case 5 for different loadings: (**a**) Δf_1; (**b**) ΔP_{tie12}; (**c**) Δf_2.

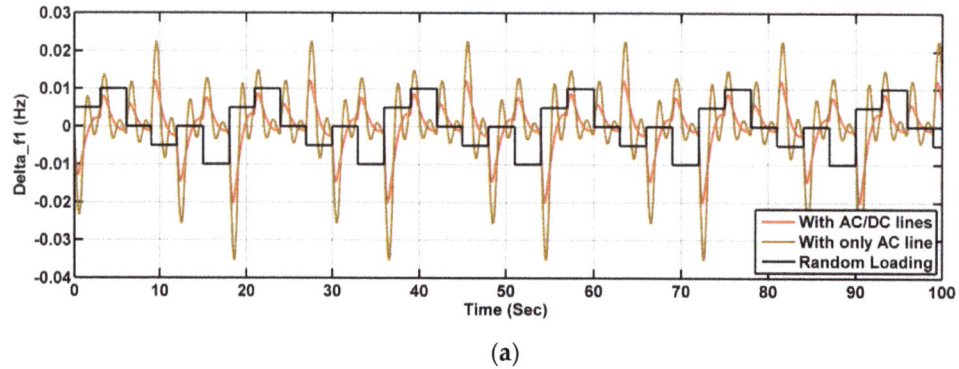

(**a**)

Figure 11. *Cont.*

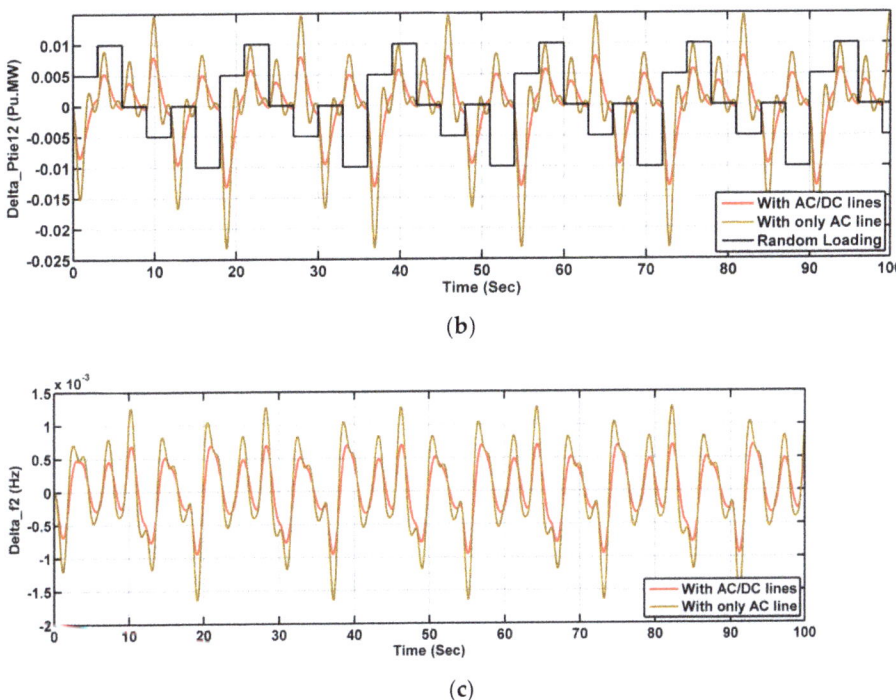

Figure 11. MAMF system responses for case 5 for random loadings: (**a**) Δf_1; (**b**) ΔP_{tie12}; (**c**) Δf_2.

7. Conclusions

In this paper, a WCA-tuned fuzzy PID controller was suggested for frequency regulation of the MAMF power system. The efficacy of fuzzy PID was demonstrated, compared with the performance of traditional PID/PIDD. The dynamical behaviour of the MAMF system was analyzed by subjecting area 1 to 10% SLD. Moreover, the investigation was performed on the MAMF system without and with consideration of CTDs, to exhibit their dominance with regard to the system performance. To further substantiate the fluctuations in the MAMF system responses due to the effect of CTDs, a territorial control strategy of AC/DC lines was operated within the system. The simulation results demonstrated the effect of the AC/DC line on the MAMF system performance in damping out the fluctuations in less time. Furthermore, considering the advantages of fuzzy PID, we suggest adopting and testing the efficacy of FO-based intelligent FLC controllers for stability analysis of interconnected power systems considering CTDs in future work.

Author Contributions: Conceptualization, C.N.S.K., M.B. and S.K.; Data curation, B.S.G., M.K.K. and E.M.A.; Formal analysis, C.N.S.K. and M.B.; Funding acquisition, B.S.G., E.M.A. and S.K.; Investigation, C.N.S.K., B.S.G., M.B. and M.K.K.; Methodology, B.S.G., E.M.A. and S.K.; Project administration, C.N.S.K. and M.B.; Resources, B.S.G., M.K.K., E.M.A. and S.K.; Software, C.N.S.K., B.S.G. and M.K.K.; Supervision, B.S.G., M.B. and S.K.; Validation, M.K.K. and E.M.A.; Visualization, C.N.S.K., M.B. and S.K.; Writing – original draft, C.N.S.K. and B.S.G.; Writing – review & editing, M.B., M.K.K., E.M.A. and S.K. All authors have read and agreed to the published version of the manuscript.

Funding: This work is funded by the Deanship of Scientific Research at Jouf University under grant No (DSR-2021-02-0307).

Institutional Review Board Statement: Not applicable.

Informed Consent Statement: Not applicable.

Data Availability Statement: Not applicable.

Conflicts of Interest: The authors declare no conflict of interest.

Abbreviations

SLD	Step load disturbance
AGC	Automatic generation control
CTDs	Communication time delays
IPS	Interconnected power system
LFC	Load frequency control
DG	Distributed generation
MAMF	Multi-area multi-fuel
GDB	Governor dead band
GRC	Generation rate constraint
HVDC	High-voltage DC line
WCA	Water cycle algorithm
COG	Center of gravity
MFs	Membership functions
ISE	Integral square error
ACE	Area control error

References

1. Cohen, N. Some aspects of tie-line bias control on interconnected power systems. *Trans. Am. Inst. Electr. Eng. Part III Power Appar. Syst.* **1957**, *75*, 1415–1436.
2. Elgerd, O.; Fosha, E. Optimum megawatt-frequency control of multi-area electric energy systems. *IEEE Trans. Power Appar. Syst.* **1970**, *84*, 556–563. [CrossRef]
3. Latif, A.; Hussain, S.M.; Das, D.C.; Ustun, T.S. State-of-the-art of controllers and soft computing techniques for regulated load frequency management of single/multi-area traditional and renewable energy based power systems. *Appl. Energy* **2020**, *266*, 114858. [CrossRef]
4. Chandrakala, K.R.M.V.; Balamurugan, S. Simulated annealing based optimal frequency and terminal voltage control of multi-source multi area system. *Int. J. Electr. Power Energy Syst.* **2016**, *78*, 823–829. [CrossRef]
5. Dogan, A. Load frequency control of two area and multi source power system using grey wolf optimization algorithm. In Proceedings of the 11th International Conference on Electrical and Electronics Engineering (ELECO), Bursa, Turkey, 28–30 November 2019; pp. 81–84.
6. Elsaied, M.M.; Attia, M.A.; Mostafa, M.A.; Mekhamer, S.F. Application of different optimization techniques to load frequency control with WECS in a multi-area system. *Electr. Power Compon. Syst.* **2018**, *46*, 739–756. [CrossRef]
7. Guha, D.; Roy, P.K.; Banerjee, S. Application of backtracking search algorithm in load frequency control of multi-area interconnected power system. *Ain Shams Eng. J.* **2018**, *19*, 257–276. [CrossRef]
8. Shabani, H.; Vahidi, B.; Ebrahimpour, M. A robust PID controller based on imperialist competitive algorithm for load-frequency control of power systems. *ISA Trans.* **2013**, *52*, 88–95. [CrossRef] [PubMed]
9. Raju, M.; Saikia, L.C.; Sinha, N. Automatic generation control of a multi-area system using ant lion optimizer algorithm based PID plus second order derivative controller. *Int. J. Electr. Power Energy Syst.* **2016**, *80*, 52–63. [CrossRef]
10. Guha, D.; Roy, P.K.; Banerjee, S. Study of differential search algorithm based automatic generation control of an interconnected thermal-thermal system with governor dead-band. *Appl. Soft Comput.* **2017**, *52*, 160–175. [CrossRef]
11. Dewangan, S.; Prakash, T.; Singh, V.P. Design and performance analysis of elephant herding optimization based controller for load frequency control in thermal interconnected power system. *Optim. Control. Appl. Methods* **2021**, *42*, 144–159. [CrossRef]
12. Chaine, S.; Tripathy, M.; Jain, D. Non dominated cuckoo search algorithm optimized controllers to improve the frequency regulation characteristics of wind thermal power system. *Eng. Sci. Technol. Int. J.* **2017**, *20*, 1092–1105. [CrossRef]
13. Abid-Elazim, S.M.; Ali, E.S. Load frequency controller design of a two-area system composing of PV grid and thermal generator via firefly algorithm. *Neural Comput. Appl.* **2018**, *30*, 607–616. [CrossRef]
14. Guha, D.; Roy, P.K.; Banerjee, S. Whale optimization algorithm applied to load frequency control of a mixed power system considering nonlinearities and PLL dynamics. *Energy Syst.* **2020**, *11*, 699–728. [CrossRef]
15. Kalyan, C.N.S.; Rao, G.S. Coordinated control strategy for simultaneous frequency and voltage stabilization of the multi-area interconnected system considering communication time delays. *Int. J. Ambient Energy* **2021**, 1–13. [CrossRef]
16. Nosratabadi, S.M.; Bornapour, M.; Gharaei, M.A. Grasshopper optimization algorithm for optimal load frequency control considering predictive function al modified PID controller in restructured multi-resource multi-area power system with redox flow battery units. *Control. Eng. Pract.* **2019**, *89*, 204–227. [CrossRef]

17. Sobhanam, A.P.; Mary, P.M.; Mariasiluvairaj, W.I.; Wilson, R.D. Automatic generation control using an improved artificial electric field in multi-area power system. *IETE J. Res.* **2021**, 1–13. [CrossRef]
18. Sahu, R.K.; Panda, S.; Padhan, S. A hybrid firefly algorithm and pattern search technique for automatic generation control of multi area power systems. *Int. J. Electr. Power Energy Syst.* **2015**, *64*, 9–23. [CrossRef]
19. Kalyan, C.N.S.; Rao, G.S. Combined frequency and voltage stabilization of multi-area multisource system by DE-AEFA optimized PID controller with coordinated performance of IPFC and RFBs. *Int. J. Ambient Energy* **2020**, 1–17. [CrossRef]
20. Sharma, J.; Hote, Y.V.; Prasad, R. Robust PID load frequency controller design with specific gain and phase margin for multi-area power systems. *IFAC-Pap.* **2018**, *51*, 627–632. [CrossRef]
21. Tasnin, W.; Saikia, L.C. Comparative performance of different energy storage devices in AGC of multi-source system including geothermal power plant. *J. Renew. Sustain. Energy* **2018**, *10*, 024101. [CrossRef]
22. Arya, Y. automatic generation control of two-area electrical power systems via optimal fuzzy classical controller. *J. Frankl. Inst.* **2018**, *355*, 2662–2688. [CrossRef]
23. Arya, Y.; Kumar, N. Design and analysis of BFOA-optimized fuzzy PI/PID controller for AGC of multi-area traditional/restructured electrical power systems. *Soft Comput.* **2017**, *21*, 6435–6452. [CrossRef]
24. Sahu, R.K.; Panda, S.; Yegireddy, N.K. A novel hybrid DEPS optimized fuzzy PI/PID controller for load frequency control of multi-area interconnected power systems. *J. Control Process* **2014**, *24*, 1596–1608. [CrossRef]
25. Sahu, P.C.; Prusty, R.C.; Panda, S. Approaching hybridized GWO-SCA based type-II fuzzy controller in AGC of diverse energy source multi area power system. *J. King Saud Univ.-Eng. Sci.* **2020**, *32*, 186–197. [CrossRef]
26. Sahoo, D.K.; Sahu, R.K.; Sekhar, G.T.; Panda, S. A novel modified differential evolution algorithm optimized fuzzy proportional integral derivative controller for load frequency control with Thyristor controlled series compensator. *J. Electr. Syst. Inf. Technol.* **2018**, *5*, 944–963. [CrossRef]
27. Pradhan, P.C.; Sahu, R.K.; Panda, S. Firefly algorithm optimized fuzzy PID controller for AGC of multi-area multi-source power systems with UPFC and SMES. *Eng. Sci. Technol. Int. J.* **2016**, *19*, 338–354. [CrossRef]
28. Nayak, J.R.; Shaw, B.; Sahu, B.K. Application of adaptive-SOS (ASOS) algorithm based interval type-2 fuzzy-PID controller with derivative filter for automatic generation control of an interconnected power system. *Eng. Sci. Technol. Int. J.* **2018**, *21*, 465–485. [CrossRef]
29. Chen, X.; Li, Y.; Zhang, Y.; Ye, X.; Xiong, X.; Zhang, F. A novel hybrid model based on an improved seagull optimization algorithm for short-term wind speed forecasting. *Processes* **2021**, *9*, 387. [CrossRef]
30. Jain, M.; Rani, A.; Pachauri, N.; Singh, V.; Mittal, A.P. Design of fractional order 2-DOF PI controller for real-time control of heat flow experiment. *Eng. Sci. Technol. Int. J.* **2019**, *22*, 215–228. [CrossRef]
31. Kalyan, C.N.S.; Rao, G.S. Frequency and voltage stabilization in combined load frequency control and automatic voltage regulation of multi area system with hybrid generation utilities by AC/DC links. *Int. J. Sustain. Energy* **2020**, *39*, 1009–1029. [CrossRef]
32. Padhy, S.; Panda, S. A hybrid stochastic fractal search and pattern search technique based cascade PI-PD controller for automatic generation of multi-source power systems in presence of plug in electric vehicles. *CAAI Trans. Intell. Technol.* **2017**, *2*, 12–25. [CrossRef]
33. Rajesh, K.S.; Dash, S.S.; Rajagopal, R. Hybrid improved firefly-pattern search optimized fuzzy aided PID controller for automatic generation control of power systems with multi-type generations. *Swarm Evol. Comput.* **2019**, *44*, 200–211. [CrossRef]
34. Lal, D.K.; Barisal, A.K.; Tripathy, M. Load Frequency Control of Multi Source Multi-Area Nonlinear Power System with DE-PSO Optimized Fuzzy PID Controller in Coordination with SSSC and RFB. *Int. J. Control. Autom.* **2018**, *11*, 61–80. [CrossRef]
35. Gheisarnejad, M. An effective hybrid harmony search and cuckoo optimization algorithm based fuzzy PID controller for load frequency control. *Appl. Soft Comput.* **2018**, *65*, 121–138. [CrossRef]
36. Kouba, N.E.Y.; Menaa, M.; Hasni, M.; Boudour, M. A novel optimal combined fuzzy PID controller employing dragonfly algorithm for solving automatic generation control problem. *Electr. Power Compon. Syst.* **2018**, *46*, 2054–2070. [CrossRef]
37. Eskander, H.; Sadollah, A.; Bahreininejad, A.; Hamdi, M. Water cycle algorithm—A novel meta-heuristic optimization method for solving constrained engineering optimization problems. *Comput. Struct.* **2012**, *110*, 151–166. [CrossRef]

Article

Artificial Intelligence in Fractional-Order Systems Approximation with High Performances: Application in Modelling of an Isotopic Separation Process

Roxana Motorga [1], Vlad Mureșan [1], Mihaela-Ligia Ungureșan [2,*], Mihail Abrudean [1], Honoriu Vălean [1] and Iulia Clitan [1]

[1] Automation Department, Technical University of Cluj-Napoca, 28 Memorandumului Street, 400114 Cluj-Napoca, Romania; roxana.motorga@campus.utcluj.ro (R.M.); vlad.muresan@aut.utcluj.ro (V.M.); mihai.abrudean@aut.utcluj.ro (M.A.); honoriu.valean@aut.utcluj.ro (H.V.); iulia.clitan@aut.utcluj.ro (I.C.)
[2] Physics and Chemistry Department, Technical University of Cluj-Napoca, 28 Memorandumului Street, 400114 Cluj-Napoca, Romania
* Correspondence: mihaela.unguresan@chem.utcluj.ro

Citation: Motorga, R.; Mureșan, V.; Ungureșan, M.-L.; Abrudean, M.; Vălean, H.; Clitan, I. Artificial Intelligence in Fractional-Order Systems Approximation with High Performances: Application in Modelling of an Isotopic Separation Process. *Mathematics* 2022, 10, 1459. https://doi.org/10.3390/math10091459

Academic Editor: Adrian Olaru

Received: 14 March 2022
Accepted: 22 April 2022
Published: 26 April 2022

Publisher's Note: MDPI stays neutral with regard to jurisdictional claims in published maps and institutional affiliations.

Copyright: © 2022 by the authors. Licensee MDPI, Basel, Switzerland. This article is an open access article distributed under the terms and conditions of the Creative Commons Attribution (CC BY) license (https://creativecommons.org/licenses/by/4.0/).

Abstract: This paper presents a solution for the modelling, implementation and simulation of the fractional-order process of producing the enriched ^{13}C isotope, through the chemical exchange between carbamate and carbon dioxide. To achieve the goal of implementation and simulation of the considered process, an original solution for the approximation of fractional-order systems at the variation of the system's differentiation order is proposed, based on artificial intelligence methods. The separation process has the property of being strongly non-linear and also having fractional-order behaviour. Consequently, in the implementation of the mathematical model of the process, the theory associated with the fractional-order system's domain has to be considered and applied. For learning the dynamics of the structure parameters of the fractional-order part of the model, neural networks, which are associated with the artificial intelligence domain, are used. Using these types of approximations, the simulation and the prediction of the produced ^{13}C isotope concentration dynamics are made with high accuracy. In order to prove the efficiency of the proposed solutions, a comparison between the responses of the determined model and the experimental responses is made. The proposed model implementation is made based on using four trained neural networks. Moreover, in the final part of the paper, an original method for the online identification of the separation process model is proposed. This original method can identify the process of fractional differentiation order variation in relation to time, a phenomenon which is quite frequent in the operation of the real separation plant. In the last section of the paper, it is proven that artificial intelligence methods can successfully sustain the system model in all the scenarios, resulting in the feasible premise of designing an automatic control system for the ^{13}C isotope concentration, a method which can be applied in the case of other industrial applications too.

Keywords: artificial intelligence; separation process; concentration; neural network; ^{13}C isotope; separation column; mathematical model; approximation; simulation; fractional-order systems

MSC: 93-10

1. Introduction

The periodic table consists of elements from nature that can be decomposed into atoms that possess several chemical properties. The isotopes are referred to as a collection of atoms that have the same chemical properties and the same name, but with different masses. There are the following two types of isotopes to be found in nature: stable ones that do not disintegrate over time, and radioactive ones that are affected by the disintegration process that makes them radioactive. In nature, carbon [1] has fifteen known isotopes (^{8}C—being radioactive, to ^{22}C), amongst which there are two stable isotopes: ^{12}C (98.9%), ^{13}C (1.1%) and one longest-lived radioactive isotope: ^{14}C (<0.0001%).

In nature, there is a small concentration of stable isotopes that are necessary for applications [2–4], so the necessity of increasing the concentrations is justified. The interest in the separation methods of the stable isotopes [5,6] (for example, as follows: carbon, oxygen, lithium, nitrogen) has shown growth in the last few years, whilst the subject has been known to be taken into consideration since the beginning of the 1960s, because of the usage of nuclear energy on an industrial scale and the need for new nuclear fuels. Along with the main fields in which the isotopes are used can be remembered as medicine (the isotopes of ^{13}C and ^{14}C are used for respiratory tests), chemistry, agriculture (efficiency in the usage of chemical fertiliser is reached by isotopes of ^{13}C, ^{15}N and ^{18}O as tracer agents), biology or engineering (for example, hydrogen with the stable isotope deuterium with applications in the moderation of nuclear reactors with natural uranium and determining groundwater flow). Some information regarding the age of the rocks or the circuit of water in nature can be found by studying the natural abundance of isotopes.

The commonly used procedure in the case of the separation of the stable isotopes [7–10] is a distillation that implies that the isotopes of the compound make an exchange in the columns with packing [11]; the isotopes can be found in columns in the gaseous or liquid phase. The procedure implies a piece of specific equipment and operation. Although there are few papers in the literature that presents the modelling and control problems for the isotopic separation [12,13], the process of the ^{13}C isotope separation is proposed to be improved in this paper. The separation column's working principle is based on the refluxing system, as follows: at the bottom of the column, the isotope is found in a liquid phase, where it is converted into a gaseous phase and re-entered into the column; at the top of the column, the isotope is converted from gaseous to liquid and re-entered into the column. The main setback of this process represents its nonlinearity, being a distributed parameter process with multiple inputs and multiple outputs, which poses a real challenge in the automation field when speaking of process modelling and control. The isotopic separation process is a consistently slow one, implying higher costs when the energy consumption of the plants may need to meet an improvement [14,15]. In the technical literature, there are some papers proposing mathematical models for the separation processes using constant parameters [16–18], where there is no necessity to implement artificial intelligence (AI) learning methods since there are no variable parameters.

The methods of artificial intelligence process modelling emphasise the efficiency of obtaining an accurate model for the separation process that can be used for controller tuning or as a reference model in the structure of automatic control systems for the concentration of the ^{13}C isotope; a main property of the model is the fact that it is designed to highlight the fractional-order behaviour [19–21] of the real process. Moreover, the technical process associated with the separation column is a distributed parameter process because its dynamics depend both on time and on the position of the elements in relation to the columns' height. On the other hand [22,23], implement solutions for learning the behaviour of some separation processes, but in their linearised form. The main approach of this research is to avoid the problem of simplification through linearisation and to consider in the proposed model the entire domains of signal variation. This aspect allows benefiting at the maximum potential from the performances of the future design of the ^{13}C isotope automatic control system, based on the proposed model. The complexity of the ^{13}C isotopic separation process results in the impossibility of learning its behaviour by only one neural network (regardless of its type), reaching the solution of interconnecting more neural networks.

There are some papers in the technical literature explaining the necessity of the implementation of fractional-order systems. Ref. [24] presents the method for obtaining stable systems for those that vary in time and that are non-linear using Caputo's definition of fractional-order derivatives, but only when the fractional differentiation order has a constant value and it is enclosed in the $(0;1)$ domain. The stability of the fractional-order systems was studied and solved using the linear feedback control in [25,26], whilst [27] presents the method of investigating the effects of fractional-order perturbation on the robust stability of linear time-invariant systems with interval uncertainty. The author of [28] states the possibility of implementing a state feedback H_∞ controller for the commensurate linear and time-invariant fractional-order systems. Moreover, in [29], the reduction problem of the H_∞ model is studied, aiming at its applicability only for positive fractional-order systems.

In practice, the fractional-order controllers, especially of the PID type (proportional-integral-derivative), have many applications. For example, an optimised method for auto-tuning procedures of PID fractional-order controllers, with application in flight control, is presented in [30]. Precise models of fractional-order processes are necessary for the tuning of fractional-order PID controllers. In this context, in [31], an example of proving the empiricism of the usage of the fractional-order systems is given based on the process of charging the circuit of a supercapacitor.

The analysis of the above-mentioned papers is concluded by offering simulation and control solutions only in those cases in which the fractional-order models of the considered lumped parameter processes are simplified and linearised. One of the main aims of this paper is to propose an original solution for the approximation of the separation column's model in order to be robust in the variation of the separation process fractional differentiation order. In the case of the fractional-order models that have the fractional differentiation order β, the actual existing methods are not allowing the model adaptation according to the variation of this parameter; more exactly, all the existent methods for the approximation of fractional-order systems with integer-order systems are valid only for constant values of β. This disadvantage is eliminated by using the original approximation method proposed by this research.

As a result of the technical literature, the finite-dimensional integer-order transfer functions are considered to be a feasible alternative for the implementation of the fractional-order transfer function. It can be stated that the integer-order transfer function has an infinite-dimensional representation of the operator s^β (fractional-order operator), where β is a real number; various approximations are proposed for a single term s^β. Consequently, the fractional-order systems are simulated or implemented by having the transfer functions replaced by the integer-order ones, which has the closest behaviour to the one that is desired, but is by far the easiest to handle.

There are different approximation solutions for the fractional-order operators, namely, for the continuous-time implementation, the Oustaloup filter (generalized, also known as a recursive approximation, or the modified version [32,33]), which is a good choice in most of the cases, the design of the FIR filter [34], and the Tustin discretisation method [35] for the discrete-time implementations, along with the methods of the retaining invariants for the impulse and step response; by selecting a frequency range of suitable interest, it is possible to easily approximate any fractional-order system with one of the above-mentioned methods.

The adaptability of the model to the actual solutions when the fractional differentiation order presents variations in relation to time, is only possible by reidentifying the structure parameters of the models, which is known to be a complex, time-consuming and laborious procedure. Using the actual approximation methods, the online identification of the process is impossible due to the impossibility of modifying the fractional differentiation.

In conclusion, there are not any elaborate methods in the technical literature that use fractional-order systems with variable fractional differentiation orders. The present research is justified due to the fact that the separation process presents in the practical operation variations of the fractional differentiation order, this aspect being highlighted in the model only if a new original approximation method is used.

Due to the complexity of the problem, the implementation of such an approximation method and implicitly a model is based on applying methods belonging to the AI (artificial intelligence) domain, namely, the neural networks. The AI methods in the last few years were applied in order to solve a lot of technical problems, as follows: predicting the evolution of the COVID-19 pandemic [36], predictions related to marketing and management solutions [37,38], education matters [39], cardiology matters [40], in power electronic systems [41], etc. The practical applicability of the proposed modelling method is proven by considering as a case study the isotopic separation process of ^{13}C.

2. The ^{13}C Isotope Separation

The laboratory plant that is used for the separation process of the ^{13}C isotope [2] is schematically presented in Figure 1a. It can be easily remarked that the system is composed of an absorber A, a separation column SC (a cylinder with $h = 300$ cm and $d = 2.5$ cm) and an R + S + H element composed of a reactor R, a stripper S and a heather H, all being interconnected by pipes. The absorber, the separation column and the stripper from Figure 1a are hachured, highlighting the fact that they contain steel packing of the Helipack type.

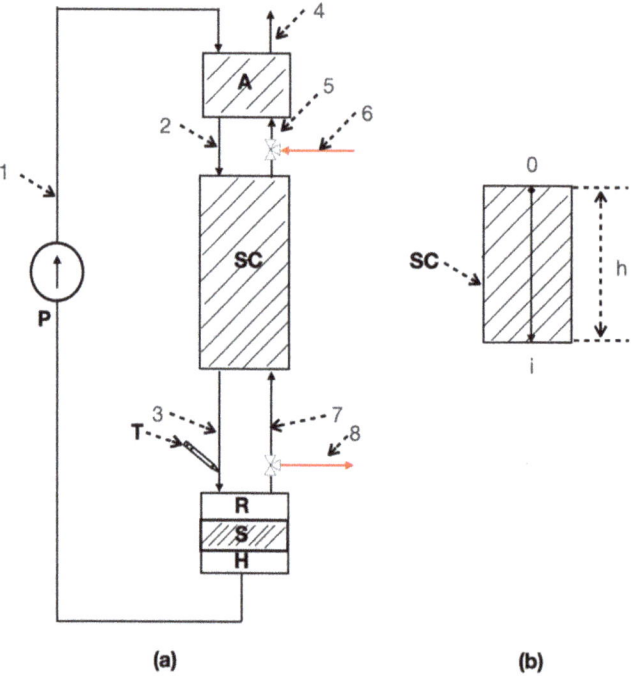

Figure 1. (a) The ^{13}C isotope separation laboratory plant; (b) The $0i$ axis.

The flow of the monoethanolamine in methanol solution, with a molar concentration of 1 M or 2 M, is engaged by the pump in the upper part of A through pipe 1. The plant can be used in the following two working regimes: In the production regime, the separation plant is supplied with carbon dioxide (CO_2) having a concentration of 99.98% using pipe 6, and the product is extracted in the gaseous phase through pipe 8 (CO_2 with an increased concentration of ^{13}C isotope); in the total reflux regime, the product is not extracted (the flow on pipe 8 is 0) from the separation plant. The carbamate results in pipe 2 after the absorption of CO_2 in monoethanolamine (the absorption phenomenon takes place in the A absorber). The separation column is supplied in the upper part (through pipe 2) with carbamate and in the lower part with CO_2 (through pipe 7). Consequently, in the separation column, the carbamate and the CO_2 are circulating in counter-current [42], the chemical exchange between them taking place. The CO_2 having an isotopic concentration lower than 1.1% of the ^{13}C natural isotopic concentration is evacuated as a waste from the absorber and implicitly from the separation plant through pipe 4. In the lower part of the column, the ^{13}C isotope concentrates in the liquid phase. The ^{13}C isotope at the desired concentration (the parameter (signal) that is desired to be monitored) can be extracted from the plant using pipe 8. The reactor is responsible for the thermal decomposition of the carbamate, which enters it through pipe 3. The concentration of the ^{13}C is measured by the T transducer—mass spectrometer. The stripper removes completely the CO_2, resulting in a pure monoethanolamine solution that is reheated using H in order to be recirculated again in the system through pipe 1, by the pump (using the pump, the absorber is continuously supplied with monoethanolamine solution). The valves from pipes 5 and 7 are three-way valves.

3. The Mathematical Modelling and the Numerical Simulation of the Separation Process

The ^{13}C concentration that is obtained from the process is strongly dependent on the position inside the SC, in relation to its height. Moreover, the ^{13}C concentration depends on time. Figure 1b presents the $0i$ axis, where the i variable highlights the position in relation to the columns' height.

In the case of the 1 M concentration solution of monoethanolamine, the identification can be carried out through an experiment when the SC is working in the total reflux regime. The input signal of the process is considered to be the input flow of the monoethanolamine solution, and the output signal is the concentration of the ^{13}C isotope at the lower part of the separation column. The experiment was made by applying at the input a step signal having a value of 350 mL/h and using T, the real-time experimental data (the real-time values of the output signal) were collected. The experimental data are presented in Table 1.

Table 1. The separation process experimental data—^{13}C concentration.

^{13}C Concentration (%)	Time (h)
1.108	0
1.65	10
1.85	20
1.91	30
2.02	40
2.05	50
2.05	60

Since there is a small amount of experimental data, the most probable curve that approximates the experimental curve has to be determined (this curve will describe the most probable separation process dynamics). The simulated curve is ought to approximate the dynamics of the time evolution of the output signal while eliminating the effect of the errors resulting from the measurement process. Due to the fact that the separation process is a fractional-order one, the most probable approximating response (curve) is obtained by using a fractional-order model.

The proposed fractional-order model that generates through simulations the most probable approximate response is represented by the following fractional-order transfer function:

$$H_1 = \frac{K}{T \cdot s^\beta + 1} \quad (1)$$

where the proportionality constant $K = 1.22$ (%·h/mL), the time constant $T = 14$ (h) and the process fractional-order $\beta = 0.91$.

The coefficients of the fractional-order transfer function from (1) are obtained using an iterative procedure, the corresponding simulations being made in the MATLAB Crone Toolbox. The graph that compares the separation process experimental curve (represented in blue) and the separation process simulated approximating response (represented in red) is presented in Figure 2.

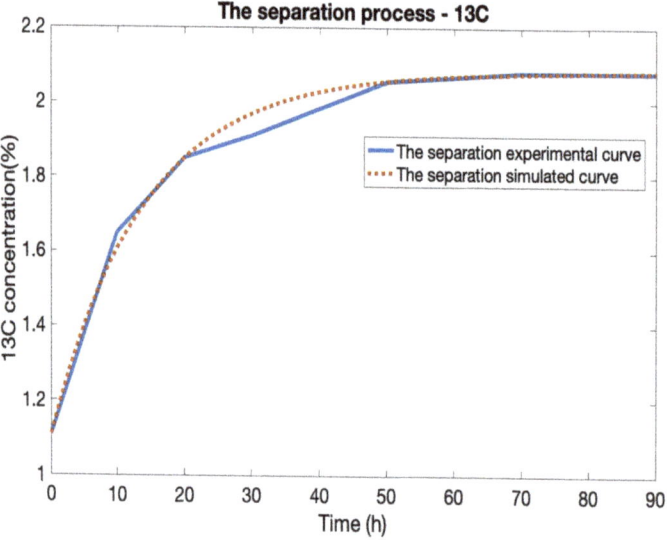

Figure 2. The separation process experimental curve and the most probable approximating response of the separation process.

It can be remarked from Figure 2 that the two curves are very close in values, meaning that the approximation's accuracy is sufficient.

Using only the approximate response obtained in Figure 2, the proof of the previously identified value of the processing time constant can be made using a classical identification method. It can be observed that the classic identification method is applicable in the case of a first-order process without dead time; the time constant of the process is determined using the tangent method [43] (the considered classic identification method), and it is presented in Figure 3.

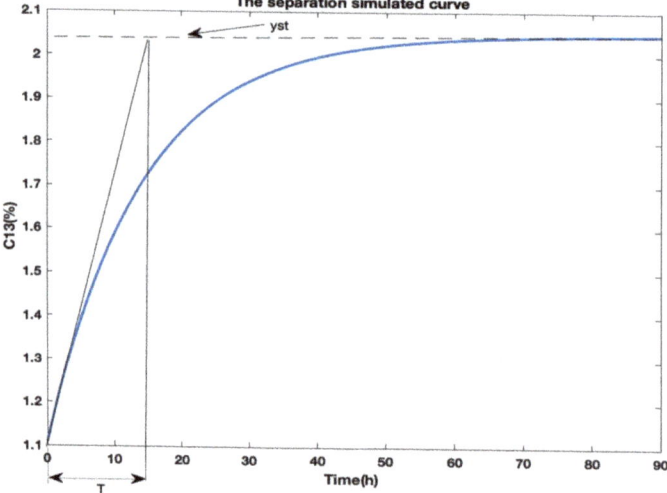

Figure 3. The tangent method—time constant computation.

It can be remarked from Figure 3 that y_{st} represents the steady-state value for the response of the process ($y_{st} = 2.05$ (%)). After applying the tangent method, the time constant $T = 14$ h is determined, the same value as it was previously determined through the procedure applied to identify the coefficients of (1).

The variation of the steady-state value of the ^{13}C isotope concentration in relation to the variation of the input monoethanolamine solution flow can be modelled through the proportionality constant K_p that can be computed using the values of the input signals associated with two different experiments and the corresponding output signal steady-state values (for $F_{in1} = 340$ mL/h the experimentally obtained steady-state ^{13}C isotope concentration is 2.05 (%) and for $F_{in1} = 460$ mL/h the experimentally obtained steady-state ^{13}C isotope concentration is 1.65 (%); the notation F_{in} is used for the input flow of the monoethanolamine solution) as follows:

$$K_p = \frac{1.65 - 2.05}{460 - 340} = -0.0033 \ (\% \cdot \text{h/mL}) \qquad (2)$$

K_p has the significance of the gradient of the approximation ramp that models the variation of the steady-state value of the ^{13}C isotope concentration due to the variation of the input flow.

The mathematical model for the separation process [44] is given by the equations below as follows:

- The output signal of the open-loop process notated with $y(t)$ as follows:

$$y(t) = s_{13C1}(t) + F_{0T}(t) \cdot u(t) \qquad (3)$$

where $F_{0T}(t)$ is an increasing exponential function having the following form:

$$F_{0T}(t) = \frac{1}{T} \cdot t^{\beta-1} \cdot \mathcal{E}_{\beta,\beta}\left(-\frac{1}{T} \cdot t^\beta\right), \qquad (4)$$

In which $\mathcal{E}_{\beta,\beta}\left(-\frac{1}{T} \cdot t^\beta\right)$ is the Mittag-Leffler function in two parameters [45] defined by $\mathcal{E}_{\beta,\beta}(m) = \sum_{k=0}^{\infty} \frac{m^k}{\Gamma(\beta k + \beta)}$, where $\mathcal{R}(\beta) > 0$; this complex form of $F_{0T}(t)$ is due to the fact that the separation process is a fractional-order one.

- Moreover, $u(t)$ represents an equivalent step-type signal (depending on the process input signal—the input monoethanolamine solution flow $F_{in}(t)$) in concentration as follows:

$$u(t) = s_{13C0}(t) - K_p \cdot (F_{in0}(t) - F_{in}(t)) - s_{13C1}(t) \qquad (5)$$

where the ^{13}C concentration (the output) has an initial value $s_{13C1}(t) = s_{13C1} = 1.108\%$, and its steady-state value (for $F_{in1} = 340$ mL/h) $s_{13C0}(t) = s_{13C0} = 2.05\%$. The steady-state value of the ^{13}C concentration varies in relation to the value of the solution flow (which is the input signal) according to K_p value; this procedure based on using the K_p constant allows to model a nonlinear process with modelling techniques that are used for linear ones.

The separation column can also be modelled using a more complex version that allows the highlighting of the influence of the position in relation to the column height. The equations for the complex version of the process model are presented below as follows:

- The height equivalent to a theoretical plate (HETP) for the separation column as follows:

$$HETP(t) = HETP_0 + K_H \cdot (F_{in}(t) - F_{in0}(t)), \qquad (6)$$

where $F_{in0}(t) = 367$ mL/h is the constant value of the monoethanolamine input flow and $F_{in}(t)$ is the instantaneous value of the monoethanolamine input flow (represented as a step input signal), $K_H = 0.0085$ (cm·h/mL)—proportionality constant (experimentally identified), $HETP_0$ —the steady-state value of the $HETP$, for the $F_{in0}(t)$. It can be remarked that the $HETP$ is directly influenced by the monoethanolamine input flow $F_{in}(t)$.

- The proportionality constant (K_H) as follows:

$$K_H = \frac{HETP_{st1} - HETP_0}{F_{in1} - F_{in0}} \qquad (7)$$

Which is responsible of the connection between the input flow of monoethanolamine and the $HETP$ and where $HETP_{st1} = 5.43$ cm is the steady-state value of the $HETP$ for $F_{in1} = 460$ mL/h.

- The number of theoretical plates ($n(t)$) as follows:

$$n(t) = \frac{h}{HETP(t)}, \qquad (8)$$

- The separation ($S(t)$):

$$S(t) = \alpha^{n(t)} \qquad (9)$$

where the elementary separation factor for the ^{13}C isotope regarding the procedure of chemical exchange is $\alpha = 1.01$.

- The equivalent input signal of the separation process as follows:

$$u_2 = y_0 \cdot (S(t) - 1) \qquad (10)$$

where the natural abundance of the ^{13}C isotope is $y_0 = 1.108\%$.

- The time constant (T) as follows:

$$T = T_{i0} + (T_{if} - T_{i0}) \cdot \frac{i}{i_f} \qquad (11)$$

where T_{i0} is the process time constant when $i = 0^+$ and T_{if} it the process time constant when $i = i_f$. As it can be remarked, the complex form of the model also highlights the variation of the process time constant in relation to the position variation in the column height.

It is considered that the final position in the columns' height is equal to the height of the column as follows:

$$i_f = h, \qquad (12)$$

- The fractional-order differential equation [45] that models the separation process dynamics as follows:

$$D^\beta F_{t(t)} = -\frac{1}{T} \cdot F_t(t) + \frac{1}{T} \cdot u_2(t) \qquad (13)$$

The $F_t(t)$ function represents the solution of (13).

- The dynamics of the concentration $F_i(i)$ in relation with i as follows:

$$F_i(i) = (y_0 \cdot \alpha - 1) + e^{\frac{i}{C+K \cdot (F_{in}(t) - F_{in0})}} \qquad (14)$$

where $C = 430$ cm is an equivalent length constant for SC and the proportionality constant $K = 0.7527$ cm·h/mL that is determined experimentally makes the mathematical connection between the input flow and the length constant of SC.

- The length constant (I) as follows:

$$I = C + K \cdot (F_{in}(t) - F_{in0}) \qquad (15)$$

- The ^{13}C isotope concentration at any point of height in SC as follows:

$$y_{an}(t,i) = y_0 + F_t(t) \cdot F_i(i, F_{in}(t)) \quad (16)$$

and it depends on the input flow $F_{in}(t)$ of monoethanolamine. In (16), the $F_i(i, F_{in}(t))$ function is given by the following: $F_i(i, F_{in}(t)) = \frac{F_i(F_{in}(t),i) - y_0}{F_i(F_{in}(t),i_f) - y_0}$.

Using the mathematical model presented in (3), the process is simulated for different input signals of $F_{in}(t) \in \{200, 275, 350, 425, 500\}$ mL/h. The comparative graph between the responses obtained by simulating the separation process is presented in Figure 4.

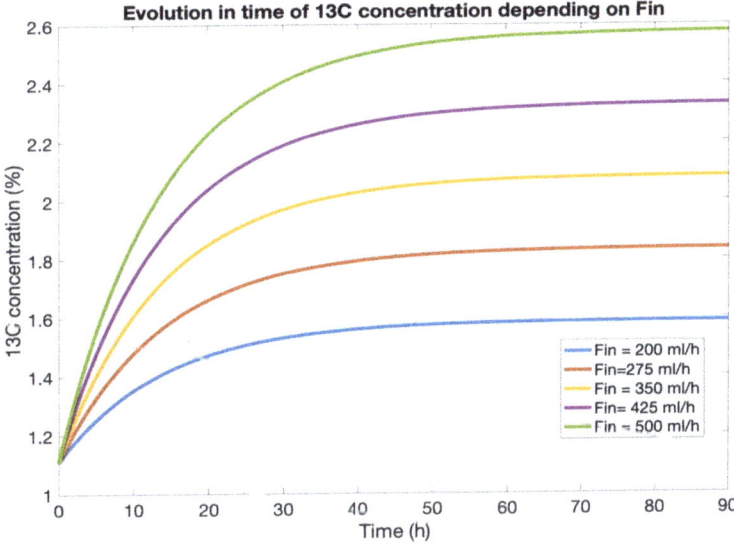

Figure 4. The comparative graph between the simulated responses of the process when the variation of the input signal occurs.

The results for the simulations from Figure 4 (more exactly the steady-state values of the five responses) are presented in Table 2.

Table 2. Simulation results centralizer.

F_{in} (mL/h)	200	275	350	425	500
^{13}C concentration in steady-state regime (%)	2.062	2.054	2.047	2.039	2.032

It can be concluded from Table 2 and Figure 4 that by decreasing the input flow F_{in} (also considered the input signal) results in an increase in the ^{13}C isotope concentration (output signal). The phenomenon can be mathematically correlated to the negative value of the proportionality constant K_p from (2). On the other hand, from the physical point of view, the chemical exchange between the carbon dioxide and the carbamate has a lower intensity when the input flow of ethanolamine is higher; there is a smaller amount of time when the two reactants come into contact). However, the extreme values of the input flow that imply extreme operation regimes for the separation plant have to be avoided (the flooding phenomenon for high input flows and the dry-column phenomenon for low input flows).

The isotopic separation processes are considered extremely slow processes. Due to the fact that the separation plant operations are affected by different parametric perturbations (for example, the following technological parameters: temperature, insulation efficiency, or other disruptive parameters encountered due to the equipment in the structure of the isotopic separation installation); therefore, the structural parameters of the separation columns present variation with respect to time. Considering the results of the proceeded experiments and the previous explanation, it was concluded that the differentiation fractional-order (β) of the separation process is strongly affected by the mentioned perturbations. The advantages of the proposed model that are likely to be considered are the following:

- The possibility to implement an automated control strategy amongst with the associated controllers based on the developed model;
- The implementation of the model as reference model in IMC (internal model control) structures;
- Simulations can be performed by employees in order to highlight the behaviour of the isotopic separation installation in different operational scenarios.

The maximum efficiency of the proposed models, both on the technological and economical aspects, can be reached by obtaining a precision as good as possible; in this context, the online adaptation of the proposed model when the differentiation fractional-order (β) presents variations (due to the mentioned parametric endogenous perturbations) is required.

4. The Proposed Solution for the Online Approximation and Adaptation of the Fractional-Order Models

In order to implement the first version of the separation process, the function with a complex structure in (4) should be approximated with high accuracy (being the representation in the time domain of a fractional-order process response).

There are more solutions proposed in [45] in order to define the fractional-order derivatives. The Riemann–Liouville definition is presented below as follows:

$$R\mathcal{D}^{\alpha} f(t) \triangleq \mathcal{D}^m \mathcal{I}^{m-\alpha} f(t) = \frac{d^m}{dt^m}\left[\frac{1}{\Gamma(m-\alpha)} \int_0^t \frac{f(\tau)}{(t-\tau)^{\alpha-m+1}} d\tau\right], \quad (17)$$

where $\mathcal{I}^{m-\alpha}$ is a fractional-order integral and m is an integer ($m-1 < \alpha < m$ and $\alpha \in \mathbb{R}^+$).

Caputo introduced an alternative method to define the following fractional-order derivative:

$$C\mathcal{D}^{\alpha} f(t) \triangleq \mathcal{I}^{m-\alpha} \mathcal{D}^m f(t) = \frac{1}{\Gamma(m-\alpha)}\left[\int_0^t \frac{f^{(m)}(\tau)}{(t-\tau)^{\alpha-m+1}} d\tau\right], \quad (18)$$

where $m \in \mathbb{N}$ and $m - 1 < \alpha < m$; the Caputo definition is more restrictive than the definition in (17), requiring the absolute integrability on the mth order derivative of the function $f(t)$.

Supposing that $t \neq 0^+$ for the first $(m-1)$th order derivatives of $f(t)$ function and for $f(t)$ it results that

$$R\mathcal{D}^{\alpha} f(t) \triangleq \mathcal{D}^m \mathcal{I}^{m-\alpha} f(t) \neq \mathcal{I}^{m-\alpha} \mathcal{D}^m f(t) \triangleq C\mathcal{D}^{\alpha} f(t), \quad (19)$$

Consequently, the relationship between the definitions in (17) and (18) is the following:

$$R\mathcal{D}^{\alpha} f(t) = C\mathcal{D}^{\alpha} f(t) + \sum_{k=0}^{m-1} \frac{t^{k-\alpha}}{\Gamma(k-\alpha+1)} f^{(k)}\left(0^+\right), \quad (20)$$

$$R\mathcal{D}^{\alpha}\left(f(t) - \sum_{k=0}^{m-1} f^{(k)}\left(0^+\right)\frac{t^k}{k!}\right) = C\mathcal{D}^{\alpha} f(t) \quad (21)$$

The generalisation of backward difference underlies the following Grünwald–Letnikov definition:

$$\mathcal{D}^\alpha f(t)|_{t=kh} = \lim_{h \to 0} \frac{1}{h^\alpha} \sum_{j=0}^{k} (-1)^j \binom{\alpha}{j} f(kh - jh), \qquad (22)$$

where $\binom{\alpha}{j}$ is the usual notation for the binomial coefficients; there is also a possibility to define Grünwald–Letnikov definition alternatively in the following integral form:

$$L\mathcal{D}^\alpha f(t) = \sum_{k=0}^{m} \frac{f^{(k)}(0^+) t^{k-\alpha}}{\Gamma(m+1-\alpha)} + \frac{1}{\Gamma(m+1-\alpha)} \int_0^t (t-\tau)^{m-\alpha} f^{(m+1)}(\tau) d\tau, \qquad (23)$$

where $m > \alpha - 1$.

By analysing the equations between (4) and (17)–(23), it is found that they imply consistent problems in terms of their numerical simulation (for example, the approximation of the Gamma function (Γ), the integral computation or the limits approximation).

Moreover, due to the fact that, in the case of the separation process, the corresponding fractional differentiation order can present variations, the previously presented mathematical operations are not feasible for the implementation of its model.

In order to obtain and use a fractional-order transfer function, the Laplace transformation (for null initial conditions) is applied to Equation (3), resulting in the following:

$$Y(s) = \frac{1}{s} \cdot [s_{13C1} + u \cdot H_1(s)], \qquad (24)$$

where H_1 is the following mentioned fractional-order transfer function:

$$H_1(s) = \frac{K}{T \cdot s^\beta + 1} \qquad (25)$$

In (25), $K = 1.22$ (%·h/mL), $\beta = 0.91$ and $T = 14$ (h) are the structural parameters of the separation process. The mathematical form from (24) is due to the fact that $u(t)$ signal from (3) is a step-type one. In order to have the possibility to simulate the equation in (24), for the H_1 transfer function, the Oustaloup approximation of fifth-order is applied. The comparison graph between the simulation of the most probable experimental curve and the simulation of the applied Oustaloup approximation is presented in Figure 5.

After a complex analysis and comparation, it was concluded that by using the proposed fractional-order mathematical model, consistently better performances are obtained than the ones presented in the case of the sixth grade polynomial in [46]. The considered quality indicator for the comparison is the mean squared error (computed based on the difference between the measured process output and the simulated process output).

The Oustaloup approximation is implemented using the MATLAB software, mainly by using the CRONE toolbox. As similar as in the case of the transfer function, the fractional-order function can be defined using "$frac\_tf$". The syntax of the $frac\_tf$ function [47], which also allows the user to modify the order of the Oustaloup approximation, is presented below as follows:

$$frac\_tf = (num, den, N, w, va, Ts, sim), \qquad (26)$$

where num—represents the numerator, being a cell, a scalar or an $frac\_poly\_exp$ object, den—represents the denominator having the same arguments as the numerator, N—is a scalar representing the order for the used Oustaloup approximation of fractional differentiator; w—a 1×2 matrix containing the lower waveband and the upper frequency for the Oustaloup approximation, va—Laplace variable corresponding character, Ts—the sampling time as a scalar and sim—the string giving the method to simulate the fractional system (in this case, $Oust$).

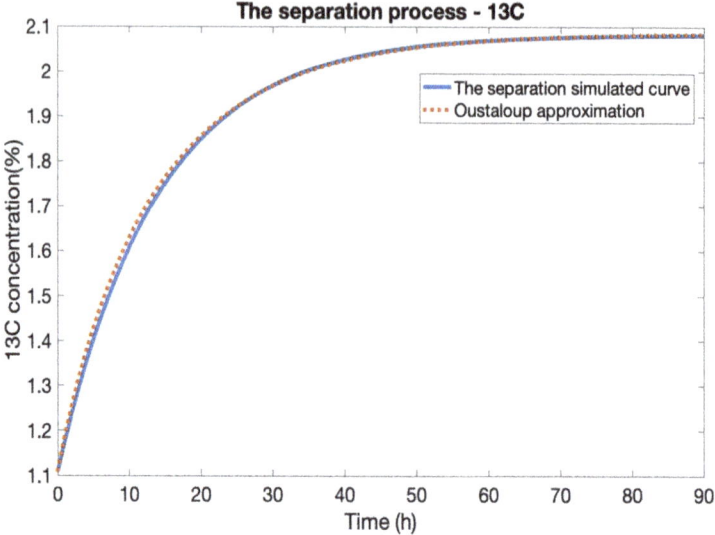

Figure 5. The most probable experimental curve dynamics and the response of the applied Oustaloup approximation.

The Oustaloup approximation can be rewritten as a ratio between two polynomials of the "s" complex variable. The two polynomials have the a coefficients at the denominator and the b coefficients at the following nominator:

$$H(s) = \frac{\sum_{i=0}^{n} b_i \cdot s^i}{\sum_{i=0}^{n} a_i \cdot s^i}, \quad (27)$$

where the coefficients a_i and b_i are depending on β ($a_i(\beta)$ and $b_i(\beta)$) and n represents the order of the Oustaloup approximation.

There are some cases when the variation of β leads to the coefficients $a_0 = 0$ or $b_0 = 0$ (for example, when β takes an integer value). In order to highlight the variations of the β parameter in the separation process model, an online identification mechanism that implements an adaptation procedure has to be used. This necessity is due to the fact that the classical identification can be applied only by retaking the experiments. More exactly, this procedure requires, in the first stage, the separation column to be turned off meaning that the so far obtained production is lost. Furthermore, the experiments are retraced each time the β parameter presents variations. The main disadvantages of the classical identification are the time loss (the separation process being an extremely slow one $T = 14$ (h)) and the product loss.

For the approached separation process, the fractional-order of the $H_1(s)$ transfer function is considered that $\beta \in (0;2]$. As an example, the evolution of the transfer functions of both b_3 and a_3 coefficients in relation to β is presented in Figure 6.

It can be remarked from Figure 6a,b that the nominator coefficients are not monotonously varying (the same conclusion can be reached from Figure 6c,d in the case of the denominator coefficients). The variation of the β parameter was highlighted using the step $\Delta\beta = 0.01$. The two different considered domains for the β parameter variation $(0;1.02]$ and $[1.03;2]$ are necessary due to the fact that for $\beta > 1.02$ the Oustaloup approximation presents a pair of complex conjugated polls, an aspect which imposes differences in the mathematical model implementation. Because of this problem, it is also necessary to divide the fractional differentiation order of the system into the two mentioned intervals in order to store the resultant values for the Oustaloup approximation coefficients (for more efficient processing of the coefficients). Near the limit between the two considered domains, the monotony variation occurs, both for the a and b coefficients.

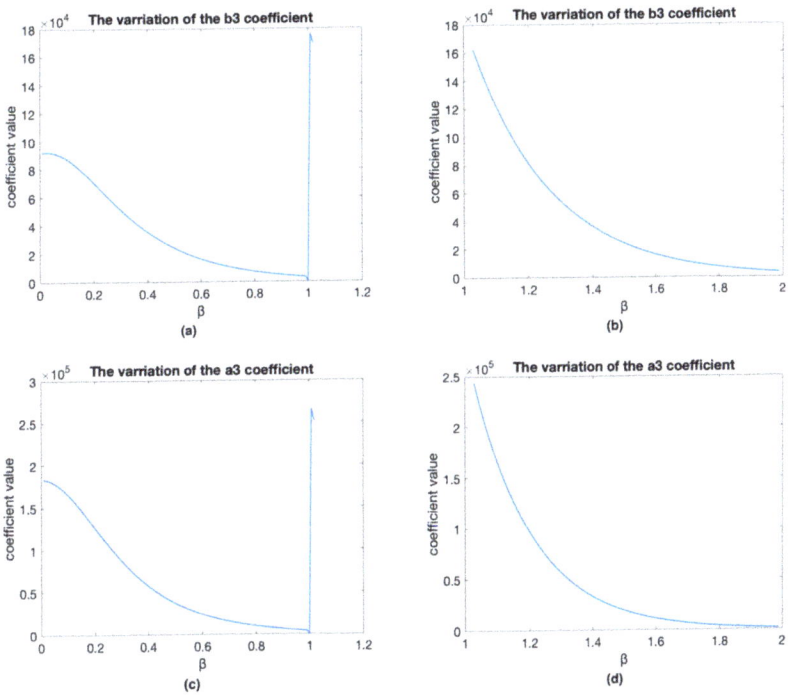

Figure 6. The evolution of the transfer function b_3 and a_3 coefficients: (**a**) The evolution of the transfer function b_3 coefficient in relation to β ($\beta \in (0; 1.02]$); (**b**) The evolution of the transfer function b_3 coefficient in relation to β ($\beta \in (1.02, 1.99]$); (**c**) The evolution of the transfer function a_3 coefficient in relation to β ($\beta \in (0; 1.02]$); (**d**) The evolution of the transfer function a_3 coefficient in relation to β ($\beta \in (1.02, 1.99]$).

Due to the strong nonlinearity of the isotopic separation process (due to the high probability of the β fractional differentiation order variation), the implementation of neural networks is required; the input-output datasets are to be obtained by sampling the signals that are used in order to train the four neural networks (the fractional-order coefficient β (using the same step-size $\Delta\beta = 0.01$) as the input signal and the coefficients of the integer-order transfer function resulted after applying the Oustaloup filter as output signals); the neural networks are able to learn all the Oustaloup approximation coefficients. Since there are two intervals determined for the fractional-order transfer function and since there is a major difference between the values of the denominator and the nominator coefficients, four neural networks are required in order to obtain the best performance when learning the Oustaloup approximation coefficients.

The neural architecture used in this paper is the feed-forward structure using the Bayesian regularization learning algorithm for training.

The feed-forward network consists of three or more layers. In the case of this application, the used neural networks each contain the input layer, only one hidden layer and an output layer. The input layer (the first layer) refers to the connections between the input signals and the neurons from Layer 2 (the hidden layer); it has no computational role; it is only taking over and dispatching the input signals. The neurons from the hidden layer have as input signals the input signals of the neural network weighted with the values of the weights that connect the input layer with the hidden layer; if the neural network had more than one hidden layer (which is not the case of the present application), the output signals of these neurons would represent the input signals for the neurons from the following hidden layer (through the weights that connect the mentioned consecutive hidden layers); the output signals from the neurons of the hidden layers of the proposed neural networks represent the input signals for the neurons of the output layer (through the weights that connect the hidden layer with the output layer). The output signals of the neurons from the output layer are the output signals generated by the proposed neural networks. However, the operation of a neural network relays on a simple principle, as follows: if a neuron is connected to another (following) neuron via a positively connected synapse (weight), it has an excitatory effect; on the other hand, if a neuron is connected to another neuron by a negative synapse (weight), it has an inhibitory effect. In the training procedure, pairs of values of the input-output signals are considered in matrix form. During the training procedure, the following two types of training signals can be highlighted: the functional signals computed by applying input reference vectors (the functional output signals are used for the computation of the errors between the desired values of the output signals and their instantaneous values); the adaptation signals, which are used for adapting the values of the neural network weights based on processing the errors resulting from using the functional signals.

The proposed feed-forward structure has the property of being a universal approximator, and the applied training algorithm is complex enough to learn the mathematical dependencies between the input signal and output signals. It can be remarked that the coefficients of the transfer functions obtained after applying the Oustaloup approximation are not recursive (their values corresponding to a certain β do not depend on values of the same coefficients corresponding to other values of β, more exactly, their instantaneous values are not dependent on their previous samples), this being the reason why recurrent neural networks are not necessary to be implemented.

Each neural structure was implemented by defining only one hidden layer. This was so to avoid increasing the complexity of the computations during the training procedures (the increase in the number of hidden layers implies a consistent increase in the computation complexity). The generated accuracy by increasing the number of hidden layers does not necessarily guarantee better performance, but as was previously mentioned, it consists of an increase in the complexity of the computations. Iteratively, it was possible to determine the number of neurons in the hidden layer by repeating the training procedure for different sizes of the hidden layer; starting with a number of four neurons in the hidden layer in each training, the number of neurons was increased by one; the iterative algorithm was stopped when, from one training to the next one, a performance decrease was remarked; using this procedure, the best training performances were obtained. The learning algorithm was stopped for each neural network when the MSEs (mean squared error) values between the approximated coefficients and their analytical values started to increase. Since the four neural networks must learn the behaviour of the parameters that are nonlinear, the activation functions for the neurons in the hidden layers are the hyperbolic tangent functions (bipolar sigmoid functions). The size of the output layer for all the four neural networks is five, each output giving a corresponding value for a denominator coefficient (in the case of the neural networks that approximate the denominator coefficients) or a nominator coefficient (in the case of the neural networks that approximate the nominator coefficients); the output signal is generally noted with c_i ($i \in \{1, 2, 3, 4, 5\}$), both for denominator and nominator coefficients, and the output neurons are linear (having linear activation functions).

The dynamics of the Oustaloup approximation coefficients could also be implemented using only one more complex neural network, but this aspect would increase the complexity of the neural solution and the computation volume necessary to obtain it. Due to the fact that the Oustaloup approximation coefficients are highly variable, and have numerous decimals, both for denominator and nominator coefficients, the implementation of four neural networks is preferred (resulting in a more efficient and accurate mathematical model).

The general structure of the four used neural networks is presented in Figure 7.

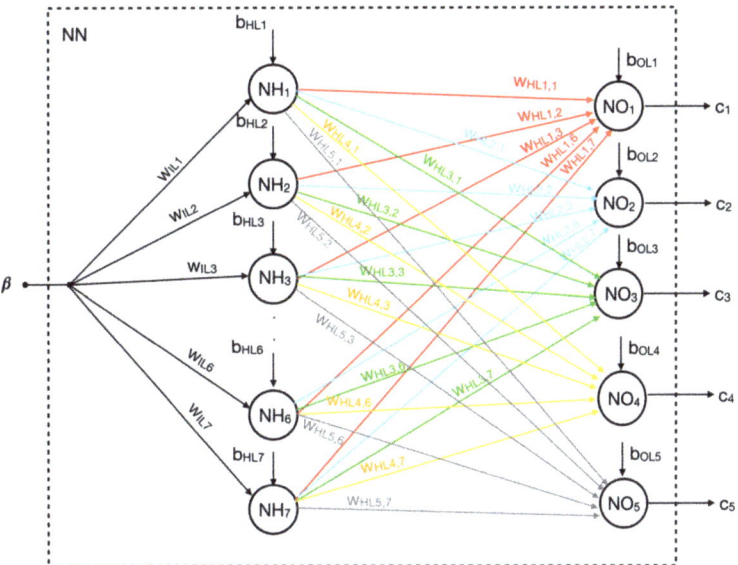

Figure 7. The general structure of the four neural networks.

In Figure 7, w_{ILi} represents the synaptic weight that connects the input signals with the ith neuron of the hidden layer ($i \in \{1, 2, \ldots, n = 7\}$) and $w_{HLj,i}$ represents the synaptic weight that connects the ith neuron of the hidden layer ($i \in \{1, 2, \ldots, n = 7\}$) with the jth neuron of the output layer ($i \in \{1, 2, \ldots, m = 5\}$)."

The hyperbolic sigmoid bipolar function used as an activation function for the NH_k neurons (the neurons from the hidden layer) is defined by $\varphi(v) = \frac{1-e^{(-\gamma v)}}{1+e^{(-\gamma v)}}$, where γ is a constant parameter.

The linear function used as an activation function for the NO_j neurons (the neurons from the output layers) is defined by $\varphi(v) = v$.

The algorithm Bayesian Regularization [48,49] is used in order to accomplish the training of the four networks and the allowed maximum number of epochs was set to 50,000, the minimum error gradient at 10^{-100} and the initial learning rate at 10^{-5}. For each learned coefficient, the MSE target value was set to 10^{-8}. The training was accomplished after 42,356 epochs when the imposed error was reached. The Levenberg–Marquardt algorithm was also implemented, but the obtained performances were significantly lower in comparison with the case of using the Bayesian Regularization. Other applied learning algorithms generated solutions that cannot be used due to their low accuracy for approximating the Oustaloup filter coefficient variation. Applying the previously presented iterative procedure, it was determined that in the hidden layer, the optimum number of neutrons is seven (in each case of all four neural networks). The implementation details of the four neural networks (their parameters) and their proposed structure are presented in Figure 8.

The trained neural networks generate an output signal as it follows:

$$y = w_{HL} \cdot [tansig(w_{IL} \cdot \beta + B_{HL})] + B_{OL} \qquad (28)$$

The high modelling accuracy generated by the proposed neural networks is proved in Appendix A.

Neural network structure: feed-forward fully connected neural network
One input layer containing the input signal: β
One hidden layer containing: n = 7 neurons (NH$_k$) where k ∈ {1, 2, ... , n}
One output layer containing: m = 5 neurons (NO$_j$) where j ∈ {1, 2, ... , m}
The activation functions: Hyperbolic Tangent Function (Bipolar Sigmoid Function) for NH$_k$ neurons and Linear Function for NO$_j$ neurons

The vectors and the matrix that contains the neural network weights and bias values:

$$w_{IL}(7 \times 1) = \begin{pmatrix} w_{IL1} \\ w_{IL2} \\ w_{IL3} \\ \vdots \\ w_{IL6} \\ w_{IL7} \end{pmatrix}; \quad B_{HL}(7 \times 1) = \begin{pmatrix} B_{HL1} \\ B_{HL2} \\ B_{HL3} \\ \vdots \\ B_{HL6} \\ B_{HL7} \end{pmatrix}; \quad B_{OL}(5 \times 1) = \begin{pmatrix} b_{OL1} \\ b_{OL2} \\ b_{OL3} \\ b_{OL4} \\ b_{OL5} \end{pmatrix}$$

$$w_{HL}(5 \times 7) = \begin{pmatrix} w_{HL1,1} & w_{HL1,2} & w_{HL1,3} & \cdots & \cdots & \cdots & w_{HL1,6} & w_{HL1,7} \\ w_{HL2,1} & w_{HL2,2} & w_{HL2,3} & \cdots & \cdots & \cdots & w_{HL2,6} & w_{HL2,7} \\ w_{HL3,1} & w_{HL13,2} & w_{HL3,3} & \cdots & \cdots & \cdots & w_{HL3,6} & w_{HL3,7} \\ w_{HL4,1} & w_{HL4,2} & w_{HL4,3} & \cdots & \cdots & \cdots & w_{HL4,6} & w_{HL4,7} \\ w_{HL5,1} & w_{HL5,2} & w_{HL5,3} & \cdots & \cdots & \cdots & w_{HL5,6} & w_{HL5,7} \end{pmatrix}$$

Figure 8. The structure and the details of the four proposed neural networks.

In Figure 9, the comparison between the response of the Oustaloup approximation implemented using the first two neural networks (corresponding to β values lower than 1.02) and the response of the fractional-order transfer function in (25) is presented. As a case study, for the fractional-order transfer function, the following parameters are considered: $\beta = 0.53$, $T = 1$ (h) and $K = 1$. This example, which is not associated with the case of the separation process, is given only to prove the feasibility and the high accuracy of the proposed modelling method.

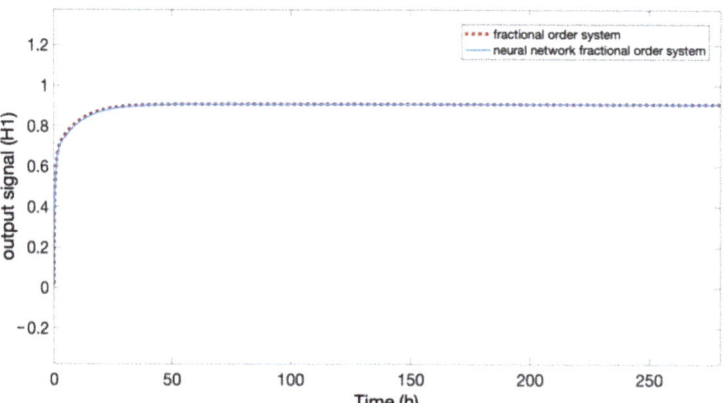

Figure 9. The comparison between the response of the Oustaloup approximation implemented using the first two neural networks and the response of the fractional-order system ($\beta = 0.53 < 1.02$).

It can be remarked from Figure 9 that the two neural networks are able to fully learn the coefficients of the Oustaloup approximation, the plots of the two functions being overlapped.

The second example is given only to prove the feasibility and high accuracy of the proposed modelling method for β values equal to or higher than 1.02. The comparison between the response of the Oustaloup approximation implemented using the second pair of neural networks and the response of the fractional-order system is presented in Figure 10 (where the considered parameters of the fractional-order system are the following: $K = 1$, $T = 1$ (h) and $\beta = 1.45$).

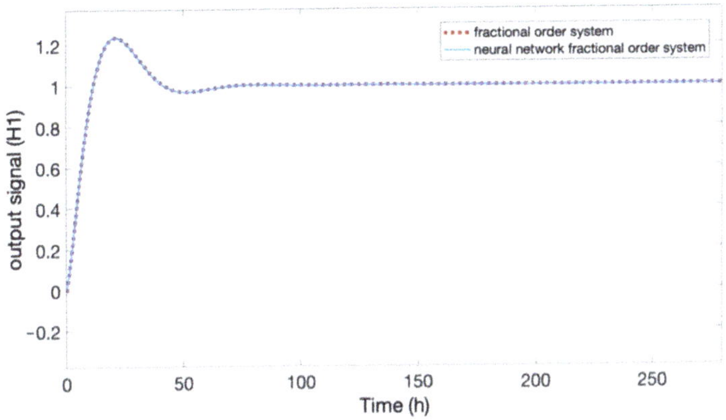

Figure 10. The comparison between the response of the Oustaloup approximation implemented using the first two neural networks and the response of the fractional-order system ($\beta = 1.45 > 1.02$).

From Figure 10, it can be concluded that the neural networks (both for the denominator and nominator coefficients) are learning with very high accuracy the coefficients for the Oustaloup approximation. The examples from Figures 9 and 10 demonstrate that the neural networks are able to learn and adapt to the desired output based on the selected input (the fractional differentiation order), and they can be used in the structure of the separation process mathematical model.

The main problem with modelling the separation process is the fact that it is a fractional-order process, and the associated differentiation order can present variations in relation to time. The proposed original solution is focused on approximating the fractional-order dynamics of the process, and it introduces the possibility to simulate the process in the case when its associated differentiation order is modified. In Figures 9 and 10, the proposed solution for approximating the model of a fractional-order process with variable differentiation order is proven as feasibile. These examples are theoretical ones, and they are considered due to the fact that they have the same fractional-order structure as the fractional-order component as the considered separation process, but without considering the technological structure parameters of the separation process. These two examples are presented in order to sustain the feasibility of the theoretical part of the proposed solution with relevant simulations.

5. Simulation Results

Some of the advantages of including the neural networks in the process modelling for the dynamics of the ^{13}C isotopic separation process include the higher accuracy obtained by implementing the neural models and the ability to design an online adaptation algorithm for the proposed model when some variations occur in the structural parameters of the separation process. Furthermore, a future approach to this system may include the intelligent control, using the same proposed procedure in the previous chapters for obtaining an adaptive fractional-order controller.

The mathematical model for the ^{13}C isotopic separation process is implemented considering the Equations (1)–(5), (24), (25) presented previously, using the MATLAB/Simulink software [47], and it runs in parallel with the proposed model implemented using the neural networks, having the same applied input signal β (the fractional-order system). The output from the separation process is the real (experimental) ^{13}C isotope concentration, and the output signal from the proposed model is the simulated ^{13}C isotope concentration curve. In order to implement the online procedure for the model adaptation, the error $(e(t,i))$

is computed as the difference between the two signals (the ^{13}C isotope experimental and simulated concentrations). It can be remarked that the obtained error signal is applied at the input of the adaptive mechanism, which consists of a PI controller generating at its output the input signal for the two neural networks (the two previously presented variation domains of β have to be separately approached). The adaptive mechanism processes the error value and further generates the adaptation signal.

The proposed adaptive structure of the isotopic separation process model using neural networks is presented in the following figure (Figure 11).

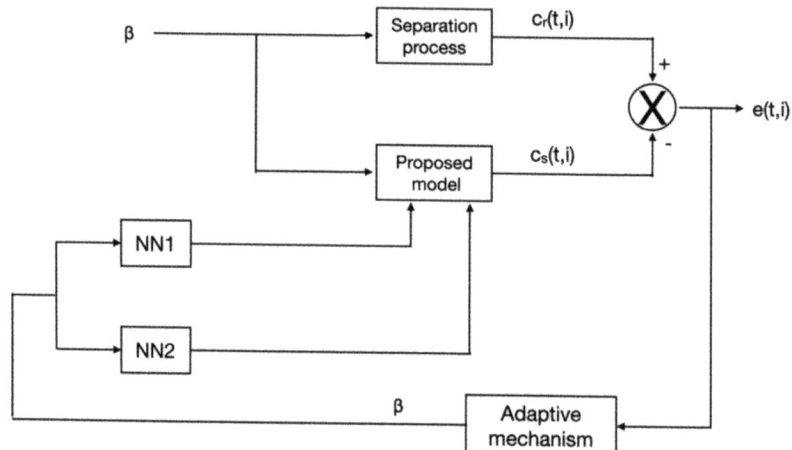

Figure 11. The proposed adaptive structure for the isotopic separation process model.

The feasibility of the online adaptation of the proposed model is proved; the proposed model is run in parallel with the separation process, having applied the same input signal (the input flow of monoethanolamine) to both entities and considering the same fractional differentiation order β. The notation $c_r(t,i)$ refers to the real (experimental) concentration of the ^{13}C isotope at the output of the separation column, whilst $c_s(t,i)$ refers to the simulated concentration obtained for the ^{13}C isotope at the output of the process model; the error signal $e(t,i)$ is computed by the difference between the following two signals: $c_r(t,i)$ and $c_s(t,i)$. When, in the case of the real process, the fractional differentiation order β presents variations, it implies the fact that the concentration of the ^{13}C isotope also presents variations in relation to the time. Consequently, it results in the necessity to adapt the proposed fractional-order model using the adaptive mechanism from Figure 11. In this case, a proportional-integral (PI) controller was chosen to implement the adaptive mechanism. Since the isotopic separation of the ^{13}C isotope is a slow process, the steady-state value of the output signal (the ^{13}C isotope concentration) is reached after long periods of time. The performance of the online identification of the process when the fractional differentiation order presents variations can be improved, for example, by using a full PID controller or a non-linear controller, more exactly by increasing the complexity of the adaptive mechanism structure.

As a future development direction, the proposed adaptive structure from Figure 11 can be extended in order to have the possibility to learn, also, the variation of the process structure parameters (for example, in some particular and very rare operation scenarios, the time constant of the process presents some significant value deviations in relation to its nominal value). Practically, the future extended form of the proposed adaptive structure will be able to learn the possible variations of the process structure parameters by equivalenting their effects with the effect of modifying the value of the fractional differentiation order of the process.

5.1. Adaptation of Differentiation Order of a Fractional-Order System

In order to prove the feasibility of the proposed adaptation solution, as case study, the following fractional-order transfer function is considered:

$$H_1(s) = \frac{1}{s^\beta + 1},\qquad(29)$$

The efficiency of the used adaptive mechanism combined with the proposed neural solutions is presented in Figure 12 (where the value of the fractional differentiation order is $\beta = 0.78$) and in Figure 13 (where $\beta = 1.45$). It can be remarked from Figure 12 that at the time moment $t = 180$ (h) the value of the fractional differentiation order presented a step-type variation from $\beta = 0.78$ to $\beta = 0.4$ having as affecting the decrease in the ^{13}C isotope concentration. Moreover, from Figure 12, it results that using the adaptive mechanism, the mathematical model of the separation process based on using the neural networks is properly adapted, its output signal tracking with high precision the output signal from the real process (in this example, the fractional-order system).

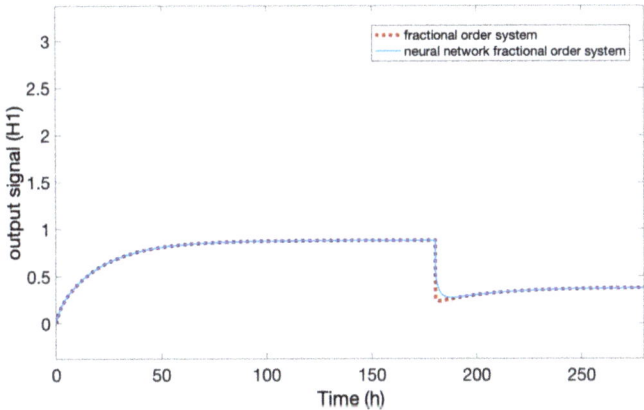

Figure 12. The proof of the proposed adaptive solution when a disturbance implies the β variation from 0.78 to 0.4 at $t = 180$ (h).

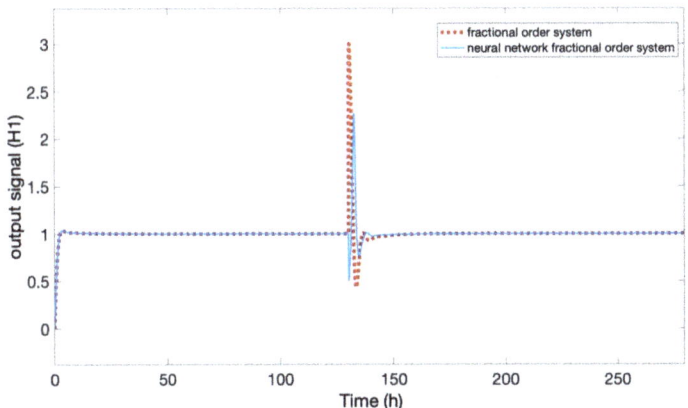

Figure 13. The proof of the proposed adaptive solution when a disturbance implies the β variation from 1.45 to 1.15 at $t = 130$ (h).

By analysing Figure 12, it can be remarked that the only visible difference between the two responses occurs after the moment when the β differentiation order varies until the adaptive mechanism accomplishes the online identification of this variation (the corresponding period being insignificant (approximatively 5 h) in relation to the process dynamics).

In Figure 13, at the time moment $t = 130$ (h), the value of the fractional differentiation order presents a negative step-type variation from $\beta = 1.45$ to $\beta = 1.15$. As in the previous case (case of Figure 12), the same main conclusion results. More exactly, the proposed adaptive mechanism combined with the proposed mathematical model using neural networks can learn with accuracy the model dynamics variation at the variation of the fractional differentiation order of the real process (which is an essential structural parameter of the separation process).

Regarding the visible difference between the two responses from Figure 13, the same conclusion as in the case of the responses from Figure 12 can be drawn. However, immediately after the moment when the β fractional differentiation order varies for a short period of time (approximately 5 h as in the case of Figure 12), the differences between the two responses are higher than the differences between the two responses from Figure 12. This aspect is due to the fact that in the case of Figure 13, the variation of the β fractional differentiation order for values higher than one is presented, a case in which the two output signals present faster variations than in the case when β has lower values than one. As it was mentioned before, these differences can be reduced by using a more complex form of the adaptive mechanism that can generate better online identification performances in a dynamic regime.

5.2. Adaptation of Differentiation Order of the Separation Process

The process model of the ^{13}C isotopic separation system presented in (24) is simulated in Figures 14 and 15. These simulations are made by considering the identified structure parameters of the process, and consequently, using the following:

$$H_1(s) = \frac{1.22}{14 \cdot s^{0.91} + 1}. \tag{30}$$

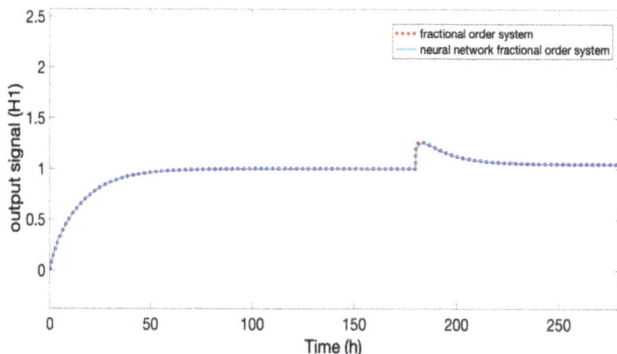

Figure 14. The proof of learning the increasing dynamics of the fractional differentiation order (from $\beta = 0.91$ to $\beta = 0.97$ at $t = 180$ (h)).

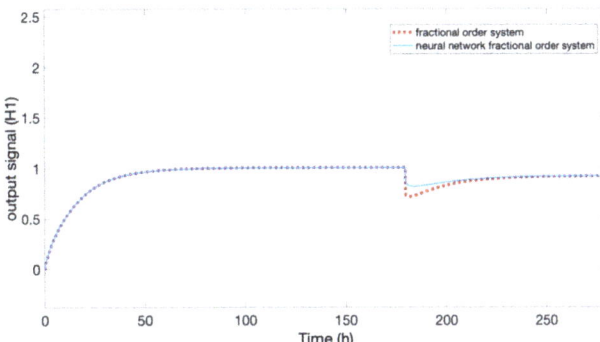

Figure 15. The proof of learning the decreasing dynamics of the fractional differentiation order (from $\beta = 0.91$ to $\beta = 0.82$ at $t = 180$ (h)).

Firstly, the efficiency of the proposed methods in approximating the $H_1(s)$ dynamics is proven, using as input signal the unit-step signal. It can be remarked from Figure 14, that the initial value determined for $\beta = 0.91$ was modified to $\beta = 0.97$ at the time moment $t = 180$ (h). Furthermore, it results that the fractional-order model implemented using neural networks and using the adaptive mechanism follows with a high accuracy the dynamics implied by $H_1(s)$.

In Figure 15, the value of $\beta = 0.91$ was modified to $\beta = 0.82$ at the time moment $t = 180$ (h). Furthermore, the efficiency of the fractional-order model implemented using the artificial intelligence techniques (neural networks) is proven again since the accuracy of learning the behaviour of the fractional-order process is almost the same as in the case of the Figure 14.

By analysing the differences between the two responses presented in Figure 14, respectively, presented in Figure 15, immediately after the variation of the β fractional differentiation order, it results in better performances in the case of Figure 14. This aspect has the following two main causes: firstly, in the case of Figure 15, the β fractional differentiation order presents a higher variation with 50% than in the case of Figure 14; secondly, in the case of Figure 14, the β fractional differentiation order presents an increasing variation from a value belonging to the neighbourhood of value 1 to a value belonging to the close neighbourhood of value 1 (this phenomenon of tending to an integer order process implies better performance for the adaptive mechanism).

5.3. Online Adaptation of the Separation Process Model

The evolution in time of the ^{13}C isotope concentration is presented in Figure 16, considering the input flow $F_{in} = 350$ mL/h. The proposed neural model performs a close tracking over the real fractional-order process, being able to perform the adaptation at the variation of the fractional differentiation order value from $\beta = 0.91$ to $\beta = 0.97$ (at the moment of time $t = 180$ (h)). It can also be remarked that by increasing the differentiation order of the fractional transfer function, the ^{13}C isotope concentration also increases.

The control signal (the fractional differentiation order β) applied by the adaptive mechanism to the NN1 and NN2 inputs in order to perform the online adaptation of the process model is presented in Figure 17.

The control effort ($\Delta\beta$) generated by the adaptive mechanism in order to perform the adaptation is presented in Figure 18; it follows from Figures 17 and 18 that the positive control effort is generated only after the β parameter variation in order to learn this variation.

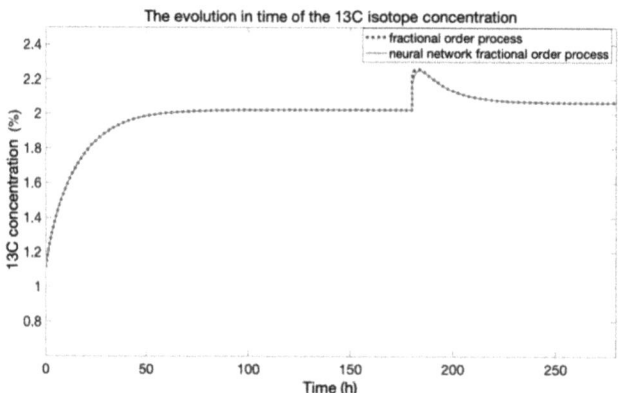

Figure 16. The proof of the proposed adaptive model efficiency in learning the increasing dynamics of the ^{13}C separation process when the fractional differentiation order varies increasingly from $\beta = 0.91$ to $\beta = 0.97$ at $t = 180$ (h).

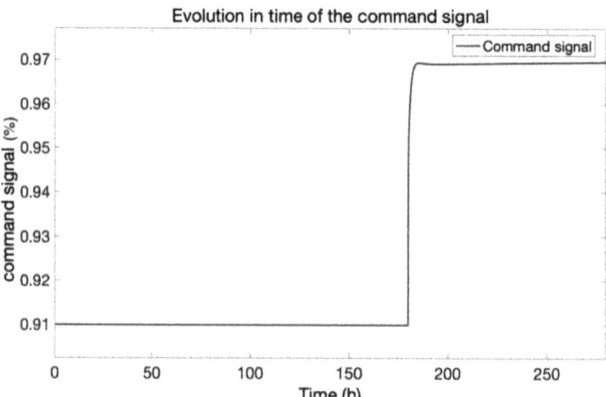

Figure 17. Evolution in time of the control signal applied in order to adapt the proposed model of the separation process when the fractional differentiation order varies from $\beta = 0.91$ to $\beta = 0.97$ at $t = 180$ (h).

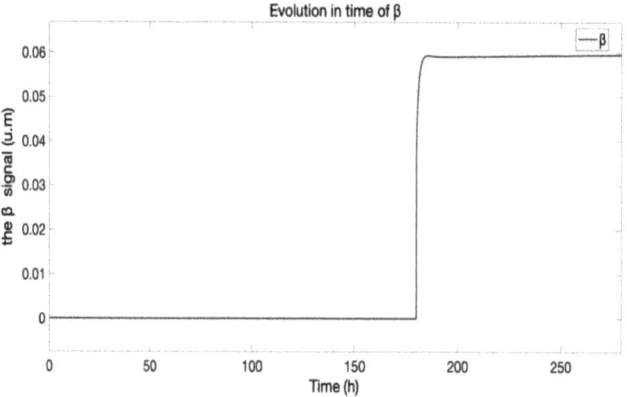

Figure 18. Evolution in time of control effort ($\Delta\beta$) if the variation of $\beta = 0.91$ to $\beta = 0.97$ at $t = 180$ (h) occurs.

The efficiency in the adaptation of the isotopic separation process model when the decreasing variation of the fractional differentiation order value occurs is proven in Figure 19. The initial value of $\beta = 0.91$ was decreased to the value of $\beta = 0.82$ at the time moment $t = 180$ (h). It can be remarked that by lowering the value of the fractional differentiation order, the obtained ^{13}C isotope concentration is also lowered, and the dynamics of the proposed model output signal follows with accuracy the real separation process output signal.

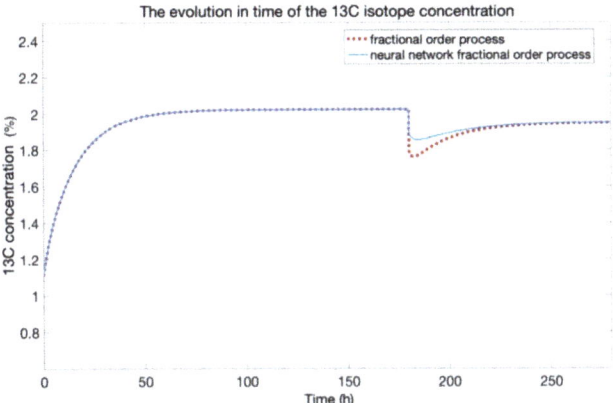

Figure 19. The proof of the proposed adaptive model efficiency in learning the increasing dynamics of the ^{13}C separation process when the fractional differentiation order varies decreasingly from $\beta = 0.91$ to $\beta = 0.82$ at $t = 180$ (h).

The control signal (the fractional differentiation order β) applied by the adaptive mechanism to the NN1 and NN2 inputs in order to perform the online adaptation of the process model is presented in Figure 20.

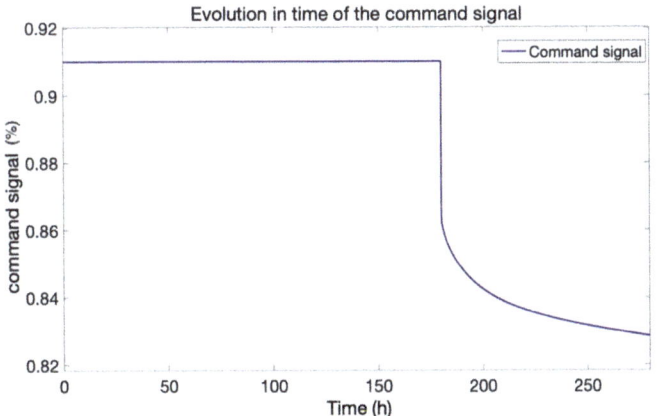

Figure 20. Evolution in time of the control signal applied in order to adapt the proposed model of the separation process when the fractional differentiation order varies from $\beta = 0.91$ to $\beta = 0.82$ at $t = 180$ (h).

The control effort ($\Delta\beta$) generated by the adaptive mechanism in order to perform the adaptation is presented in Figure 21. It follows from Figures 20 and 21 that the negative control effort is generated only after the β parameter variation in order to learn this variation.

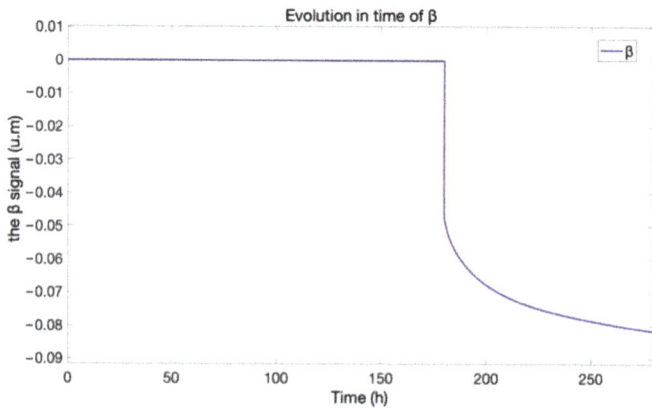

Figure 21. Evolution in time of control effort ($\Delta\beta$) if the variation of $\beta = 0.91$ to $\beta = 0.82$ at $t = 180$ (h) occurs.

It can be remarked by comparing the results presented in Figures 16 and 19, which in the case of the β parameter increases, the online adaptation is visible more efficient than in the case when the β parameter decreases. This aspect is due to the fact that the tuning of the adaptive mechanism is made for the case when the β parameter increases. In order to obtain the same performance for the online adaptation when the β decreases the adaptive mechanism can be augmented with a control subsystem tuned in order to optimise this case.

By comparing the differences between the responses presented in Figures 16 and 19, the same conclusions as in the case of Figures 14 and 15 can be drawn. The better performances obtained in the cases of Figures 14 and 16 are a consequence of the much faster evolution and stabilisation of the control signal presented in Figure 17 than the evolution and stabilisation of the control signal presented in Figure 20 (this control signal is associated with the simulation from Figure 19, but it can be associated as a variation form to the simulation from Figure 15, too).

These conclusions are proven through the values of the mean squared errors (MSE) presented in Table 3.

Table 3. The MSE values between the presented responses of the separation process.

	Figure 14		Figure 15	Figure 16		Figure 19
MSE	0.00137	<<	0.00615	0.00215 (%)	<<	0.0105 (%)

The errors presented in Table 3 are computed for each figure considering the 318 pairs of samples of the two corresponding responses.

5.4. The Effect of the Neural Networks in Processing the Experimental Data

In order to prove the efficiency of the proposed methods based on the usage of neural networks, another experiment was conducted on the considered separation column is approached.

The experimental curve for the 2 M (molar) input flow of monoethanolamine in methanol is presented in Figure 22. The experiment consists of applying at the input of the process a step signal having a value of 700 mL/h. As an important remark is the fact that the previously presented experiment (Figure 2) was made by considering the 1 M (molar) input flow of monoethanolamine in methanol. This is the reason why in the new experiment higher values of the input flow are used compared to in the first one.

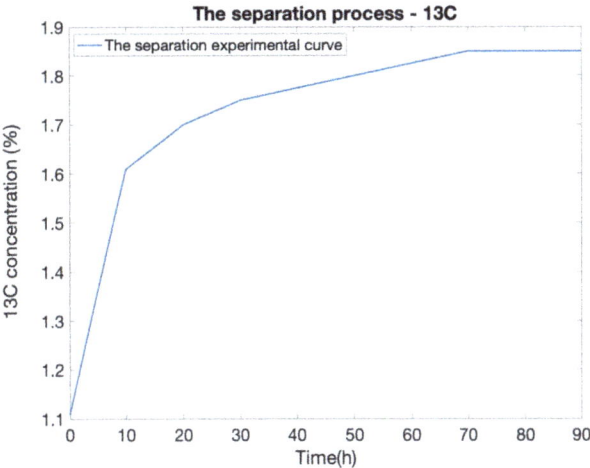

Figure 22. The experimental curve for the 2 M input flow of monoethanolamine in methanol.

The next step consists of the online identification of the response from Figure 22 by using the adaptive structure (designed based on the proposed methods) from Figure 11. In order to run the adaptive system, the searched fractional-order part of the model having the structure defined in (25) is initialised with the same value of the time constant as in the case of the first experiment ($T = 14$ (h)), with the proportionality constant ($K = 1.22$ (%·h/mL)) also being the same as in the previous case, and the fractional differentiation order $\beta = 0.57$ (a value lower than 1, randomly chosen). Moreover, the constant K_p was recomputed for the case of using 2 M of input monoethanolamine flow. Consequently, by running the adaptive system from Figure 11, the appropriate value of the β fractional differentiation order has to be identified. The evolution in relation to time of the β parameter during the running of the adaptive structure is presented in Figure 23.

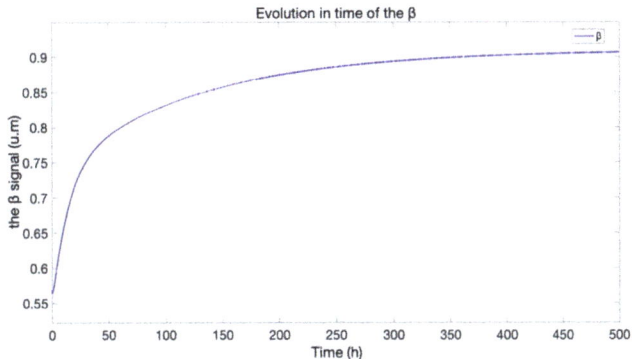

Figure 23. Evolution in time of the β parameter during the running of the adaptive structure.

From Figure 23, it results that β varies from the value of 0.57 (the initialisation value) to the value of 0.91 (obtained in the steady-state regime), which represents the final result of the identification. It can be remarked that the identified value of the β parameter is the same as in the case of the first experiment. This aspect is due to the fact that the same separation plant is considered and also the same separation process (in both experiments). The usage of the 2 M input monoethanolamine flow in the case of the second experiment does not change physically the order (fractional-order in this case) of the process and, obviously, not mathematically.

The comparative graph between the experimental response associated with the second experiment and the response of the identified mathematical model for this case is presented in Figure 24.

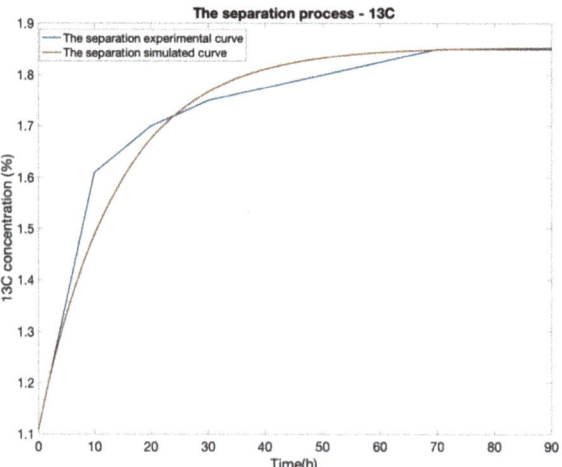

Figure 24. The separation process experimental curve and the most probable approximating response of the separation process (the case of the second experiment).

By analysing Figure 24, the high quality of the identification can be remarked. The approximating response follows the process dynamics with accuracy, and the steady-state value of the two curves from Figure 24 is equal. Consequently, the efficiency of the proposed method based on neural networks is again proved. The use of neural networks allows the simulation of the fractional-order systems when their fractional differentiation order presents variations, and by having this possibility, the fractional-order systems can be identified online (also the fractional differentiation order can be identified online). Both these approaches are original ones.

6. Conclusions

The benefit of using the neural networks in order to learn the dynamics of the isotopic separation process structure parameters in relation to the input value of the fractional differentiation order is represented by the high accuracy of the proposed model; the proposed solution for modelling the fractional-order systems is an original one and introduces important advantages in the simulation of these types of systems.

Section 3 proves the feasibility of the implementation of the proposed mathematical model of the separation process as a fractional-order one, whilst in Section 4 the approach based on neural networks is presented.

In this paper, the mathematical modelling [50–53], the simulation [54–57] and the on-line model adaptation of the ^{13}C isotopic separation process are approached; the proposed solution can be implemented and adapted to the case of the other separation processes, such as the ones for obtaining the ^{15}N, ^{18}O, ^{10}B isotopes [58]. The adaptation of the developed methods is efficient for being implemented in the cases as follows:

- The separation processes are distributed parameter ones;
- The separation processes are strongly nonlinear;
- The concentration of the isotope to be separated depends on time and on the "length" variable (the position in the separation column in relation to the columns height);
- The processes are very slow, and the time constants are varying depending on the intensity of the operation of the separation system.

There are some differences to be mentioned in the procedures applied to obtain other isotope separations, which can imply complications in the model adaptation as follows: other isotope production requires different chemical substances to be used, different equipment or even different structures of the separation plants.

The isotopic separation process operation is improved by implementing an adaptive mechanism in order to obtain the proposed model adaptation when the variation of the fractional differentiation order of the real process presents variations.

The proposed mathematical model for the separation process uses neural networks (which belong to the artificial intelligence domain) to generate at the output each value of the coefficients of the Oustaloup approximation of the fractional-order system. The efficiency of the neural networks is proven since the fractional differentiation order can vary between any value from 0 to 2, resulting in 200 Oustaloup approximation functions, each of them consisting of five coefficients for the nominator and five or six (in the case of the pairs of complex conjugated polls) coefficients for the denominator.

The developed system is improved by the implementation of the adaptive mechanism, which is able to adapt the proposed model during the evolution of the process (online) when the separation process fractional differentiation order presents variations.

An important future development possibility is to apply the proposed solution for approximating the dynamics of fractional-order systems in relation to the fractional differentiation order in the case of fractional-order controllers and to implement, based on this idea, fractional-order adaptive controllers. The implementation in practice of a future fractional-order adaptive controller is feasible from the perspective of processing power vs. accuracies due to two important aspects. Firstly, for a certain practical application, the training of the neural networks that are used for approximating the variation of the Oustaloup filter coefficients in relation to the fractional differentiation order is made, for example, in MATLAB, on a computer that is not integrated into the control loop. Consequently, the implementation of the practical control system does not need much computation processing power in order to train the neural solutions. Secondly, the fractional-order adaptive controller implementation, for example on a micro-controller, consists of the implementation of the recurrence relations associated with the neural solution's operation. These recurrence relations that describe the neural solution's operation (previously obtained after applying the training procedures) contain only basic mathematical operations, and they do not imply an increase in the computation processing power. Consequently, the necessary accuracy can be obtained by using acceptable computation processing power, and it can be improved by increasing the number of decimals of the coefficients that occur in the recurrence relations that describe the neural solution's operation.

Author Contributions: R.M., V.M., M.-L.U., M.A. and H.V.; methodology, R.M., V.M., M.-L.U., M.A., H.V. and I.C.; software, R.M., V.M., M.-L.U., M.A., H.V. and I.C.; validation, R.M., V.M. and M.A.; formal analysis, R.M., V.M., M.-L.U., and M.A.; investigation, R.M., V.M., M.-L.U., M.A., H.V. and I.C.; resources, R.M., V.M., M.-L.U., M.A. and H.V.; data curation, R.M., V.M., M.A., H.V. and I.C.; writing—original draft preparation, R.M., V.M., M.-L.U. and I.C.; writing—review and editing, R.M., V.M. and I.C.; visualization, R.M., M.A. and I.C.; supervision, R.M., V.M. and M.A.; project administration, R.M., V.M., M.-L.U., M.A. and H.V.; funding acquisition, V.M. and H.V. All authors have read and agreed to the published version of the manuscript.

Funding: The APC was funded by Technical University of Cluj-Napoca, Romania.

Conflicts of Interest: The authors declare no conflict of interest.

Nomenclature

i	the length constant
h	the separation columns' height
H_1	fractional-order transfer function
K	proportionality constant of the fractional-order transfer function

T	time constant
β	the process fractional-order
y_{st}	steady-state value of the response of the process (^{13}C isotope concentration)
K_p	proportionality constant responsible of the variation of the ^{13}C isotope concentration in relation to the input of the monoethanolamine solution flow
F_{in}	input flow of the monoethanolamine solution
$y(t)$	the output signal of the open loop process
$F_{0T}(t)$	an increasing exponential function
$\mathcal{E}_{\beta,\beta}\left(-\frac{1}{T}\cdot t^{\beta}\right)$	the Mittag-Leffer function in two parameters
u(t)	Step-type signal depending on input flow of the monoethanolamine solution
$s_{13C1}(t)$	the initial value of the ^{13}C concentration
$s_{13C0}(t)$	the steady-state value of the ^{13}C concentration when F_{in} = 340 mL/h
HETP(t)	the height equivalent to a theoretical plate
$HETP_0$	the steady-state value of the HETP determined for F_{in0}
K_H	a proportionality constant determined experimentally
F_{in0}	a constant value of the input flow of the monoethanolamine solution
n(t)	the number of theoretical plates
S(t)	the separation
α	The elementary separation factor for the ^{13}C isotope regarding the chemical exchange procedure
y_0	Natural abundance of the ^{13}C isotope
u_2	the equivalent input signal of the separation process
T_{i0}	process time constant when $i = 0^+$
T_{if}	process time constant when $i = i_f$
$D^{\beta}F_{t(t)}$	the fractional-order differential equation
$F_{t(t)}$	the solution of the fractional-order differential equation
$F_{i1}(i)$	the dynamics of the ^{13}C isotope concentration in relation to i
C	equivalent length constant for the separation column
K	proportionality constant for the separation column
$y_{an}(t,i)$	the ^{13}C isotope concentration at any point of height in the separation column
m	an integer
$RD^{\alpha}f(t)$	the Riemann–Liouville definition of the fractional-order derivative
$\mathcal{I}^{m-\alpha}$	fractional-order integral
$CD^{\alpha}f(t)$	the Caputo definition of the fractional-order derivative
$LD^{\alpha}f(t)$	the Grunwald–Letnikov definition of the fractional-order derivative
$\Gamma()$	Gamma function
Y(s)	fractional-order transfer function
fract_tf	MATLAB function used in order to implement the Oustaloup approximation
num	the numerator, being a cell, a scalar or an $frac\_poly\_exp$ object
den	the denominator having the same arguments as the numerator
N	a scalar representing the order for the used Oustaloup approximation of fractional differentiator
w	a 1×2 matrix containing the lower waveband and the upper frequency for the Oustaloup approximation
va	Laplace variable corresponding character
Ts	the sampling time as a scalar
sim	the string giving the method to simulate the fractional system
H(s)	Oustaloup approximation represented as a ratio between two polynomial functions of "s" complex variable
a_i	The denominator coefficients for the H(s) function
b_i	The nominator coefficients for the H(s) function

Appendix A

In order to prove the high performances of the proposed neural networks regarding their accuracy, the comparative simulations from Figure A1 are presented.

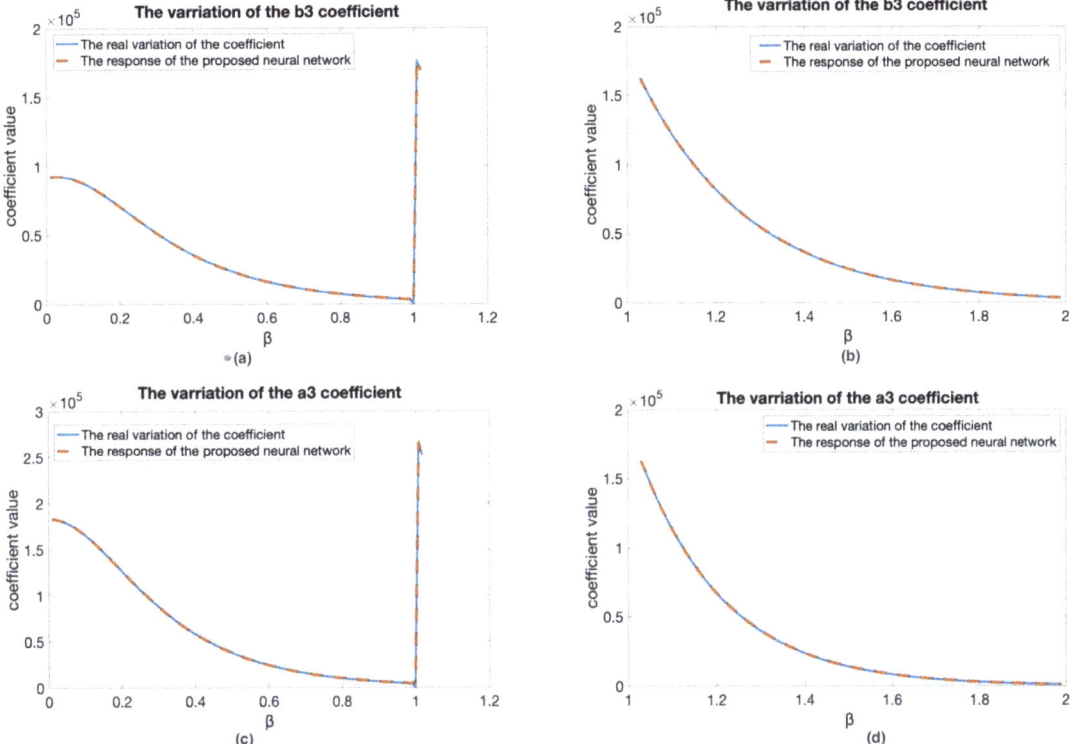

Figure A1. Proof of the proposed neural networks accuracy: (**a**) The evolution of the transfer function b_3 coefficient in relation to β ($\beta \in (0; 1.02]$) and the response of the proposed neural network; (**b**) The evolution of the transfer function b_3 coefficient in relation to β ($\beta \in (1.02, 1.99]$) and the response of the proposed neural network; (**c**) The evolution of the transfer function a_3 coefficient in relation to β ($\beta \in (0; 1.02]$) and the response of the proposed neural network; (**d**) The evolution of the transfer function a_3 coefficient in relation to β ($\beta \in (1.02, 1.99]$) and the response of the proposed neural network.

In Figure A1, the variation of the same coefficients as in Figure 6 is presented, but compared with the responses of the proposed neural networks that approximate them. From Figure A1, the differences between the responses from each graph are superposed with high accuracy; practically, they could not be distinguished without using consistent zoom options. The high accuracy generated by the proposed neural solutions is proved again considering the very small values of the quality indicator (MSE).

In Table A1, the following are centralized: the MSE values between the responses from each graph from Figure A1; the coefficients average values (CAV) for each of the four cases; the ratios between the MSE values and CAV values for each graph case. By analysing the MSE values, these are insignificant compared to the corresponding CAV values. In the cases of graphs (a) and (c), the MSE values are consistently higher than in the cases of graphs (b) and (d). This aspect is due to the high variation of the coefficients a_3 and b_3 when the β fractional differentiation order takes value near the close neighbourhood of value 1 (due to this high variation, the difference between the two signals of graphs (a) and (c) is higher in the mentioned neighbourhood).

Table A1. The centralizer of the errors.

Figure A1	(a)	(b)	(c)	(d)
MSE	39.80	4.88×10^{-3}	29.705	9.24×10^{-2}
CAV	37987.68	41624.22	65840.79	33028.35
MSE/CAV	1.04×10^{-3}	1.17×10^{-7}	4.51×10^{-4}	2.79×10^{-6}

In order to prove that these variations do not influence consistently the approximation accuracy, the ratio MSE/CAV is computed and presented also in Table A1. The obtained values are insignificant (lower than 0.11%). Consequently, the approximations generated by the proposed neural solutions are accurate on the entire domains of definition and they are accurate enough for being usable in practice, even in the worst scenarios (in this case, when the β fractional differentiation order takes value in the close neighbourhood of value 1).

These conclusions explain the high accuracy obtained in modelling the considered fractional-order isotopic separation process by using neural networks.

References

1. Grocke, D.R. *Chapter One—Carbon Isotope Stratigraphy: Principles and Applications*; Stratigraphy & Timescales; Academic Press: Cambridge, MA, USA, 2020; Volume 5, pp. 1–40.
2. Axente, D.; Abrudean, M.; Bâldea, A. *^{15}N, ^{18}O, ^{10}B, ^{13}C Isotopes Separation trough Isotopic Exchange*; Sci. Book House: Cluj-Napoca, Romania, 1994; pp. 122–238.
3. Van Rompay, P.A.; Zhang, Z.; Nees, J.A.; Mourou, G.A.; Pronko, P.P. Angular dependence of isotope enrichment in ultrafast laser ablation plumes. *CLEO Tech. Dig. Postconf.* **2001**, *56*, CThL9.
4. Zhu, G.; Shangguan, Z.; Deng, L. Dynamics of water-stable aggregates associated organic carbon assessed from delta C-13 changes following temperate natural forest development in China. *Soil Tillage Res.* **2021**, *205*, 104782. [CrossRef]
5. Badoud, F.; Goeckener, B.; Severin, K.; Ernest, M.; Romero, R.; Alzieu, T.; Glabasnia, A.; Hamel, J.; Buecking, M.; Delatour, T. Fate of acrylamide during coffee roasting and in vitro digestion assessed with carbon 14- and carbon 13-labeled materials. *Food Chem.* **2020**, *320*, 126601. [CrossRef] [PubMed]
6. Malani, R.S.; Choudhury, H.A.; Moholkar, V.S. *Chapter 13—Waste Biorefinery Based on Waste Carbon Sources: Case Study of Biodiesel Production Using Carbon-Based Catalysts and Mixed Feedstocks of Nonedible and Waste Oils*; Waste Biorefinery; Elsevier: Amsterdam, The Netherlands, 2020; pp. 337–378.
7. Mori, S.; Akatsuka, H.; Suzuki, M. Carbon and oxygen isotope separation by plasma chemical reactions in carbon monoxide glow discharge. *J. Nucl. Sci. Technol.* **2001**, *38*, 850–858. [CrossRef]
8. Ching, K.; Baker, A.; Tanaka, R.; Zhao, T.; Su, Z.; Ruoff, R.S.; Zhao, C.; Chen, X.J. Liquid-phase water isotope separation using graphene-oxide membranes. *Carbon* **2022**, *186*, 344–354. [CrossRef]
9. Naseri, F.; Ali Faal Rastegar, S.; Salek, N.; Charkhi, A.; Yadollahi, A. Effective isolation of europium impurities from 153Sm using electro amalgamation approach based on response surface methodology. *Sep. Purif. Technol.* **2021**, *279*, 119701. [CrossRef]
10. Matecha, R.M.; Capo, R.C.; Stewart, B.W.; Thompson, R.L.; Hakala, J.A. A single column separation method for barium iso-tope analysis of geologic and hydrologic materials with complex matrices. *Geochem. Trans.* **2021**, *22*, 4. [CrossRef]
11. Li, H.L.; Ju, Y.L.; Li, L.J.; Xu, D.G. Separation of isotope C-13 using high-performance structured packing. *Chem. Eng. Process* **2010**, *49*, 255–261. [CrossRef]
12. Borisov, A.V.; Gvertiteli, I.G.; Kucerov, R.Y. *Dritte Arbeitstagung uber Stabile Isotope, Leipzig 1963*; Akademie-Verlag: Berlin, Germany, 1965; p. 171.
13. Abrudean, M.; Dronca, S.; Axente, D.; Bâldea, A. Modelling and simulation of 13C separation column by isotopic exchange in CO_2-amine carbamate system. In Proceedings of the International Conference on Automatic and Quality Control, Cluj-Napoca, Romania, 1–4 June 1998.
14. Ghate, M.R.; Taylor, T.I. Production of ^{13}C by Chemical Exchange Reaction between Amine Carbamate and Carbon Dioxide in a Solvent-Carrier System. *Sep. Sci.* **1975**, *10*, 547–569.
15. Fenby, D.V.; Kooner, Z.S.; Khurma, J.R. Deuterium isotope effects in liquid—liquid phase diagrams: A review. *Fluid Phase Equilibria* **1981**, *7*, 327–338. [CrossRef]
16. Iraola, E.; Nougues, J.M.; Sedano, L.; Feliu, J.A.; Batet, L. Dynamic simulation tools for isotopic separation system modeling and design. *Fusion Eng. Des.* **2021**, *169*, 112452. [CrossRef]
17. Wang, G.; Chu, J.; Zhuang, Y.; Gulik, W.; Noorman, H. A dynamic model-based preparation of uniformly-13C-labeled internal standards facilitates quantitative metabolomics analysis of Penicillium chrysogenum. *J. Biotechnol.* **2019**, *299*, 21–31. [CrossRef] [PubMed]
18. Lin, W.; Wang, Z.; Huang, M.; Zhuang, Y.; Zhang, S. On structural identifiability analysis of the cascaded linear dynamic systems in isotopically non-stationary 13C labelling experiments. *Math. Biosci.* **2018**, *300*, 122–129. [CrossRef] [PubMed]

19. Akgül, A.; Rajagopal, K.; Durdu, A.; Pala, M.A.; Boyraz, O.F.; Yildiz, M.Z. A simple fractional-order chaotic system based on memristor and memcapacitor and its synchronization application. *Chaos Solitons Fractals* **2021**, *152*, 111306. [CrossRef]
20. Ha, S.; Chen, L.; Liu, H.; Zhang, S. Command filtered adaptive fuzzy control of fractional-order nonlinear systems. *Eur. J. Control.* **2022**, *63*, 48–60. [CrossRef]
21. Zhu, Z.; Lu, J.-G. Robust stability and stabilization of hybrid fractional-order multi-dimensional systems with interval uncertainties: An LMI approach. *Appl. Math. Comput.* **2021**, *401*, 232–249. [CrossRef]
22. Bassam, A.; Conde-Gutierrez, R.A.; Castillo, J.; Laredo, G.; Hernandez, J.A. Direct neural network modeling for separation of linear and branched paraffins by adsorption process for gasoline octane number improvement. *Fuel* **2014**, *124*, 158–167. [CrossRef]
23. Lai, C.K.; Lim, S.K.; Teh, P.C.; Yeap, K.H. Modeling Electrostatic Separation Process Using Artificial Neural Network (ANN). *Procedia Comput. Sci.* **2016**, *91*, 372–381. [CrossRef]
24. Camacho, N.-A.; Duarte-Mermoud, M.A.; Gallegos, J.A. Lyapunov functions for fractional order systems. *Commun. Nonlinear Sci. Numer. Simul.* **2014**, *19*, 2951–2957. [CrossRef]
25. Wang, Z.; Yang, D.; Ma, T. Stability analysis for nonlinear fractional-order systems based on comparison principle. *Nonlinear Dyn.* **2014**, *75*, 387–402. [CrossRef]
26. Rivero, M.; Rogosin, S.V.; Tenreiro Machado, J.A.; Trujillo, J.J. Stability of Fractional Order Systems. *New Chall. Fract. Syst.* **2013**, *2013*, 356215. [CrossRef]
27. Alagoz, B.B.; Yeroglu, C.; Senol, B.; Ates, A. Probabilistic robust stabilization of fractional order systems with interval uncertainty. *ISA Trans.* **2015**, *75*, 101–110. [CrossRef] [PubMed]
28. Shen, J.; Lam, J. State feedback H_∞ control of commensurate fractional-order systems. *Int. J. Syst. Sci.* **2014**, *45*, 363–372. [CrossRef]
29. Shen, J.; Lam, J. H_∞ Model Reduction for Positive Fractional Order Systems. *Asian J. Control.* **2014**, *16*, 441–450. [CrossRef]
30. Alagoz, B.; Ates, A.; Yeroglu, C. Auto-tuning of PID controller according to fractional-order reference model approximation for DC rotor control. *Mechatronics* **2013**, *23*, 789–797. [CrossRef]
31. Latawiec, K.J.; Stanislawski, R.; Lukaniszyn, M.; Czuczwara, W.; Rydel, M. Fractional-order modeling of electric circuits: Modern empiricism vs. classical science. In Proceedings of the 2017 Progress in Applied Electrical Engineering (PAEE), Koscielisko, Poland, 25–30 June 2017; IEEE: Koscielisko, Poland, 2017; pp. 1–4.
32. Gao, Z.; Liao, X. Improved Oustaloup approximation of fractional-order operators using adaptive chaotic particle swarm optimization. *J. Syst. Eng.* **2016**, *23*, 145–153. [CrossRef]
33. Djouambi, A.; Charef, A.; Besancon, A.V. Optimal approximation, simulation and analog realization of the fundamental fractional order transfer function. *Int. J. Appl. Math. Comput. Sci.* **2007**, *17*, 455–462. [CrossRef]
34. Karam, L.J.; McClellan, J.H. Complex Chebyshev approximation for FIR filter design. *IEEE Trans. Circuits Syst. II Analog. Digit. Signal Processing* **1995**, *4*, 207–216. [CrossRef]
35. Mandava, S.; Gudipalli, A.; Amutha Prabha, N.; Rajini, G. Control of micro-grid by discretized PR controller using tustin frequency pre-wrapping method. In *Advances in Automation, Signal Processing, Instrumentation, and Control*; Komanapalli, V.L.N., Sivakumaran, N., Hampannavar, S., Eds.; Springer: Singapore, 2021; Volume 700, pp. 2301–2311.
36. Clitan, I.; Puscasiu, A.; Muresan, V.; Unguresan, M.L.; Abrudean, M. Web Application for Statistical Tracking and Predicting the Evolution of Active Cases with the Novel Coronavirus (SARS-CoV-2). *Int. J. Modeling Optim.* **2021**, *11*, 70–74. [CrossRef]
37. Huang, M.H.; Rust, R.T. A strategic framework for artificial intelligence in marketing. *J. Acad. Mark. Sci.* **2021**, *49*, 30–50. [CrossRef]
38. Haefner, N.; Wincent, J.; Parida, V.; Gassmann, O. Artificial intelligence and innovation management: A review, framework, and research agenda. *Technol. Forecast. Soc. Change* **2021**, *162*, 120392. [CrossRef]
39. Chen, L.; Chen, P.; Lin, Z. Artificial Intelligence in Education: A Review. *IEEE Access* **2020**, *8*, 75264–75278. [CrossRef]
40. Johnson, K.W.; Soto, J.T.; Glicksberg, B.S.; Shameer, K.; Miotto, R.; Ali, M.; Ashley, E.; Dudley, J.T. Artificial Intelligence in Cardiology. *J. Am. Coll. Cardiol.* **2018**, *71*, 23. [CrossRef] [PubMed]
41. Zhao, S.; Blaabjerg, F.; Wang, H. An Overview of Artificial Intelligence Applications for Power Electronics. *IEEE Trans. Power Electron.* **2021**, *36*, 4633–4658. [CrossRef]
42. Dugas, R.; Rochelle, G. Absorption and desorption rates of carbon dioxide with monoethanolamine and piperazine. *Energy Procedia* **2009**, *1*, 1163–1169. [CrossRef]
43. Love, J. *Process Automation Handbook*, 1st ed.; Springer Publishing House: New York, NY, USA, 2007; p. 1200.
44. Muresan, V.; Abrudean, M.; Valean, H.; Colosi, T.; Unguresan, M.-L.; Sita, V.; Clitan, I.; Moga, D. Neural modeling and control of a 13C isotope separation process. In Proceedings of the 12th International Conference on Informatics in Control, Automation and Robotics (ICINCO), Colmar, France, 21–23 July 2015; pp. 254–263.
45. Monje, C.A.; Chen, Y.; Vinagre, B.M.; Xue, D.; Feliu, V. Fractional-order systems and controls. In *Fundamentals and Applications*; Springer: New York, NY, USA, 2010; pp. 3–9.
46. Kovendi, Z.; Muresan, V.; Abrudean, M.; Clitan, I.; Unguresan, M.-L.; Colosi, T. Modeling a Chemical Exchange Process for the ^{13}C Isotope Enrichment. *Appl. Mech. Mater.* **2015**, *772*, 27–32. [CrossRef]
47. User Guide. MATLAB (R2021a. Available online: https://www.mathworks.com/help/matlab/release-notes-R2021a.html#responsive_o_canvas (accessed on 23 October 2021).
48. Shrestha, A.; Mahmood, A. Review of Deep Learning Algorithms and Architectures. *IEEE Access* **2019**, *7*, 53040–53065. [CrossRef]

49. Chen, Y.; Ren, J.; Yi, C. Neural Networks for the Output Tracking-Control Problem of Nonlinear Strict-Feedback System. *IEEE Access* **2017**, *5*, 26257–26266. [CrossRef]
50. Dronca, S.; Axente, D.; Baldea, A.; Abrudean, M. Adsorption of carbon dioxide in the solution of Di-n-butylamine in nonaqueous solvent. *Rev. Chim.* **1998**, *49*, 775.
51. Axente, D.; Bâldea, A.; Abrudean, M. Isotope separation by chemical exchange. In Proceedings of the International Symposium of Isotope Separation and Chemical Exchange Uranium Enrichment, Tokyo, Japan, 29 October 1990; pp. 1–11.
52. Coloşi, T.; Abrudean, M.; Naşcu, I.; Dulf, E.; Ungureşan, M.L. A variant of approximation for IC and CF in numerical modelling and simulation of distributed parameter process. In Proceedings of the International Conference on Quality Control, Automation and Robotics, Tome II, Cluj-Napoca, Romania, 19–20 May 2000; pp. 45–50, ISBN 973–686-058-2.
53. Abrudean, M.; Dulf, E.-H.; Folea, S.; Nascu, I.; Colosi, T. The Use of a Modelling and Simulation Method for Thermo-Chemical Processes (With Distributed Parameters). International Conference on Control Systems and Computer Science 13; Bucureşti, Romania, 2001.
54. Colosi, T.; Abrudean, M.; Nascu, I.; Dulf, E.-H.; Folea, S. Examples of Numerical Simulation and Modeling through Taylor Series for Distributed ISSN 1224-600X, Parameters Processes, CONTI 2002, Periodica Politehnica. *Trans. Autom. Control. Comput. Sci.* **2001**, *47*, 93–96.
55. Abrudean, M.; Dulf, E.; Coloşi, T. Block schemes for analogical modelling and numerical simulation through local-iterative linearization. In Proceedings of the IEEE-TTTC-International Conference on Automation, Quality and Testing, Robotics, Cluj-Napoca, Romania, 13–15 May 2004; ISBN 973-713-046-4.
56. Dulf, E.; Abrudean, M.; Coloşi, T. The Taylor LIL method for analogical modelling and numerical simulation for linear processes. In Proceedings of the IEEE-TTTC-International Conference on Automation, Quality and Testing, Robotics, AQTR 2004 (THETA 14), Cluj-Napoca, Romania, 13–15 May 2004; ISBN 973-713-046-4.
57. Axente, D.; Bâldea, A.; Teacă, C.; Horga, R.; Abrudean, M. 15N separation in the nitrox system under pressure. In Proceedings of the International Conference on Isotopic and Molecular Processes, Cluj-Napoca, Romania, 23–25 September 1999.
58. Abrudean, M.; Axente, D.; Baldea, A. Enrichment of 15N and 18O by chemical exchange reaction between nitrogen oxide (NO, NO_2) and aqueous nitric acid. *Isot. Isot. Environ. Health Stud.* **2008**, *17*, 377–382. [CrossRef]

Article

Log Transformed Coherency Matrix for Differentiating Scattering Behaviour of Oil Spill Emulsions Using SAR Images

Kinjal Prajapati [1], Ratheesh Ramakrishnan [2], Madhuri Bhavsar [1,*], Alka Mahajan [3], Zunnun Narmawala [1], Archana Bhavsar [4], Maria Simona Raboaca [5,*] and Sudeep Tanwar [1,*]

[1] Department of Computer Science and Engineering, Institute of Technology, Nirma University, Ahmedabad 382481, India; 19PTVPHDE201@nirmauni.ac.in (K.P.); zunnun.narmawala@nirmauni.ac.in (Z.N.)
[2] Space Application Center, ISRO, Ahmedabad 380015, India; ratheeshr@sac.isro.gov.in
[3] SVKM's Mukesh Patel School of Technology, Management, and Engineering, Mumbai 400056, India; alka.mahajan@nmims.edu
[4] Department of Computer Engineering, SSBT'S College of Engineering and Technology, Bambhori, Jalgaon 425001, India; asgujar@rediffmail.com
[5] National Research and Development Institute for Cryogenic and Isotopic Technologies—ICSI Râmnicu Valcea, Uzinei Street, No. 4, P.O. Box 7 Raureni, 240050 Râmnicu Vâlcea, Romania
* Correspondence: madhuri.bhavsar@nirmauni.ac.in (M.B.); simona.raboaca@icsi.ro (M.R.S.); sudeep.tanwar@nirmauni.ac.in (S.T.)

Abstract: Oil spills on the ocean surface are a serious threat to the marine ecosystem. Automation of oil spill detection through full/dual polarimetric Synthetic Aperture Radar (SAR) images is considered a good aid for oil spill disaster management. This paper uses the power of log transformation to discern the scattering behavior more effectively from the coherency matrix (T3). The proposed coherency matrix is tested on patches of the clean sea surface and four different classes of oil spills, viz. heavy sedimented oil, thick oil, oil-water emulsion, fresh oil; by analyzing the entropy (H), anisotropy (A), and mean scattering angle alpha (α), following the $H/A/\alpha$ decomposition. Experimental results show that not only does the proposed T3 matrix differentiate between Bragg scattering of the clean sea surface from a random scattering of thick oil spills but is also able to distinguish between different emulsions of oil spills with water and sediments. Moreover, unlike classical T3, the proposed method distinguishes concrete-like structures and heavy sedimented oil even though both exhibit similar scattering behavior. The proposed algorithm is developed and validated on the data acquired by the UAVSAR full polarimetric L band SAR sensor over the Gulf of Mexico (GOM) region during the Deepwater Horizon (DWH) oil spill accident in June 2010.

Keywords: oil spill detection; UAVSAR; Deep Water Horizon; weathered oil; oil characterization; SAR Polarimetry

MSC: 49M27; 54B15

1. Introduction

During the last few decades, oil spills on the ocean surface, either accidental or deliberate discharges by ships, have grown with the increase in maritime transportation. It has been estimated that 457,000 tonnes of oil are released by shipping or accidents into the ocean every year [1]. Several oil spill accidents have been reported in the last few years, from the Deepwater Horizon oil spill in the year 2010, with 134 million gallons of oil spilled into the ocean, to the Mauritius oil spill in the year 2020, with 1200 tonnes of oil spilled into the ocean, leaving huge and long-lasting damage on the marine life and coastal region. Developing a cost-effective oil spill detection system has been the subject of research for the past two decades [2–5] for contingency planning, mitigation, and remediation to save the marine ecosystem from toxic oils.

Oil slicks can spread quickly on the sea surface through transportation both horizontally on the surface and vertically within the water column. After the oil spill, the weathering effects such as evaporation, emulsification, submerged oil sinking, dispersion, sedimentation, dissolution, oil-mineral aggregation, photolysis, etc. can cause a loss of material through the evaporation or concentration of material into emulsions that can persist for a long time in the environment [6,7]. The oil spill may drift on the sea surface for many days, weeks, or even months, during which its chemical composition changes due to weathering [8]. Hence, to reduce or clean the oil spill, one needs to know its source, the spill extent, the estimate of the quantity, the range of probable transport paths, and current and future meteorological and sea conditions.

State-of-the-art remote sensing technologies with various sensors such as optical, infrared, thermal, microwave, etc., have been successfully used for effective data acquisition of oil spill [9]. Each sensor has proved its capabilities for efficient oil spill detection over the ocean surface, but each has its limitations. For example, optical sensors are limited to image acquisition during cloud coverage and daylight dependency. Microwave SAR sensors provide a potential alternative due to their all-weather and day-night imaging capability [10,11]. Oil spill detection using SAR data was carried out using single polarimetric SAR data using dark spot detection. However, with the development of multi-polarized SAR images, oil spill detection was much improved [12]. The multi-polarimetric SAR data have phase information and amplitude and intensity, which helps in a detailed analysis of the image resulting in better classification and discrimination of the type of oil spill. Promising technologies without a rapid response capability were largely not useful during the spill, although important data were collected for post-spill interpretation.

1.1. Motivation

An oil spill on the ocean surface not only pollutes the ocean water but also has adverse effects on the marine ecosystem and coastal region; hence, the major objective of oil spill detection and characterization is immediate dissipation of the oil spill information to the rightful stack-holder for the mitigation process. In response to a spill, accurate and rapid information on spill magnitude, location, and spread enables more effective and efficient cleanup, reducing the impact of oil spills on the marine ecosystem and cleanup cost. Most effective techniques for oil spill mitigation other than manual cleanup include oil booms, skimmers, sorbents, dispersants, burning in-situ, bio-remediation, and chemical stabilization. Here the type of sorbents, dispersants, and bio-remediation and chemical stabilization techniques are dependent on the chemical composition of the identified oil spill. Hence, the major issue with the existing offshore oil pollution treatment is the lack of information about the type of oil spill, amount of oil spill, and spread area. The majority of the research work has defined and successfully implemented various approaches for oil spill detection on the ocean surface. Still, comparatively least efforts have been made for the characterization of oil spill based on their physical and chemical properties that varies based on the weathering effect. Here in our research work, we propose a log transformation approach that can help estimate the physical-chemical properties of the oil spill based on the thickness and weathering using remote sensing SAR data which can be further used for effective cleanup and mitigation process by offshore pollution treatment authorities.

Various remote sensing technologies are analyzed together to address the rapid response to oil spill detection, including the type of oil spill and weathering effect on the oil spill. Oil spill detection using a single polarized SAR image aims toward identifying dark spots in the image due to reduced back scattered area generated due to dampening of small capillary and gravity waves over the oil-covered area. However, other than oil spills, various other oceanic phenomena result in low backscatter area and thus generating look-alikes of the oil spill in the image [8,13]. Various ancillary data from other sensors, geometric and contextual features of low backscattered areas can help to categorize dark formations into oil spills and look-alikes with high confidence [14,15]. Studies show that due to strong reliance on the suitable threshold, number of training samples, and ancillary data, single polarized SAR images are used in limited capacity. Further, the majority of research work is focused on oil spill detection with minimal emphasis on characterization of oil spill based on weathering effect on oil spill resulting into change physical and chemical properties of the oil. Moreover, differentiation between different emulsions of oil spills and their physical-chemical characteristics is difficult using the optical and single polarimetric SAR data. Hence, the use of multipolarmtric SAR data is much preferred for better classification and characterization of various types of the oil spill. Rapid Response Products were key to response utilization data needs are time-critical; thus, a high technological readiness level is critical to the operational use of remote sensing products such as multipolarimetric SAR data.

1.2. Novelty and Scientific Contribution

In this paper, the log transformation over the coherency matrix followed by eigenvalue-eigenvector based $H/A/\alpha$ decomposition of SAR image for efficient oil spill detection and characterization of various types of oil is used. Extensive research has already been conducted for efficient oil spill detection using various remote sensing data [7,8,16,17] but comparatively less research has been conducted on studying and discriminating the type of weathered oil [18,19]. The majority of the research work on SAR images for oil spill detection until now has been carried out on the coherency matrix T3 followed by the decomposition algorithm. Here in our case, we propose to apply the log transformation on the building pillars of polarimetric images, i.e., its Coherency Matrix T3. We have applied the log transformation on each element of the T3 matrix which has shown a major impact on the standard decomposition algorithm, which takes the T3 matrix as input for further processing. Here we have used the well renowned $H/A/\alpha$ Decomposition algorithm for oil spill detection [20,21], but the discriminating type of oil spill was difficult here. The proposed log transformation over the coherency matrix obtained from the input UAVSAR full polarimetric has shown extraordinary effect in the discrimination of weathered oil. The $H/A/\alpha$ decomposition using the proposed log-transformed coherency matrix effectively detects and discriminates the type of weathered oil spill and highlights the minor features of the image with unique signatures as compared to traditional $H/A/\alpha$ decomposition. Further, this log-transformed T3 can be used to derive other traditionally established polarimetric parameters and another decomposition algorithm as per requirement.

Various chemical, physical and biological processes on the oil spill plays a significant role in the spread and behavior of oil spill on the ocean surface. The DWH oil spill continued from April 2010 to August 2010 with a time span of 84 days. During this period, the oil spill has undergone various physical and chemical degradation(weathering) and emulsification with water. To relate the DWH oil spill signature, researchers have collected the samples of the various types of oil, including weathered oil, from different locations (i.e., surface oil and oil collected at coastal regions) of DWH oil spill at a fixed interval of time. In [22], the chemical composition of weathered oil of DWH oil spill incident was analyzed where collected emulsified oil samples during the spill period (May 2010), and they found it resolved n-alkanes $\geq$ C14 compared to our samples which had an average of C13 n-alkanes. Moreover, in [23] analysis of n-alkane and PAH concentrations showed that four of the post-capping samples were less weathered than the six pre-capping samples. The trajectory map of oil spill spread can be generated using the physical and chemical properties of the oil spill. In [24] researchers developed the model that predicted locations and amounts of shoreline oiling were compared to the documentation of stranded oil by shoreline assessment teams. The model-estimated daily average water surface area affected by floating oil >1.0 g/m^2 was 6720 km^2, within the range of uncertainty for the 11,200 km^2 estimate based on remote sensing for DWH oil spill. In [18], the researchers carried out Lab Testing in the OHMSETT lab to evaluate the signatures of optical, thermal, and SAR sensors concerning various thicknesses and chemical composition of the oil spill. They compared the results with the DWH oil spill results for analyzing relativity with real-time events. Hence extensive study on the physical and chemical composition of weathered oil and its significant signature over SAR images has been performed in the literature. Hence, the proposed approach for oil spill characterization based on weathering effect can be further evaluated and combined with the available ground truth information as a base for future oil spill characterization for further research and prediction of physical-chemical properties of oil spill.

1.3. Organization

In this research paper, an effort has been made to detect oil spills on the ocean surface and distinguish the various types of weathered oil-based using the full polarimetric L-band SAR data with high accuracy. The State-of-Art of the oil spill detection using SAR Polarimetry which includes various approaches carried out by the renowned researcher has been discussed in Section 2. Further, the proposed log transformation over the coherency matrix has been discussed in detail in Section 3. The input L band full polarimetric UAVSAR dataset is discussed in Section 3.1. The significance of Log transformation over the coherency matrix of SAR image for oil spill detection is explained in Section 3.2. The detailed experimentation of the proposed approach carried out has been discussed in Section 4. The impact of the proposed log-transformed T3 for oil spill detection is tested using the $H/A/\alpha$ decomposition, and its comparison with the conventional approach is presented in Section 4.2. The statistical analysis and accuracy assessment of the proposed approach using SVM classification is discussed in Section 4.3. Finally, the research work has been concluded with future work in Section 5.

2. State-of-the-Art

Traditionally oil spill on the ocean surface was detected based on the dark spot signature using various remote sensing sensors such as optical, thermal, Single Polarimetric SAR data [9]. Further, the ability of multi-polarized SAR technology to record multiple polarization responses of the scatterer and thereby help in studying and understanding their scattering behavior has led to an increase in usage of multi polarized images in several application areas along with oil spill detection. Figure 1 shows the fundamental steps involved in polarimetric SAR data processing for oil spill detection. Here, the input Single Look Complex/Multi Look Complex image is transformed into the second-order descriptors such as 3 × 3 Hermitian average coherency (T3) and covariance (C3) matrices, which are further decomposed into independent scattering descriptors using the incoherent decomposition algorithms such as the Freeman [25,26], the Huynen, and the Eigenvector-eigenvalue decomposition [20,21], etc. for better physical interpretation. A broad number of polarimetric features such as entropy, anisotropy, scattering angle, degree of polarization, correlation coefficient, pedestal height, etc. [19,27,28] are then extracted from the decomposed components, which are feed into the supervised or unsupervised classifier for oil spill detection and characterization resulting into discrimination of oil spill from water and lookalikes.

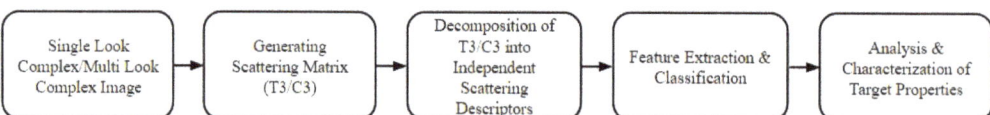

Figure 1. Flow of Multi-Polarized SAR Image Processing.

Various research works have been reported in the literature, which talk about different methodologies to detect oil spills using single and multi polarized SAR images [8,16,29]. A summary of a few recent research work relevant to the usage of optical and SAR data for oil spill detection and classification is discussed in Table 1. The significance of the polarimetric features such as Backscattered Intensity (span), Entropy (H), Anisotropy (A), Conformity Coefficient (μ), Pedestal Height (P), mean scattering angle (α) for efficient oil spill detection were demonstrated in various research articles [28,30]. It was further observed that joint use of multiple fully polarimetric features as input to the classifier could provide higher accuracy than single fully polarimetric features [31]. In our recent work [32], the selective polarimetric features of Pauli and $H/A/\alpha$ decomposition were combined for efficient oil spill detection and discrimination of oil spill from lookalikes.. However, very few papers have tested the sensitivity of SAR to discriminate between oil slicks of different thicknesses and at different weathering/emulsification stages. For example, Jones, Holt, and Minchew in [7,33,34] have shown the effectiveness of L-band Airborne UAVSAR radar in detecting oil and differentiating mixed/weathered oil concentrated in the bay area from freshly released oil. The author of [18] experimented at the OHMSETT Lab environment for using optical as well as SAR sensors for the identification of various thicknesses of oil spill. Then, Singha in [35] investigated the use of fully polarimetric space-born C (RADARSAT-2) and X (TERASAR-X) band images to decaffeinate between look-alike, emulsion, crude oil, and ocean water by developing ANN-based classifier; They have used 10 polarimetric features reported in the literature [27] were used to study their capability in distinguishing classes and showed that Scattering Diversity, Surface Scattering Fraction and Span features are more suitable.

Table 1. Summary of recent research on oil spill detection using SAR Polarimetry.

Ref.	Dataset	Approach	Objective and Outcome
[8]	Envisat ASAR, ERS-1 ERS-2, AVHRR	Oil spill Detection and Lookalike Discrimination	• Parameters used Normalized Radar Cross-Section, position and texture of spill, Co-polarized Phase difference, radar backscatter, image intensity, Dielectric constant. • Supporting Ancillary data such as surface temperature, wind speed, chlorophyll content used.
[30]	RadarSat-2	Oil Spill Detection and Classification	• Optimization of the Back-propagation Neural Network Classifier to Optimized Wavelet Neural Network • Polarimetric features used : (H), (A), (μ), (P), (α), Backscattered Intensity(SPAN).
[7]	Full Pol UAVSAR	Oil Spill Thickness discrimination	• Type of oil analysed-Weathered Oil, oil penetrated into the coastal wetlands and inter-coastal waterways based on Variation in the intensity of the radar backscatter • Effect of Incidence angle on radar properties of oil and water • Average Intensity and Anisotropy at incidence angle $\angle 45°$ to $50°$ are better suited for discrimination of thickness of oil spill as compared to Entropy.
[18]	UAVSAR, RADARSAT-2, Worldview-2	Oil Spill Thickness Classification	• OHMSETT Lab Experimental study on vivid signature of SAR and Optical sensors for different thickness of oil • Accuracy assessment using Maximum Likelihood classifier
[36]	Dual-Pol TerraSAR-X	Oil spill detection and Lookalike Discrimination	• Use of Combination of Traditional and Polarimetric Features for oil spill detection and discrimination from lookalike • Features used-H, A, α, μ, σ, min contrast, max contrast, Span etc. • The feature combination Surface scattering diversity, surface scattering fraction and Span was observed to have better accuracy of 90% using SVM classifier
[37]	C Band Sentinel-1	Oil Spill detection and Segmentation using Deep Learning	• Analysis of oil spill detection using semantic segmentation using various deep learning architectures such as UNet, LinkNet, PSPNet, DeepLabv2, and DeepLabv3+. • DeepLabv3+ was observed to have better performance for oil spill detection and discrimination from lookalikes.
[28]	Radarsat-2, UAVSAR	Oil spill detection and Lookalike Discrimination	• Combination of proposed self similarity feature with 7 polarimetric features, i.e., $p, DoP, A_{12}, V, \mu\, R_{CO}$, etc. • Random Forest Classifier and Combination of DeepCNN with Superpixel Classification (Accuracy achieved-92.99% and 82.25% for each dataset) • J-M Distance and F1 score for accuracy assessment

Table 1. Cont.

Ref.	Dataset	Approach	Objective and Outcome
[19]	RADARSAT 2	Oil Spill Classification based on thickness	• Discrimination of oil based on thickness using various combination of H, A and proposed A_{12} polarimetric parameters. • Accuracy assessment using parameters such as Michelson Contrast, J-M Distance and Random Forest Classification
[38]	RADARSAT-2	Impact of seasons on oil spill detection	• 6 Machine Learning approaches such as ANN, RF, Decision Tree, NavieBayes, LDA and Logistic Regression studied. • Impact of seasons i.e. Winter, Fall, Summer, Spring for acquiring oil spill image and prediction of source of oil spill (natural or anthropic) • Best case-winter season with Random Forest classifier
[39]	Deep SAR Oil Dataset	Oil Spill Segmentation using CBD-Net	• Approach to improve the feature representation of complex oil spills in SAR images using proposed CBD-Net edge detection algorithm. • Proposed manually generated Deep SAR Oil dataset.
[40]	ERS SAR, ENVISAT 2 SAR	Feature Selection for efficient Oil spill Detection	• Comparison of 5 feature selection method Correlation-based feature selection (CFS), Consistency-based filter, Information Gain, ReliefF and Recursive Feature Elimination for Support Vector Machine (SVM-RFE). • Selected Feature Evaluated using SVM Classification • 5 features SVM-RFE showed best feature selection with 87.1% classification accuracy
[41]	RADARSAT-2, SIR-C/X SAR	Oil spill Detection	• Use of Polarimetric Decomposition, i.e., $H/A/\alpha$, Yamaguchi-4 Component, Freeman-Durden • Polarimetric Parameters-SERD, μ, Corelation Coefficient • SLIC superpixel segmentation with CNN classification

The classification of remote sensing data is daunting as most of the supervised classification methods require a sufficiently large number of training samples along with well-verified test samples. Moreover, receiving the well-calibrated remote sensing data for oil spill incidents and the verified ground truth or ancillary data are critical. Still, Researchers have tried to use various supervised a and unsupervised classification algorithms such as K-means clustering, maximum likelihood, Artificial Neural Network, Random forest, KNN, SVM, etc. for oil spill detection and discrimination for look alikes [10,31,36,37]. The researcher in [38] evaluated the impact of 6 machine learning approaches such as ANN, RF, Decision Tree, Navie Bayes, LDA, Logistic Regression for effective oil spill detection and develops an algorithm for prediction of the best season for image acquisition of oil spill for Gulf of Mexico region. Among all traditional approaches, ANN and SVM have been majorly used by researchers for oil spill detection and characterization. Along with providing high accuracy with smaller training samples, SVM strikes the right balance between accuracy attained on a given finite amount of training patterns and the ability to generalize to unseen data. Its reported accuracy of SVM in oil spill studies ranges from 71% to 97% [10]. In [40], the authors have used five feature selection techniques by discarding irrelevant features for oil spill detection. These selected features are fed to the SVM classifier resulting in an accuracy of 87%. Hence, the SVM classification algorithm is majorly considered while dealing with remote sensing data, especially in the case of oil spill detection where there is a limitation of least availability input training samples leading towards the higher performance of the oil spill detection and classification for SAR Polarimetric data.

3. Proposed Approach

The flow of the proposed approach for identification and characterization of various types of the weathered oil spill is shown in Figure 2. The full polarimetric L band UAVSAR data acquired near the Barataria Bay region of the Gulf of Mexico is used as input data. It includes various stages of weathered oil with verified ground truth. The input data set is first pre-processed to remove speckle noise using Refined Lee Filter. Further, the Hermitian Coherency (T3) matrix is generated using Stokes parameters obtained from the radar backscatter image. Additionally, the polarimetric decomposition is performed on the T3 matrix leading to the effective physical interpretation of the target object and classification. In the first phase, the standard polarimetric decomposition algorithms, i.e., eigenvalue-based decomposition algorithm, $H/A/\alpha$ decomposition, are applied to the T3 matrix to study their efficiency in oil spill detection and discrimination of types of the oil spill. Here, H stands for entropy that signifies the randomness of the backscattering from the ocean surface, A, i.e., Anisotropy shows multiple backscattering behavior over the surface, and the mean scattering angle (α) defines the dominance of the specific scattering behavior over the surface. Finally, the same polarimetric decomposition algorithm is applied to the proposed log-transformed coherency matrix for enhanced oil spill discrimination especially discriminating the type of the weathered oil. The proposed approach is finally evaluated and analyzed using the various performance parameters such as Michelson Contrast, M-statistic, J-M distance and finally classification of weathered oil using SVM classification.

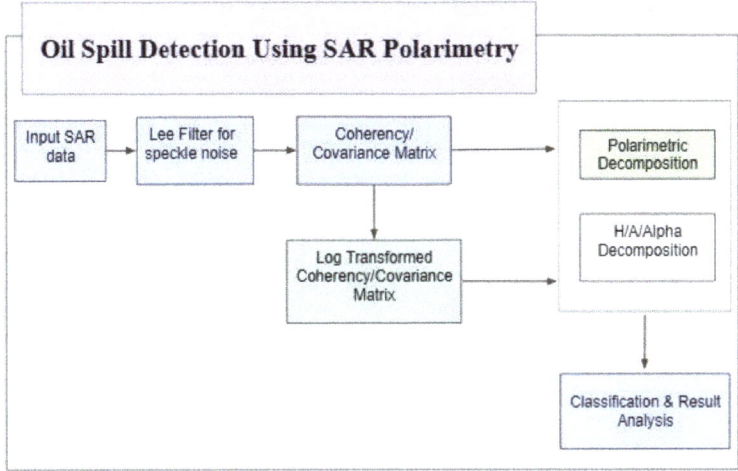

Figure 2. The proposed Log Transformation approach for efficient Oil Spill Detection using SAR Polarimetry.

3.1. Input Dataset

Following the Deepwater Horizon Oil spill disaster in the Gulf of Mexico (GoM) in April 2010 [42], NASA deployed the full polarimetric Uninhabited Aerial Vehicle Synthetic Aperture Radar (UAVSAR) L band radar to cover the oil affected areas of GoM and nearby coastal wetlands mainly in Barataria Bay(BB), Louisiana [33,43]. Images/Photographs captured by various space-borne and airborne sensors have shown large variations in slick properties in terms of thickness and states of weathering/emulsification over the large affected area [15]. The DWH oil spill continued from April 2010 to August 2010 with heavy spread over the ocean surface, while in the meantime, Oil slick processes on a day to week timescales, i.e., a typical oil spill response that includes horizontal and vertical transportation and surface diffusion, sedimentation and dissolution into the water column, emulsification, evaporation, and photochemical and biological degradation including weathering [9]. Along with the aerial photography, remote sensing sensors such as MODIS, LandSAT, AVRIS, Sentinel, RadarSat, UAVSAR, etc. were used to capture the spread of the DWH oil spill [9,17,44] building a strong repository of the dataset with confirmed oil spill and supporting ground truth and ancillary data. The researchers Cathleen Jones, B. Holt and team in [43] studied the signature of weathered oil transported to the coastal region of Barataria Bay(BB) using L UAVSAR data and ground truth data. The polarimetric features average intensity and entropy were used to analyze the impact of weathered oil over the BB coastal region, confirming the presence of weathered oil in the UAVSAR image as shown in Figure 3. Further, a detailed study on the characteristics of the weathered oil collected at BB during the DWH oil spill incident has been carried out by various researchers in [7,18,45].

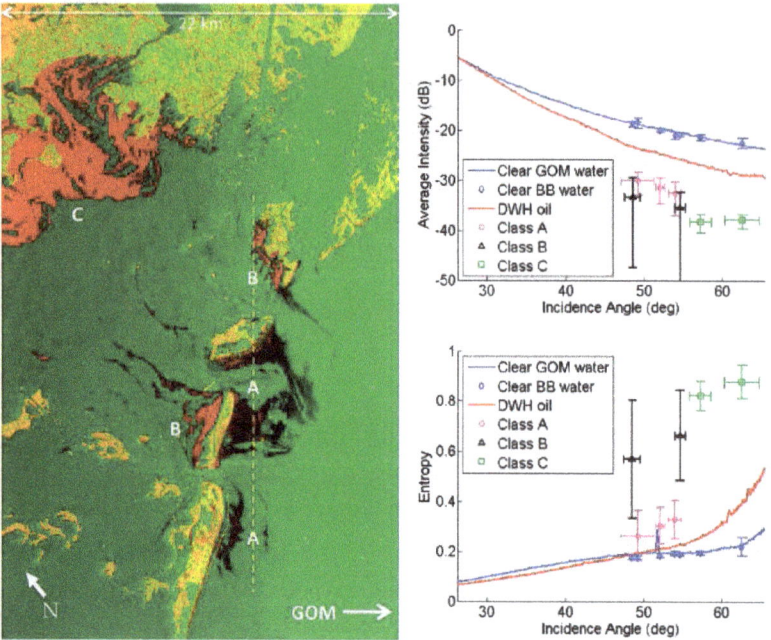

Figure 3. (**left**) Image with combination of Polarimetric features Average IntensityΛ(Red) and Entropy(Green) divided into 3 classes (**A**)-Thick Weathered oil, (**B**) Weathered oil mixed with Sediment near BB coastline and (**C**) Weathered oil heavily mixed with sediment . (**Right**) Λ(top) and entropy (bottom) plotted as a function of incidence angle for clean water in the GOM and in BB, oil in the main slick near the DWH site (DWH oil), and oil classes A, B, and C. [43].

As the aim is to study variations in oil characteristics due to differences in oil emulsification, the study of 3 images labeled A, B and C showed in Figure 4 are considered. Here, image A is the weathered oil image mentioned in Figure 3 is the includes an oil patch at various stages of weathering effect such as emulsion, weathered oil, and sedimented oil(mixed with sediment) as it was captured in June 2010 after 2 months of the oil spill. Image A also includes the oil transported over the coastal region, which by the time has undergone weathering effect and mixed with sediment after reaching coastline. Images B and C in Figure 4 cover the DWH rig site spotting the fresh released oil due to the removal of the containment cap. The presence of oil spill and its various stage of weathered oil were confirmed by researchers in [7,8]. Further, authors have estimated that the upper layer of the oil slick was a mixture of approximately 80% oil and 20% seawater, with a range in the volumetric oil concentration from 65% to 90% across the slick near the DWH site [15]. Figure 5a shows the combination of cropped part of images B and C of Figure 4 consisting of clean water and oil-contaminated water near the rig site labeled as fresh released oil.

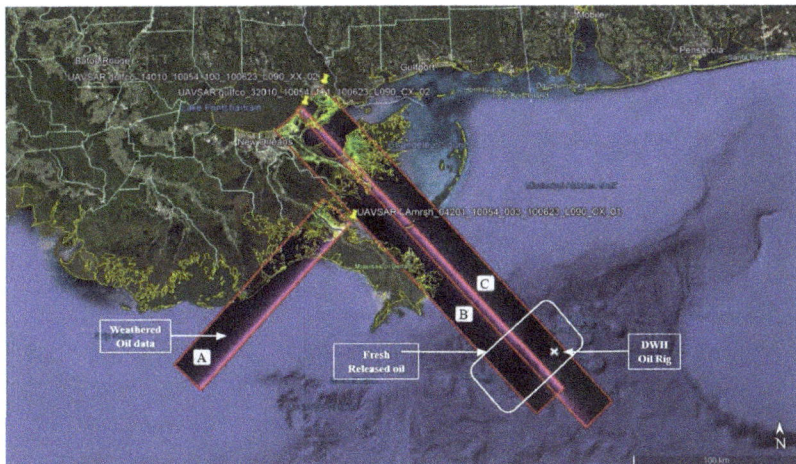

Figure 4. Study area: (**B**,**C**) UAVSAR L band multi-polarization images of main slick of DWH spill-gulfco_14010 (23 June 2010 20:42 UTC) and gulfco_32010 (23 June 2010 21:08 UTC). (**A**) UAVSAR multi-polarization images of Barataria Bay (BB), Lousiana and the barrier islands at the entrance to BB; BB is in the upper part of the image – Lamrsh_04201 (23 June 2010 23:05 UTC). The colors are a composite of the HH-polarization intensity image (red), the VV (black) and the HV (green).

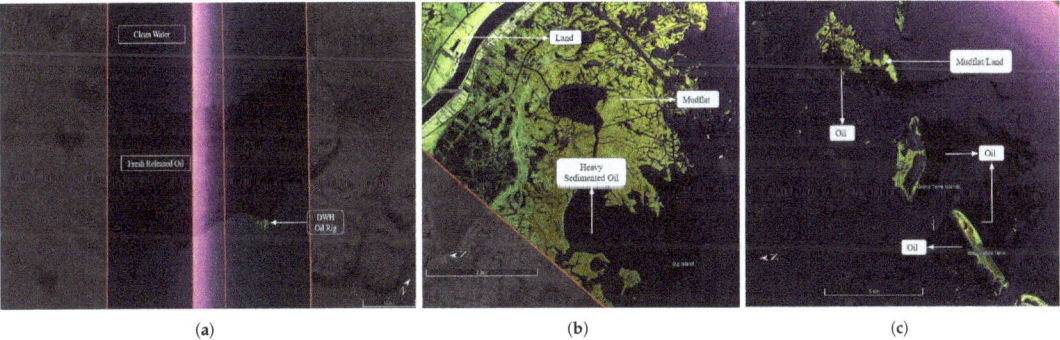

Figure 5. Patches of UAVSAR images considered in study: (**a**) shows surface oil and clean water near DWH rig site; (**b**) shows oil heavily mixed with sediment and other surfactants that has moved into the interior bay labeled as Heavy Sedimented Oil. (**c**) shows weathered oil on the GOM side of the barrier islands partially mixed with sediment labeled as oil [43].

Image A covers oil concentrated in coastal wetlands in BB and at barrier islands at the entrance to BB, which is believed to be several days older than the capture time. During this period, the oil's chemical and physical properties may have changed due to weathering/emulsification, and the oil have mixed with suspended sediment and other surfactants near the shore, further altering its bulk physical properties [National Research Council, 2003]. Hence, to characterize all these variants of oil, two patches of image A in Figure 4 are taken as shown in Figures 5b,c representing different amount of emulsified oil, further verified in papers [33,43]. The patch labeled as heavy sedimented oil in Figure 5b is defined as weathered oil on the GOM side of the barrier islands, patch labeled as oil in Figure 5a is oil on the immediate bay side of the barrier islands that has partially mixed with sediment and other surfactants.

3.2. Significance of Log Transformed T3 Matrix

Log transformation of data has shown its successful applicability in various domains ranging from medical image processing in various linear regression models to satellite image processing. Depending on the type of data and application area, researchers have applied log transformation taking advantage of different facts such as: (i) it reduces skewness of the data and makes data fit as input in regressions, (ii) reduces multiplicative speckle noise into additive speckle in SAR image [46], (iii) compresses the dynamic range of data by enhancing lower intensity pixels which ultimately helps to improve the quality of satellite images to capture and analyze unseen features in the low-intensity region of the image clearly [47]. Log transformation increases the processing speed as it compresses the dynamic range of images with large variations in intensity values [48].

For fully polarimetric SAR data, the backscattering properties of the object are described using the backscattering matrix as given in Equation (1)

$$S = \begin{bmatrix} S_{HH} & S_{HV} \\ S_{VH} & S_{VV} \end{bmatrix} \quad (1)$$

where S_{XY} is the scattering component with x as transmit polarization and y as receive polarization. Here H stands for horizontal polarization while V stands for vertical polarization.

Since the oil spill in the SAR image appears as dark signatures as shown in Figure 5, the use of log transformation over the SAR image enhances and highlights the oil spill signatures in the input SAR image. Hence, this paper proposes using log-transformation on T3 matrix elements for oil spill characterization using SAR data. The conventional T3 matrix is shown in Equation (2), where the 3 diagonal elements represent the dominant scattering behavior, i.e., surface scattering, double-bounce scattering, and volume scattering, respectively. The log-transformed T3 is shown in Equation (3), where the log transformation is applied to each element of the T3 matrix, forming a new log transformed T3 matrix.

$$\langle [T] \rangle = \begin{bmatrix} \langle |S_{HH}+S_{VV}|^2 \rangle & \langle (S_{HH}+S_{VV})(S_{HH}-S_{VV})^* \rangle & 2\langle (S_{HH}+S_{VV})S_{HV}^* \rangle \\ \langle (S_{HH}-S_{VV})(S_{HH}+S_{VV})^* \rangle & \langle |S_{HH}-S_{VV}|^2 \rangle & 2\langle (S_{HH}-S_{VV})S_{HV}^* \rangle \\ 2\langle S_{HV}(S_{HH}+S_{VV})^* \rangle & 2\langle S_{HV}(S_{HH}-S_{VV})^* \rangle & 4\langle |S_{HV}|^2 \rangle \end{bmatrix} \quad (2)$$

$$\langle [T^*] \rangle = \begin{bmatrix} \langle 10log_{10}|S_{HH}+S_{VV}|^2 \rangle & \langle 10log_{10}((S_{HH}+S_{VV})(S_{HH}-S_{VV})^*) \rangle & 2\langle 10log_{10}((S_{HH}+S_{VV})S_{HV}^*) \rangle \\ \langle 10log_{10}((S_{HH}-S_{VV})(S_{HH}+S_{VV})^*) \rangle & \langle 10log_{10}(|S_{HH}-S_{VV}|^2) \rangle & 2\langle 10log_{10}((S_{HH}-S_{VV})S_{HV}^*) \rangle \\ 2\langle 10log_{10}(S_{HV}(S_{HH}+S_{VV})^*) \rangle & 2\langle 10log_{10}(S_{HV}(S_{HH}-S_{VV})^*) \rangle & 4\langle 10log_{10}(|S_{HV}|^2) \rangle \end{bmatrix} \quad (3)$$

Initially, during the statistical analysis of the elements of the T3 matrix, it was observed that the T3 element value range of each aspect, such as ocean water or oil, was very low. Here the identification of oil spill was possible, but discrimination of type of oil spill was difficult due to minor variation in pixel range value It is found that the application of log transformation on each of 9 elements of the T3 matrix improvised the separability of the element range value for the vivid object of the image. For more clarity to the proposed idea, the histogram of diagonal elements (T11, T22, T33) of standard T3, as well as log-transformed T3 for the patch of water region of the image, was generated as shown in Figure 6. It is observed from Figure 6a,b The range of water for standard T3 elements, i.e., T11 (0.01 to 0.03), has improved from (−25 to −15) providing larger scope of separability for each object to be identified or discriminated.

The three obtained eigenvalues ($\lambda1, \lambda2, \lambda3$) are related to strength of three different scattering mechanisms namely surface scattering which is mainly observed in ocean surface; double-bounce scattering majorly observed in urban area, mudflats and man-made structures such as ships, buildings, etc.; volume scattering prominently seen in forests respectively. Figure 7 shows images of three eigenvalues computed using both conventional and log transformed T3 for a cropped input UAVSAR image A of Figure 4. The images i.e.,

Figure 7a,c,e correspond to eigenvalues computed using conventional T3 while other 3 images, i.e., Figure 7b,d,f correspond to eigenvalues computed using log transformed T3.

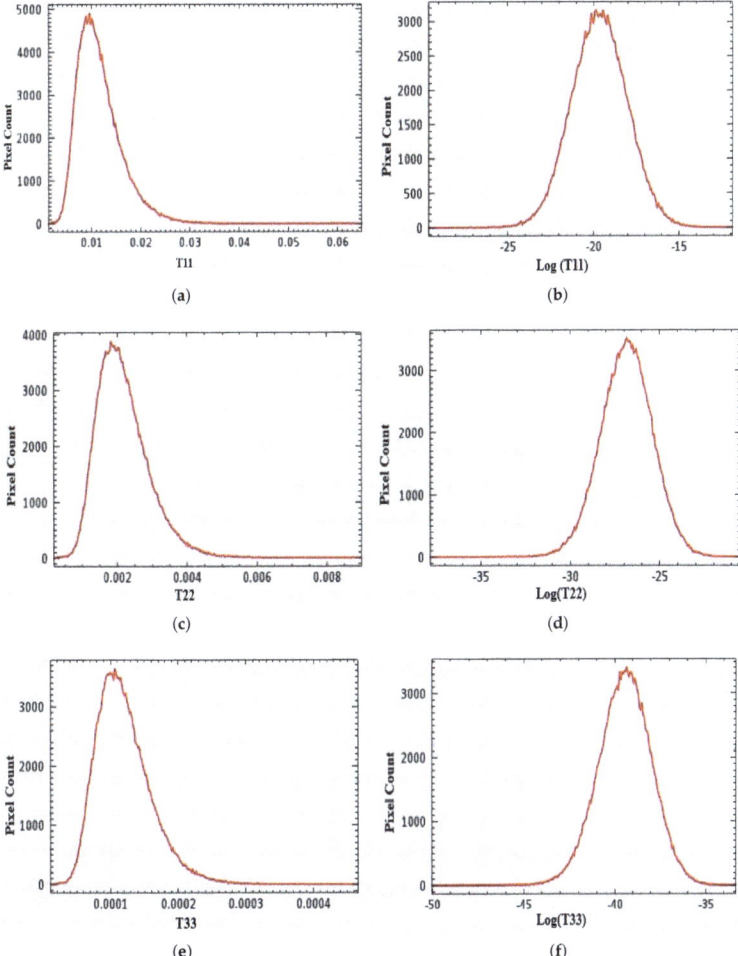

Figure 6. Histogram of elements of conventional T3 (**a**) T11, (**c**) T22, (**e**) T33 and Log transformed T3 (**b,d,f**) for a clean water patch.

The comparison and interpretation of images of respective eigenvalues are as follows:

(i) It is observed from the $\lambda 1$ computed using conventional T3 in Figure 7a and using log-transformed T3 in Figure 7b that oil slicks are clearly visible and easily distinguishable from surrounding water in log-transformed version as compared to the conventional version. In Figure 7a, all the features of the water and oil are suppressed in the dark region due to low backscatter, and the area of water and oil are not discriminated due to minor variation in their ranges. The log-transformed version gives superior results due to the enhancement of lower pixel values which enhances the ranges of oil and water in the image resulting in the proper visible distinction between oil and water in the image as shown in Figure 7a.

(ii) Comparison of $\lambda 2$ using conventional T3 and log-transformed T3 in Figure 7c,d has led to a very interesting and important observation: Image of $\lambda 2$ of log-transformed T3 also highlights slicks of oil along with mudflats and man-made houses present on along sides of canal structure seen at the top of the image. As the oil slicks present in these patches are mixed with sediments (refer Section 3.1) and thus exhibit double-bounce scattering along with surface scattering. $\lambda 2$ of conventional T3 fails to capture this signature.

(iii) Image of $\lambda 3$ Figure 7f calculated using log-transformed T3 reveals no particular structure as there may not be any object present that exhibits volume scattering dominantly. Thus, a clear distinction of features is possible due to eigenvalues of log scaled T3, resulting in better discrimination among different emulsified slicks based on the calculated Entropy, Anisotropy, and Alpha angle.

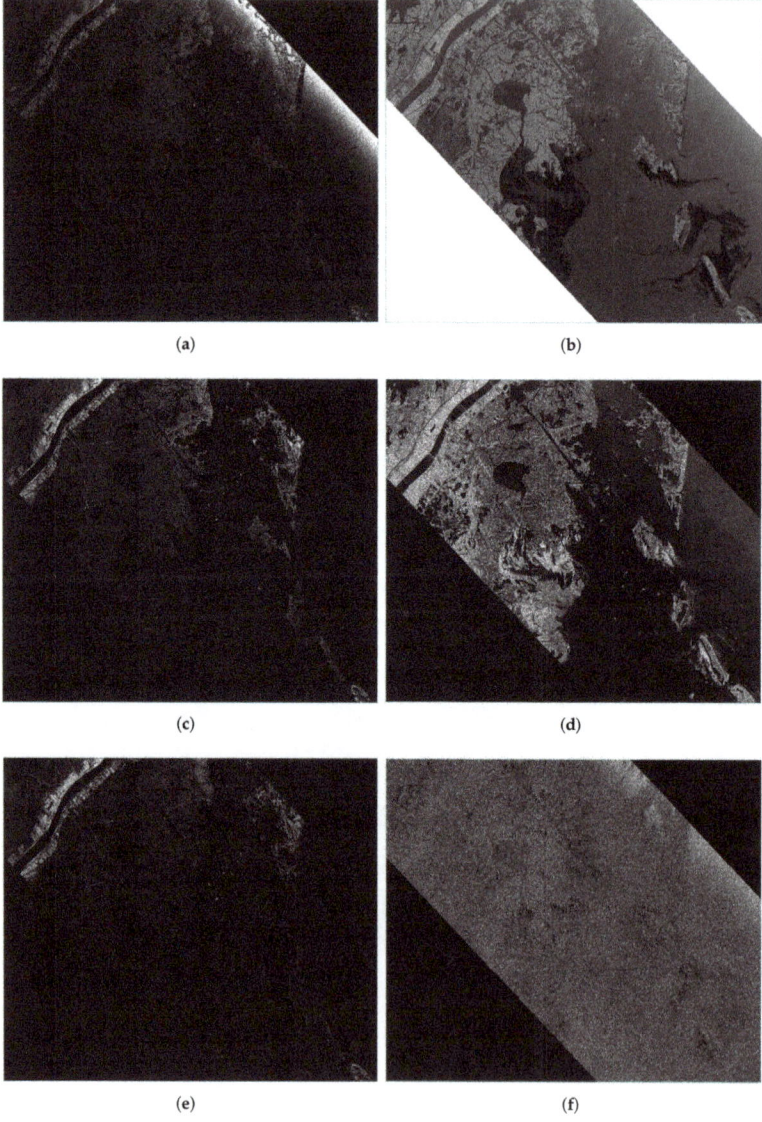

Figure 7. Comparative Analysis of Eigenvalues obtained form conventional T3, i.e., (**a**) T11, (**c**) T22, (**e**) T33 and Log Scaled T3 (**b**) T11, (**d**) T22, (**f**) T33.

3.3. H/A/α Decomposition

Further, to validate the effectiveness of log scaled T3 matrix, Eigen-value based $H/A/\alpha$ decomposition algorithm was applied using both conventional and log-transformed T3. The rotation invariant $H/A/\alpha$ parameters (Entropy, Anisotropy (A) and Scattering angle (α) are calculated based on the eigenvalues as shown in Equations (4)–(6), respectively [20].

$$H = -\sum_{i=1}^{3} P_i \log_3 P_i \quad \text{with} \quad P_i = \lambda_i / (\lambda_1 + \lambda_2 + \lambda_3) \quad (4)$$

Entropy (4) value signifies the randomness in the backscattered radiation using pseudo probability of the eigenvalues P_i. Further, the amount of multiple backscattering behaviour of the target object is evaluated using anisotropy (A) which is calculated as (5)

$$A = \frac{\lambda_2 - \lambda_3}{\lambda_2 + \lambda_3} \quad (5)$$

The mean scattering angle α shows the most dominant scattering behaviour of the target object signifying the presence of various type of objects in image, i.e., surface scattering for water, double bounce or volume scattering for metallic object such as ships on the ocean surface.

$$\bar{\alpha} = \sum_{i=1}^{3} p_i \alpha_i \quad (6)$$

The resultant image of $H/A/\alpha$ decomposition using conventional T3 matrix for Deep Water Horizon oil spill incident image with various type of weathered oil confirmed by various researcher is shown Figure 8. Here $H/A/\alpha$ is taken as RGB components of the image where H stands for R component and similarly for A and α for G and B component respectively.

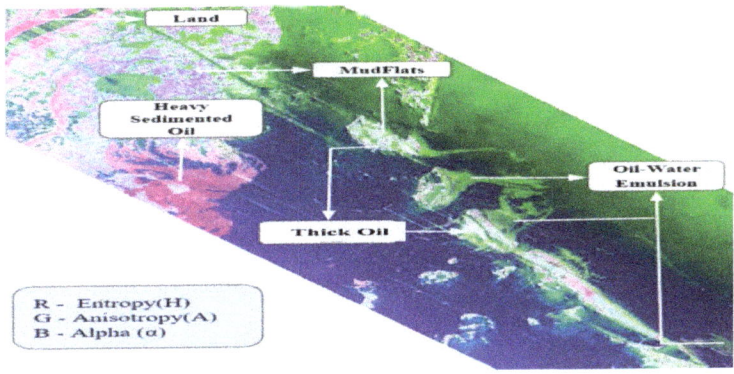

Figure 8. $H/A/\alpha$ decomposition using Conventional T3.

4. Experiments and Results Analysis

In this section we describe the experimental settings and performance analysis of the results obtained for detecting and characterization of oil spill using the proposed methodology.

4.1. Experimental Setup and Parameters

The L band full polarimetric SAR images for DWH oil spill incident consisting of various weathered oil and freshly released oil which is discussed in Section 3.1 has been used as input data. This quad pol UAVSAR data are fed as input to the PolSAR pro tool for speckle filtering (Refined Lee filter) for noise removal, followed by generation of Coherency matrix T3 from the scattering matrix. This (3 × 3) T3 matrix is generated for each image pixel, resulting in m × n × 9 dimensions of the input data. A Matlab code is developed for the calculation of Eigen value-based polarimetric parameters Entropy (H), Anisotropy (A), and mean scattering angle (α) using this T3 matrix as input. In parallel to this, another Matlab code is generated to deploy the proposed log transformation of the T3 matrix followed by $H/A/\alpha$ polarimetric decomposition. The evaluation of the effectiveness of the proposed log transformation approach has been performed using some well-established statistical analysis methods such as Michelson Contrast for target separability evaluation, M statistic for calculating the degree of discrimination and SVM classification for accuracy assessment of the proposed approach.

The performance parameters used for evaluation and comparison of the proposed log transformation methodology are described as follows

- Michelson Contrast (MC)

  MC is one of the general criteria for evaluating target separability. It has thus been used to quantitatively define and evaluate contrasts between oil slicks and seawater under various polarimetric feature spaces [19]. MC is calculated as Equation (7).

$$MC = \frac{I_{max} - I_{min}}{I_{max} + I_{min}} \quad (7)$$

Here I_{min} and I_{max} indicate the maximum and minimum mean polarimetric feature values between the two target samples being tested, respectively, and the value range of MC is [0, 1].

- M-Statistic (MS)

  The MS assesses the degree of discrimination between the two-pixel groups. It operates by evaluating the separation between the histograms produced by plotting the frequency of all the pixel values within the two classes [49]. The M-statistic can be calculated using the mean μ and standard deviation σ of two targets to be tested, respectively, as shown in Equation (8)

$$M = \frac{\mu_a - \mu_b}{\sigma_a + \sigma_b} \quad (8)$$

A value of M < 1 denotes that the histograms significantly overlap and the ability to separate (or discriminate) the two regions is poor. A value of M > 1 denotes that the histogram means are well separated and that the two regions are relatively easy to discriminate.

4.2. H/A/α Decomposition Result Analysis

To assess the efficiency of log transformed coherency matrix in detecting and differentiating oil slicks of varying characteristics, variations in $H/A/\alpha$ parameters have been calculated and analyzed using both conventional T3 and log transformed T3. Figures 9 and 10 shows the $H/A/\alpha$ decomposition results of the identified cropped image consisting of fresh released surface oil and various types of weathered oil in Figure 5 of the UAVSAR dataset, using both conventional T3 and log transformed T3. The top three images, i.e., Figure 9a–c correspond to $H/A/\alpha$ decomposition computed using conventional T3 while the bottom three images, i.e., Figure 9d–f corresponds to $H/A/\alpha$ decomposition computed using log transformed T3. The results of image acquired near rig site with fresh released oil and clean water are shown in Figure 9a,b,d,e while the results of image acquired near BB consisting of various stage of weathered oil labeled as oil water emulsion, thick oil and heavy sedimented oil and land and mudflats are shown in Figures 9c,f and 10a,b.

It is observed from the Figure 9a,b that the signature of freshly released oil near the rig site labeled as fresh released oil is almost similar to water in the case of a conventional approach while in the case of a log-transformed approach, the fresh released oil is distinguished signature as compared to water in Figure 9c,f.

However, due to similar backscattering behavior, the signature of thick oil and mudflats (pinkish white) in Figure 9c is getting mixed. At the same time, the oil-water emulsion (light-green) is quite distinguished from the conventional approach. However, in the case of the log-transformed approach, the oil-water emulsion, thick oil (dark red), and mudflats have clear, distinct signatures in Figure 9f. The $H/A/\alpha$ decomposition result of another patch of image A in Section 3.1, consisting of weathered oil which is heavily mixed with sediment labeled as heavy sedimented oil, is shown in Figure 10. It is observed that the signatures of heavy sedimented oil (dark red) and land (light red) are different in the case of the log-transformed approach, while these signatures are getting mixed in the case of the conventional approach. Since the oil accumulated near the coast is heavily mixed with the sediment, the physical properties of the oil are changed such that the backscattering properties of heavy sedimented oil are similar to that of land in conventional $H/A/\alpha$ decomposition. Hence, due to the enhancement of the dark features of oil using the log transformation, every minor feature or variation in the oil spill is captured, resulting in efficient oil spill detection and characterization. Other land features, such as mudflats, buildings and ships show clear, distinct features in the proposed log-transformed approach.

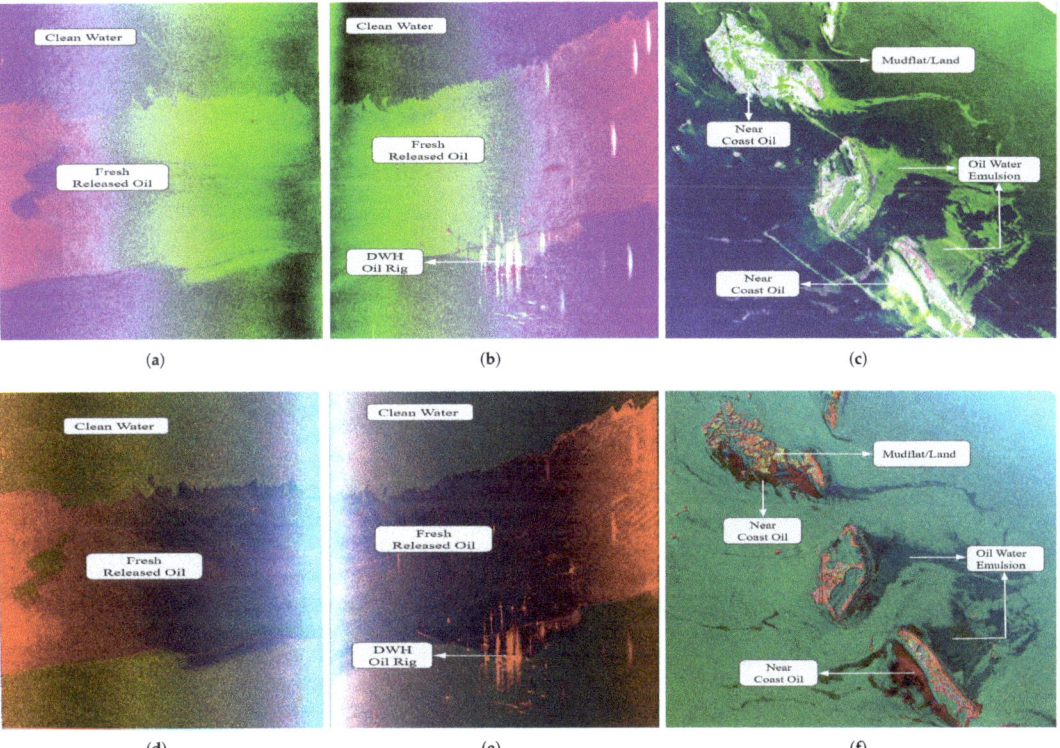

Figure 9. Comparative analysis of image generated using combination of entropy (red), anisotropy (green) and alpha (black) ($H/A/\alpha$) using conventional T3 (**a**–**c**) and log transformed T3 (**d**–**f**) showing their capability in detecting and differentiating different emulsions of oil.

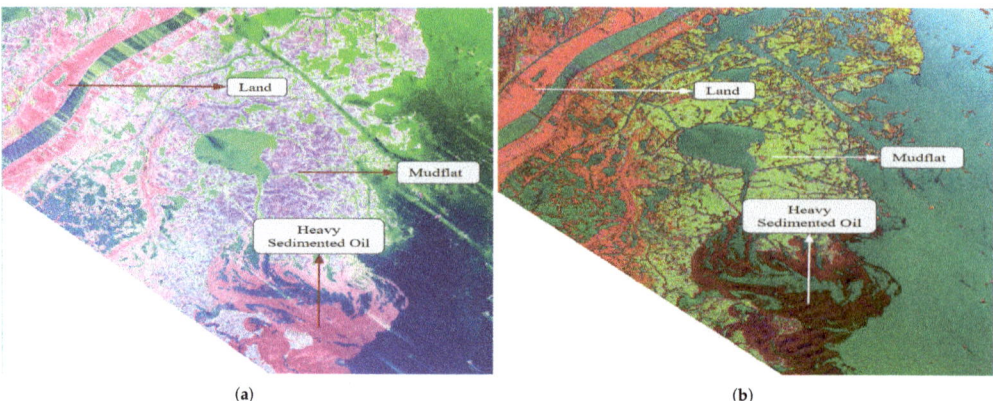

Figure 10. Comparative analysis of images generated by combining entropy (red), anisotropy (green) and alpha(black) ($H/A/\alpha$) using conventional T3 (**a**) and log transformed T3 (**b**) showing their capability in differentiating between highly sedimented oil and mudflat/building.

Figure 11 shows the plots of entropy, anisotropy, alpha parameters calculated for different classes of oil emulsions (Oil-water Emulsion (red), thick Oil (Green), Heavy Sedimented oil (pink), Land/Mudflat (black)) for statistical analysis of the proposed approach. The observation from these plots are as follows.

- Entropy calculated using log-transformed T3 Figure 11d captures subtle contrast changes in oil-contaminated patches resulting due to different stages of emulsification which is not the case with entropy calculated using classical T3 Figure 11a. As shown in the histogram in Figure 11d, the oil-water emulsion has a range of 0.74 to 0.76 in the log-transformed approach. It can also differentiate between oil-water emulsion, thick oil, and heavy sedimented oil with an extended upper bound of the range. Further, the entropy values increase gradually from moderate weathering stage oil to high emulsified oil. However, the entropy range calculated using classical T3 Figure 11a for oil-water emulsion is 0.2 to 0.4, roughly which is the same as clean water and surface oil1. This indicates that it does not differentiate between fresh and weakly weathered oil. Further, it also fails to capture minor changes in physical and electrical properties of thick oil and heavy sedimented oil as both have the same range. The blue line in the histogram is for a sample taken of mudflat/shrub/building present near Barataria Bay (BB), Louisiana. It can be clearly seen that the log-transformed T3 gives a different entropy range for highly mixed sedimented oil and mudflat/building regions even though both exhibit a similar scattering mechanism - moderate entropy double bounce. The separation between values of entropy for highly mixed sedimented oil and mudflat/building region is not that clear in the case of classical T3.
- Anisotropy values in Figure 11e calculated using log-transformed T3 show opposite behaviour than classical T3 in Figure 11b. Anisotropy calculated using log-transformed T3 has higher values for clean water and surface oil, which reduce from weakly emulsified oil to highly emulsified oil. However, the anisotropy values calculated using classical T3 cannot differentiate between clean water and any oil sample; it does not show a separate range for building/mudflat samples. On the other hand, anisotropy calculated using log-transformed T3 differentiates between clean water/surface water (Bragg scattering) from different emulsified oils (non-Bragg scattering). However, it fails to differentiate between building/mudflat and oil mixed with partial sediments.
- Alpha values Figure 11f calculated using log-transformed T3 do not show any favorable result in capturing differences between the type of scattering mechanism exhibited by water and different emulsified oils. It shows that clean water and all

kinds of oil samples were taken to follow the double bounce scattering. On the other hand, though, Alpha values Figure 11c calculated using classical T3 show surface scattering for clean water and surface oil; double-bounce scattering for oil mixed with sediments. However, it fails to differentiate between thick oil from surface oil/clean water and mudflat/building from oil mixed with sediments.

4.3. Statistical Analysis and Accuracy Assessment

It is observed from Figure 12 that the range of polarimetric features such as H, A, and α derived using conventional T3 are low (range from 0 to 0.45) for the majority of the cases while in the case of those derived using log-transformed T3 ranges from 0.2 to 0.8 on average. The important aspect observed here is the inseparability of some weathered oil observed for a conventional T3 approach such as emulsion and thick oil, thick oil and heavy sedimented oil, heavily sedimented oil and land shows a good separability in the case of the proposed log-transformed approach, respectively.

It is observed from Figure 13 that the range of polarimetric features such as H, A, and α derived using conventional T3 are low (range -0 to 3) for the majority of the cases while in the case of those derived using log-transformed T3 ranges from 3 to 10 on average. The important aspect observed here is the inseparability of some type of weathered oil observed for conventional T3 approach such as emulsion and thick oil, thick oil and heavy sedimented oil, heavily sedimented oil and land shows good discrimination in the case of the proposed log-transformed approach, respectively.

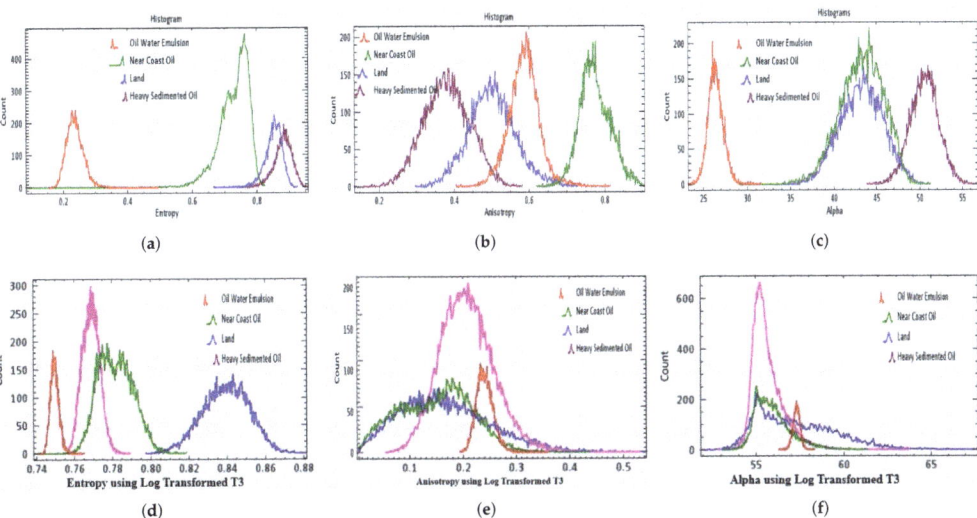

Figure 11. Statistical analysis of results of $H/A/\alpha$ decomposition using conventional T3 and log transformed T3, i.e., Histogram of Entropy H (**a,d**), Anisotropy A (**b,e**) and Scattering Angle α (**c,f**) for different patches showing ranges for Oil water Emulsion (Red), thick Oil (Green), Heavy Sedimented oil (Pink), Land/Mudflat (black).

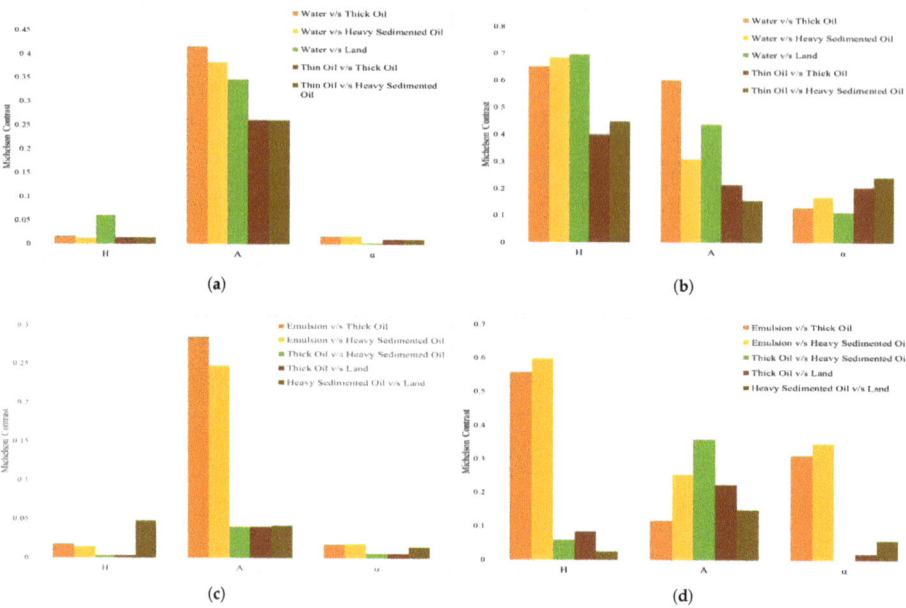

Figure 12. Michelson Contrast result analysis with respect to different types of polarimetric feature. For Conventional T3 (**a**) Different types of oil slick versus seawater& (**c**) Comparison of Different type Weathered Oil slick & look-alikes. For Proposed Log Transformed T3 (**b**) Different types of oil slick versus seawater& (**d**) Comparison of Different type Weathered Oil slick & look-alikes.

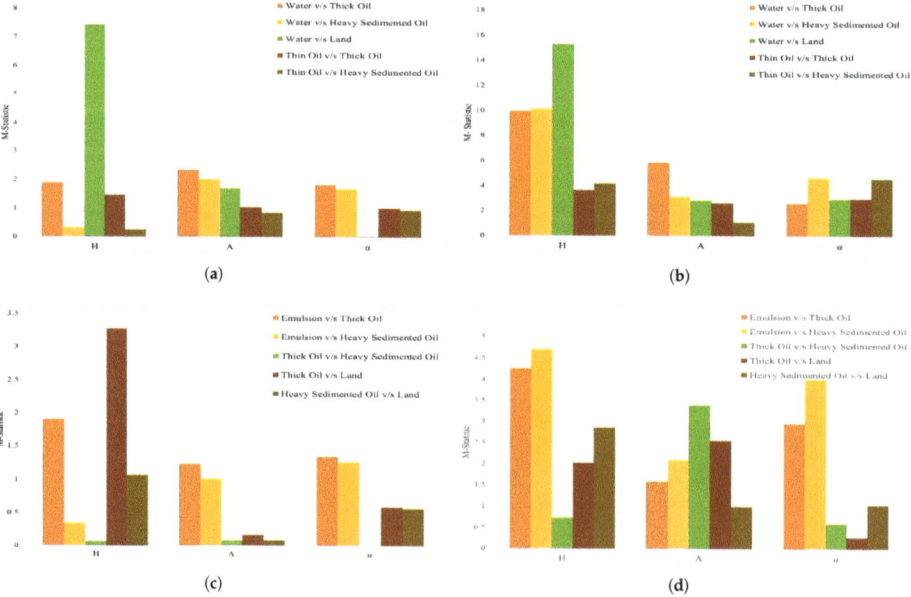

Figure 13. M-Statistic result analysis with respect to different types of polarimetric feature. For Conventional T3 (**a**) Different types of oil slick versus seawater& (**c**) Comparison of Different type Weathered Oil slick and look-alikes. For Proposed Log Transformed T3 (**b**) Different types of oil slick versus seawaterand (**d**) Comparison of Different type Weathered Oil slick and look-alikes.

4.4. SVM Classification

SVM classification algorithm is majorly used for accuracy assessment and classification of the remote sensing data due to its important features such as self-adaptability, swift learning pace, and a limited requirement on training samples. Hence SVM is best suited here for the classification of the oil spill. The SVM classification has been carried out with 6 class ROI (Region of Interest) that includes Water, thin oil, Oil-Water Emulsion, Thick Oil, Heavy Sedimented Oil, and Land. The input features H, A, α have been used here. We have optimized three hyper-parameters to achieve the best performance for oil spill characterization. The three major parameters include kernel, regularization parameter (C), and kernel coefficient parameter (Gamma). The kernel is a core function that transforms the input space from a lower dimension to a higher dimension in a non-linear fashion. The regularization parameter (C) is the penalty parameter that indicates the misclassification boundary of different classes. The kernel coefficient parameter (Gamma) indicates the distance impact on the line of different class separations. The best-case hyperparameters are Kernel-Sigmoid, Regularization Parameter(C)-0.9 with pyramid level 3, and Gamma value was set to 0.333. The SVM classification result for the $H/A/alpha$ decomposition algorithm using the proposed log-transformed T3 is shown in Figure 14. The researcher in [40] achieved an accuracy of 87% using SVM classification for oil spill detection using SAR images, while the researcher in [19] attained the kappa coefficient accuracy of 76% for discrimination of various types of oil slick based on its thickness. The overall accuracy of 97% is achieved with kappa coefficient 0.9607 using SVM classification for the proposed approach of log transformation of the coherency matrix for discrimination of various types of weathered oil using the $H/A/\alpha$ decomposition algorithm, proving the significance of proposed approach over other existing algorithms.

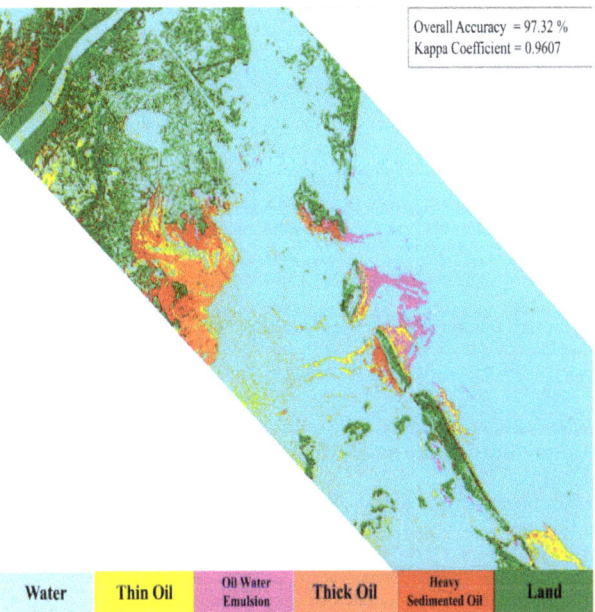

Figure 14. SVM Classification image for proposed log transformed approach.

5. Conclusions

The advantage of log transformation to enhance the dark features of oil in the SAR image is used in this paper. Log transformation has been applied to each element of the coherency matrix to generate the log-transformed coherency matrix (T3) of the full polarimetric SAR image. The eigenvalue-eigenvector-based $H/A/\alpha$ decomposition algorithm analyzes the effect of the proposed log transformation. The proposed algorithm offers a major accuracy improvement in detecting various types of weathered oil spills on the ocean surface, significantly advancing the current state of the practice with an accuracy of 97%. Further, compared to the conventional approach, the land features are also distinguished with enhanced representation. The proposed algorithm can be further enhanced using the deep learning approach to classify various types of weathered oil spills efficiently.

Author Contributions: Conceptualization: K.P. and R.R.; writing—original draft preparation: M.B., Z.N. and S.T.; methodology: A.M. and R.R.; writing—review and editing: A.M. and A.B.; Investigation: K.P., M.S.R. and Z.N.; Supervision: M.B., R.R. and S.T.; Visualization: R.R., A.B. and A.M.; Software: S.T., M.S.R. and K.P. All authors have read and agreed to the published version of the manuscript.

Funding: The research work was carried out as a part of the ASAR L and S band project entitled "SAR Polarimetry for Detecting Ocean Surface Target" funded by Indian Space Research Organisation (ISRO) at Institute of Technology, Nirma University, Ahmedabad. And the APC was funded by the Subprogram 1.1. Institutional performance-Projects to finance excellence in RDI, Contract No. 19PFE/30.12.2021 and a grant of the National Center for Hydrogen and Fuel Cells (CNHPC)—Installations and Special Objectives of National Interest (IOSIN).

Institutional Review Board Statement: Not applicable.

Informed Consent Statement: Not applicable.

Data Availability Statement: No data is associated with this reserach work

Conflicts of Interest: The authors declare no conflict of interest.

References

1. Transportation Research Board and National Research Council. *Oil in the Sea III: Inputs, Fates, and Effects*; National Academies Press (US): Washington, DC, USA, 2003.
2. Skrunes, S.; Brekke, C.; Eltoft, T. Characterization of marine surface slicks by radarsat-2 multipolarization features. *IEEE Trans. Geosci. Remote Sens.* **2014**, *52*, 5302–5319. [CrossRef]
3. Velotto, D.; Migliaccio, M.; Nunziata, F.; Lehner, S. Dual-polarized TerraSAR-X data for oil-spill observation. *IEEE Trans. Geosci. Remote Sens.* **2011**, *49*, 4751–4762. [CrossRef]
4. Kudryavtsev, V.N.; Chapron, B.; Myasoedov, A.G.; Collard, F.; Johannessen, J.A. On dual co-polarized SAR measurements of the ocean surface. *IEEE Geosci. Remote Sens. Lett.* **2012**, *10*, 761–765. [CrossRef]
5. Skrunes, S.; Brekke, C.; Eltoft, T.; Kudryavtsev, V. Comparing near-coincident C-and X-band SAR acquisitions of marine oil spills. *IEEE Trans. Geosci. Remote Sens.* **2014**, *53*, 1958–1975. [CrossRef]
6. ASCE Task Committee on Modeling of Oil Spills. State-of-the-art review of modeling transport and fate of oil spills. *J. Hydraul. Eng.* **1996**, *122*, 594–609. [CrossRef]
7. Jones, C.E.; Holt, B. Experimental L-band airborne SAR for oil spill response at sea and in coastal waters. *Sensors* **2018**, *18*, 641. [CrossRef]
8. Alpers, W.; Holt, B.; Zeng, K. Oil spill detection by imaging radars: Challenges and pitfalls. *Remote Sens. Environ.* **2017**, *201*, 133–147. [CrossRef]
9. Leifer, I.; Lehr, W.J.; Simecek-Beatty, D.; Bradley, E.; Clark, R.; Dennison, P.; Hu, Y.; Matheson, S.; Jones, C.E.; Holt, B.; et al. State of the art satellite and airborne marine oil spill remote sensing: Application to the BP Deepwater Horizon oil spill. *Remote Sens. Environ.* **2012**, *124*, 185–209. [CrossRef]
10. Al-Ruzouq, R.; Gibril, M.B.A.; Shanableh, A.; Kais, A.; Hamed, O.; Al-Mansoori, S.; Khalil, M.A. Sensors, features, and machine learning for oil spill detection and monitoring: A review. *Remote Sens.* **2020**, *12*, 3338. [CrossRef]
11. Masud, M.; Alshehri, M.; Alroobaea, R.; Mohammad, S. Leveraging Convolutional Neural Network for COVID-19 Disease Detection Using CT Scan Images. *Intell. Autom. Soft Comput.* **2021**, *29*, 1–13. [CrossRef]
12. Topouzelis, K.; Singha, S. Oil spill detection: Past and future trends. In Proceedings of the ESA Living Planet Symposium, Prague, Czech Republic, 9–13 May 2016; European Space Agency (Special Publication): Paris, Frence, 2016.
13. Zhang, Y.; Li, Y.; Lin, H. Oil-Spill Pollution Remote Sensing by Synthetic Aperture Radar. In *Advanced Geoscience Remote Sensing*; IntechOpen: London UK, 2014; pp. 27–50. [CrossRef]
14. Müllenhoff, O.; Bulgarelli, B.; Ferraro, G.; Perkovic, M.; Topouzelis, K.; Sammarini, V. Geospatial modelling of metocean and environmental ancillary data for the oil spill probability assessment in SAR images. *Remote Sens. Environ. Monit. Gis Appl. Geol. VIII* **2008**, *7110*, 71100R. [CrossRef]

15. Leifer, I.; Clark, R.; Jones, C.; Holt, B.; Svejkovsky, J.; Swayze, G. Satellite and airborne oil spill remote sensing: State of the art and application to the BP DeepWater Horizon oil spill. In Proceedings of the 34th AMOP Technical Seminar on Environmental Contamination and Response, Banff, AB, Canada, 4–6 October 2011; pp. 270–295.
16. Carvalho, G.d.A.; Minnett, P.J.; Ebecken, N.F.; Landau, L. Oil Spills or Look-Alikes? Classification Rank of Surface Ocean Slick Signatures in Satellite Data. *Remote Sens.* **2021**, *13*, 3466. [CrossRef]
17. Sun, S.; Hu, C. The challenges of interpreting oil–water spatial and spectral contrasts for the estimation of oil thickness: Examples from satellite and airborne measurements of the deepwater horizon oil spill. *IEEE Trans. Geosci. Remote Sens.* **2018**, *57*, 2643–2658. [CrossRef]
18. Garcia-Pineda, O.; Staples, G.; Jones, C.E.; Hu, C.; Holt, B.; Kourafalou, V.; Graettinger, G.; DiPinto, L.; Ramirez, E.; Streett, D.; et al. Classification of oil spill by thicknesses using multiple remote sensors. *Remote Sens. Environ.* **2020**, *236*, 111421. [CrossRef]
19. Li, G.; Li, Y.; Hou, Y.; Wang, X.; Wang, L. Marine Oil Slick Detection Using Improved Polarimetric Feature Parameters Based on Polarimetric Synthetic Aperture Radar Data. *Remote Sens.* **2021**, *13*, 1607. [CrossRef]
20. Cloude, S.R.; Pottier, E. A review of target decomposition theorems in radar polarimetry. *IEEE Trans. Geosci. Remote Sens.* **1996**, *34*, 498–518. [CrossRef]
21. Cloude, S.R.; Pottier, E.; Boerner, W. Unsupervised Image Classification using the Entropy/Alpha/Anisotropy Method in Radar Polarimetry. In Proceedings of the NASA-JPL, AIRSAR-02 Workshop, Pasadena, CA, USA, 4–6 March 2002; Volume 44, pp. 4–6.
22. Belore, R.; Trudel, K.; Morrison, J. Weathering, emulsification, and chemical dispersibility of Mississippi Canyon 252 crude oil: field and laboratory studies. In Proceedings of the International Oil Spill Conference Proceedings (IOSC), Virtual, 10–14 May 2011; American Petroleum Institute: Washington, DC, USA, 2011; Volume 2011, p. abs247.
23. Kolian, S.R.; Porter, S.A.; Sammarco, P.W.; Birkholz, D.; Cake, E.W.; Subra, W.A. Oil in the Gulf of Mexico after the capping of the BP/Deepwater Horizon Mississippi Canyon (MC-252) well. *Environ. Sci. Pollut. Res.* **2015**, *22*, 12073–12082. [CrossRef]
24. French-McCay, D.P.; Spaulding, M.L.; Crowley, D.; Mendelsohn, D.; Fontenault, J.; Horn, M. Validation of oil trajectory and fate modeling of the Deepwater Horizon oil spill. *Front. Mar. Sci.* **2021**, *8*, 136. [CrossRef]
25. An, W.; Cui, Y.; Yang, J.; Member, S. Three-Component Model-Based Decomposition for Polarimetric SAR Data. *IEEE Trans. Geosci. Remote Sens.* **2014**, *48*, 2732–2739. [CrossRef]
26. Freeman, A.; Member, S.; Durden, S.L. A Three-Component Scattering Model for Polarimetric SAR Data. *IEEE Trans. Geosci. Remote Sens.* **1998**, *36*, 963–973. [CrossRef]
27. Migliaccio, M.; Nunziata, F.; Buono, A. SAR polarimetry for sea oil slick observation. *Int. J. Remote Sens.* **2015**, *36*, 3243–3273. [CrossRef]
28. Tong, S.; Liu, X.; Chen, Q.; Zhang, Z.; Xie, G. Multi-feature based ocean oil spill detection for polarimetric SAR data using random forest and the self-similarity parameter. *Remote Sens.* **2019**, *11*, 451. [CrossRef]
29. Li, G.; Li, Y.; Liu, B.; Hou, Y.; Fan, J. Analysis of Scattering Properties of Continuous Slow-Release Slicks on the Sea Surface Based on Polarimetric Synthetic Aperture Radar. *ISPRS Int. J. -Geo-Inf.* **2018**, *7*, 237. [CrossRef]
30. Song, D.; Ding, Y.; Li, X.; Zhang, B.; Xu, M. Ocean oil spill classification with RADARSAT-2 SAR based on an optimized wavelet neural network. *Remote Sens.* **2017**, *9*, 799. [CrossRef]
31. Shamsudeen, T.Y. Advances in remote sensing technology, machine learning and deep learning for marine oil spill detection, prediction and vulnerability assessment. *Remote Sens.* **2020**, *12*, 3416.
32. Prajapati, K.; Prajapati, P.; Ramakrishnan, R.; Mahajan, A.; Bhavsar, M. Feature Combination of Pauli and H/A/Alpha Decomposition for Improved Oil Spill Detection Using SAR. In Proceedings of the International Conference on Recent Trends in Image Processing and Pattern Recognition, Aurangabad, India, 3–4 January 2020; pp. 134–147.
33. Minchew, B.; Jones, C.E.; Holt, B. Polarimetric analysis of backscatter from the deepwater horizon oil spill using l-band synthetic aperture radar. *IEEE Trans. Geosci. Remote Sens.* **2012**, *50*, 3812–3830. [CrossRef]
34. Angelliaume, S.; Dubois-Fernandez, P.C.; Jones, C.E.; Holt, B.; Minchew, B.; Amri, E.; Miegebielle, V. SAR imagery for detecting sea surface slicks: Performance assessment of polarization-dependent parameters. *IEEE Trans. Geosci. Remote Sens.* **2018**, *56*, 4237–4257. [CrossRef]
35. Singha, S.; Ressel, R.; Velotto, D.; Lehner, S. A Combination of Traditional and Polarimetric Features for Oil Spill Detection Using TerraSAR-X. *IEEE J. Sel. Top. Appl. Earth Obs. Remote Sens.* **2016**, *9*, 4979–4990. [CrossRef]
36. Singha, S.; Ressel, R. Offshore platform sourced pollution monitoring using space-borne fully polarimetric C and X band synthetic aperture radar. *Mar. Pollut. Bull.* **2016**, *112*, 327–340. [CrossRef]
37. Krestenitis, M.; Orfanidis, G.; Ioannidis, K.; Avgerinakis, K.; Vrochidis, S.; Kompatsiaris, I. Oil spill identification from satellite images using deep neural networks. *Remote Sens.* **2019**, *11*, 1762. [CrossRef]
38. Matias, Í.d.O.; Genovez, P.C.; Torres, S.B.; Ponte, F.F.d.A.; Oliveira, A.J.S.d.; Miranda, F.P.d.; Avellino, G.M. Improved Classification Models to Distinguish Natural from Anthropic Oil Slicks in the Gulf of Mexico: Seasonality and Radarsat-2 Beam Mode Effects under a Machine Learning Approach. *Remote Sens.* **2021**, *13*, 4568. [CrossRef]
39. Zhu, Q.; Zhang, Y.; Li, Z.; Yan, X.; Guan, Q.; Zhong, Y.; Zhang, L.; Li, D. Oil Spill Contextual and Boundary-Supervised Detection Network Based on Marine SAR Images. *IEEE Trans. Geosci. Remote Sens.* **2021**, *60*, 5213910. [CrossRef]
40. Mera, D.; Bolon-Canedo, V.; Cotos, J.M.; Alonso-Betanzos, A. On the use of feature selection to improve the detection of sea oil spills in SAR images. *Comput. Geosci.* **2017**, *100*, 166–178. [CrossRef]

41. Zhang, J.; Feng, H.; Luo, Q.; Li, Y.; Wei, J.; Li, J. Oil spill detection in quad-polarimetric SAR Images using an advanced convolutional neural network based on SuperPixel model. *Remote Sens.* **2020**, *12*, 944. [CrossRef]
42. Fornaro, G.; Verde, S.; Reale, D.; Pauciullo, A. CAESAR: An approach based on covariance matrix decomposition to improve multibaseline-multitemporal interferometric SAR processing. *IEEE Trans. Geosci. Remote Sens.* **2015**, *53*, 2050–2065. [CrossRef]
43. Jones, C.E.; Minchew, B.; Holt, B.; Hensley, S. Studies of the Deepwater Horizon Oil Spill With the UAVSAR Radar. In *Monitoring and Modeling the Deepwater Horizon Oil Spill: A Record Breaking Enterprise*; Geophysical Monograph. No.195; American Geophysical Union: Washington, DC, USA, 2013; pp. 33–50. [CrossRef]
44. Svejkovsky, J.; Hess, M.; Muskat, J.; Nedwed, T.J.; McCall, J.; Garcia, O. Characterization of surface oil thickness distribution patterns observed during the Deepwater Horizon (MC-252) oil spill with aerial and satellite remote sensing. *Mar. Pollut. Bull.* **2016**, *110*, 162–176. [CrossRef]
45. Garcia-Pineda, O.; MacDonald, I.R.; Li, X.; Jackson, C.R.; Pichel, W.G. Oil spill mapping and measurement in the Gulf of Mexico with textural classifier neural network algorithm (TCNNA). *IEEE J. Sel. Top. Appl. Earth Obs. Remote Sens.* **2013**, *6*, 2517–2525. [CrossRef]
46. Xu, B.; Cui, Y.; Li, Z.; Zuo, B.; Yang, J.; Song, J. Patch Ordering-Based SAR Image Despeckling Via Transform-Domain Filtering. *IEEE J. Sel. Top. Appl. Earth Obs. Remote Sens.* **2015**, *8*, 1682–1695. [CrossRef]
47. Gonzalez, R.C.; Woods, R.E. *Digital Image Processing*; Pearson Education Inc.: Upper Saddle River, NJ, USA, 2002.
48. Sumaiya, M.N.; Kumari, R.S.S. Logarithmic mean-based thresholding for SAR image change detection. *IEEE Geosci. Remote Sens. Lett.* **2016**, *13*, 1726–1728. [CrossRef]
49. Kaufman, Y.J.; Remer, L.A. Detection of forests using mid-IR reflectance: an application for aerosol studies. *IEEE Trans. Geosci. Remote Sens.* **1994**, *32*, 672–683. [CrossRef]

Article

RST Digital Robust Control for DC/DC Buck Converter Feeding Constant Power Load

Akram M. Abdurraqeeb *, Abdullrahman A. Al-Shamma'a *, Abdulaziz Alkuhayli, Abdullah M. Noman and Khaled E. Addoweesh

Electrical Engineering Department, College of Engineering, King Saud University, Riyadh 11421, Saudi Arabia; aalkuhayli@ksu.edu.sa (A.A.); anoman@ksu.edu.sa (A.M.N.); khaled@ksu.edu.sa (K.E.A.)
* Correspondence: amohammed6@ksu.edu.sa (A.M.A.); ashammaa@ksu.edu.sa (A.A.A.-S.)

Abstract: The instability of DC microgrids is the most prominent problem that limits the expansion of their use, and one of the most important causes of instability is constant power load CPLs. In this paper, a robust RST digital feedback controller is proposed to overcome the instability issues caused by the negative-resistance effect of CPLs and to improve robustness against the perturbations of power load and input voltage fluctuations, as well as to achieve a good tracking performance. To develop the proposed controller, it is necessary to first identify the dynamic model of the DC/DC buck converter with CPL. Second, based on the pole placement and sensitivity function shaping technique, a controller is designed and applied to the buck converter system. Then, validation of the proposed controller using Matlab/Simulink was achieved. Finally, the experimental validation of the RST controller was performed on a DC/DC buck converter with CPL using a real-time Hardware-in-the-loop (HIL). The OPAL-RT OP4510 RCP/HIL and dSPACE DS1104 controller board are used to model the DC/DC buck converter and to implement the suggested RST controller, respectively. The simulation and HIL experimental results indicate that the suggested RST controller has high efficiency.

Keywords: DC microgrids; robust RST digital controller; DC/DC buck converter; constant power load (CPL); hardware-in-the-loop (HIL)

MSC: 93D09; 93D15; 93C10

Citation: Abdurraqeeb, A.M.; Al-Shamma'a, A.A.; Alkuhayli, A.; Noman, A.M.; Addoweesh, K.E. RST Digital Robust Control for DC/DC Buck Converter Feeding Constant Power Load. *Mathematics* **2022**, *10*, 1782. https://doi.org/10.3390/math10101782

Academic Editor: Adrian Olaru

Received: 16 April 2022
Accepted: 19 May 2022
Published: 23 May 2022

Publisher's Note: MDPI stays neutral with regard to jurisdictional claims in published maps and institutional affiliations.

Copyright: © 2022 by the authors. Licensee MDPI, Basel, Switzerland. This article is an open access article distributed under the terms and conditions of the Creative Commons Attribution (CC BY) license (https://creativecommons.org/licenses/by/4.0/).

1. Introduction

Microgrids are increasingly being used as a result of environmental concerns such as CO_2 emissions and global climate change [1]. A microgrid is a small power grid that connects various sources and loads. A microgrid is composed of several components, including renewable energy sources such as solar, wind, and fuel cells, as well as energy storage technologies such as super capacitors, batteries, and power electronic converters [2]. The architecture of the microgrid can be classified into three types: AC, DC, and hybrid microgrid. DC microgrids are preferred over AC microgrids due to higher reliability, no reactive power losses, no harmonics, no requirement for synchronization, no frequency challenges, good compatibility, high efficiency, and direct connection of DC loads [3,4]. In DC microgrids, the DC/DC converters is critical for connecting distributed renewable sources and energy storage systems (ESSs) to loads [5]. The typical construction of a DC microgrid is depicted in Figure 1. Despite the advantages of DC microgrids, stability is a critical problem that might bring the entire system down. The main cause of stability issue in DC microgrids is the constant power loads (CPLs). The CPL is a nonlinear load with an incremental negative impedance (INI) characteristic, which implies the load current decrease/increase with the increase/decrease in its terminal voltage. Various CPLs, such as electric motors, actuators, and power electronic converters, should be regulated to maintain a constant output power [6]. A CPL has the ability to reduce system damping and make DC microgrids unstable [7,8].

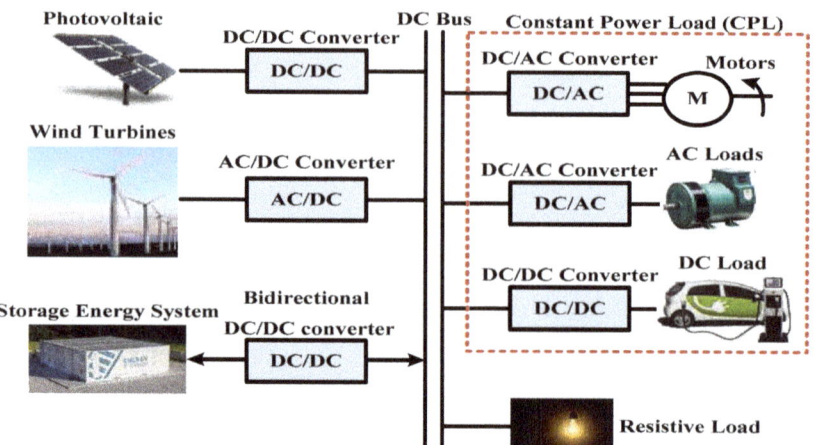

Figure 1. The structure of a DC microgrid with various loads and sources.

Numerous control strategies have been suggested for addressing the instability problem in DC microgrids with CPLs. In [8–10], the authors proposed passive-damping methods to increase the damping factor by adding passive components such as resistors, capacitors, or inductors, to the DC/DC converter. However, this approach diminishes system efficiency by producing excessive power losses The authors in [11–13] developed active-damping approaches by modifying control loops with virtual impedance to allow the system poles to lie on the left side without changing the system hardware. This approach is effective in ensuring system stability when CPL is prevalent. However, the original control loop of the converter will be changed, affecting the dynamic responsiveness of the entire system. For both passive and active damping approaches, small-signal analysis is being used in the design and analysis process. When a broad range of operating conditions and disturbances are present, poor performance is inevitable [14]. Due to the non-linear nature of the DC/DC converters, several nonlinear controllers that are suggested to ensure the stability of DC microgrids in the presence of CPL have been implemented [15]. The authors of [16,17] presented model predictive control (MPC) to stabilize DC microgrids with CPLs. In [18], a nonlinear fuzzy MPC with effective control performance for nonlinear systems is formed by combining a Takagi-Sugeno (TS) fuzzy model with a linear model predictive controller (MPC). However, the computational burden of such controllers, which involve maximizing a predefined cost function, restricts their widespread application in real time. The authors in [19–23] proposed a robust based PWM slide mode controller (SMC) to stabilize a DC/DC boost converter system feeding CPLs, where the duty cycle of the boost converter is estimated using a nonlinear polynomial sliding surface. However, SMC has the disadvantage of driving the power converter at a variable switching frequency, which degrades power quality. In [24], a fixed frequency SMC with a novel double integral type sliding manifold is presented for voltage regulation of a DC microgrid. In [25], an adaptive backstepping controller is designed for a DC microgrid feeding non-ideal CPLs through a third-degree cubature kalman filter. The proposed controller is designed for large signal stabilization through the recursive lyapunov design procedure. The authors of [26] addressed the voltage regulation issue of the DC/DC converter with CPL by integrating a composite nonlinear controller with a backstepping approach and a disturbance observer. The most recent nonlinear control techniques for stabilizing DC microgrids and resolving the tracking problem are passivity-based controllers (PBCs) [27]. Two primary categories of PBC have been identified in the literature [28]. The traditional PBC selects the energy function to be assigned and then builds a controller to minimize the energy function. In the second category of PBC, an explicitly defined control structure, such as Euler-Lagrange (EL) or Port-Controlled Hamiltonian (PCH), should be chosen first, and then all assignable energy and power functions should be characterized. In [29,30], an adaptive energy shaping algorithm combining standard PBC and immersion and invariance (I&I) parameter estimator was utilized to handle the difficult challenge of regulating the output voltage of a DC/DC buck-boost converters feeding an unknown power CPL. The I&I estimator is utilized to compute online the extracted load power, which is complicated to measure in practical applications. In [31], a standard PBC is presented to reshape the system energy and compensate for the negative impedance and a proportion-integration (PI) action is added around the passive output to boost disturbance rejection performance. In [32], an H-infinity robust controller based on the glover doyle optimization algorithm (GDOA) to prevent system instability due to the CPLs is proposed. However, in some cases, GDOA provides a robust controller with a higher order of the denominator, which may be challenging to implement.

To the best of our knowledge, no study has employed the RST digital robust controller to overcome instability problems in DC microgrid caused by CPL. As a result, this paper presents a new robust controller for stabilizing DC/DC buck converter fed a DC microgrid with CPLs. The main contributions to this article are the following:

1. An RST controller is proposed to stabilize the DC/DC buck converter with CPL;
2. All perturbations caused by changes in input voltage and current fluctuations are rejected, resulting in very good tracking;
3. Use hardware-in-the-loop (HIL) to model the DC/DC buck converter with CPL using OPAL-RT OP4510 RCP/HIL and to implement the proposed RST controller in dSPACE 1104.

The remainder of this paper is organized as follows: in Section 2, the modeling of a buck converter with CPL is presented. The RST robust controller is designed in Section 3. In Sections 4 and 5, the simulation and real-time HIL results are presented, respectively. Finally, the conclusion and some future work prospects are presented in Section 5.

2. Modeling of the DC/DC Buck Converter with CPL

The typical circuit for a DC/DC buck converter with a CPL is depicted in Figure 2, where the CPLs (such as cascaded DC/AC or DC/DC converter) can be modelled as controlled current source [33].

$$I_{CPL} = \frac{P_{CPL}}{V_{out}} \quad (1)$$

where I_{CPL} is current of CPL, P_{CPL} is power, and V_{out} is the output voltage of DC/DC buck converter. The state-space model of the converter with CPL is obtained by considering the continuous conduction mode (CCM) and by using Kirchhoff's current and voltage laws, as follows [34]:

$$d\frac{V_{in}}{L} - \frac{V_{out}}{L} = \frac{di_L}{dt} \quad (2)$$

$$\frac{i_L}{C} - \frac{V_{out}}{R_L C} - \frac{P_{CPL}}{V_{out} C} = \frac{dV_{out}}{dt} \quad (3)$$

where V_{in}, V_{out}, i_L, and $d \in [0, 1]$ are the input voltage, output voltage, inductor current, and duty ratio, respectively.

The design of the output LC filter for the DC/DC buck converter is designed on the basis of the following conditions: continuous-current conduction operation of the converter, ripple on the output voltage that does not exceed a few percent [35].

$$L \geq \frac{V_o(1-d)}{f \Delta i_L} \quad (4)$$

$$C \geq \frac{1-d}{8L \frac{\Delta V_o}{V_o} f^2} \quad (5)$$

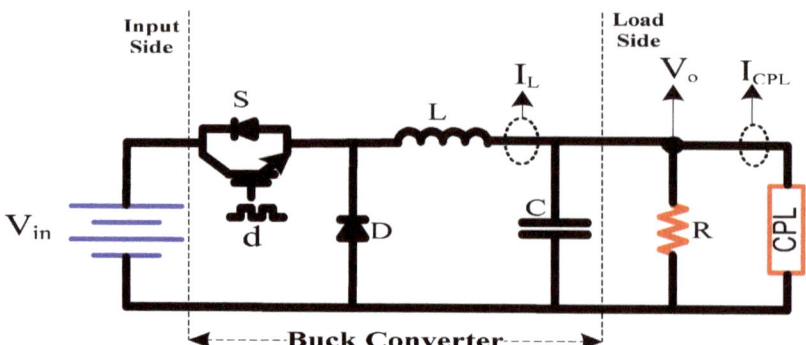

Figure 2. The typical circuit for a DC/DC buck converter with CPL.

By using average switch modeling, the transfer function of duty cycle to the output voltage of the buck converter in S domain is given as:

$$G(s) = \frac{V_{out}}{d} \tag{6}$$

$$G(s) = \frac{\frac{V_{in}}{LC}}{s^2 + \left(\frac{1}{RC} - \frac{P_{CPL}}{V_{out}^2 C}\right)s + \frac{1}{LC}} \tag{7}$$

where d is the duty ratio and V_{out} is the output voltage.

Assuming that the system parameters are $C = 220\ \mu F$, $L = 2.7$ mH, $R_{CPL} = -9.6\ \Omega$, $P = 20.4$ W, $V_{out} = 14$ V, $V_{in} = 28$ V, $R = 470\ \Omega$, and by substituting these values into the transfer function of the system given of in (7), the result is as shown in (8).

$$G(s) = \frac{4.714 \times 10^7}{s^2 - 463.8\ s\ + 1.684 \times 10^6} \tag{8}$$

The characteristic equation obtained from (7) demonstrates that the increment negative impedance (INI) of the CPL pushes poles to the right-half plane (RHP) and makes the system unstable, as indicated in (8). To improve the stability of the system and robustness to disturbances when changes occur in CPL, as well as to achieve good reference tracking performance, an RST digital robust controller is presented in the next section.

3. RST Robust Digital Controller Design

3.1. System Identification Workflow

Figure 3 illustrates the principle of discrete-time model identification. Using MATLAB identification toolbox, a discrete-time model with adjustable parameters is implemented. A parameter-adaptation technique uses the prediction error, the difference between the system output at time t, y(t), and the output predicted by the model, ŷ(t), to adjust the model parameters at each sampling time in order to reduce this error. The system is excited via the discrete sequence u(t) t = 0, 1, 2, ... n. This discrete signal is made continuous by the Zero Order Hold (ZOH). After obtaining the model, statistical tests on the prediction error e(t) and the predicted output yL could be used to do objective validation (t). The validation test allows the optimum algorithm for parameter estimate to be determined.

The sampling frequency is set based on the bandwidth of the continuous-time plant and, more specifically, the bandwidth required for the closed loop. The general rule is:

$$f_s = (6\ to\ 25) f_B^{Cl} \tag{9}$$

where f_s is the sampling frequency and f_B^{Cl} is the desired bandwidth of the closed loop.

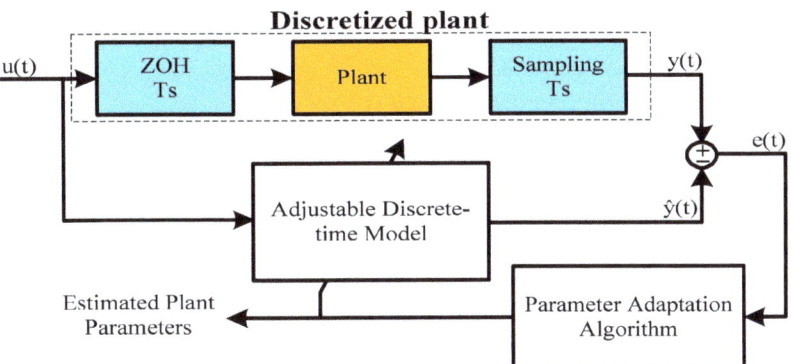

Figure 3. Parameter estimation of discrete-time models.

3.2. The R-S-T Digital Controller

To design the RST controller, a region of uncertainties must be defined based on the interval parameter variation of the plant model. To choose the RST polynomials that better fit the control system requirements can be a very difficult numerical problem, especially in auto- and self-tuning control systems. Due to these limitations, general RST controller design for industrial applications remains challenging [36]. In this section, the RST robust digital feedback controller is designing by integrating pole placement with sensitivity function shaping [37]. This design methodology is utilized here to improve the performance of the closed-loop system and disturbance rejection at the same time. The RST controller architecture is depicted in Figure 4.

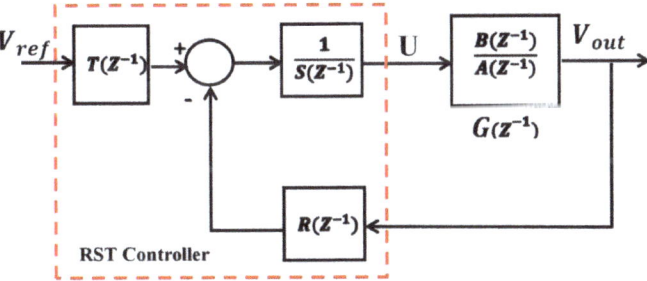

Figure 4. Block diagram of RST robust digital feedback controller with plant.

In Figure 4, the parameters R, S, and T represent polynomials of the controller and G represents the dynamic model of the buck converter. The discrete time plant model (G), which is utilized in the design of digital controllers, is obtained by the discretization of the model in (8) using the ZOH transformation as depicted in Figure 3. The discrete time plant model is rewritten in this case as shown in (10).

$$G\left(z^{-1}\right) = \frac{B\left(z^{-1}\right)}{A\left(z^{-1}\right)} = \frac{0.239 + 0.2428z^{-1}}{1 - 2.03\ z^{-1} + 1.047z^{-2}} \quad (10)$$

The R and S digital polynomials are designed to achieve the desired regulation performance, and the T is designed to provide the required tracking performance. The three polynomials of the proposed RST digital controller are as follows:

$$R\left(z^{-1}\right) = r_0 + r_1\ z^{-1} + r_2\ z^{-2} + \cdots + r_{nR}\ z^{-nR} \quad (11)$$

$$S(z^{-1}) = s_0 + s_1\ z^{-1} + s_2\ z^{-2} + \cdots + s_{ns}\ z^{-ns} \tag{12}$$

$$T(z^{-1}) = t_0 + t_1\ z^{-1} + t_2\ z^{-2} + \cdots + t_{nt}\ z^{-nt} \tag{13}$$

However, $T(z^{-1})$ will be set equal to $R(1)$, implying that the gain of the $T(z^{-1})$ will equal to the sum of $R(z^{-1})$ coefficients in order to maintain a unit gain between the desired and actual outputs in steady state.

The desired performance of the DC/DC buck converter system is to achieve precise reference tracking while maintaining robustness and stability. These desired performances can be achieved using constraints on the shape of closed-loop sensitivity functions [38,39]. The output sensitivity function (S_0) between the load variation disturbance and plant output is given by:

$$S_0(z^{-1}) = \frac{A(z^{-1})S(z^{-1})}{A(z^{-1})S(z^{-1}) + B(z^{-1})R(z^{-1})} \tag{14}$$

The complementary sensitivity function (T_0) between the disturbance measurement noise and plant output is given by:

$$T_0(z^{-1}) = \frac{B(z^{-1})T(z^{-1})}{A(z^{-1})S(z^{-1}) + B(z^{-1})R(z^{-1})} \tag{15}$$

The input sensitivity function (S_i) between the disturbance of control signal and plant input is given by:

$$S_i(z^{-1}) = \frac{A(z^{-1})R(z^{-1})}{A(z^{-1})S(z^{-1}) + B(z^{-1})R(z^{-1})} \tag{16}$$

Table 1 summarizes the limits on the shapes of closed-loop sensitivity functions that have been addressed [37,39].

Table 1. Constraints on sensitivity function shapes.

Constraints	Conditions	Condition Description	Purpose
Constraint 1	$\|S_0(z^{-1})\|_\infty < 6$ dB, $\forall \omega$	The maximum output sensitivity function should be less than 6 dB.	For ensure adequate stability margins and robustness margins.
Constraint 2	$\|T_0(z^{-1})\|_\infty < 3.5$ dB, $\forall \omega$	The maximum of the complementary sensitivity function should be less than 3.5 dB.	For ensure adequate stability margins, as this will also maintain a good robustness margin.
Constraint 3	$\|S_i(z^{-1})\|_\infty \leq 0$ dB, $\forall \omega$	The maximum of input sensitivity function should be equal or less than 0 dB.	To ensure the output of controller between zero and one.

The closed-loop sensitivity function is shaped by selecting desired closed loop poles and introducing pre-specified polynomials into the controller. From the expressions of sensitivity functions, it can be noted that the 3 sensitivity functions have the same denominator $P(z^{-1}) = A(z^{-1})S(z^{-1}) + B(z^{-1})R(z^{-1})$ which determines the closed-loop poles and can be distinguished to the dominant and auxiliary closed-loop poles as given in (17).

$$P(z^{-1}) = P_A(z^{-1})P_D(z^{-1}) \tag{17}$$

where $P_A(z^{-1})$ denotes the auxiliary poles and $P_D(z^{-1})$ denotes the desired dominant poles of the closed loop system. The pre-specified polynomials of the $R(z^{-1})$ and $S(z^{-1})$ are introduced as shown in (18) and (19):

$$R(z^{-1}) = H_R(z^{-1})R'(z^{-1}) \tag{18}$$

$$S(z^{-1}) = H_S(z^{-1})S'(z^{-1}) \tag{19}$$

where $H_R(z^{-1})$ and $H_S(z^{-1})$ are polynomials that have been pre-specified. The anonymous polynomials of the controller $R'(z^{-1})$ and $S'(z^{-1})$ produced by solving the following equations:

$$P(z^{-1}) = A(z^{-1})S(z^{-1}) + B(z^{-1})R(z^{-1}) \qquad (20)$$

$$P_D(z^{-1}) \cdot P_A(z^{-1}) = A(z^{-1})H_S(z^{-1})S'(z^{-1}) + B(z^{-1})H_S(z^{-1})R'(z^{-1}) \qquad (21)$$

Figure 5 displays the required steps that must be performed in order to build the RST controller [36].

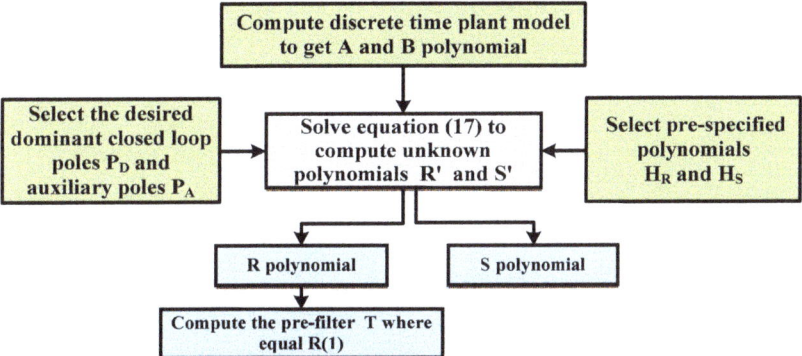

Figure 5. Block diagram of the controller design steps.

The polynomials for the RST controller derived by solving (20) are as follows:

$$R(z^{-1}) = 0.2923 - 0.3061z^{-1} - 0.2624z^{-2} + 0.3076z^{-3} - 0.0284z^{-4} \qquad (22)$$

$$S(z^{-1}) = 1 - 1.1640z^{-1} - 0.2094z^{-2} - 0.0520z^{-3} + 0.0066z^{-4} \qquad (23)$$

$$T(z^{-1}) = 0.003 \qquad (24)$$

Figure 6 demonstrates all of the considered sensitivity functions with the RST digital controller. It can be observed that the recommended RST digital controller completely fits all three of the aforementioned restrictions in Table 1.

4. Simulation Results and Discussion

In this section, the simulation study was carried out to validate the efficacy of the suggested controller for DC/DC buck converter with CPL using the Matlab/Simulink (2016). The CPL is modeled as a current-controlled source, and the parameters of the system have been described and mentioned in Section 2. The switching frequency is set at 20 kHz. The simulation results in Figure 7 demonstrate how CPL affects the DC/DC buck converter, causing the system to become unstable in open loop. To mitigate this issue, the system is equipped with an RST digital robust controller. The output voltage in Figure 8 demonstrates the ability of the proposed controller to maintain system stability and keep the output voltage within the desired reference range. As shown in Figure 9, the tracking error between the desired reference and the output voltage of the buck converter is very small and negligible.

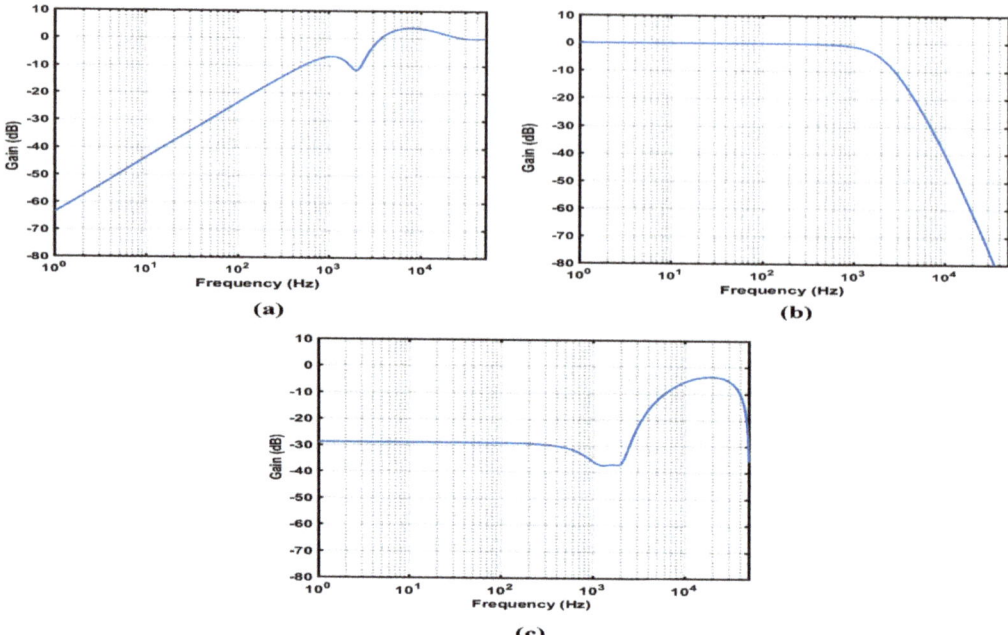

Figure 6. (a) Output sensitivity (S_0), (b) Complementary sensitivity (T_0), (c) Input sensitivity (S_i).

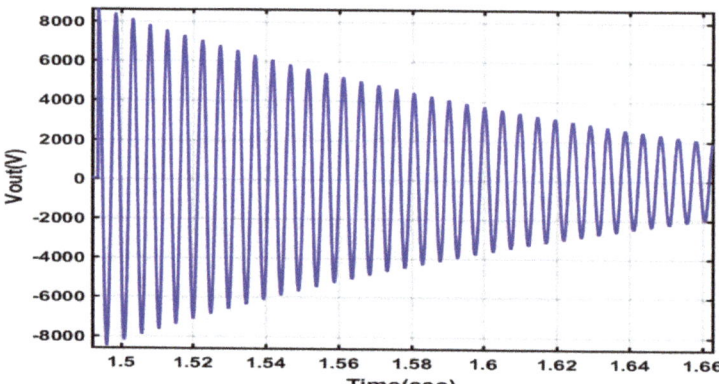

Figure 7. Dynamic response of the buck converter with CPL in an open loop mode.

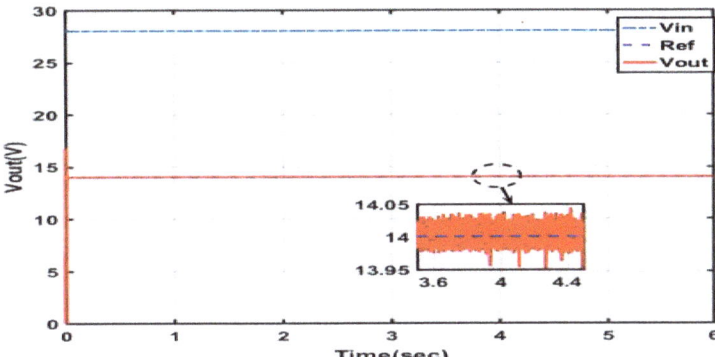

Figure 8. Dynamic response of the buck converter with CPL closed loop mode using RST controller.

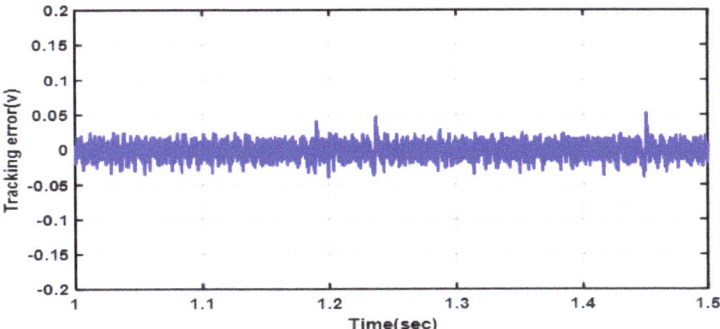

Figure 9. Tracking error between reference voltage and measured voltage.

The effectiveness and robustness of the proposed controller is depicted in Figure 10, where the desired voltage of the system is set at 14 V and the output voltage of the system remains stable despite changes in power consumed. The sudden change in power CPL causes a tiny transient variation in the output voltage, but after that, the output voltage is able to track the reference voltage with reasonable accuracy. Furthermore, the control signal (duty cycle) remains constant at 0.5 with a small fluctuation, but it is still within the range of 0 and 1. Figure 11 shows the effectiveness and robustness of the proposed controller in reducing the effects of a change in the source voltage on the output voltage where the influence is negligible.

5. HIL Experimental Results and Discussion

This section describes the HIL experimental testbed that is used to validate the MATLAB simulation findings achieved before. The OPAL-RT real-time simulator is used to connect the MATLAB Simulink model to the digital signal processor (DSP). The experimental setup and the block diagram are shown in Figures 12 and 13, respectively. This platform is consisting of OP4510 simulator, dSPACE DS1104 controller box, RT-LAB monitor console, dSPACE control desk monitor, and digital oscilloscope. In the HIL design of experiments, two cases are examined to validate the effectiveness of the proposed RST controller: one with a change in CPL and the other with a change in input voltage.

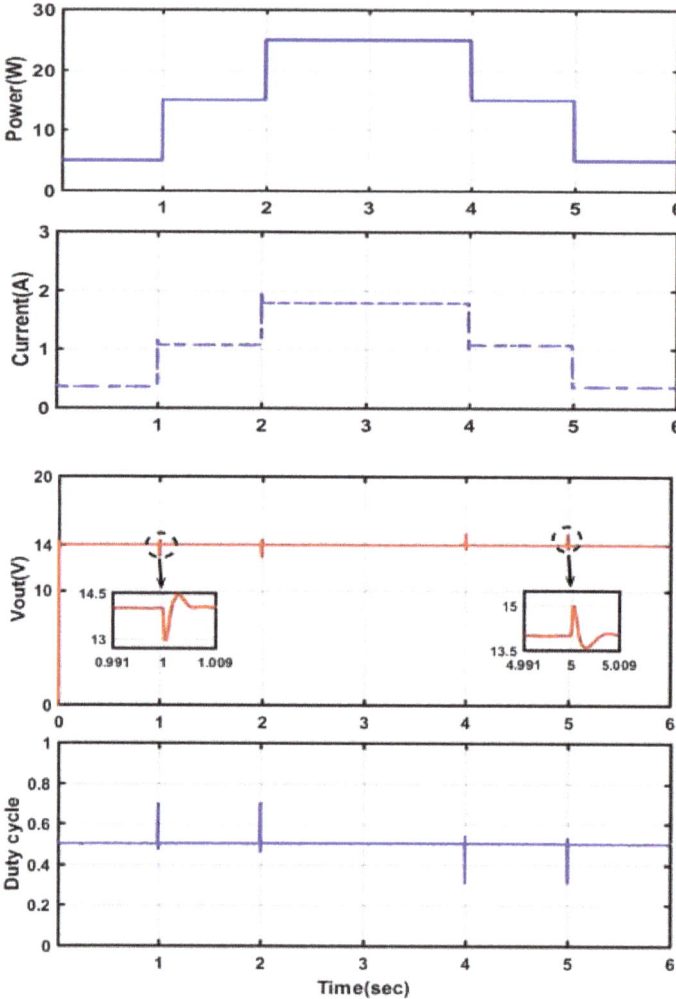

Figure 10. Changes in output voltage and duty cycle with an RST controller in response to CPL variation.

In this testbed, the RST controller is performed in the dSPACE DS1104 R&D controller board, while the DC/DC Buck converter with a CPL under MATLAB/Simulink operates in the OPAL-RT in real-time. The system output signal is sent from the analog port of the OPAL-RT to the ADC module of dSPACE DS1104. In order to keep the system running in the next cycle, the PWM signal is computed by the RST controller and supplied to the OPAL-RT through the digital input port. The analoge signals used in the experiments are scaled down since the output and input ranges of both the dSPACE and the OPAL-RT are constrained to -10 V to $+10$ V, and -16 V to $+16$ V, respectively. To achieve this limitation, the output and input voltages are divided by 4 V, and the CPL by 2 W. Meanwhile, due to the computational power of the OPAL-RT, the switching frequency is set to 20 kHz and the step size is set to 10^{-5} s.

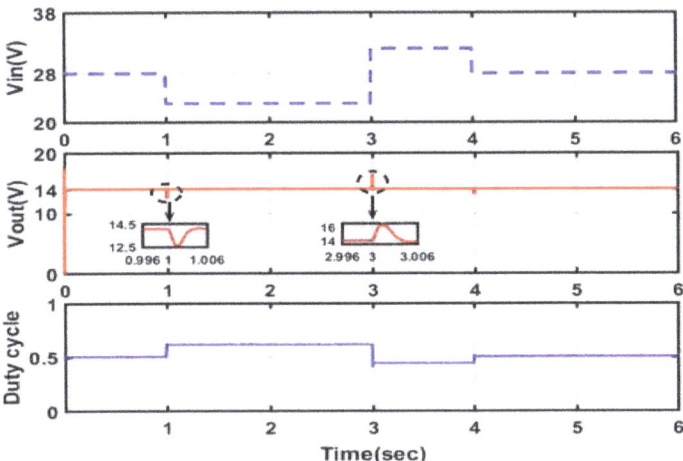

Figure 11. Changes in output voltage and duty cycle with an RST controller in response to input voltage variation.

Figure 12. The experimental testbed. 1—OP4510 simulator; 2—dSPACE ds1104 Controller Box; 3—RT-LAB monitor console; 4—dSPACE control desk monitor; 5—Digital oscilloscope.

The suggested RST controller has been proved to be both robust and dynamically efficient, using the HIL experimental findings presented in Figures 14 and 15. The impact of varying the CPL on the output voltage is depicted in Figure 14, where we can see that the suggested RST controller operates accurately throughout the CPL fluctuation, and the output voltage remains stable and fast-tracked to the reference voltage of the system at 14 V. The duty cycle signal, as can be observed, is stable at 0.5 V. Figure 14 illustrates the effect of input voltage fluctuation on the output voltage; it can be seen that the proposed RST controller performs quite correctly when the input voltage changes, while the output voltage remains stable and fast-tracked to the reference voltage of 14 V. When the input voltage changes, the duty cycle signal changes from 0.5 V to 0.62 V, then to 0.44 V, and finally back to 0.5.

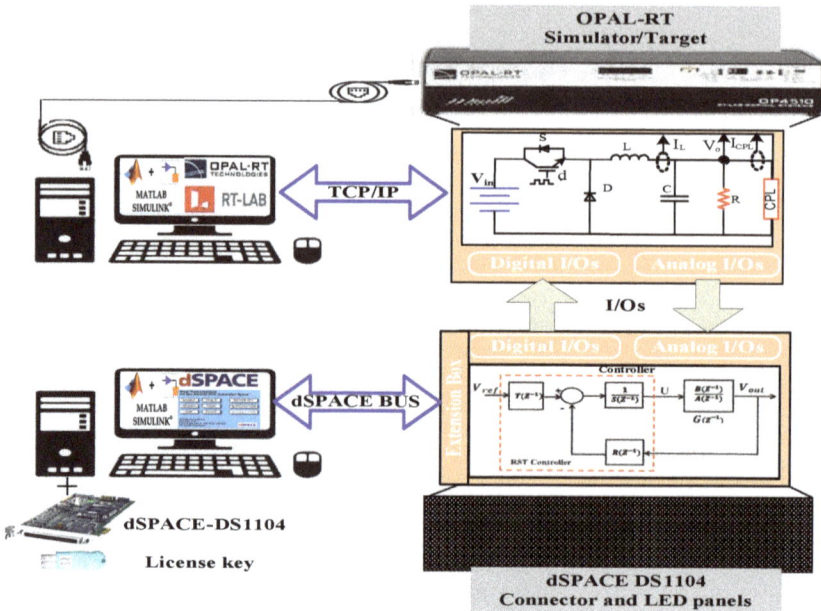

Figure 13. Block diagram of experimental HIL.

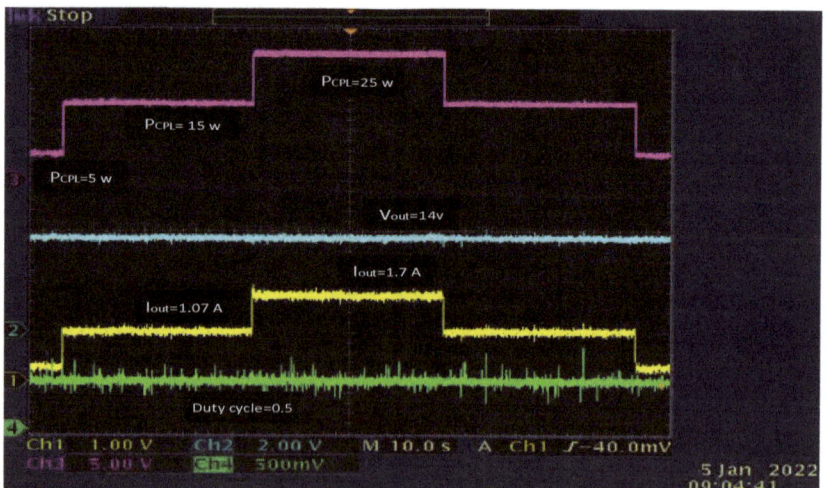

Figure 14. HIL experimental results of system with CPL variation.

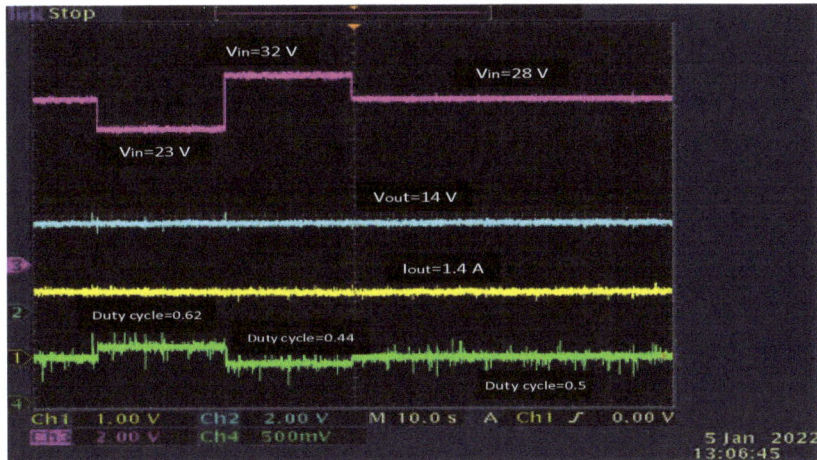

Figure 15. HIL experimental results of system with input voltage variation.

6. Conclusions

This article discussed the instability issue that arises when a DC/DC buck power converter is used to power a CPL in DC microgrid systems. The study proposed and implemented an RST digital feedback controller to stabilize the system and minimize steady-state error induced by system disturbances such as input voltage and load variations. To begin, a model of the system was developed. Then, to regulate the system, a robust digital RST controller was built by combining pole placement with a sensitivity function shaping method. To evaluate the control performance, MATLAB/Simulink simulations were used to compare the conventional closed loop PI linear controller to the proposed RST. Additionally, the RST controller was validated on the and HIL real-time experimental platforms to be both robust and dynamically efficient. According to the findings, the proposed control strategy may demonstrate good performance in terms of recovery, settling time, and overshoot when the load and input voltage are changed. The droop control scheme for DC microgrids with multiple energy storage devices to assure both voltage regulation and equal load sharing might be a useful study area for future work.

Author Contributions: Conceptualization, A.A. and K.E.A.; Data curation, A.M.A., A.M.N. and K.E.A.; Formal analysis, A.M.A., A.A.A.-S. and A.M.N.; Funding acquisition, A.A. and A.M.N.; Investigation, A.M.A., A.A.A.-S., A.A. and K.E.A.; Methodology, A.M.A., A.A.A.-S., A.A. and K.E.A.; Project administration, A.A.A.-S., A.A., A.M.N. and K.E.A.; Resources, A.M.A., A.A.A.-S., A.A. and A.M.N.; Software, A.M.A., A.A.A.-S. and A.M.N.; Supervision, A.A.A.-S., A.A., A.M.N. and K.E.A.; Validation, A.M.A. and A.A.A.-S.; Visualization, A.M.A. and A.A.A.-S.; Writing—original draft, A.M.A. and A.A.A.-S.; Writing—review & editing, A.M.A., A.A.A.-S., A.A., A.M.N. and K.E.A. All authors have read and agreed to the published version of the manuscript.

Funding: This research received no external funding.

Institutional Review Board Statement: Not applicable.

Informed Consent Statement: Not applicable.

Data Availability Statement: The data presented in this study are available on request from the corresponding author.

Acknowledgments: This work was supported by the Researchers Supporting Project number (RSP-2021/258) King Saud University, Riyadh, Saudi Arabia.

Conflicts of Interest: The authors declare no conflict of interest.

References

1. Ayadi, F.; Colak, I.; Garip, I.; Bulbul, H.I. Impacts of Renewable Energy Resources in Smart Grid. In Proceedings of the 2020 8th International Conference on Smart Grid (icSmartGrid), Paris, France, 17–19 June 2020; pp. 183–188.
2. Bayindir, R.; Hossain, E.; Kabalci, E.; Perez, R. A comprehensive study on microgrid technology. *Int. J. Renew. Energy Res.* **2014**, *4*, 1094–1107.
3. Xu, Q.; Vafamand, N.; Chen, L.; Dragičević, T.; Xie, L.; Blaabjerg, F. Review on Advanced Control Technologies for Bidirectional DC/DC Converters in DC Microgrids. *IEEE J. Emerg. Sel. Top. Power Electron.* **2021**, *9*, 1205–1221. [CrossRef]
4. Dragičević, T.; Lu, X.; Vasquez, J.C.; Guerrero, J.M. DC Microgrids—Part II: A Review of Power Architectures, Applications, and Standardization Issues. *IEEE Trans. Power Electron.* **2016**, *31*, 3528–3549. [CrossRef]
5. Yang, J.; Cui, H.; Li, S.; Zolotas, A. Optimized Active Disturbance Rejection Control for DC-DC Buck Converters with Uncertainties Using a Reduced-Order GPI Observer. *IEEE Trans. Circuits Syst. I Regul. Pap.* **2018**, *65*, 832–841. [CrossRef]
6. Rahimi, A.M.; Emadi, A. An Analytical Investigation of DC/DC Power Electronic Converters with Constant Power Loads in Vehicular Power Systems. *IEEE Trans. Veh. Technol.* **2009**, *58*, 2689–2702. [CrossRef]
7. Hossain, E.; Perez, R.; Bayindir, R. Implementation of hybrid energy storage systems to compensate microgrid instability in the presence of constant power loads. In Proceedings of the IEEE International Conference on Renewable Energy Research and Applications (ICRERA), Birmingham, UK, 20–23 November 2016; pp. 1068–1073. [CrossRef]
8. Kwasinski, A.; Onwuchekwa, C.N. Dynamic Behavior and Stabilization of DC Microgrids with Instantaneous Constant-Power Loads. *IEEE Trans. Power Electron.* **2011**, *26*, 822–834. [CrossRef]
9. Cespedes, M.; Xing, L.; Sun, J. Constant-Power Load System Stabilization by Passive Damping. *IEEE Trans. Power Electron.* **2011**, *26*, 1832–1836. [CrossRef]
10. Liu, X.; Bian, Y.; Fan, S. Active stabilization control strategy for storage system paralleled with constant power loads. In Proceedings of the 20th International Conference on Electrical Machines and Systems (ICEMS), Sydney, Australia, 8 November 2017; pp. 1–5. [CrossRef]
11. Lu, X.; Sun, K.; Huang, L.; Guerrero, J.M.; Vasquez, J.C.; Xing, Y. Virtual impedance based stability improvement for DC microgrids with constant power loads. In Proceedings of the IEEE Energy Conversion Congress and Exposition (ECCE), Pittsburgh, PA, USA, 14–18 September 2014; pp. 2670–2675. [CrossRef]
12. Cai, W.; Fahimi, B.; Cosoroaba, E.; Yi, F. Stability analysis and voltage control method based on virtual resistor and proportional voltage feedback loop for cascaded DC-DC converters. In Proceedings of the IEEE Energy Conversion Congress and Exposition (ECCE), Pittsburgh, PA, USA, 14–18 September 2014; pp. 3016–3022.
13. Zhang, X.; Ruan, X.; Zhong, Q.-C. Improving the Stability of Cascaded DC/DC Converter Systems via Shaping the Input Impedance of the Load Converter with a Parallel or Series Virtual Impedance. *IEEE Trans. Ind. Electron.* **2015**, *62*, 7499–7512. [CrossRef]
14. Singh, S.; Gautam, A.R.; Fulwani, D. Constant power loads and their effects in DC distributed power systems: A review. *Renew. Sustain. Energy Rev.* **2017**, *72*, 407–421. [CrossRef]
15. Emadi, A.; Khaligh, A.; Rivetta, C.H.; Williamson, G.A. Constant power loads and negative impedance instability in automotive systems: Definition modeling stability and control of power electronic converters and motor drives. *IEEE Trans. Veh. Technol.* **2006**, *55*, 1112–1125. [CrossRef]
16. Dragicevic, T. Dynamic Stabilization of DC Microgrids With Predictive Control of Point-of-Load Converters. *IEEE Trans. Power Electron.* **2018**, *33*, 10872–10884. [CrossRef]
17. Andres-Martinez, O.; Flores-Tlacuahuac, A.; Ruiz-Martinez, O.F.; Mayo-Maldonado, J.C. Nonlinear Model Predictive Stabilization of DC–DC Boost Converters with Constant Power Loads. *IEEE J. Emerg. Sel. Top. Power Electron.* **2021**, *9*, 822–830. [CrossRef]
18. Vafamand, N.; Khooban, M.H.; Dragicevic, T.; Blaabjerg, F. Networked Fuzzy Predictive Control of Power Buffers for Dynamic Stabilization of DC Microgrids. *IEEE Trans. Ind. Electron.* **2019**, *66*, 1356–1362. [CrossRef]
19. Oucheriah, S.; Guo, L. PWM-Based Adaptive Sliding-Mode Control for Boost DC–DC Converters. *IEEE Trans. Ind. Electron.* **2013**, *60*, 3291–3294. [CrossRef]
20. Zhao, Y.; Qiao, W.; Ha, D. A Sliding-Mode Duty-Ratio Controller for DC/DC Buck Converters with Constant Power Loads. *IEEE Trans. Ind. Appl.* **2014**, *50*, 1448–1458. [CrossRef]
21. Singh, S.; Fulwani, D.; Kumar, V. Robust sliding-mode control of dc/dc boost converter feeding a constant power load. *IET Power Electron.* **2015**, *8*, 1230–1237. [CrossRef]
22. Martinez-Treviño, B.A.; El Aroudi, A.; Vidal-Idiarte, E.; Cid-Pastor, A.; Martinez-Salamero, L. Sliding-mode control of a boost converter under constant power loading conditions. *IET Power Electron.* **2019**, *12*, 521–529. [CrossRef]
23. El Aroudi, A.; Martínez-Treviño, B.A.; Vidal-Idiarte, E.; Cid-Pastor, A. Fixed Switching Frequency Digital Sliding-Mode Control of DC-DC Power Supplies Loaded by Constant Power Loads with Inrush Current Limitation Capability. *Energies* **2019**, *12*, 1055. [CrossRef]
24. Yasin, A.R.; Ashraf, M.; Bhatti, A.I. Fixed Frequency Sliding Mode Control of Power Converters for Improved Dynamic Response in DC Micro-Grids. *Energies* **2018**, *11*, 2799. [CrossRef]
25. Yousefizadeh, S.; Bendtsen, J.D.; Vafamand, N.; Khooban, M.H.; Blaabjerg, F.; Dragicevic, T. Tracking Control for a DC Microgrid Feeding Uncertain Loads in More Electric Aircraft: Adaptive Backstepping Approach. *IEEE Trans. Ind. Electron.* **2019**, *66*, 5644–5652. [CrossRef]

26. Xu, Q.; Zhang, C.; Wen, C.; Wang, P. A Novel Composite Nonlinear Controller for Stabilization of Constant Power Load in DC Microgrid. *IEEE Trans. Smart Grid* **2017**, *10*, 752–761. [CrossRef]
27. Ortega, R.; Perez, J.A.L.; Nicklasson, P.J.; Sira-Ramirez, H.J. *Passivity-Based Control of Euler-Lagrange Systems: Mechanical, Electrical and Electromechanical Applications*; Springer Science & Business Media: London, UK, 1998.
28. Hilairet, M.; Ghanes, M.; Béthoux, O.; Tanasa, V.; Barbot, J.-P.; Normand-Cyrot, D. A passivity-based controller for coordination of converters in a fuel cell system. *Control Eng. Pr.* **2013**, *21*, 1097–1109. [CrossRef]
29. Soriano-Rangel, C.A.; He, W.; Mancilla-David, F.; Ortega, R. Voltage Regulation in Buck–Boost Converters Feeding an Unknown Constant Power Load: An Adaptive Passivity-Based Control. *IEEE Trans. Control Syst. Technol.* **2021**, *29*, 395–402. [CrossRef]
30. Pang, S.; Nahid-Mobarakeh, B.; Pierfederici, S.; Phattanasak, M.; Huangfu, Y.; Luo, G.; Gao, F. Interconnection and Damping Assignment Passivity-Based Control Applied to On-Board DC–DC Power Converter System Supplying Constant Power Load. *IEEE Trans. Ind. Appl.* **2019**, *55*, 6476–6485. [CrossRef]
31. He, W.; Namazi, M.M.; Koofigar, H.R.; Amirian, M.A.; Blaabjerg, F. Stabilization of DC–DC buck converter with unknown constant power load via passivity-based control plus proportion-integration. *IET Power Electron.* **2021**, *14*, 2597–2609. [CrossRef]
32. Boukerdja, M.; Chouder, A.; Hassaine, L.; Bouamama, B.O.; Issa, W.; Louassaa, K. H∞ based control of a DC/DC buck converter feeding a constant power load in uncertain DC microgrid system. *ISA Trans.* **2020**, *105*, 278–295. [CrossRef]
33. Wu, M.; Lu, D.D.-C. A Novel Stabilization Method of LC Input Filter with Constant Power Loads Without Load Performance Compromise in DC Microgrids. *IEEE Trans. Ind. Electron.* **2015**, *62*, 4552–4562. [CrossRef]
34. AL-Nussairi, M.K.; Bayindir, R.; Padmanaban, S.; Mihet-Popa, L.; Siano, P. Constant Power Loads (CPL) with Microgrids: Problem Definition, Stability Analysis and Compensation Techniques. *Energies* **2017**, *10*, 1656. [CrossRef]
35. Di Piazza, M.C.; Vitale, G. Photovoltaic field emulation including dynamic and partial shadow conditions. *Appl. Energy* **2010**, *87*, 814–823. [CrossRef]
36. Landau, I. The R-S-T digital controller design and applications. *Control Eng. Pract.* **1998**, *6*, 155–165. [CrossRef]
37. Landau, I.D.; Langer, J.; Rey, D.; Barnier, J. Robust control of a 360/spl deg/ flexible arm using the combined pole placement/sensitivity function shaping method. *IEEE Trans. Control Syst. Technol.* **1996**, *4*, 369–383. [CrossRef]
38. Seborg, D.E.; Edgar, T.F.; Mellichamp, D.A.; Doyle, F.J. *Process Dynamics and Control*; John Wiley & Sons: Hoboken, NJ, USA, 2016.
39. Ahmad, I.; Abdurraqeeb, A. Tracking control of a piezoelectric actuator with hysteresis compensation using RST digital controller. *Microsyst. Technol.* **2017**, *23*, 2307–2317. [CrossRef]

Article

Force Tracking Impedance Control of Hydraulic Series Elastic Actuators Interacting with Unknown Environment

Yong Nie [1,2], Jiajia Liu [2,3], Gang Liu [4], Litong Lyu [5,*], Jie Li [5,*] and Zheng Chen [1,2,3]

1. The State Key Laboratory of Fluid Power and Mechatronic Systems, Zhejiang University, Hangzhou 310027, China
2. Hainan Instruction of Zhejiang University, Sanya 572025, China
3. Ocean College, Zhejiang University, Zhoushan 316021, China
4. No.2 Research Department, Wuhan Second Ship Design and Research Institute, Wuhan 430205, China
5. School of Mechanical Engineering, Shijiazhuang Tiedao University, Shijiazhuang 050043, China
* Correspondence: litong_lyu@stdu.edu.cn (L.L.); lijie@stdu.edu.cn (J.L.)

Abstract: Force tracking control for hydraulic series elastic actuators (SEAs) is the demand in robots interacting with the surrounding world. However, the inherent nonlinearities and uncertainties of the hydraulic system, as well as the unknown environment, make it difficult to achieve precise contact force control of hydraulic SEAs. Therefore, in this study, force tracking impedance control of hydraulic SEAs is developed considering interaction with an unknown environment in which the force tracking performance can be guaranteed in theory. Based on the typical force tracking impedance frame, the force tracking performance is improved by introducing backstepping control into the inner position controller to deal with the high-order nonlinear dynamics of the hydraulic SEA. In addition, the environment parameters are also estimated online by the adaptive method. Finally, comparative simulation is conducted with different interacting environments, which verifies the advantages of the proposed method.

Keywords: force tracking; impedance control; electro-hydrostatic actuator; hydraulic series elastic actuators

MSC: 70Q05; 70K20

1. Introduction

Force control has been the fundamental capacity and a hot topic research area for actuators due to its wider applications in industry and robot systems. These research issues may be broadly classified into two types: compliance and precision. For the case of compliance force control, this is commonly used in the collaboration between humans and robots, tele-robotic systems, and walking robots, which have been reported in the literature [1–3]. For the case of precise force control, this is usually applied in force loading simulation [4]. An important control method of compliance force control is impedance control presented in [5,6], which adjusts the contract force by using the relationship between force and position/velocity error. Impedance control avoids dangerousness when the actuators interact with the external environment. However, the force tracking performance is not satisfactory, especially in an unknown environment.

With the growing interest in providing force tracking capability for impedance control, force tracking impedance control was proposed by Seraji and Colbaugh [7]. The main contribution of this method presents accurate steady-state force tracking performance and flexibility when the external environment changes rapidly. Therefore, it is widely employed in hole operation, deburring, grinding, etc. A special device for precise force control is hydraulic series elastic actuators (SEAs), which are equipped with a spring between the power output shaft and the environment. The advantages of hydraulic SEAs can be summarized two aspects according to [8–11]. On the one hand, it provides high force fidelity, shock tolerance, and force sensing for interaction control. On the other hand, it enjoys the property of high power density compared with electric SEA. However, to our knowledge, the studies on the precise force tracking for hydraulic SEAs have not yet been established. In the existing literature, there is some research on modeling and controller design. Shen et al. [12] established the hydraulic SEAs model based on flow equations [13] and Newton's second law. Then they applied the impedance method to the hydraulic series elastic actuator using an outer loop feedback position and inner feedback force to achieve force control. Mustalahti et al. [14] established a fifth-order state space model for the hydraulic SEAs considering the non-linear dynamics of hydraulic systems, and the full stated feedback position controller was designed. However, the environment was regarded as known and rigid, which decreased the application of the proposed control. Furthermore, the force tracking performance is not satisfactory in the above papers. In order to improve force performance, force tracking impedance control is an available method. The main difficulties applying this control method to the hydraulic SEAs are as follows. Firstly, a position tracking error due to unknown dynamic uncertainties of hydraulic systems should be minimized. Secondly, the controller must be robust enough to deal with unknown environment stiffness.

These problems will also emerge when applying the force tracking impedance to electronic SEAs. Many efforts have been made to solve these problems. For the of case control frame, Zhao et al. [15] proposed a controller design criterion, which is composed of outer impedance and inner torque feedback loops for SEAs. For the detail control methods, based on disturbance observer control is applicable with overcoming the model uncertainty. For instance, Oh and Kong [16] applied a disturbance observer and feedforward controller to achieve the high-precision force control for the SEA system by utilizing the two-mass dynamic model. Sun et al. [17] proposed nonlinear observer-based force control for electro-hydraulic actuators, which does not require the cylinder position and velocity information. In addition, adaptive control is another method to deal with the model uncertainties. Liu et al. [18] proposed a Lyapunov-based parameter adaption control algorithm to compensate for parameter uncertainties. Baigzadehnoe et al. [19] and Wang et al. [20] used the adaptive fuzzy control method to achieve the force/position hybrid control for a robot manipulator. However, these literature concentrate on the electrical drive machinery system using the motor torque control close-ring. Unfortunately, the hydraulic SEAs system generally does not have a force closed loop. This is because the hydraulic system behaves with higher nonlinearity, stronger parameter uncertainties, and a higher dynamic model compared with electronic SEAs. In spite of this, many control methods have been proposed to achieve precise position control for hydraulic systems, for example, adaptive control, robust control, adaptive robust control [21–24], disturbance control based on the extended state observer [25,26], backstepping control [27], the sign of the error (RISE) control [28], sliding mode control [29] and so on. These theories have not been integrated into force tracking control to achieve perfect force tracking performance. Moreover, the adaptive techniques using force tracking errors have been proposed to estimate environment parameters (stiffness and damping). Misra et al. [30,31] applied adaptive techniques to bilateral manipulators for estimating environment parameters. Calanca et al. [32] developed an environment-adaptive force controller by estimating the environment dynamics online and continuously adjusting the control law accordingly. These theories provide a basis for this paper.

The purpose of this paper is to propose a force tracking impedance control method for the hydraulic series elastic actuators. It is robust with respect to uncertainties in both hydraulic dynamic model and environment stiffness. The main idea is to minimize force error by using an advanced position controller and a parameter adaptive method for an unknown environment.

This paper is organized as follows. The dynamic model of the nonlinear hydraulic SEAs is derived in Section 2. Section 3 demonstrates the design of the force tracking impedance controller. In Section 4, the simulation utilizing a hydraulic SEAs system verifies the high performance of the proposed controller. The conclusion and further research are presented in Section 5.

2. Modeling of the Hydraulic Series Elastic Actuators
2.1. Hydraulic SEAs Modeling

The structure of single-rod electro-hydrostatic series elastic actuators is shown in Figure 1. The environment is represented by a linear spring and a damper. Thus, the mathematical dynamics model of hydraulic SEAs is represented [8] as follows:

$$\begin{aligned} m_{cyl}\ddot{x}_{cyl} + B_{cyl}\dot{x}_{cyl} + K_s(x_{cyl} - x_{load}) - F_1 &= 0, \\ m_{load}\ddot{x}_{load} + B_e\dot{x}_{load} + (K_s + K_e)x_{load} - K_s x_{cyl} &= 0, \end{aligned} \quad (1)$$

where m_{cyl} and m_{load} are the mass of the piston and load in [kg], respectively. x_{cyl} and x_{load} are the position of the piston and load in [m], respectively; K_s is the spring stiffness of SEA in [N/mm]; B_{cyl} is the viscous damping coefficient of the piston in [Ns/m]; K_e is a linear spring stiffness and B_e a damping coefficient; and F_1 is the hydraulic driven force in [N].

The hydraulic driven force F_1 satisfies:

$$\begin{aligned} F_1 &= P_1 A_1 - P_2 A_2, \\ \dot{F}_1 &= \alpha(x_{cyl}, t) w_p + \beta(x_{cyl}, t) \dot{x}_{cyl} + \varphi(x_{cyl}, t) F_1 + \gamma(x_{cyl}, \dot{x}_{cyl}), \end{aligned} \quad (2)$$

where P_1, P_2 are the pressures of both chambers for hydraulic cylinders in [N/m^2]; A_1, A_2 are the areas of both chambers for hydraulic cylinders in [m^2]; w_P is the speed of the pump in [rad/s]; and $\alpha(x_{cyl}, t)$, $\beta(x_{cyl}, t)$, and $\varphi(x_{cyl}, t)$ are the parameters of the pump control hydraulic cylinder satisfying [26]:

$$\alpha(x_{cyl}, t) = \left(\frac{V_1}{A_1} + \frac{V_2}{A_2}\right)\beta_e D_p, \quad (3)$$

$$\beta(x_{cyl}, t) = \left(\frac{A_1^2}{V_1} + \frac{A_2^2}{V_2}\right)\beta_e, \quad (4)$$

$$\varphi(x_{cyl}, t) = \left(\frac{1}{V_1} + \frac{1}{V_2}\right)L_P \beta_e, \quad (5)$$

where D_P is the volumetric capacity of the pump in [m^3/rad], L_P is the total leakage coefficient of the pump and cylinder in [m^5/Ns], β_e is the effective bulk modulus of the systems in [N/m^2], and $V_1(x_{cyl}) = V_{A0} + A_1 x_{cyl}$ and $V_2(x_{cyl}) = V_{B0} - A_2 x_{cyl}$ are the volumes of chambers A and B in [m^3], respectively. x_{cyl} and x_{load} are physically bound as:

$$\begin{aligned} -x_{lim1} &\leq x_{cyl} \leq x_{lim1}, \\ -x_{lim2} &\leq x_{laod} \leq x_{lim2}, \end{aligned} \quad (6)$$

where x_{lim1}, x_{lim2} are positive constants. The ranges of $V_1(x_{cyl}), V_2(x_{cyl})$ are defined as:

$$\begin{aligned} V_{A0} - A_1 x_{lim1} = V_{Amin} &\leq V_1(x_{cyl}) \leq V_{Amax} = V_{A0} + A_1 x_{lim1}, \\ V_{B0} - A_2 x_{lim1} = V_{Bmin} &\leq V_2(x_{cyl}) \leq V_{Bmax} = V_{B0} + A_2 x_{lim2}. \end{aligned} \quad (7)$$

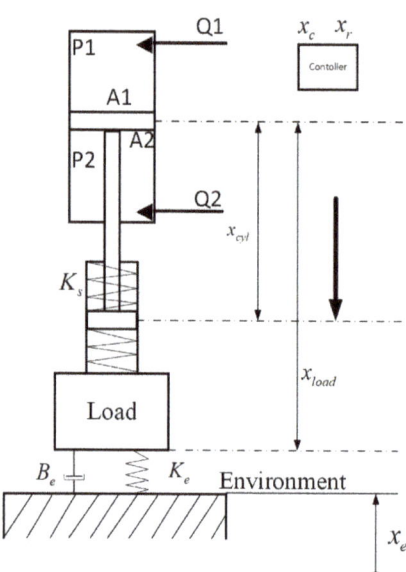

Figure 1. The structure of the single-rod electro-hydrostatic series elastic actuators. P_1 and P_2 are the pressures of both chambers for hydraulic cylinders, Q_1 and Q_2 are the flow of the two chambers, K_s is the spring stiffness of SEAs, and K_e and B_e are the environment stiffness and damping coefficient, respectively. x_{cyl} and x_{load} are the position of the piston and load, respectively; x_r and x_c are the reference and commanded position trajectories, respectively, and x_e is the location of the environment.

Remark 1. *In B_{cyl}, K_s, A_1, A_2, V_1, and V_2 can be easily known because they are mechanically fixed parameters. However, the β_e varies with the temperature and working time. In addition, considering the unmeasured states γ, the total model uncertainty can be defined as d_1, including γ and $\Delta\beta_e$. The d_1 is also bounded since V_{A0}, V_{B0}, and x_{cyl} are bounded.*

2.2. Problem Formulation

The new state variable x is defined as:

$$x = \begin{bmatrix} x_1 \\ x_2 \\ x_3 \\ x_4 \\ x_5 \end{bmatrix} = \begin{bmatrix} x_{load} \\ x_{cyl} \\ \dot{x}_{load} \\ \dot{x}_{cyl} \\ F_1 \end{bmatrix}.$$

Form the relationships (1) and (2), the hydraulic cylinder dynamics are obtained as:

$$\begin{aligned}
\dot{x}_1 &= x_3, \\
\dot{x}_2 &= x_4, \\
\dot{x}_3 &= \frac{-B_{load}x_3 - (K_s + K_e)x_1 + K_s x_2}{m_{load}}, \\
\dot{x}_4 &= \frac{-B_{cyl}x_4 - K_s(x_2 - x_1) + x_5}{m_{cyl}}, \\
\dot{x}_5 &= \alpha(x_2, t)w_p + \beta(x_2, t)x_4 + \varphi(x_2, t)x_5 + d_1.
\end{aligned} \quad (8)$$

The main goal in the controller design is the force tracking impedance control based on the advance position tracking control interacting with an unknown environment.

3. Force Tracking Impedance Control of SEAs Based on Dynamic Models

In this section, the force tracking impedance control is designed, which includes an inner position controller, environment estimation, and the desired impedance model. Its frame is shown in Figure 2. In this picture, some notations are defined as follows: x_r and x_c are the reference and commanded position trajectories, respectively. x_p is the output of the desired impedance model. w_p is the controller output. F_r is the desired contact forces, F_s is the hydraulic SEAs output torque computed by evaluating the spring displacement, and E is the force tracking error. F_e is the actual contact force acting on the environment, which can be measured with force senors. F_s and F_e drive the load dynamic system.

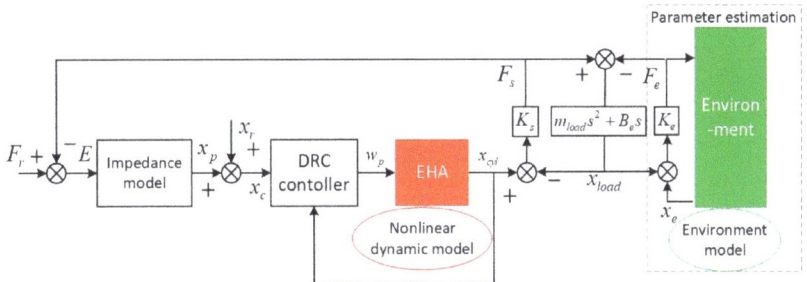

Figure 2. Frame of force tracking impedance control for hydraulic SEAs. Including designed impedance model, inner position controller (DRC), and environment parameters estimation. F_r is the desired contact forces, F_s is the hydraulic SEA output torque, F_e is the actual contact force acting on the environment, E is the force tracking error, and x_p is the output of the desired impedance model based on the force tracking error.

3.1. Inner Position Controller Design

A precise position controller is fundamental for improving the force tracking performance. According to the dynamic model, the direct robust position control (DRC) is designed via the backstepping method to deal with the high-order dynamics and nonlinearities of the hydraulic system. Assuming the system all state can be obtained, the three steps of the controller are as follows.

Step 1: The position tracking error is defined as $z_1 = x_2 - x_c(t)$. Then, it is defined z_2 as:

$$z_2 = \dot{z}_1 + k_1 z_1 = x_4 - x_{4eq}, \quad x_{4eq} = \dot{x}_c - k_1 z_1, \tag{9}$$

where x_c represents the command trajectory, which can be given later, and k_1 is the a positive stabilizing feedback gain.

Step 2: The error dynamic of z_2 is written as:

$$\dot{z}_2 = \frac{-B_{cyl} x_4 - K_s(x_2 - x_1) + x_5}{m_{cyl}} - \dot{x}_{4eq}. \tag{10}$$

Here, x_{5eq} is defined as the desired value of x_5. For the virtual control input for Step 2, the control law is:

$$\begin{aligned}
x_{5eq} &= x_{5eqa} + x_{5eqs1}, \\
x_{5eqa} &= m_{cyl}[(B_{cyl} x_4) + K_s(x_2 - x_1)] + \dot{x}_{4eq}, \\
x_{5eqs1} &= -k_2 z_2,
\end{aligned} \tag{11}$$

where x_{5eqa} is a physical-model-based compensation term, and x_{5eqs1} is the stabilizing feedback term. k_2 is the positive stabilizing feedback gain.

Step 3: We defined $z_3 = x_5 - x_{5eq}$ as the input discrepancy of Step 2. Let the pump speed w_p be the control input of Step 3 to make z_3 converge to zero or a small value. The error dynamics of z_3 is written as:

$$\dot{z}_3 = \alpha(x_2, t)w_p + \beta(x_2, t)x_v + \varphi(x_2, t)x_5 + d_1 - \dot{x}_{5eq}. \tag{12}$$

Considering the nonlinearities and uncertainties, the direct robust control law is designed as:

$$\begin{aligned} w_p &= \frac{w_a + w_{s1} + w_{s2}}{\alpha(x_2, t)}, \\ w_a &= -\beta(x_2, t)x_4 - \varphi(x_2, t)x_5 + \dot{x}_{5eq}, \\ w_{s1} &= -k_3 z_3, \\ w_{s2} &= -k_{3s2} z_3, \end{aligned} \tag{13}$$

where w_a is a physical-model-based compensation term, w_{s1} is the stabilizing feedback term, w_{s2} is the robust feedback term, k_3 is the positive stabilizing feedback gain, and k_{3s2} is the positive nonlinear robust feedback gain, which is chosen to satisfy the following robust conditions:

$$(i)\ z_3(k_{3s2} - d_1) \leq \epsilon_3, \qquad (ii)\ z_3 k_{3s2} \leq 0, \tag{14}$$

where ϵ_3 is a small enough and positive number.

Proposition 1. *The hydraulic SEA is equipped with an "almost perfect" inner position control loop such that the commanded position x_c is achieved, i.e., $x_{cyl} \approx x_c$.*

Proof. The positive definite function is:

$$V_3 = \frac{1}{2}z_1^2 + \frac{1}{2}z_2^2 + \frac{1}{2}z_3^2. \tag{15}$$

Taking a derivative in both sides of (15), it follows from (9), (10), (12), and the backstepping control laws (11) and (13) that

$$\begin{aligned} \dot{V}_3 &= -k_1 z_1^2 - k_2 z_2^2 - k_3 z_3^2 + z_3(k_{3s2} - d_1) \\ &\leq -k_1 z_1^2 - k_2 z_2^2 - k_3 z_3^2 + \epsilon_3 \\ &\leq -2\lambda V_3 + \epsilon_3. \end{aligned} \tag{16}$$

Consequently, the transient performance is quantified by:

$$V_3 \leq \exp(-2\lambda t)V_3(0) + \frac{\epsilon_3}{2\lambda}[1 - \exp(-2\lambda t)], \tag{17}$$

where $\lambda = \min\{k_1, k_2, k_3\}$.

The position tracking error of the inner position controller will converge to an arbitrarily small domain when $t \to \infty$, which completes the proof. □

3.2. Environment Parameters Estimation

Accurate knowledge of the environment parameters is also necessary for precise force tracking. The parameters' adaptive control aims to compute the estimated environment stiffness K_e and damping coefficient M_e online, which will be used to compute the reference trajectory x_r. Here, the desired trajectory is rewritten in terms of the estimated environment parameters:

$$x_r = \frac{F_r}{K_{es}} + x_e. \tag{18}$$

where K_{es} is a parameter relate to K_e and K_s. Considering the estimate force:

$$\hat{F}_e = \hat{K}_e(x_{load} - x_e) + \hat{B}_e(\dot{x}_{load}), \qquad (19)$$

the contact force estimation error is written as:

$$\hat{F}_e - F_e = (\hat{K}_e - K_e)(x_{load} - x_e) + (\hat{B}_e - B_e)(\dot{x}_{load}). \qquad (20)$$

We define $\tilde{F}_e = \hat{F}_e - F_e$; hence, the error can be written as:

$$\tilde{F}_e = \phi^T \tilde{\theta}, \qquad (21)$$

where $\phi = \begin{bmatrix} x_{load} - x_e \\ \dot{x}_{load} \end{bmatrix}$ and $\tilde{\theta} = \begin{bmatrix} \hat{K}_e - K_e \\ \hat{B}_e - B_e \end{bmatrix}$.

Define the parameter adaptive law as follows:

$$\dot{\hat{\theta}} = -\Gamma^{-1} \phi \tilde{F}_e, \qquad (22)$$

where Γ is a positive, definite, and symmetric gain matrix.

Proposition 2. *If F_e satisfies the persistent exciting (PE) condition, the environment parameters K_e and B_e can converge to an actual value.*

Proof. The Lyapunov function is denoted by:

$$V = \tilde{\theta}^T \Gamma \tilde{\theta}. \qquad (23)$$

Taking a derivative of (23) with respect to t, we conclude by parameter adaption law (22) that

$$\dot{V} = 2\tilde{\theta}^T \Gamma \dot{\tilde{\theta}} = -2\tilde{\theta}^T \phi \phi^T \tilde{\theta} < 0. \qquad (24)$$

Therefore, the estimation parameter $\hat{K}_e \to K_e$, $\hat{B}_e \to B_e$ when $t \to +\infty$, which completes the proof. □

Remark 2. *The DRC controller deals with the dynamic uncertainty of the hydraulic SEAs system, achieving the perfect position tracking, $x_{cyl} \approx x_c$, and the adaptive control methods estimate the unknown environment stiffness to produce the desired trajectory x_r.*

3.3. Force Tracking Impedance Controller Design

In this subsection, the impedance model is designed based on force tracking error. Then, the force tracking impedance control is developed.

The force tracking error is defined by;

$$E = F_r - F_s. \qquad (25)$$

The defined impedance (or called admittance) model is a second-order linear system with the transfer-function

$$Z_t(s) = M_t s^2 + B_t s + K_t.$$

where M_t, B_t, and K_t are the designed model parameters. The dynamical relationship between the force tracking error E and the position perturbation x_p mimics a mass–spring–damper system shown as:

$$x_p = \frac{E}{Z_t(s)} = \frac{E}{M_t s^2 + B_t s + K_t}. \qquad (26)$$

In order to achieve a precise force tracking performance, we set x_c and x_r satisfying:

$$x_c = x_r + x_p, \tag{27}$$

$$x_r = x_e + \frac{F_r}{K_{es}}, \tag{28}$$

where K_{es} satisfies:

$$K_{es} = \frac{K_e K_s}{K_e + K_s}. \tag{29}$$

With the above preparation, the main result is provided based on Propositions 1 and 2.

Theorem 1. *If the control input of inner position x_c is designed as (27) and the reference input x_r satisfies (28), then the force tracking error e_{ss} converges to 0 as $t \to +\infty$.*

Proof of Theorem 1. According to the system model, F_s and F_e can be written as:

$$\begin{aligned} F_s &= K_s(x_m - x_{load}), \\ F_e &= K_e(x_{load} - x_e), \\ F_s - F_e &= m_{load}\ddot{x}_{load} + B_e \dot{x}_{load}. \end{aligned} \tag{30}$$

Performing Laplace transform and Proposition 1, it is concluded by (30) that

$$F_s(s) = \frac{Z_e(s) K_s(s)}{Z_e(s) + K_s} X_c(s) + \frac{K_s K_e}{Z_e(s) + K_s} X_e(s), \tag{31}$$

where $Z_e = m_{load}s^2 + B_e s + k_e$.

Using Laplace transform for (25), one has:

$$\begin{aligned} E_s(s) &= F_r(s) - F_s(s) \\ &= F_r(s) - \frac{Z_e(s) K_s(s)}{Z_e(s) + K_s}(X_r(s) + X_p(s)) - \frac{K_s K_e}{Z_e(s) + K_s} X_e(s). \end{aligned} \tag{32}$$

Submitting (26) and (28) to (32), we obtain:

$$E_s(s) = \frac{Z_t(s)(Z_e(s) + K_s)}{Z_t(s) Z_e(s) + K_s(Z_t(s) + Z_e(s))} [F_r(s) - \frac{Z_e(s) K_s}{Z_e(s) + K_s} X_r(s) - \frac{K_s K_e}{Z_e(s) + K_s} X_e(s)]. \tag{33}$$

Thus, the steady-state force tracking error satisfies:

$$e_{ss} = \frac{K_t}{K_t + K_{es}}(F_r - K_{es} x_r - K_{es} x_e), \tag{34}$$

Assuming the environment can be regarded as quasi-static, $\dot{x}_e = 0$. Then, it is concluded that $e_{ss} \to 0$ when the reference position trajectory is chosen as (28). □

Remark 3. *The force tracking performance can be guaranteed in theory considering the interaction of hydraulic system uncertainties with an unknown environment.*

4. Simulations Result

In this section, the performance of the proposed method is evaluated using simulations by Simulink Toolbox of Matlab. Two different simulation cases were conducted. Case 1: the relation between the inner position controller and the force tracking performance is evaluated considering hydraulic SEAs interacting with a rigid environment. Case 2: the environment parameters estimation performance and force tracking performance are evaluated by different pre-set values of environment stiffness.

4.1. Configuration of Simulations

The configuration parameters of fundamental sample time are chosen as 0.001 s. Using s-function established the mathematical model of the nonlinear dynamic system and controller model.

4.1.1. Controller Set Up

Four different force tracking controller settings were implemented, such as Controller 1 (C_1), Controller 2 (C_2), Controller 3 (C_3), Controller 4 (C_4). Among them, the impedance model parameters were designed as:

$$Z_t(s) = 10s^2 + 100s + 250. \tag{35}$$

The control gains were tuned to obtain the best tracking performances in both methods. The controller parameters were designed as follows:
C_1: Inner position controller with DRC:

$$k_1 = 100, \ k_2 = 50{,}000, \ k_3 = 600, \ k_{3s2} = -\frac{1}{4\epsilon_3}, \ \epsilon_3 = 0.001. \tag{36}$$

C_2: Inner position controller with PID:

$$u = k_{p2}(x_{cyl} - x_r) + k_{i2}\int_0^t (x_{cyl} - x_r) + k_{d2}(\dot{x}_{cyl} - \dot{x}_r), \tag{37}$$

where the control gains $k_{p2} = 9200$, $k_{i2} = 5000$ and $k_{d2} = 100$.
C_3: Direct force feedback PID controller:

$$u = k_{p3}(F_e - F_r) + k_{i3}\int_0^t (F_e - F_r) + k_{d3}(\dot{F}_e - \dot{F}_r), \tag{38}$$

where the control gains $k_{p3} = 100$, $k_{i3} = 10$, and $k_{d3} = 0.1$.
C_4: Inner PID position controller without impedance model. The PID controller has the same parameters as the C_2 controller, except without an impedance model.

4.1.2. Model Parameter

The hydraulic SEAs model parameters used are listed in Table 1, which include some mechanical parameters and viscous damping. d_1 used in the simulation was designed as:

$$d_1 = (100 + 1000\exp(-0.1(t-1)))\sin(t). \tag{39}$$

The β_e used in controller is 7×10^8, which is different from the model. The desired tracking trajectory is designed as implementing a linear ramp up profile, which has a third-order derivative, as shown in Figure 3.

Table 1. The model parameters.

Parameter	Value	Parameter	Value
m_{cyl}	20	A_1	2.3758×10^{-3}
m_{load}	100	A_2	1.76×10^{-3}
B_{cyl}	2000	V_{A0}	1.924×10^{-4}
β_e	7×10^8	V_{B0}	5.702×10^{-4}
K_s	10,000	L_P	2.4×10^{-11}

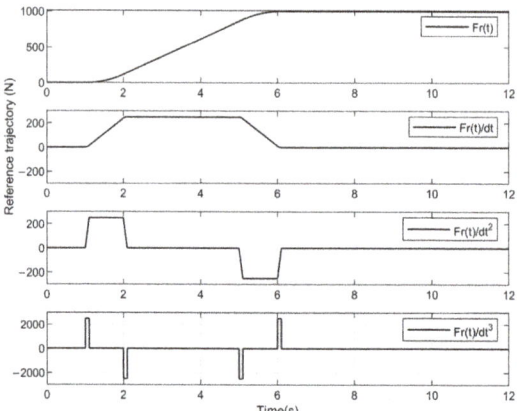

Figure 3. Reference force tracking trajectory including F_r, $\dot{F}_r$, $\ddot{F}_r$, and $\dddot{F}_r$ used in controller design.

4.2. HSEA in Contact with a Rigid Environment

If the environment stiffness is infinite or much greater than the stiffness of the HSEAs, then $K_{es} \approx K_s$, which is often used in some work situations. The tracking performances of the controllers are shown in Figures 4 and 5. Comparing the C_2 and C_1 controllers, the C_1 controller, which is equipped with the DRC position inner controller, behaves with a smaller steady-state error and faster transient performance. This is because the advanced position controller overcomes the hydraulic nonlinearity and uncertainty, which decreased the position tracking errors. Therefore, the force tracking performance is improved. Moreover, the C_4 controller shows worse performance because the force feedback information is not used by the impedance outer controller. Furthermore, the role of the impedance controller is shown in Figure 6, and x_p varies drastically for the C_2 controller, which is due to the slow convergence rate. However, x_p only comes into play at the turning point for the C1 controller, which is based on the perfect transient response. Therefore, the proposed method with an advanced position controller and force impedance controller can achieve precise force tracking control. The force tracking result is better compared with that in [8].

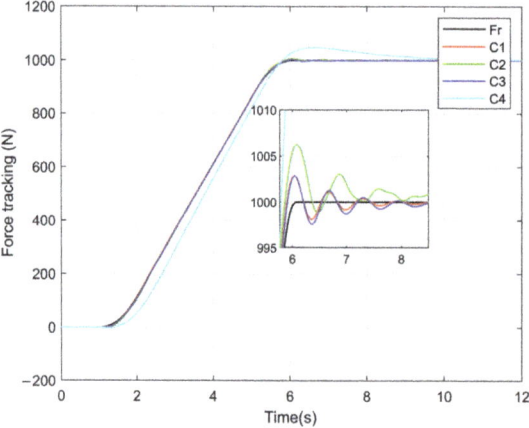

Figure 4. Force tracking performance in contact with the rigid environment. Fr is the reference force tracking trajectory. C_1 controller behaves with a smaller steady-state error and faster transient performance compared with other controllers.

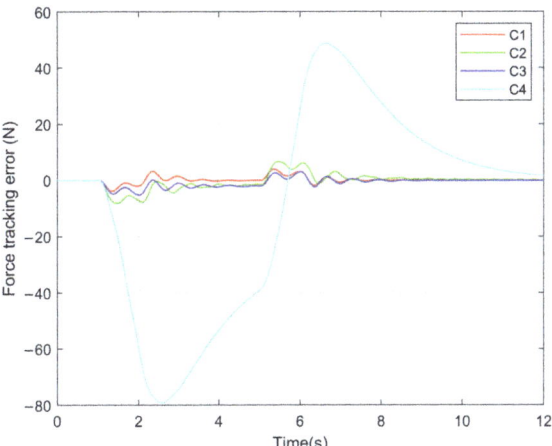

Figure 5. Force tracking errors in contact with the rigid environment. C_4 controller presents the largest force tracking error. C_1 controller has a fast speed of force tracking error coverage to zero.

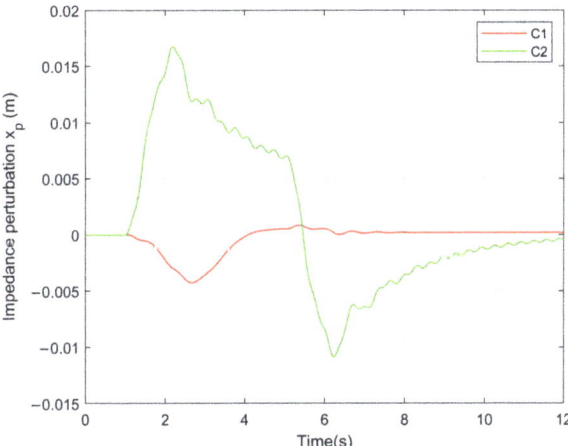

Figure 6. Position perturbation. x_p plays a role in the turning point to make the actuator present compliance.

4.3. HSEA Adaptive Environment Parameter

If the environmental stiffness is similar to the HSEAs and the environmental parameters are unknown, adaptive technology is an effective method to achieve force tracking control. The tracking performances based on environment parameter estimation are shown in Figure 7. The parameter estimation performance is shown in Figure 8. The C_2 controller had a larger force-tracking error than the proposed C_1 controller, especially at the outset and the stabilization phase. The stiffness of the environment and damping coefficients are estimated by the proposed adaptive technology. The adaptive gain was $[1000, 0; 0, 66]$. The estimation parameters satisfactorily follow the actual parameters $[10^4; 200]$.

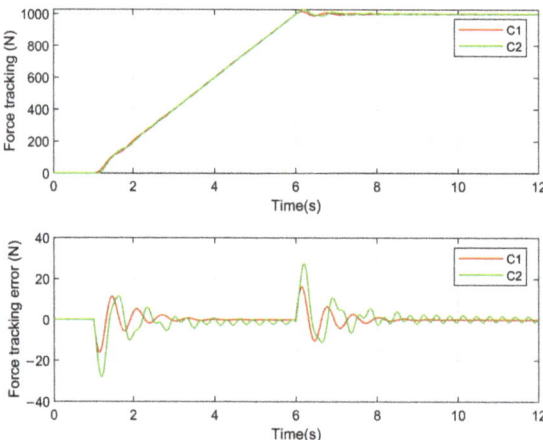

Figure 7. Force tracking performance considering unknown and invariant environment-adaptive parameters. This picture shows that adaptive technology is an effective method to achieve force tracking control.

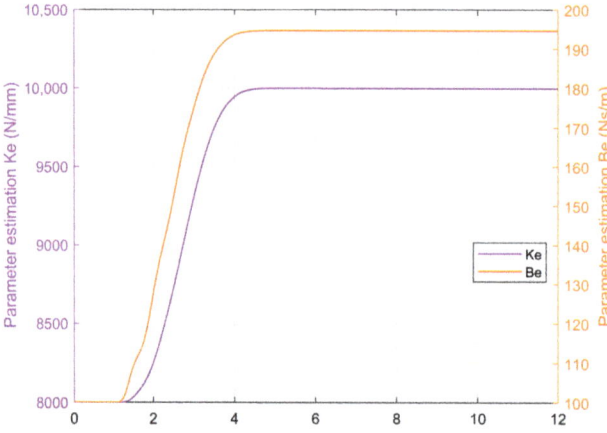

Figure 8. Environment parameter estimation performance in case of invariant stiffness. Environment parameter can be converged to actual value as the theory shows.

Furthermore, the variable stiffness case is analyzed as follows. The stiffness of the environment changes from 1.0×10^4 to 1.2×10^4 in 5 s. The force tracking performances are shown in Figure 9, and the estimated parameters are in Figure 10. Obviously, this parameter estimation has good validity, and the force tracking performance is also verified. The peaking phenomenon occurred because the environment stiffness suddenly changes, which shows the role of impedance control, that is, to a certain degree of compliance.

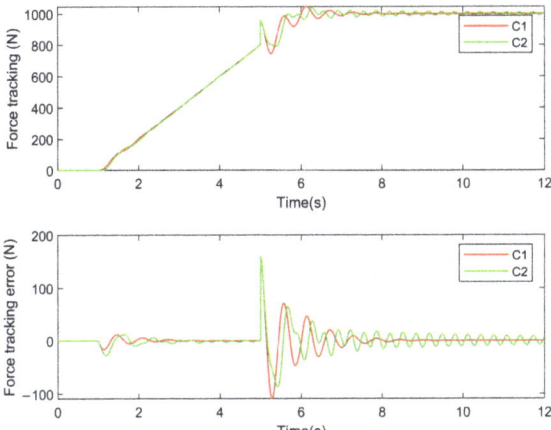

Figure 9. Force tracking performance for variable stiffness. The stiffness of the environment changes from 1.0×10^4 to 1.2×10^4 in 5 s. C_1 Controller presents faster transience and softer compliance performance.

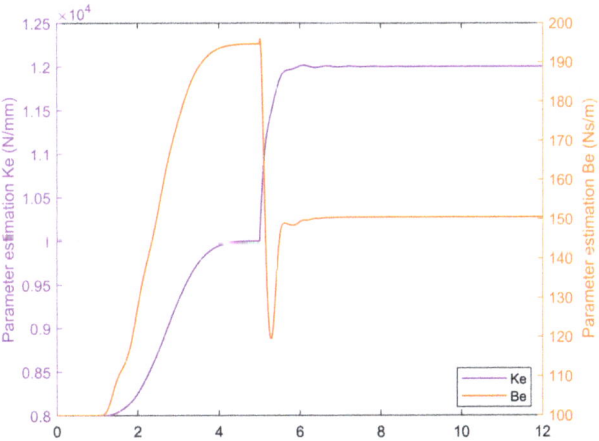

Figure 10. Environment parameter estimation performance for variable stiffness. The stiffness of the environment changes from 1.0×10^4 to 1.2×10^4 in 5 s, in which the environment parameter estimation performance is verified.

5. Conclusions

In this paper, a precise force tracking impedance control with an advanced position inner controller and an adaptive environment parameter was developed for hydraulic SEAs. In comparison with [8], the application is expanded due to the online environment parameters estimation. Furthermore, steady-state performance can be guaranteed. In addition, the force tracking precision has been improved due to the inner position control being modified by integrating the direct robust control method based on the force tracking impedance control frame. The direct robust control overcame the model uncertainty and the nonlinear and higher-order dynamic property of the hydraulic system via a backstepping procedure. The performance of the proposed method was validated using simulation. In the future, we will conduct experiments in actual systems, and the frequency characteristics will be tested. In addition, on the basis of this study [33–35], the energy control, coordinated/synchronized control and fault-Tolerant Control will be conducted.

Author Contributions: Investigation, Y.N. and G.L.; methodology, Y.N., J.L. (Jiajia Liu), L.L. and Z.C.; project administration, Z.C.; resources, Y.N., G.L. and J.L. (Jie Li); software, J.L. (Jiajia Liu); supervision, Z.C.; validation, J.L. (Jiajia Liu); writing—original draft, J.L. (Jiajia Liu); writing—review and editing, L.L. and J.L. (Jie Li). All authors have read and agreed to the published version of the manuscript.

Funding: This work was funded by the S&T Program of Hebei (E2021210011), the National Natural Science Foundation of China (52105065), the Hainan Special PhD Scientific Research Foundation of Sanya Yazhou Bay Science and Technology City (No. HSPHDSRF-2022-04-004), the Open Foundation of the State Key Laboratory of Fluid Power and Mechatronic Systems (GZKF-202127), and the Hainan Provincial National Natural Science Foundation of China (No. 521MS065).

Institutional Review Board Statement: Not applicable.

Informed Consent Statement: Not applicable.

Data Availability Statement: Not applicable.

Acknowledgments: We wish to thank Xiaoyan Li's help in science writing.

Conflicts of Interest: The authors declare no conflict of interest.

References

1. Jung, S.; Hsia, T.C. Neural network impedance force control of robot manipulator. *IEEE Trans. Ind. Electron.* **1998**, *45*, 451–461. [CrossRef]
2. Chen, Z.; Huang, F.; Chen, W.; Zhang, J.; Sun, W.; Chen, J.; Gu, J.; Zhu, S. RBFNN-Based Adaptive Sliding Mode Control Design for Delayed Nonlinear Multilateral Telerobotic System With Cooperative Manipulation. *IEEE Trans. Ind. Inform.* **2020**, *16*, 1236–1247. [CrossRef]
3. Yu, B.; Liu, R.; Zhu, Q.; Huang, Z.; Jin, Z.; Wang, X. High-Accuracy Force Control With Nonlinear Feedforward Compensation for a Hydraulic Drive Unit. *IEEE Access* **2019**, *7*, 101063–101072. [CrossRef]
4. Li, X.; Zhu, Z.C.; Rui, G.C.; Cheng, D.; Shen, G.; Tang, Y. Force Loading Tracking Control of an Electro-Hydraulic Actuator Based on a Nonlinear Adaptive Fuzzy Backstepping Control Scheme. *Symmetry* **2018**, *10*, 155. [CrossRef]
5. Jung, S.; Hsia, T.C.; Bonitz, R.G. Force Tracking Impedance Control of Robot Manipulators Under Unknown Environment. *IEEE Trans. Control. Syst. Technol.* **2004**, *12*, 474–483. [CrossRef]
6. Alleyne, A.; Liu, R.; Wright, H. On the limitations of force tracking control for hydraulic active suspensions. In Proceedings of the American Control Conference (IEEE Cat. No.98CH36207), Philadelphia, PA, USA, 24–26 June 1998; Volume 1, pp. 43–47. [CrossRef]
7. Seraji, H.; Colbaugh, R. Force tracking in impedance control. In Proceedings of the IEEE International Conference on Robotics and Automation. Atlanta, GA, USA, 2–6 May 1993; Volume 2, pp. 499–506. [CrossRef]
8. Mustalahti, P.; Mattila, J. Position-Based Impedance Control Design for a Hydraulically Actuated Series Elastic Actuator. *Energies* **2022**, *15*, 2503. [CrossRef]
9. Cao, X.; Aref, M.; Mattila, J. Design and Control of a Flexible Joint as a Hydraulic Series Elastic Actuator For Manipulation Applications. In Proceedings of the IEEE International Conference on Cybernetics and Intelligent Systems (CIS) and IEEE Conference on Robotics, Automation and Mechatronics (RAM), Bangkok, Thailand, 18–20 November 2019; pp. 553–558. [CrossRef]
10. Paine, N.; Oh, S.; Sentis, L. Design and Control Considerations for High-Performance Series Elastic Actuators. *IEEE/ASME Trans. Mechatron.* **2014**, *19*, 1080–1091. [CrossRef]
11. Calanca, A.; Muradore, R.; Fiorini, P. A Review of Algorithms for Compliant Control of Stiff and Fixed-Compliance Robots. *IEEE/ASME Trans. Mechatron.* **2016**, *21*, 613–624. [CrossRef]
12. Shen, K.; Zhang, C.; Cheng, Y.; Wang, J.; Wei, Q.; Ma, H. Impedance control of hydraulic series elastic actuation. In Proceedings of the Chinese Automation Congress (CAC), Shanghai, China, 6–8 November 2020; pp. 2393–2398. [CrossRef]
13. Sohail, M.; Nazir, U.; El-Zahar, E.R.; Park, C.; Jamshed, W.; Mukdasai, K.; Galal, A.M. Galerkin finite element analysis for the augmentation in thermal transport of ternary-hybrid nanoparticles by engaging non-Fourier's law. *Sci. Rep.* **2022**, *12*, 13497. [CrossRef]
14. Mustalahti, P.; Mattila, J. Impedance Control of Hydraulic Series Elastic Actuator with a Model-Based Control Design. In Proceedings of the IEEE/ASME International Conference on Advanced Intelligent Mechatronics (AIM), Boston, MA, USA, 6–9 July 2020; pp. 966–971. [CrossRef]
15. Zhao, Y.; Paine, N.; Jorgensen, S.J.; Sentis, L. Impedance Control and Performance Measure of Series Elastic Actuators. *IEEE Trans. Ind. Electron.* **2018**, *65*, 2817–2827. [CrossRef]

16. Oh, S.; Kong, K. High-Precision Robust Force Control of a Series Elastic Actuator. *IEEE/ASME Trans. Mechatron.* **2017**, *22*, 71–80. [CrossRef]
17. Sun, H.; Chiu, G.T.-C. Nonlinear observer based force control of electro-hydraulic actuators. In Proceedings of the American Control Conference (Cat. No. 99CH36251), San Diego, CA, USA, 2–4 June 1999; pp. 764–768. [CrossRef]
18. Liu, R.; Alleyne, A. Nonlinear force/pressure tracking of an electro-hydraulic actuator. *IFAC Proc. Vol.* **1999**, *32*, 952–957. [CrossRef]
19. Baigzadehnoe, B.; Rahmani, Z.; Khosravi, A.; Rezaie, B. On position/force tracking control problem of cooperative robot manipulators using adaptive fuzzy backstepping approach. *ISA Trans.* **2017**, *70*, 432–446. [CrossRef] [PubMed]
20. Wang, Z.; Zou, L.; Su, X.; Luo, G.; Li, R.; Huang, Y. Hybrid force/position control in workspace of robotic manipulator in uncertain environments based on adaptive fuzzy control. *Robot. Auton. Syst.* **2021**, *145*, 103870. [CrossRef]
21. Helian, B.; Chen, Z.; Yao, B. Precision Motion Control of a Servomotor-Pump Direct-Drive Electrohydraulic System With a Nonlinear Pump Flow Mapping. *IEEE Trans. Ind. Electron.* **2020**, *67*, 8638–8648. [CrossRef]
22. Helian, B.; Chen, Z.; Yao, B.; Lyu, L.; Li, C. Accurate Motion Control of a Direct-Drive Hydraulic System With an Adaptive Nonlinear Pump Flow Compensation. *IEEE/ASME Trans. Mechatron.* **2021**, *26*, 2593–2603. [CrossRef]
23. Lyu, L.; Chen, Z.; Yao, B. Advanced Valves and Pump Coordinated Hydraulic Control Design to Simultaneously Achieve High Accuracy and High Efficiency. *IEEE Trans. Control Syst. Technol.* **2021**, *29*, 236–248. [CrossRef]
24. Lyu, L.; Chen, Z.; Yao, B. Development of Pump and Valves Combined Hydraulic System for Both High Tracking Precision and High Energy Efficiency. *IEEE Trans. Ind. Electron.* **2019**, *66*, 7189–7198. [CrossRef]
25. Guo, Q.; Zhang, Y.; Celler, B.G.; Su, S.W. Backstepping Control of Electro-Hydraulic System Based on Extended-State-Observer With Plant Dynamics Largely Unknown. *IEEE Trans. Ind. Electron.* **2016**, *63*, 6909–6920. [CrossRef]
26. Nie, Y.; Liu, J.; Lao, Z.; Chen, Z. Modeling and Extended State Observer-Based Backstepping Control of Underwater Electro Hydrostatic Actuator with Pressure Compensator and External Load. *Electronics* **2022**, *11*, 1286. [CrossRef]
27. Temporelli, R.; Boisvert, M.; Micheau, P. Control of an Electromechanical Clutch Actuator Using a Dual Sliding Mode Controller: Theory and Experimental Investigations. *IEEE/ASME Trans. Mechatron.* **2019**, *24*, 1674–1685. [CrossRef]
28. Deng, W.; Yao, J. Asymptotic Tracking Control of Mechanical Servosystems With Mismatched Uncertainties. *IEEE/ASME Trans. Mechatron.* **2021**, *26*, 2204–2214. [CrossRef]
29. Shen, W.; Wang, J. An integral terminal sliding mode control scheme for speed control system using a double-variable hydraulic transformer. *ISA Trans.* **2022**, *124*, 386–394. [CrossRef]
30. Misra, S.; Okamura, A.M. Environment parameter estimation during bilateral telemanipulation. In Proceedings of the 14th Symposium on Haptic Interfaces for Virtual Environment and Teleoperator Systems, Alexandria, VA, USA, 25–26 March 2006; pp. 301–307. [CrossRef]
31. Haddadi, A.; Hashtrudi-Zaad, K. Online contact impedance identification for robotic systems. In Proceedings of the IEEE/RSJ International Conference on Intelligent Robots and Systems, Nice, France, 22–26 September 2008; pp. 974–980. [CrossRef]
32. Calanca, A.; Fiorini, P. Understanding Environment-Adaptive Force Control of Series Elastic Actuators. *IEEE/ASME Trans. Mechatron.* **2018**, *23*, 413–423. [CrossRef]
33. Lin, T.; Lin, Y.; Ren, H.; Chen, H.; Li, Z.; Chen. Q,. A double variable control load sensing system for electric hydraulic excavator. *Energy* **2021**, *223*, 119999. [CrossRef]
34. Ding, R.; Cheng, M.; Jiang, L.; Hu, G. Active Fault-Tolerant Control for Electro-Hydraulic Systems With an Independent Metering Valve Against Valve Faults. *IEEE Trans. Ind. Electron.* **2021**, *68*, 7221–7232. [CrossRef]
35. Chen, Z.; Li, C.; Yao, B.; Yuan, M.; Yang, C. Integrated Coordinated/Synchronized Contouring Control of a Dual-Linear-Motor-Driven Gantry. *IEEE Trans. Ind. Electron.* **2020**, *67*, 3944–3954. [CrossRef]

Data-Driven Event-Triggered Platoon Control under Denial-of-Service Attacks

Zengwei Li, Lin Zhu, Zhenling Wang * and Weiwei Che

Shandong Key Laboratory of Industrial Control Technology, School of Automation, Qingdao University, Qingdao 266071, China
* Correspondence: wangzhenling@qdu.edu.cn

Abstract: This paper proposes an event-triggered model-free adaptive platoon control (MFAPC) solution for non-linear vehicle systems under denial-of-service (DoS) attacks. First, the non-linear vehicle system is transformed into an equivalent linear data model using the dynamic linearization technique. Second, to save limited communication resources and reduce the influence of cyber attacks, a novel event-triggered mechanism and attack compensation method are designed. Then, based on the equivalent linear data model, a new resilient event-triggered MFAPC algorithm is developed to achieve the vehicle platoon control objective under DoS attacks. Finally, the effectiveness of the proposed control scheme is verified using an example.

Keywords: model-free adaptive platoon control; event-triggered; non-linear vehicle system; attack compensation; DoS attacks

MSC: 93D25

1. Introduction

With the rapid development of human society and the economy, automobiles have become increasingly widely used and important in our lives. However, the increased number of cars inevitably brings with it a variety of problems, such as environmental pollution, energy shortages, traffic congestion, traffic accidents and so on, which have a serious impact on the development of society. In recent years, various intelligent traffic control methods have been applied to vehicle systems aiming to solve these problems. For example, longitudinal dynamics control for autonomous driving of intelligent vehicles using a sliding mode controller based on a radial basis function neural network was investigated in [1]. In [2], a new application framework for intelligent transportation systems (ITS) based on 5G network slicing was proposed. In [3], an intelligent traffic control scheme using cloud computing and big-data mining for ITS was developed.

Vehicle platoon control, as an intelligent control method, has been applied in vehicle systems. In [4], the vehicle platoon control problem of linear heterogeneous vehicle systems subject to disturbances was investigated and an H_∞ control scheme was developed to guarantee the string stability of the platoon. Under the condition of input saturation, the vehicle platoon control problem was examined using a variable time headway strategy in [5]. In [6], the vehicular platoon control problem was investigated, with an event-triggered distributed adaptive observer used to ensure that the platoon achieved a stable state asymptotically. The authors of [7] proposed a longitudinal platoon controller for connected vehicles. In [8], a distributed consensus platooning problem affected by time-varying, heterogeneous and wireless communication delays was discussed. It is worth noting that the above studies are based on system models. However, many system models cannot be accurately applied in real scenarios. Thus, data-based control methods have been developed to address vehicle platoon control problems. A vehicle platoon control strategy to reduce energy consumption based on a reinforcement learning algorithm was proposed in [9]. The cooperative adaptive cruise control (CACC) problem was examined in [10]. In addition, the vehicle eco-adaptive cruise control problem was examined in [11] and an optimal control scheme to ensure the safe distance of the vehicles was proposed using a reinforcement learning method.

Model-free adaptive control (MFAC), as a kind of data-driven method, was first proposed in 1994 and has been widely applied [12–20]. The main feature of the MFAC method is that the plant can achieve its control objective based on measurement data for the system inputs/outputs. In [13], a dynamic linearization technique for single-input and single-output (SISO) non-linear discrete-time systems was proposed. In [14], a brief overview of the MFAC was presented. The data-driven MFAC problem for multiple-input and multiple-output (MIMO) non-linear discrete-time systems was discussed in [15]. In [17], the MFAC problem was solved using a full-form dynamic linearization technique. The MFAC problem for MIMO non-affine systems with unknown non-linear dynamics was investigated, and verified experimentally, in [18]. In [20], a model-free adaptive integral sliding mode controller was devised for non-linear discrete-time systems. In addition, in recent years, MFAC methods have been applied to vehicle systems. In [21], the model-free adaptive integral sliding-mode-constrained-control problem of autonomous vehicle parking systems was investigated. A novel dual successive projection-based MFAC approach was proposed and applied to autonomous cars in [22]. In [23,24], the heading control of unmanned surface vehicles was investigated using the MFAC method.

It should be noted that network communication resources are limited. To save resources, an event-triggered control scheme has been proposed for the controller design. There has been some research on event-triggered model-free adaptive control. The design problem of an event-triggered MFAC controller was studied in [25,26]. An event-triggered disturbance observer was designed to estimate the disturbance using intermittent system information in [27]. Additionally, the event-triggered model-free adaptive iterative learning control problem was investigated in [28]. It should be pointed out, however, that the event-triggered conditions under which results to date have been obtained [25–28] are complexed, which leads to an increase in computational costs. Therefore, it is necessary to design a simple event-triggered condition, which is a primary purpose of this paper.

With the development of networked communication technology, increasing attention has been paid to networked control systems [29–33]. In networked control systems, the system states measured by sensors are transmitted to the controller via a wireless network. Some network effects may occur during data transmission, such as time-delays, packet dropouts and malicious attacks, etc., which will degrade, or even destroy, system performance [34,35]. Consequently, some work has been carried out to solve these problems. In [36], the distributed consensus tracking problem under malicious denial-of-service (DoS) attacks was investigated. In [37], a class of networked non-linear systems affected by packet disorder and network-induced delay was discussed; [38] extended the result to the two-channel packet dropout case. In addition, the MFAC problem of non-linear systems suffering from fading measurements was studied in [39]. It is noted that cyber attacks are inevitable, threatening system safety and performance. There have been some investigations focusing on network attacks in relation to the MFAC problem. A resilient control scheme for non-linear systems suffering from fading measurements was designed in [40]. In [41], an MFAC scheme based on an attack predictor was devised against jamming attacks for non-linear cyber-physical systems. In [42], the data-based MFAC problem for non-linear cyber-physical systems with event-triggered communication scheduling was investigated. However, in [41,42], the time-varying parameters used to estimate the non-linear characteristics were assumed not to be attacked, which is a strong assumption. Therefore, it is worth exploring how this assumption might be avoided.

Motivated by the above analyses, the event-triggered model-free adaptive platoon control (MFAPC) problem of non-linear vehicle systems under DoS attacks was investigated in this paper. First, the non-linear vehicle systems were transformed into a linear data model via linearization. Then, a resilient event-triggered MFAPC scheme was designed to achieve the vehicle platoon control target under DoS attacks. The contributions of this paper are as follows:

(1) In contrast to existing MFAC-based vehicle control methods [21–24], a novel MFAC framework for vehicle platoon control under DoS attacks is established. To mitigate the effects of DoS attacks, a new attack compensation mechanism is proposed using the latest available data. Then, a resilient event-triggered MFAPC algorithm is designed to enable simultaneous velocity and path tracking.

(2) Compared with existing event-triggered MFAC results reported in [26,28], where the event-triggered condition requires an additional tracking error trigger condition, the proposed event-triggered condition removes additional conditions, so that the event-triggered design is less conservative.

The remainder of this paper is arranged as follows: The MFAPC framework and formulation of the problem are described in Section 2. The security analysis undertaken and the control algorithm design are described in Section 3. The simulation results and conclusions are presented in Section 4 and Section 5, respectively.

2. MFAPC Framework and Problem Formulation

The system framework for a non-linear vehicle system under DoS attacks is illustrated in Figure 1. The sensor measures the system output, i.e., the position and velocity of the vehicle. The estimator is used to estimate the adaptive parameter. The system outputs $y(p)$ and estimated adaptive parameter $\hat{\psi}(p)$ are packaged and transmitted to the controller via a wireless network that may be attacked.

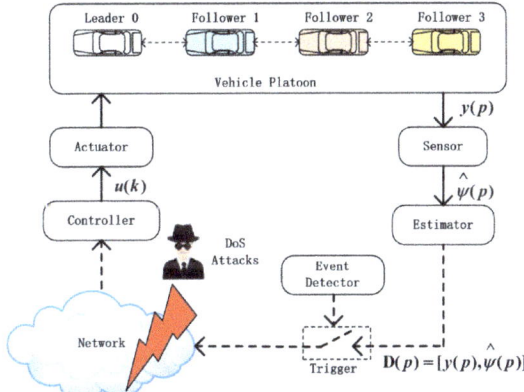

Figure 1. System framework with DoS attacks.

2.1. Vehicle System Modeling

Considering the platoon control problem for vehicles moving along the road, the dynamic model of the ith vehicle is described by

$$\begin{aligned} \dot{x}_i(t) &= v_i(t), \\ \dot{v}_i(t) &= u_i(t) + f_i(x_i(t), v_i(t)), i \in N, \end{aligned} \quad (1)$$

where $x_i(t) \in \mathbb{R}$, $v_i(t) \in \mathbb{R}$ and $u_i(t) \in \mathbb{R}$ represent the position, velocity and control input of the ith vehicle, respectively. $f_i(\cdot, \cdot) \in \mathbb{R}^2 \mapsto \mathbb{R}$ is an unknown non-linear function.

Convert (1) to the following discrete-time system [23,43]:

$$\begin{aligned} x_i(p+1) &= x_i(p) + Tv_i(p), \\ v_i(p+1) &= v_i(p) + Tu_i(p) + Tf_i(x_i(p), v_i(p)), \end{aligned} \quad (2)$$

where T denotes the sampling time.

The leading vehicle is described as

$$\begin{aligned} x_0(k+1) &= x_0(k) + Tv_0(k), \\ v_0(k+1) &= v_0(k) + Tf_0(x_0(k), v_0(k)). \end{aligned} \quad (3)$$

Remark 1. *The leading vehicle provides reference signals to the following vehicle. Therefore, the control input of the leading vehicle is not considered in this paper. Moreover, it is assumed that the information for the leading vehicle is not affected by network attacks.*

The following assumptions and lemmas are used:

Assumption 1. *The partial derivative of $f_i(\cdot, \cdot)$ with respect to $u_i(p)$ is continuous [14].*

Assumption 2. *The non-linear systems satisfy the generalized Lipschitz condition that the output changes $|\Delta y_i(p+1)| \leq k_i |\Delta u_i(p)|$ with $\Delta y_i(p+1) = y_i(p+1) - y_i(p)$, $\Delta u_i(p) = u_i(p) - u_i(p-1)$, and $k_i > 0$ is a constant [14].*

Lemma 1. *For non-linear systems that satisfy Assumptions 1, 2 and $|\Delta u_i(p)| \neq 0$ for all p, there exists a time-varying pseudo-partial derivative (PPD) parameter $\psi_i(p)$ such that the non-linear systems can be converted to the following compact-form dynamic linearization data model [15]:*

$$\Delta y_i(p+1) = \psi_i(p) \Delta u_i(p), \quad (4)$$

where $\psi_i(p)$ is bounded and satisfies $|\psi_i(p)| \leq k_i$, with k_i being a constant. If $\Delta u_i(p) = 0$, then define $\Delta y_i(p+1) = 0$.

Assumption 3. *The sign of the PPD parameter $\psi_i(p)$ remains unchanged for all p and satisfies $\psi_i(p) > \sigma_i > 0$ or $\psi_i(p) < -\sigma_i$ for all p, where σ_i is a constant.*

For the purpose of studying the vehicle platoon control problem, redefine the output of the vehicle platoon system (2) as $y_i(p+1) = x_i(p+1) + K_i v_i(p+1)$ with $K_i > 0$ being determined later, then the increment form $\Delta y_i(p+1)$ is calculated as $\Delta y_i(p+1) = \Delta x_i(p+1) + K_i \Delta v_i(p+1)$. According to (2), we can get $\Delta x_i(p+1) = \Delta x_i(p) + T \Delta v_i(p)$ and $\Delta v_i(p+1) = \Delta v_i(p) + T \Delta u_i(p) + T \Delta f_i(x_i(p), v_i(p))$. Then, we have

$$\begin{aligned} \Delta y_i(p+1) &= \Delta x_i(p+1) + K_i \Delta v_i(p+1) \\ &= \Delta x_i(p) + T \Delta v_i(p) + K_i [\Delta v_i(p) + T \Delta u_i(p) + T \Delta f_i(x_i(p), v_i(p))] \\ &= \left[\frac{\Delta x_i(p) + T \Delta v_i(p)}{\Delta u_i(p)} \right] \Delta u_i(p) + K_i \left[\frac{\Delta v_i(p) + T \Delta f_i(x_i(p), v_i(p))}{\Delta u_i(p)} + T \right] \Delta u_i(p) \\ &= \psi_i(p) \Delta u_i(p), \end{aligned} \quad (5)$$

with $\psi_i(p) = K_i \left[\frac{\Delta v_i(p) + T \Delta f_i(x_i(p), v_i(p))}{\Delta u_i(p)} + T \right] + \left[\frac{\Delta x_i(p) + T \Delta v_i(p)}{\Delta u_i(p)} \right]$, $\Delta x_i(p+1) = x_i(p+1) - x_i(p)$, $\Delta v_i(p+1) = v_i(p+1) - v_i(p)$. Similar to [23,24], and according to Lemma 1 and Assumptions 2 and 3, one has $\psi_i(p) > 0$ and $|\psi_i(p)| < k_i$.

2.2. MFAPC Algorithm Design

The actual value $\psi_i(p)$ is generally difficult to obtain. Therefore, an estimator is designed to estimate $\psi_i(p)$ to solve this problem. Then, the performance function is defined as follows:

$$J_1[\psi_i(p)] = [\Delta y_i(p) - \psi_i(p) \Delta u_i(p-1)]^2 + \mu [\psi_i(p) - \hat{\psi}_i(p-1)]^2, \quad (6)$$

where $\hat{\psi}_i(p)$ is the estimated value of $\psi_i(p)$ and μ is a weighting constant.

Taking the derivative of $J_1[\hat{\psi}_i(p)]$ with respect to $\hat{\psi}_i(p)$ and letting the result equal 0, one gets

$$\hat{\psi}_i(p) = \hat{\psi}_i(p-1) + \frac{\eta[\Delta y_i(p) - \hat{\psi}_i(p-1)\Delta u_i(p-1)]\Delta u_i(p-1)}{\Delta u_i^2(p-1) + \mu} \quad (7)$$

with the step factor $\eta \in (0,1]$ being introduced to make algorithm (7) more flexible and general.

To accomplish the vehicle platoon control task, the performance function with respect to $u_i(p)$ is defined as follows:

$$J_2[u_i(p)] = [y_0(p+1) - y_i(p+1) + d_{i0}]^2 + \lambda[u_i(p) - u_i(p-1)]^2, \quad (8)$$

where $y_0(p+1) = x_0(p+1) + v_0(p+1)$ is a given reference output according to (3). λ is a weighting constant. $d_{i0} > 0$ represents the safety distance between the ith vehicle and the leading vehicle.

Minimizing the performance function (8) with respect to $u_i(p)$, one gets

$$u_i(p) = u_i(p-1) + \frac{\rho \psi_i(p)}{\psi_i^2(p) + \lambda}[y_0(p+1) + d_{i0} - y_i(p)], \quad (9)$$

where the role of ρ is the same as η in (7).

Remark 2. *In this controller, the distances d_{i0} are assumed to be available, which can also be obtained using between-vehicle sensing distances via $d_{i0} = d_{i,i-1} + d_{i-1,i-2} + \cdots + d_{2,1} + d_{1,0}$. Moreover, this controller is a theoretical formulation. In practice, the "future" data $y_0(k+1)$ can be obtained via estimation techniques, possibly with acceptable small errors.*

2.3. Event-Triggered Mechanism Design

The MFAC scheme devised above communicates continuously, which wastes network communication resources. To save network resources, event-triggered control is used. Assuming that the set of the event-triggered instants is determined as $\{k_i, i = 0, 1, \ldots\}$, then, the event-triggered mechanism is designed as follows:

$$\begin{cases} Y_i(p) = |m_i(p)| - \zeta_i |e_i(p)| \\ \Psi_i(p) = |n_i(p)| - \xi_i |\Delta y_i(p)| \end{cases} \quad (10)$$

where $\zeta_i > 0$ and $\xi_i > 0$ are the event-triggered thresholds. $m_i(p) = y_i(p) - y_i(p_i)$ and $n_i(p) = \Delta y_i(p) - \Delta y_i(p_i)$ with $\Delta y_i(p_i) = y_i(p_i) - y_i(p_{i-1})$ are the measurement errors. $e_i(p) = y_i^*(p) - y_i(p)$ is the tracking error.

The controller receives packets at the event-triggered instant $\{p_i, i = 0, 1, \ldots\}$, which is generated by the following event-triggered condition:

$$p_{i+1} = \inf\{p \in \mathbb{N} | p > p_i, Y_i(p) > 0 \text{ or } \Psi_i(p) > 0\}. \quad (11)$$

Then, the control input $u_i(p)$ is updated as follows:

$$u_i(p) = u_i(p-1) + \frac{\rho \psi_i(p_i)}{\psi_i^2(p_i) + \lambda}[y_0(p+1) + d_{i0} - y_i(p_i)] \quad (12)$$

2.4. MFAPC Modeling under DoS Attacks

For a system framework under DoS attacks, we know that the DoS attacks intend to destroy system performance by blocking the data packets $D(p)$ transmitted between the controller and the sensor/estimator. If the wireless network is attacked, the controller will not receive the data packets $D(p)$, i.e., $D(p) = 0$. Otherwise, the data packets $D(p)$ can be received by the controller. When DoS attacks occur, the redefined system $y_i(p_i)$ will be converted to the following form:

$$y_{ai}(p_i) = \theta_i(p_i) y_i(p_i), \tag{13}$$

where $\theta_i(p_i)$ is an indicator function that represents the consequence of DoS attacks in the communication network, with $\theta_i(p_i) = 0$ indicating that the DoS attacks to the communication are completely successful, and $\theta_i(p_i) = 1$ otherwise. Assume that $\theta_i(p_i)$ conforms to the Bernoulli distribution, with probabilities of the successful and the failing DoS attacks being $\mathbb{P}\{\theta_i(p_i) = 0\} = \theta_i$ and $\mathbb{P}\{\theta_i(p_i) = 1\} = 1 - \theta_i$, respectively.

An attack compensation mechanism is proposed as

$$y_{ai}(p_i) = \theta_i(p_i) y_i(p_i) + [1 - \theta_i(p_i)] y_i(p_{i-1}). \tag{14}$$

Remark 3. *The compensation mechanism can reduce the impact of DoS attacks. When there are DoS attacks in communication networks, the indicator function $\theta_i(p_i) = 0$ and $y_{ai}(p_i) = y_i(p_{i-1})$; that is, using the latest received system output $y_i(p_{i-1})$ stored in the buffer, the impacts of DoS attacks will be compensated for. The sensor measures the vehicle output $y(p)$ and the estimator estimates the time-varying parameter based on $y(p)$ to obtain $\hat{\psi}(p)$. Then, the system output $y(p)$ and estimated time-varying parameter $\hat{\psi}(p)$ are packaged and transmitted to the controller via an event detector and the wireless network that may be attacked. The buffer is embedded into the controller as an attack compensator to reduce the influence of network attacks. Once the packets are transmitted to the buffer they will be stored and used to compensate for lost packets during network attacks.*

According to the above analysis, the designed MFAPC algorithm is given as follows:

$$\begin{cases} \hat{\psi}_i(p) = \hat{\psi}_i(p-1) + \frac{\eta \Delta y_i(p) \Delta u_i(p-1)}{\Delta u_i^2(p-1)+\mu} - \frac{\eta \hat{\psi}_i(p-1) \Delta u_i^2(p-1)}{\Delta u_i^2(p-1)+\mu}; & \text{others} \\ \hat{\psi}_i(p) = \hat{\psi}_i(0), \text{ if } |\hat{\psi}_i(p)| \leq \sigma_i \text{ or } |\Delta u_i(p-1)| \leq \sigma_i \text{ or } sign(\hat{\psi}_i(p)) \neq sign(\hat{\psi}_i(0)) \end{cases} \tag{15}$$

$$u_i(p) = u_i(p-1) + \frac{\rho \hat{\psi}_i(p_i)}{\hat{\psi}_i^2(p_i) + \lambda} [y_0(p+1) + d_{i0} - y_{ai}(p_i)], \tag{16}$$

where $\sigma_i > 0$ represents a small constant.

Remark 4. *The designed algorithm includes two aspects: the estimation algorithm and the reset algorithm (15), and the control algorithm (16). First, the estimation algorithm calculates the estimated PPD parameter $\hat{\psi}_i(p)$ and the reset algorithm (15) is used to reset $\hat{\psi}_i(p) = \hat{\psi}_i(0)$ if the reset condition is satisfied. Then, the control algorithm (16) calculates the control input based on the estimated PPD parameter, system output and the reference output.*

Remark 5. *The proposed control strategy does not require a system model and only uses the inputs/outputs data of the closed-loop system in the design of the controller. This represents a necessary supplement to the model-based method when the dynamic model is difficult and inaccurate to obtain.*

Problem 1. *For a non-linear vehicle system (2) under DoS attacks, the goal is to devise a resilient MFAPC scheme to accomplish the vehicle platoon task in the mean square sense, i.e., $e_i(p) = y_0(p) + d_{i0} - y_i(p)$ converges into the following small bounded set:*

$$\{e_i(p) \mid \mathbb{E}\{|e_i(p)|\} \leq \epsilon_i\}, \tag{17}$$

where ϵ_i is the upper bound of the tracking error.

3. Security Analysis

An analysis is presented below of the stability of the vehicle platoon system and determination of the control algorithm parameters.

Theorem 1. *If Assumptions 1–3 are satisfied, then Problem 1 can be solved using the MFAPC scheme (15) and (16) for some parameters $\lambda > \lambda_{min} > 0$, $\rho \in (0,1]$, $\eta \in (0,1]$, $\mu > 0$, $\zeta_i > 0$ and $\xi_i \in (0, M)$ with $M \in (0,1)$.*

Proof. The proof consists of two parts. First, the estimation error of the PPD parameter is uniformly bounded. Then, based on the boundedness of the estimated PPD parameter, the tracking error is uniformly bounded in the mean square sense.

(1) Defining $e_{\psi_i}(p) = \hat{\psi}_i(p) - \psi_i(p)$, and subtracting the PPD parameter $\psi_i(p)$ from both sides of Equation (15), we get

$$e_{\psi_i}(p) = e_{\psi_i}(p-1) - \frac{\eta e_{\psi_i}(p-1)\Delta u_i^2(p-1)}{\Delta u_i^2(p-1) + \mu} + \psi_i(p-1) - \psi_i(p). \tag{18}$$

Then, taking the absolute value of (18),

$$|e_{\psi_i}(p)| \leq \left|1 - \frac{\eta \Delta u_i^2(p-1)}{\Delta u_i^2(p-1) + \mu}\right| |e_{\psi_i}(p-1)| + |\psi_i(p-1) - \psi_i(p)|. \tag{19}$$

It is clear that $\frac{\eta \Delta u_i^2(p-1)}{\Delta u_i^2(p-1)+\mu}$ is monotonically increasing for $\Delta u_i^2(p-1)$ and its minimum value is $\frac{\eta \sigma_i^2}{\mu + \sigma_i^2}$ according to (15). Then, the following inequality holds for $0 < \eta \leq 1$ and $\mu > 0$:

$$\left|1 - \frac{\eta \Delta u_i^2(p-1)}{\Delta u_i^2(p-1) + \mu}\right| \leq 1 - \frac{\eta \sigma_i^2}{\mu + \sigma_i^2} \triangleq d_1 < 1, \tag{20}$$

where d_1 is a constant. According to Lemma 1, one has $|\psi_i(p)| \leq k_i$. Thus, $|\psi_i(p-1) - \psi_i(p)| \leq 2k_i$. Then, according to (20), (19) is rewritten as

$$\begin{aligned} |e_{\psi_i}(p)| &\leq d_1 |e_{\psi_i}(p-1)| + 2k_i \\ &\leq d_1^2 |e_{\psi_i}(p-2)| + 2d_1 k_i + 2k_i \\ &\leq \cdots \\ &\leq d_1^p |e_{\psi_i}(0)| + \frac{2k_i(1-d_1^p)}{1-d_1}. \end{aligned}$$

Therefore, the estimation error $e_{\psi_i}(p)$ is uniformly bounded. Since $\psi_i(p)$ is bounded, $\hat{\psi}_i(p)$ is bounded.

(2) Substituting control input (16) into $\Delta y_i(p+1) = \psi_i(p)\Delta u_i(p)$, obtained from (5), leads to

$$y_i(p+1) = y_i(p) + \frac{\rho \psi_i(p)\hat{\psi}_i(p_i)}{\hat{\psi}_i^2(p_i) + \lambda}[y_0(p+1) + d_{i0} - y_{ai}(p_i)]. \tag{21}$$

Then, the error system is obtained as

$$\begin{aligned} e_i(p+1) &= y_0(p+1) + d_{i0} - y_i(p) - \frac{\rho \psi_i(p)\hat{\psi}_i(p_i)}{\hat{\psi}_i^2(p_i) + \lambda}[y_0(p+1) + d_{i0} - y_{ai}(p_i)] \\ &= \Delta y_0(p+1) + e_i(p) - \frac{\rho \psi_i(p)\hat{\psi}_i(p_i)}{\hat{\psi}_i^2(p_i) + \lambda}[\Delta y_0(p+1) + e_i(p) \\ &\quad -(\theta_i(p_i)-1)\psi_i(p-1)\Delta u_i(p-1) + (\theta_i(p_i)-1)n_i(p) + m_i(p)], \end{aligned} \tag{22}$$

where the following transformation is used:

$$\begin{aligned}
y_0(p+1)+d_{i0}-y_{ai}(p_i) &= \Delta y_0(p+1) + y_0(p) + d_{i0} - \theta_i(p_i)y_i(p_i) - [1-\theta_i(p_i)]y_i(p_{i-1})\\
&= \Delta y_0(p+1) + y_0(p) + d_{i0} - [\theta_i(p_i)\Delta y_i(p_i) - \Delta y_i(p_i) + y_i(p_i)]\\
&= \Delta y_0(p+1) + y_0(p) + d_{i0} - [(\theta_i(p_i)-1)\Delta y_i(p_i) + y_i(p_i)]\\
&= \Delta y_0(p+1) - (\theta_i(p_i)-1)\Delta y_i(p) + (\theta_i(p_i)-1)n_i(p) - y_i(p_i) + m_i(p)\\
&= \Delta y_0(p+1) + e_i(p) - (\theta_i(p_i)-1)\psi_i(p-1)\Delta u_i(p-1)\\
&\quad + (\theta_i(p_i)-1)n_i(p) + m_i(p),
\end{aligned} \qquad (23)$$

with $\Delta y_i(p) = \psi_i(p-1)\Delta u_i(p-1)$ obtained from (5).
Then, taking the absolute value and expectation of (22), one has

$$\begin{aligned}
\mathbb{E}\{|e_i(p+1)|\} &\leq \left|1 - \frac{\rho\psi_i(p)\hat{\psi}_i(p_i)}{\hat{\psi}_i^2(p_i)+\lambda}\right|\left[\mathbb{E}\{|e_i(p)|\} + |\Delta y_0(p+1)|\right]\\
&\quad + \left|\frac{\rho\psi_i(p)\hat{\psi}_i(p_i)}{\hat{\psi}_i^2(p_i)+\lambda}\right||\theta_i-1||\psi_i(p-1)||\Delta u_i(p-1)|\\
&\quad + \left|\frac{\rho\psi_i(p)\hat{\psi}_i(p_i)}{\hat{\psi}_i^2(p_i)+\lambda}\right||\theta_i-1||n_i(p)| + \left|\frac{\rho\psi_i(p)\hat{\psi}_i(p_i)}{\hat{\psi}_i^2(p_i)+\lambda}\right||m_i(p)|.
\end{aligned} \qquad (24)$$

According to the event-triggered condition, one gets

$$\begin{aligned}
\mathbb{E}\{|e_i(p+1)|\} &\leq \left|1 - \frac{\rho\psi_i(p)\hat{\psi}_i(p_i)}{\hat{\psi}_i^2(p_i)+\lambda}\right|\left[\mathbb{E}\{|e_i(p)|\} + |\Delta y_0(p+1)|\right]\\
&\quad + \left|\frac{\rho\psi_i(p)\hat{\psi}_i(p_i)}{\hat{\psi}_i^2(p_i)+\lambda}\right||\theta_i-1||\psi_i(p-1)||\Delta u_i(p-1)|\\
&\quad + \zeta_i\left|\frac{\rho\psi_i(p)\hat{\psi}_i(p_i)}{\hat{\psi}_i^2(p_i)+\lambda}\right||\theta_i-1||\Delta y_i(p)| + \zeta_i\left|\frac{\rho\psi_i(p)\hat{\psi}_i(p_i)}{\hat{\psi}_i^2(p_i)+\lambda}\right|\mathbb{E}\{|e_i(p)|\}\\
&\leq \left|1 - \frac{\rho\psi_i(p)\hat{\psi}_i(p_i)}{\hat{\psi}_i^2(p_i)+\lambda}\right|\left[\mathbb{E}\{|e_i(p)|\} + |\Delta y_0(p+1)|\right]\\
&\quad + \left|\frac{\rho\psi_i(p)\hat{\psi}_i(p_i)}{\hat{\psi}_i^2(p_i)+\lambda}\right||\theta_i-1||\psi_i(p-1)||\Delta u_i(p-1)|\\
&\quad + \zeta_i\left|\frac{\rho\psi_i(p)\hat{\psi}_i(p_i)}{\hat{\psi}_i^2(p_i)+\lambda}\right||\theta_i-1||\psi_i(p-1)||\Delta u_i(p-1)|\\
&\quad + \zeta_i\left|\frac{\rho\psi_i(p)\hat{\psi}_i(p_i)}{\hat{\psi}_i^2(p_i)+\lambda}\right|\mathbb{E}\{|e_i(p)|\}.
\end{aligned} \qquad (25), (26)$$

Consequently, $\psi_i(p) > 0$ and $|\psi_i(p)| \leq k_i$. According to Lemma 1 and Assumption 3, there exists a positive constant $0 < M_i < 1$ such that

$$0 < M_i \leq \frac{\psi_i(p)\hat{\psi}_i(p_i)}{\lambda + \hat{\psi}_i^2(p_i)} \leq \frac{k_i\hat{\psi}_i(p_i)}{\lambda + \hat{\psi}_i^2(p_i)} \leq \frac{k_i\hat{\psi}_i(p_i)}{2\sqrt{\lambda}\hat{\psi}_i(p_i)}. \qquad (27)$$

Letting $\lambda_{min} = \frac{k_i^2}{4}$, the following inequality holds for all $\lambda > \lambda_{min}$:

$$\frac{k_i\hat{\psi}_i(p_i)}{2\sqrt{\lambda}\hat{\psi}_i(p_i)} < \frac{k_i}{2\sqrt{\lambda_{min}}} = 1. \qquad (28)$$

Then, one can get

$$\left|1 - \frac{\rho\psi_i(p)\hat{\psi}_i(p_i)}{\hat{\psi}_i^2(p_i) + \lambda}\right| = 1 - \frac{\rho\psi_i(p)\hat{\psi}_i(p_i)}{\hat{\psi}_i^2(p_i) + \lambda} \leq 1 - \rho M_i \triangleq d_2 < 1, \quad (29)$$

where d_2 is a constant. Since the control input cannot change too fast in the actual system, the increment of the control input $\Delta u_i(p)$ should be bounded, denoted as $|\Delta u_i(p)| < \varepsilon_i$ for all p with $\varepsilon_i > 0$ being a constant. Then, one gets

$$(1 + \xi_i)\left|\frac{\rho\psi_i(p)\hat{\psi}_i(p_i)}{\hat{\psi}_i^2(p_i) + \lambda}\right| |\theta_i - 1||\psi_i(p-1)||\Delta u_i(p-1)| \leq (1 + \xi_i)\rho k_i \varepsilon_i \triangleq d_3, \quad (30)$$

where d_3 is a constant. Additionally, the increment of the desired output $\Delta y_0(p+1)$ should be bounded, denoted as $|\Delta y_0(p+1)| < d_4$, where d_4 is a constant. Then, (25) can be converted to the following inequality:

$$\mathbb{E}\{|e_i(p+1)|\} \leq (1 - M + \zeta_i)\mathbb{E}\{|e_i(p)|\} + d_2 d_4 + d_3. \quad (31)$$

Additionally, the following inequality can be obtained if $0 < \zeta_i < M$:

$$1 - M + \zeta_i = 1 - (M - \zeta_i) \triangleq d_5 < 1. \quad (32)$$

Then, it follows from (31) that

$$\begin{aligned}\mathbb{E}\{|e_i(p+1)|\} &\leq d_5\mathbb{E}\{|e_i(p)|\} + d_2 d_4 + d_3 \\ &\leq d_5^2\mathbb{E}\{|e_i(p-1)|\} + d_5(d_2 d_4 + d_3) + d_2 d_4 + d_3 \\ &\leq \ldots \\ &\leq d_5^{p+1}\mathbb{E}\{|e_i(0)|\} + \frac{(d_2 d_4 + d_3)(1 - d_5^{p+1})}{1 - d_5}.\end{aligned} \quad (33)$$

Therefore, the tracking error is uniformly bounded in the mean square sense, i.e., $e_i(p)$ converges to the following set:

$$\left\{e_i(p) \mid \mathbb{E}\{|e_i(p)|\} \leq \frac{d_2 d_4 + d_3}{1 - d_5}\right\}.$$

□

Remark 6. *In contrast to the stability analysis of the data-driven platoon control scheme for non-linear vehicles [44], in the error system (22), the introduction of the measurement errors $m_i(p)$ and $n_i(p)$ caused by the event-triggered mechanism will make the stability analysis more complicated. Specifically, compared with the traditional control scheme where $\psi_i(p)$ and $y_i(p)$ are used in the controller, the trigger instant values $\psi_i(p_i)$ and $y_i(p_i)$ are used in the event-triggered control scheme (16). Then, by introducing the measurement error $m_i(p) = y_i(p) - y_i(p_i)$ and $n_i(p) = \Delta y_i(p) - \Delta y_i(p_i)$, $\psi_i(p_i)$ is replaced by $\psi_i(p)$ and $m_i(p)$, and $y_i(p_i)$ is replaced by $y_i(p)$ and $n_i(p)$. This transformation will lead to additional terms $\left|\frac{\rho\psi_i(p)\hat{\psi}_i(p_i)}{\hat{\psi}_i^2(p_i) + \lambda}\right| |\theta_i - 1||n_i(p)| + \left|\frac{\rho\psi_i(p)\hat{\psi}_i(p_i)}{\hat{\psi}_i^2(p_i) + \lambda}\right| |m_i(p)|$ appearing. To handle these two terms, the event-triggered condition (11) is designed. Then, the main difficulty is how to design its trigger condition. If the event-triggered condition with the additional term cannot be solved, this will affect the stability analysis.*

4. Simulation and Experimental Results

An example is provided to test the effectiveness of the proposed control algorithm.

Consider the following vehicle platoon system:

$$\dot{x}_i(t) = v_i(t),$$
$$\dot{v}_i(t) = u_i(t) - 3v_i^3(t) + 0.1x_i(t), i \in N.$$

The dynamic model of the leading vehicle is considered as

$$\dot{x}_0(t) = v_0(t),$$
$$\dot{v}_0(t) = -3v_0^3(t) + 0.1x_0(t).$$

The vehicle platoon control scheme is presented in Figure 2. The distances between the ith vehicle and the leading vehicle are $d_{10} = 1$ metre, $d_{20} = 3$ metre and $d_{30} = 5$ metre, respectively, and the initial values are $x_i(0) = 0.1$, $v_i(0) = 0$, $u_i(0) = 0$ and $\hat{\psi}_i(0) = [0.5, 0.5]^T (i = 1, 2, 3)$. By Theorem 1, the control parameters are $\mu = 50$, $\eta = 1$, $\rho = 0.35$, $\lambda = 5$ and $K_i = 1$. The sampling period is $T = 0.005$ and the probability of successful DoS attacks is $\theta_i = 0.6$. The parameters of the event-triggered mechanism are selected as $\zeta_i = 0.2$ and $\bar{\zeta}_i = 0.1$.

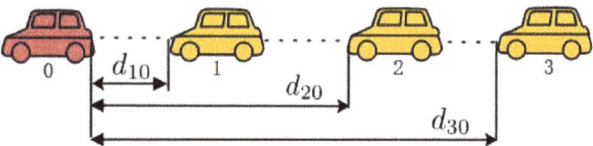

Figure 2. The vehicle platoon control scheme.

Figure 3 shows a comparison of the control scheme proposed here and in [13]. The vehicular platoon control objective is achieved using the proposed method under DoS attacks; that is, there is a safety distance between the following vehicles and the leading vehicle, and the velocity of the following vehicles can track the velocity of the leading vehicle at the same time. However, the vehicular control objective cannot be achieved using the control method designed in [13] under DoS attacks. The event-triggered instants of all vehicles are illustrated in Figure 4; Figure 4a–c denote the event-triggered instants for vehicle 1, 2 and 3. By calculation, the number of communication packets of vehicles 1, 2 and 3 are 598, 433 and 393 (number of communication packets under time-triggered: 2000), respectively, which implies that the packet transmission rate is reduced by 70.1%, 78.35% and 80.35%, respectively. Therefore, the designed event-triggered mechanism can effectively reduce the network communication.

Table 1. The 2-norms of the tracking errors of the position and velocity.

	This Paper	[13]
$\|e_{x_1}(t)\|$	26.18	1.33×10^3
$\|e_{x_2}(t)\|$	58.83	1.48×10^3
$\|e_{x_3}(t)\|$	98.72	2×10^3
$\|e_{v_1}(t)\|$	25.77	75.96
$\|e_{v_2}(t)\|$	46.04	119.80
$\|e_{v_3}(t)\|$	67.34	176.21

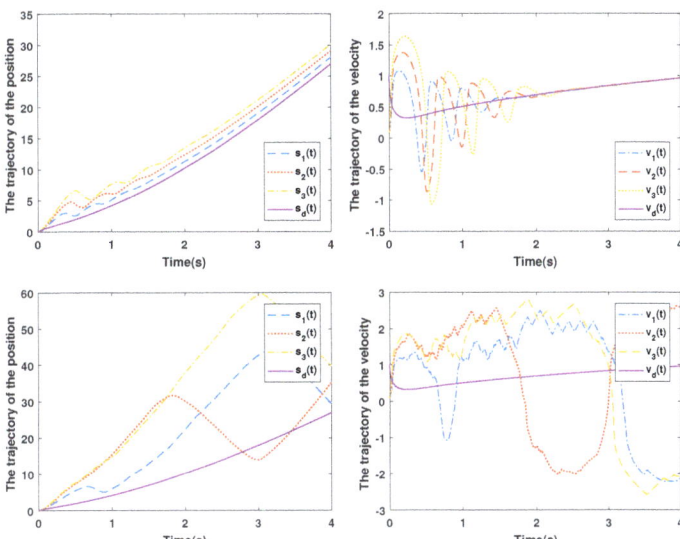

Figure 3. The trajectories of the position and velocity of the vehicular platoon system between the proposed method (**up**) and the method in [13] (**down**).

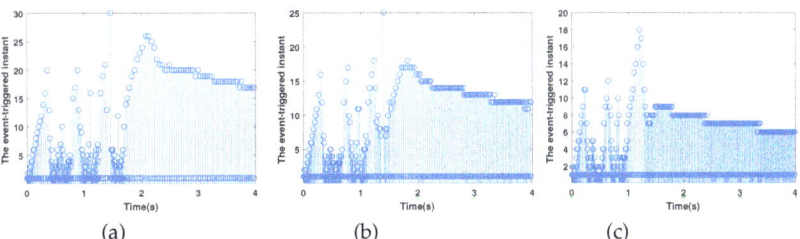

Figure 4. The event-triggered instant. (**a**–**c**) denote the event-triggered instants for vehicle 1, 2 and 3.

In contrast to the existing vehicle platoon control result [44], the event-triggered mechanism is introduced into the vehicle platoon control scheme to save the limited network communication resources. By simulation, the number of communication packets without using the event-triggered mechanism [44] were 2000, 2000, 2000 (i.e., time-trigger) for vehicles 1, 2 and 3, but the number of communication packets for vehicles 1, 2 and 3 using the proposed event-triggered mechanism were 598, 433 and 393. Therefore, compared with the vehicle platoon control scheme without considering the event-triggered mechanism [44], the proposed event-triggered vehicle platoon control scheme can achieve the control task with limited network communication resources.

The effectiveness of the proposed method is more clearly illustrated in Figure 5. The 2-norms of the errors between the method proposed and [13] are shown in Table 1, where $\|e_{v_i}(k)\|$ and $\|e_{x_i}(k)\|$ are the 2-norms of the tracking errors of the velocity and position in the ith vehicle, respectively.

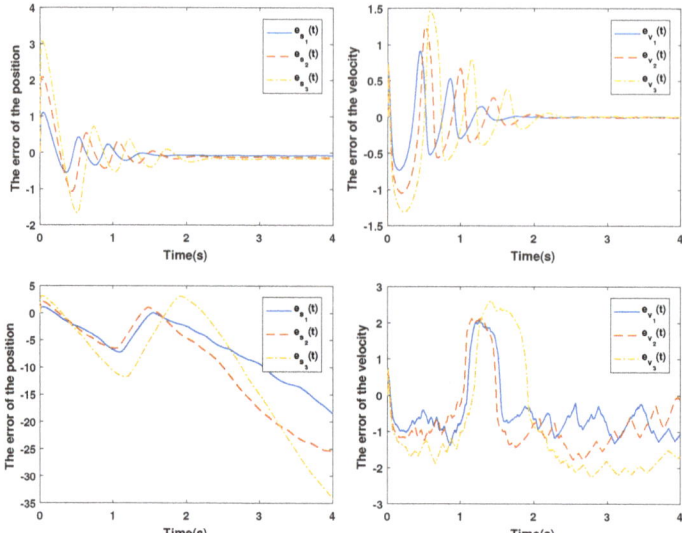

Figure 5. The errors of the position and velocity for the vehicular platoon system between the proposed method (**up**) and the method in [13] (**down**).

5. Conclusions

The data-driven event-triggered platoon control problem was addressed for non-linear vehicle systems under DoS attacks. The input-output equivalent linear data model for a non-linear vehicle system was established using a dynamic linearization technique and the event trigger mechanism was used to save communication resources. Then, a novel resilient control scheme was developed to resist DoS attacks. In this scheme, a new attack compensation mechanism was designed to reduce the impact of DoS attacks based on the latest received system information. The simulation results show that the algorithm was able to achieve the platoon control target under DoS attacks well and save communication resources effectively. Future work will mainly focus on the dynamic event-triggered platoon control problem under a class of aperiodic DoS attacks.

Author Contributions: Conceptualization, L.Z. and W.C.; methodology, Z.W. and W.C.; software, L.Z.; validation, Z.W. and W.C.; formal analysis, Z.L.; writing—original draft preparation, Z.L.; writing—review and editing, Z.L., L.Z. and Z.W.; supervision, W.C.; funding acquisition, W.C. All authors have read and agreed to the published version of the manuscript.

Funding: This research was funded by the National Natural Science Foundation of China grant number 62273191; the Natural Science Foundation of Shandong Province grant number ZR2020KF034.

Conflicts of Interest: The authors declare no conflict of interest.

References

1. Wang, S.; Hui, Y.; Sun, X.; Shi, D. Neural network sliding mode control of intelligent vehicle longitudinal dynamics. *IEEE Access* **2019**, *7*, 162333–162342. [CrossRef]
2. Saraiva, T.D.V.; Campos, C.A.V.; Fontes, R.D.R.; Rothenberg, C.E.; Sorour, S.; Valaee, S. An application-driven framework for intelligent transportation systems using 5G network slicing. *IEEE Trans. Intell. Transp. Syst.* **2021**, *22*, 5247–5260. [CrossRef]
3. Mu, S.; Xiong, Z.; Tian, Y. Intelligent traffic control system based on cloud computing and big data mining. *IEEE Trans. Ind. Inform.* **2019**, *15*, 6583–6592.
4. Xu, L.; Zhuang, W.; Yin, G.; Bian, C.; Wu, H. Modeling and robust control of heterogeneous vehicle platoons on curved roads subject to disturbances and delays. *IEEE Trans. Veh. Technol.* **2019**, *68*, 11551–11564. [CrossRef]
5. Chen, J.; Liang, H.; Li, J.; Lv, Z. Connected automated vehicle platoon control with input saturation and variable time headway strategy. *IEEE Trans. Intell. Transp. Syst.* **2020**, *22*, 4929–4940. [CrossRef]

6. Zhang, H.; Liu, J.; Wang, Z.; Yan, H.; Zhang, C. Distributed adaptive event-triggered control and stability analysis for vehicular platoon. *IEEE Trans. Intell. Transp. Syst.* **2021**, *22*, 1627–1638. [CrossRef]
7. Li, Y.; Zhong, Z.; Song, Y.; Sun, Q.; Sun, H.; Wang, Y. Longitudinal platoon control of connected vehicles: Analysis and verification. *IEEE Trans. Intell. Transp. Syst.* **2020**, *23*, 4225–4235. [CrossRef]
8. di Bernardo, M.; Salvi, A.; Santini, S. Distributed consensus strategy for platooning of vehicles in the presence of time-varying heterogeneous communication delays. *IEEE Trans. Intell. Transp. Syst.* **2015**, *16*, 102–112. [CrossRef]
9. Li, M.; Cao, Z.; Li, Z. A reinforcement learning-based vehicle platoon control strategy for reducing energy consumption in traffic oscillations. *IEEE Trans. Neural Netw. Learn. Syst.* **2021**, *32*, 5309–5322. [CrossRef]
10. Song, X.; Feng, D.; Feng, X. Data-driven optimal cooperative adaptive cruise control of heterogeneous vehicle platoons with unknown dynamics. *Sci. China-Inf. Sci.* **2020**, *63*, 9. [CrossRef]
11. Li, G.; Görges, D. Ecological adaptive cruise control for vehicles with step-gear transmission based on reinforcement learning. *IEEE Trans. Intell. Transp. Syst.* **2020**, *21*, 4895–4905. [CrossRef]
12. Hou, Z.; Jin, S. *Model Free Adaptive Control: Theory and Applications*; CRC Press: Boca Raton, FL, USA, 2013.
13. Hou, Z.; Jin, S. A novel data-driven control approach for a class of discrete-time nonlinear systems. *IEEE Trans. Control Syst. Technol.* **2011**, *19*, 1549–1558. [CrossRef]
14. Hou, Z.; Chi, R.; Gao, H. An overview of dynamic-linearization-based data-driven control and applications. *IEEE Trans. Ind. Electron.* **2017**, *64*, 4076–4090. [CrossRef]
15. Hou, Z.; Jin, S. Data-driven model-free adaptive control for a class of MIMO nonlinear discrete-time systems. *IEEE Trans. Neural Netw.* **2011**, *22*, 2173–2188. [PubMed]
16. Chi, R.; Zhang, H.; Huang, B.; Hou, Z. Quantitative Data-Driven Adaptive Iterative Learning Control: From Trajectory Tracking to Point-to-Point Tracking. *IEEE Trans. Cybern.* **2020**, *52*, 4859–4873. [CrossRef] [PubMed]
17. Hou, Z.; Xiong, S. On model-free adaptive control and its stability analysis. *IEEE Trans. Autom. Control* **2019**, *64*, 4555–4569. [CrossRef]
18. Xiong, S.; Hou, Z. Model-free adaptive control for unknown MIMO nonaffine nonlinear discrete-time systems with experimental validation. *IEEE Trans. Neural Netw. Learn. Syst.* **2020**, *33*, 1727–1739. [CrossRef]
19. Bu, X.; Yu, W.; Yu, Q.; Hou, Z.; Yang, J. Event-Triggered Model-Free Adaptive Iterative Learning Control for a Class of Nonlinear Systems Over Fading Channels. *IEEE Trans. Cybern.* **2021**, *52*, 9597–9608. [CrossRef]
20. Liu, D.; Yang, G. Prescribed performance model-free adaptive integral sliding mode control for discrete-time nonlinear systems. *IEEE Trans. Neural Netw. Learn. Syst.* **2019**, *30*, 2222–2230. [CrossRef]
21. Xu, D.; Shi, Y.; Ji, Z. Model-free adaptive discrete-time integral sliding-mode-constrained-control for autonomous 4WMV parking systems. *IEEE Trans. Ind. Electron.* **2018**, *65*, 834–843. [CrossRef]
22. Liu, S.; Hou, Z.; Tian, T.; Deng, Z.; Li, Z. A novel dual successive projection-based model-free adaptive control method and application to an autonomous car. *IEEE Trans. Neural Netw. Learn. Syst.* **2019**, *30*, 3444–3457. [PubMed]
23. Jiang, Q.; Liao, Y.; Li, Y.; Fan, J.; Miao, Y. Heading control of unmanned surface vehicle with variable output constraint model-free adaptive control algorithm. *IEEE Access* **2019**, *7*, 131008–131018. [CrossRef]
24. Liao, Y.; Jiang, Q.; Du, T.; Jiang, W. Redefined output model-free adaptive control method and unmanned surface vehicle heading control. *IEEE J. Ocean. Eng.* **2020**, *45*, 714–723. [CrossRef]
25. Liu, D.; Yang, G. Neural network-based event-triggered MFAC for nonlinear discrete-time processes. *Neurocomputing* **2018**, *272*, 356–364. [CrossRef]
26. Lin, N.; Chi, R.; Huang, B. Event-triggered model-free adaptive control. *IEEE Trans. Syst. Man, Cybern. Syst.* **2019**, *51*, 3358–3369. [CrossRef]
27. Li, H.; Wang, Y.; Zhang, H. Data-driven-based event-triggered tracking control for non-linear systems with unknown disturbance. *IET Control Theory Appl.* **2019**, *13*, 2197–2206. [CrossRef]
28. Lin, N.; Chi, R.; Huang, B.; Hou, Z. Event-triggered nonlinear iterative learning control. *IEEE Trans. Neural Netw. Learn. Syst.* **2020**, *32*, 5118–5128. [CrossRef]
29. Mao, J.; Sun, Y.; Yi, X.; Liu, H.; Ding, D. Recursive filtering of networked nonlinear systems: A survey. *Int. J. Syst. Sci.* **2021**, *52*, 1110–1128. [CrossRef]
30. Ding, D.; Han, Q.L.; Ge, X.; Wang, J. Secure state estimation and control of cyber-physical systems: A survey. *IEEE Trans. Syst. Man, Cybern. Syst.* **2020**, *51*, 176–190. [CrossRef]
31. Deng, C.; Zhang, D.; Gang, F. Resilient practical cooperative output regulation for MASs with unknown switching exosystem dynamics under DoS attacks. *Automatica* **2022**, *139*, 110172. [CrossRef]
32. Li, Z.; Che, W. Event-triggered asynchronous periodic distributed secondary control of microgrids under DoS attacks. *J. Frankl. Inst.* **2022**. [CrossRef]
33. Yue, B.; Che, W. Data-Driven dynamic event-triggered fault-tolerant platooning control. *IEEE Trans. Ind. Inform.* **2022**. [CrossRef]
34. Ma, Y.; Che, W.; Deng, C.; Wu, Z. Observer-based event-triggered containment control for MASs under DoS attacks. *IEEE Trans. Cybern.* **2021**. [CrossRef] [PubMed]
35. Ma, Y.; Che, W.; Deng, C.; Wu, Z. Distributed model-free adaptive control for learning nonlinear MASs under DoS attacks. *IEEE Trans. Neural Netw. Learn. Syst.* **2021**. [CrossRef] [PubMed]

36. Wan, Y.; Wen, G.; Yu, X.; Huang, T. Distributed Consensus Tracking of Networked Agent Systems under Denial-of-Service Attacks. *IEEE Trans. Syst. Man, Cybern. Syst.* **2021**, *51*, 61836196. [CrossRef]
37. Pang, Z.; Liu, G.; Zhou, D.; Sun, D. Data-based predictive control for networked nonlinear systems with network-induced delay and packet dropout. *IEEE Trans. Ind. Electron.* **2016**, *63*, 1249–1257. [CrossRef]
38. Pang, Z.; Liu, G.; Zhou, D.; Sun, D. Data-based predictive control for networked non-linear systems with two-channel packet dropouts. *IET Control. Theory Applocations* **2015**, *9*, 1154–1161. [CrossRef]
39. Yu, W.; Wang, R.; Bu, X.; Hou, Z. Model free adaptive control for a class of nonlinear systems with fading measurements. *J. Frankl. Inst.-Eng. Appl. Math.* **2020**, *357*, 7743–7760. [CrossRef]
40. Yu, W.; Wang, R.; Bu, X.; Hou, Z.; Wu, Z. Resilient Model-Free Adaptive Iterative Learning Control for Nonlinear Systems under Periodic DoS Attacks via a Fading Channel. *IEEE Trans. Syst. Man, Cybern. Syst.* **2021**, *52*, 4117–4128. [CrossRef]
41. Qiu, X.; Wang, Y.; Xie, X. Resilient model-free adaptive control for cyber-physical systems against jamming attack. *Neurocomputing* **2020**, *413*, 422–430. [CrossRef]
42. Wang, Y.; Qiu, X.; Zhang, H.; Xie, X. Data-driven-based event-triggered control for nonlinear CPSs against jamming attacks. *IEEE Trans. Neural Netw. Learn. Syst.* **2021**, *33*, 3171–3177. [CrossRef] [PubMed]
43. Sun, H.; Hou, Z.; Li, D. Coordinated iterative learning control schemes for train trajectory tracking with overspeed protection. *IEEE Trans. Autom. Sci. Eng.* **2013**, *10*, 323–333. [CrossRef]
44. Yue, B.; Che, W. Data-driven resilient platooning control for vehicular platooning systems with denial-of-service attacks. *Int. J. Robust Nonlinear Control* **2022**, *32*, 7099–7112. [CrossRef]

Article

Two-Step Neural-Network-Based Fault Isolation for Stochastic Systems

Liping Yin [1,2], Jianguo Liu [1], Hongquan Qu [3] and Tao Li [1,2,*]

[1] Shoool of Ationautom, Nanjing University of Information Science & Techonlogy, Nanjing 210044, China
[2] Jiangsu Collaborative Innovation Center on Atmospheric Environment and Equipment Technology, Nanjing 210044, China
[3] School of Information, North China University of Technology, Langfang 065000, China
* Correspondence: litaojia@nuist.edu.cn; Tel.: +86-025-58731409

Abstract: This paper studies a fault isolation method for an optical fiber vibration source detection and early warning system. We regard the vibration sources in the system as faults and then detect and isolate the faults of the system based on a two-step neural network. Firstly, the square root B-spline expansion method is used to approximate the output probability density functions. Secondly, the nonlinear weight dynamic model is established through a dynamic neural network. Thirdly, the nonlinear filter and residual generator are constructed to estimate the weight, analyze the residual, and estimate the threshold, so as to detect, diagnose, and isolate the faults. The feasibility criterion of fault detection and isolation is given by using some linear matrix inequalities, and the stability of the estimation error system is proven according to the Lyapunov theorem. Finally, simulation experiments based on a optical fiber vibration source system are given to verify the effectiveness of this method.

Keywords: fault detection; fault isolation; B-spline; filter; probability density functions

MSC: 93E10

1. Introduction

With the development of industrial automation, the scale and complexity of modern control systems are increasing rapidly. During operation, the sensor, actuator, and some components might fail due to aging, wearing, or other reasons [1–4]. If the faults of the system cannot be detected and eliminated in time in the process of operation, this may lead to system failure, paralysis, and even catastrophic consequences [5]. Therefore, in the past few decades, the theory of fault detection and isolation (FDI) has developed rapidly [6–10].

The purpose of fault detection and isolation is that, when multiple faults occur in the system, we can find and isolate these faults in time and estimate the size of each fault [6]. At present, many research achievements have been made in fault detection and fault isolation [11–17]. Classical fault detection and isolation methods include the T-S fuzzy model [11], the independent component analysis fault isolation method [12], the detection filter method [13], minimum variance fault estimation [14], etc.

In fact, actual industrial systems are stochastic systems [18–21]. Due to the nonlinearity of the system, even if the input obeys a Gaussian distribution, the output of the system will also obey a non-Gaussian distribution [18]. At present, there are many research results that focus on fault diagnosis and isolation for stochastic distribution systems. For example, in [8], an adaptive fault diagnosis observer was used to diagnose actuator faults and accurately estimate the fault size. In [19], fault diagnosis schemes for stochastic distributed systems were studied based on the minimum entropy principle. In [20], a fault isolation method based on entropy optimization filtering was studied for nonlinear non-Gaussian systems with unmeasurable outputs.

As we know, in order to monitor the operation of oil or gas pipelines, a commonly used method is to embed the oil or gas pipelines together with optical fibers in the same ditch. The conditions of the oil or gas pipelines can be monitored by observing the optical fiber's output data in one end of the fiber if we input light at the other end [22–24]. However, In the optical fiber vibration source detection and early warning system, the sensors are quite sensitive due to inevitable non-stationary interferences from the environment, which often brings false alarms. To reduce the false alarm rate, we regard the vibration sources, such as pickaxe planing of mechanical excavation, as faults, and the objective is then transferred into detecting and isolating the faults. Different from the literature in the optical fiber vibration source detection field [22,23], we use a two-step neural network to model the optic data collected from the end of the fiber. The false alarm rate is controlled below the threshold, and the different vibration sources are estimated and isolated by using filter designing, convex optimization, Lyapunov theorems, etc.

This paper is organized as follows: In Section 2, the static modeling is carried out with the help of square root B-splines, and the nonlinear weighted dynamic model is established through the neural network to describe the FDI problem. In Section 3, based on the adaptive filter, the fault detection problem of the transformed nonlinear weighted dynamic model is studied. In Section 4, according to the adaptive fault diagnosis method, the size of different faults is estimated to achieve the purpose of fault isolation. The simulation is given in Section 5 to illustrate the feasibility of the results.

2. Static Modeling and Weighted Dynamic Modeling

For the optical fiber vibration source detection system, although the output value cannot be measured directly, the output PDFs can be estimated by the kernel density method [23]. Next, the output PDF at each sampling time is approximated by B-splines, and the weight of each B-splines is calculated.

2.1. Output PDFs' Static Modeling

As in Figure 1, let $u(t) \in R^m$ be the input of the nonlinear stochastic optical fiber vibration detection system, $y(t) \in [a, b]$ be the output light intensity, F_1 and F_2 be the fault vectors (vibration sources) to be detected and diagnosed, and the probability distribution of the output $y(t)$ of the stochastic dynamic system in the interval $[a, \xi]$ satisfy the condition $P(a \leq y(t) \leq \xi) = \int_a^\xi \gamma(z, u(t), F_1, F_2) dz$. We can use the square root B-spline model with approximate error as shown in (1) to statically model the output PDFs [8]:

$$\sqrt{\gamma(z, u(t), F_1, F_2)} = \sum_{i=1}^n v_i(u(t), F_1, F_2) b_i(z) + \omega_0(z, u(t), F_1, F_2) \quad (1)$$

where $v_i(u(t), F_1, F_2)(i = 1, 2, \cdots, n)$ are the corresponding weights of B-spline expansion and $b_i(z)(i = 1, 2, \cdots, n)$ are the pre-specified basis functions on interval $[a, b]$. For all $\{z, u(t), F_1, F_2\}$, the term $\omega_0(z, u(t), F_1, F_2)$ represents the model uncertainty or the error term on the approximation of the PDFs, which is supposed to satisfy $|\omega_0(z, u(t), F_1, F_2)| \leq \delta_0$, where δ_0 is assumed to be a known positive number. Denote

$$B(z) = [b_1(z), b_2(z), \cdots, b_{n-1}(z)]$$

$$V(t) = [v_1(u(t), F_1, F_2), v_2(u(t), F_1, F_2), \cdots, v_{n-1}(u(t), F_1, F_2)]$$

and

$$\Lambda_1 = \int_a^b B^T(z) B(z) dz \quad (2)$$

$$\Lambda_2 = \int_a^b B^T(z) b_n(z) dz \quad (3)$$

$$\Lambda_3 = \int_a^b (b_n)^2(z) dz \quad (4)$$

where $\Lambda_1 \in R^{(n-1)\times(n-1)}$, $\Lambda_2 \in R^{(n-1)\times 1}$, and $\Lambda_3 \in R^{1\times 1}$ are known matrices or constants. In the following, for simplicity, $V(u(t), F_1, F_2)$ is written as $V(t)$. According to the properties of the probability density function, for any $\gamma(z, u(t), F_1, F_2)$, the constraint condition $\int_a^\zeta \gamma(z, u(t), F_1, F_2)dz = 1$ is always true, and only $n-1$ weight vectors in the weight $\{v_i(u(t), F_1, F_2) : i = 1, 2, \cdots, n\}$ are independent. Let $\Lambda_0 = \Lambda_1 \Lambda_3 - \Lambda_2^T \Lambda_2$, then the following inequality holds [8]:

$$(1 - \omega_1(z, u(t), F_1, F_2))\Lambda_3 - V^T(t)V(t) \geq 0 \tag{5}$$

where

$$\omega_1(z, u(t), F_1, F_2) = 2\omega_0^2(z, u(t), F_1, F_2) \times \left[\left(\int_a^b B(z)dz\right)V(t) \right.$$
$$\left. + \left(\int_a^b b_n(z)dz\right)v_n(t)\right] + \omega_0^2(z, u(t), F_1, F_2)(b-a)$$

From (5), we can obtain:

$$V^T(t)\Lambda_0 V(t) \leq (1 - \omega_1(z, u(t), F_1, F_2))\Lambda_3 \tag{6}$$

where

$$\Lambda_0 > 0, 1 - \omega_1(z, u(t), F_1, F_2) > 0 \tag{7}$$

According to (6), we can know $V(t)$ is bounded and $\|V(t)\|^2 \leq \tilde{\delta} = \left\|\Lambda_0^{-1}\right\|\Lambda_3$ holds. Therefore, (1) can be rewritten as:

$$\sqrt{\gamma(z, u(t), F_1, F_2)} = B(z)V(t) + h_0(V(t), \omega_1)B_n(z) \tag{8}$$

where $h_0(V(t), \omega_1)$ is a function of $V(t)$ and $\omega_1(z, u(t), F_1, F_2)$, as shown in (9):

$$h_0(V(t), \omega_1) = \frac{1}{\Lambda_3}\sqrt{(1-\omega_1)\Lambda_3 - V^T(t)\Lambda_0 V(t)} - \frac{\Lambda_2 V(t)}{\Lambda_3} \tag{9}$$

In order to simplify the B-spline model represented by (8), $h_0(V(t), \omega_1)$ can be further approximated as:

$$\sqrt{\gamma(z, u(t), F_1, F_2)} = B(z)V(t) + h(V(t))b_n(z) + \omega(z, u(t), F_1, F_2) \tag{10}$$

Equation (10) is a nonlinear output equation with uncertainty, and the term $h(V(t))$ satisfies

$$h(V(t)) = \frac{1}{\Lambda_3}(-\Lambda_2 \pm \sqrt{\Lambda_3 - V^T(t)\Lambda_0 V(t)}) \tag{11}$$

As $V(t)$ is bounded and $|\omega_0(z, u(t), F_1, F_2)| \leq \delta_0$, it can be concluded that $|\omega(z, u(t), F_1, F_2)| \leq \delta$ holds for all $\{z, u(t), F_1, F_2\}$. For $h(V(t))$ in (11), it is supposed that, for any $V_1(t)$ and $V_2(t)$, there exists a known matrix U_1, such that:

$$\|h(V_1(t)) - h(V_2(t))\| \leq \|U_1(V_1(t) - V_2(t))\| \tag{12}$$

2.2. Nonlinear Dynamic Weight Model

After the B-spline expansion of the output PDFs, the next task is to find the dynamic relationship between $u(t)$ and γ. As $V(t)$ is a nonlinear function of $u(t)$, we perform the modeling with the help of a neural network as in [25] and study the following weight dynamic system:

$$\begin{cases} \dot{x}(t) = Ax(t) + Gg(x(t)) + Hu(t) + F_1 + F_2 \\ V(t) = Dx(t) \end{cases} \tag{13}$$

where $x(t) \in R^m$ is the state vector, A, G, H, and D represent the known parameter matrices, and $g(x(t))$ is a nonlinear function. Supposing $g(0) = 0$ and for any $x_1(t)$, $x_2(t)$, the following inequality holds [8]:

$$\|g(x_1(t)) - g(x_2(t))\| \le \|U_2(x_1(t) - x_2(t))\| \quad (14)$$

where U_2 is a known matrix. According to (13), (10) can be rewritten as:

$$\sqrt{\gamma(z, u(t), F_1, F_2)} = B(z)Dx(t) + h(Dx(t))b_n(z) + \omega(z, u(t), F_1, F_2) \quad (15)$$

Because there exist nonlinear terms in the weighted dynamic system, the design of the nonlinear filter is the key in the process of fault detection and isolation. In this paper, the fault detection and fault diagnosis filters are designed, respectively, according to $u(t)$, as well as the output PDFs $\gamma(z, u(t), F_1, F_2)$, so as to achieve the task of fault isolation.

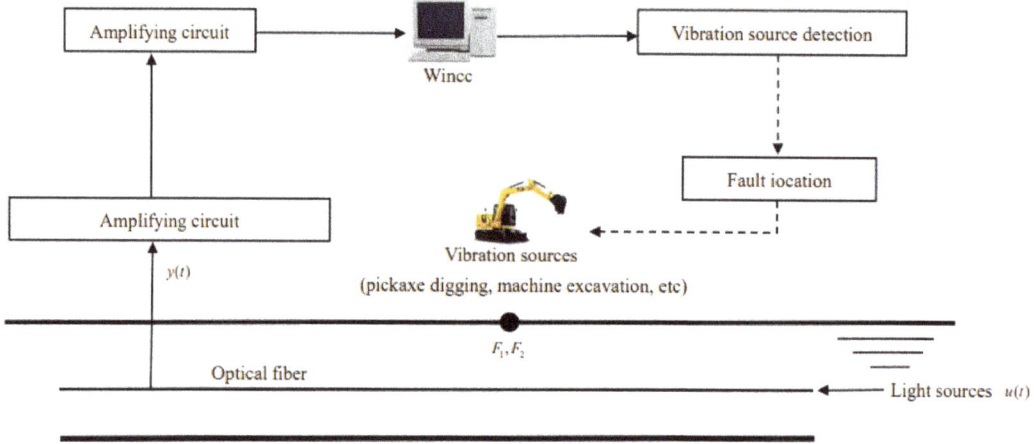

Figure 1. Fiber vibration source detection system.

3. Fault Detection Filter Design

In order to detect the faults based on the changes of the output PDFs, we construct the following nonlinear filter:

$$\begin{cases} \dot{\hat{x}}(t) = A\hat{x}(t) + Gg(\hat{x}(t)) + Hu(t) + L\varepsilon(t) \\ \varepsilon(t) = \int_a^b \sigma(z)[\sqrt{\gamma(z, u(t), F_1, F_2)} - \sqrt{\hat{\gamma}(z, u(t))}]dz \\ \sqrt{\hat{\gamma}(z, u(t))} = B(z)D\hat{x}(t) + h(D\hat{x}(t))b_n(z) \end{cases} \quad (16)$$

where $\hat{x}(t)$ is the estimated value of the state vector $x(t)$, $L \in R^{m \times p}$ is the gain of the detection observer to be determined, $\sigma(z) \in R^{p \times 1}$ is the pre-specified weighting vector defined on $[a, b]$, and the residual $\varepsilon(t)$ represents the integral of the difference between the measured PDFs $\gamma(z, u(t), F_1, F_2)$ and the estimated PDFs $\hat{\gamma}(z, u(t))$ [26]. Denote $e(t) = x(t) - \hat{x}(t)$, then the first derivative of $e(t)$ with respect to time t is:

$$\begin{aligned}\dot{e}(t) = \dot{x}(t) - \dot{\hat{x}}(t) = (A - L\Gamma_1)e(t) + [Gg(x(t)) - Gg(\hat{x}(t))] \\ -L\Gamma_2[h(Dx(t)) - h(D\hat{x}(t))] + F_1 + F_2 - L\Delta(t)\end{aligned} \quad (17)$$

where
$$\begin{cases} \Gamma_1 = \int_a^b \sigma(z)B(z)dz \\ \Gamma_2 = \int_a^b \sigma(z)b_n(z)dz \\ \Delta(t) = \int_a^b \sigma(z)\omega(z,u(t),F_1,F_2)dz \end{cases} \quad (18)$$

As shown in (10) and (16), it is clear that the residual $\varepsilon(t)$ is a nonlinear function of $e(t)$, $x(t)$, and $\hat{x}(t)$. According to (18), the residual $\varepsilon(t)$ can be further expressed as

$$\begin{aligned} \varepsilon(t) &= \int_a^b \sigma(z)B(z)De(t)dz + \int_a^b \sigma(z)[h(Dx(t))-h(D\hat{x}(t))]b_n(z)dz \\ &\quad + \int_a^b \sigma(z)\omega(z,u(t),F_1,F_2)dz \\ &= \Gamma_1 e(t) + \Gamma_2[h(Dx(t))-h(D\hat{x}(t))] + \Delta(t) \end{aligned} \quad (19)$$

Recall $|\omega(z,u(t),F_1,F_2)| < \delta$, and combine it with (18); we can obtain that

$$|\Delta(t)| < \tilde{\delta} \quad (20)$$

where $\tilde{\delta} = \delta \left\| \int_a^b \sigma(z)dz \right\|$. In (16), $\sigma(z)$ can be any constant vector, and it is required that (A, Γ_1) is observable. In the fault detection stage, according to Theorem 1 in [8], if there exist parameters $\lambda_i (i=1,2)$, matrices $P > 0$, R, and constant $\eta > 0$, then if $F_1 = F_2 = 0$, the system (17) with gain $L = P^{-1}R$ is stable, and the error satisfies:

$$\|e(t)\| \leq \alpha_0 = \max\left\{\|e(0)\|, 2\eta^{-1}\tilde{\delta}\|R\|\right\} \quad (21)$$

In order to detect the faults, we select $\varepsilon(t)$ as the residual signal. According to [8], the faults can be detected as follows:

$$\varepsilon(t) > \alpha = \alpha_0(\|\Gamma_1\| + \|\Gamma_2\|\|U_1\|) + \tilde{\delta} \quad (22)$$

4. Fault Isolation Filter Design

Once the faults are detected according to the method in Section 2, it is necessary to carry out fault diagnosis and estimate the size of different faults, respectively, so as to achieve fault isolation. For this purpose, we construct the following adaptive filter as shown in (23):

$$\begin{cases} \dot{\hat{x}}(t) = A\hat{x}(t) + Gg(\hat{x}(t)) + Hu(t) + \begin{bmatrix} 1 & 1 \end{bmatrix} \begin{bmatrix} \hat{F}_1 \\ \hat{F}_2 \end{bmatrix} + L\varepsilon(t) \\ \begin{bmatrix} \dot{\hat{F}}_1 \\ \dot{\hat{F}}_2 \end{bmatrix} = \begin{bmatrix} -\Lambda_5 & 0 \\ 0 & -\Lambda_7 \end{bmatrix} \begin{bmatrix} \hat{F}_1 \\ \hat{F}_2 \end{bmatrix} + \begin{bmatrix} \Lambda_6 \\ \Lambda_8 \end{bmatrix} \varepsilon(t) \\ \varepsilon(t) = \int_a^b \sigma(z)[\sqrt{\gamma(z,u(t),F_1,F_2)} - \sqrt{\hat{\gamma}(z,u(t))}]dz \\ \sqrt{\hat{\gamma}(z,u(t))} = B(z)D\hat{x}(t) + h(D\hat{x}(t))b_n(z) \end{cases} \quad (23)$$

where $\hat{F}_1$ and $\hat{F}_2$ are the estimates of faults F_1 and F_2. In (23), $\Lambda_i (i=5,6,7,8)$ is the learning operator with respect to $\hat{F}_1$, $\hat{F}_2$, and the fault estimation errors.

Let $e(t) = x(t) - \hat{x}(t)$, and define the fault estimation errors as $\tilde{F}_1 = F_1 - \hat{F}_1$, $\tilde{F}_2 = F_2 - \hat{F}_2$, then the estimation errors can be shown as in (24):

$$\begin{cases} \dot{e}(t) = (A - L\Gamma_1)e(t) + [Gg(x(t)) - Gg(\hat{x}(t))] \\ \quad - L\Gamma_2[h(Dx(t)) - h(D\hat{x}(t))] + \tilde{F}_1 + \tilde{F}_2 - L\Delta(t) \\ \dot{\tilde{F}}_1 = -\Lambda_5 \tilde{F}_1 + \Lambda_5 F_1 - \Lambda_6 \varepsilon(t) \\ \dot{\tilde{F}}_2 = -\Lambda_7 \tilde{F}_2 + \Lambda_7 F_2 - \Lambda_8 \varepsilon(t) \\ \varepsilon(t) = \Gamma_1 e(t) + \Gamma_2[h(Dx(t)) - h(D\hat{x}(t))] + \Delta(t) \end{cases} \quad (24)$$

Supposing $\|F_1\| \leq M_1/2$, $\|F_2\| \leq M_2/2$, the following theorem will show that, by selecting the appropriate filter gains $\Lambda_5, \Lambda_6, \Lambda_7,$ and Λ_8, the fault estimation errors can be controlled in a small range.

Theorem 1. *If there exist $\lambda_i > 0 (i = 1, 2)$, matrices $P > 0$, R, and $\Lambda_i (i = 5, 6, 7, 8)$, and constants $\kappa > 0$, $\theta_1 > 0$, $\theta_2 > 0$, and θ_3 satisfying:*

$$\begin{bmatrix} \Pi_0 + \kappa I & P - \Gamma_1^T \Lambda_6^T & P - \Gamma_1^T \Lambda_8^T & \Pi_2 & 0 & 0 & D^T U_1^T \\ P - \Lambda_6 \Gamma_1 & -2\Lambda_5^T & 0 & 0 & \Pi_3 & 0 & 0 \\ P - \Lambda_8 \Gamma_1 & 0 & -2\Lambda_7^T & 0 & 0 & \Pi_4 & 0 \\ \Pi_2^T & 0 & 0 & -I & 0 & 0 & 0 \\ 0 & \Pi_3^T & 0 & 0 & -I & 0 & 0 \\ 0 & 0 & \Pi_4^T & 0 & 0 & -I & 0 \\ U_1 D & 0 & 0 & 0 & 0 & 0 & -\frac{1}{2}\theta_3^2 I \end{bmatrix} < 0 \quad (25)$$

where

$$\Pi_2 = [\; \lambda_1 R \Gamma_2 \;\; \lambda_2 PG \;\; \theta_1 \; R\;]$$
$$\Pi_3 = [\; \theta_2 \Lambda_6 \;\; \theta_3 \Lambda_6 \Gamma_2 \;]$$
$$\Pi_4 = [\; \theta_2 \Lambda_8 \;\; \theta_3 \Lambda_8 \Gamma_2 \;]$$
$$\Pi_0 = (PA - R\Gamma_1) + (PA - R\Gamma_1)^T + \tfrac{1}{\lambda_1^2} D^T U_1^T U_1 D + \tfrac{1}{\lambda_2^2} U_2^T U_2$$

then, with gain $L = P^{-1}R$, the error system (24) is stable in the presence of F_1, F_2, and the estimation error satisfies

$$\|e(t)\|^2 \leq \min\{\|e(0)\|^2, \kappa^{-1}((\theta_1^{-2} + 2\theta_2^{-2})\tilde{\delta}^2 + \|\Lambda_5\|M_1^2 + \|\Lambda_7\|M_2^2)\} \quad (26)$$

for all $t \in [0, +\infty)$.

Proof. Consider the following Lyapunov function:

$$\Pi(e(t), x(t), \hat{x}(t), \tilde{F}_1, \tilde{F}_2, t) = \Phi(e(t), x(t), \hat{x}(t), t) + \tilde{F}_1^T \tilde{F}_1 + \tilde{F}_2^T \tilde{F}_2 \quad (27)$$

where

$$\Phi(e(t), x(t), \hat{x}(t), t) = e^T(t) P e(t) + \frac{1}{\lambda_2^2} \int_0^t [\|U_2 e(\tau)\|^2 - \|gx(\tau) - g(\hat{x}(\tau))\|]d\tau \quad (28)$$
$$+ \frac{1}{\lambda_1^2} \int_0^t [\|U_1 D e(\tau)\|^2 - \|h(Dx(\tau)) - h(D\hat{x}(\tau))\|^2]d\tau$$

To simplify the proof, we abbreviate $\Phi(e(t), x(t), \hat{x}(t), t)$ to Φ. Let $R = PL$; we obtain:

$$\dot{\Phi} \leq e^T(t) \Psi_0 e(t) - 2e^T(t) PL\Delta(t) + 2e^T(t) P\tilde{F}_1 + 2e^T(t) P\tilde{F}_2 \quad (29)$$
$$\leq e^T(t) \Psi_1 e(t) + \theta_1^{-2} \Delta^T(t) \Delta(t) + 2e^T(t) P\tilde{F}_1 + 2e^T(t) P\tilde{F}_2$$

where

$$\Psi_1 = \Psi_0 + \theta_1^2 RR^T$$
$$\Psi_0 = P(A - L\Gamma_1) + (A - L\Gamma_1)^T P + \lambda_2^2 PGG^T P$$
$$+ \lambda_1^2 PL\Gamma_2 \Gamma_2 LP + \tfrac{1}{\lambda_1^2} D^T U_1^T U_1 D + \tfrac{1}{\lambda_2^2} U_2^T U_2$$

From (24) and (29), the first derivative of Π is:

$$\dot{\Pi} = e^T(t)\Psi_1 e(t) + \theta_1^{-2}\Delta^T(t)\Delta(t) + 2e^T(t)P\tilde{F}_1 + 2e^T(t)P\tilde{F}_2 + 2\tilde{F}_1^T\dot{\tilde{F}}_1 + 2\tilde{F}_2^T\dot{\tilde{F}}_2$$
$$\leq e^T(t)[\Psi_1 + 2\theta_3^{-2}D^T U_1^T U_1 D]e(t) + 2e^T(t)P\tilde{F}_1 + 2e^T(t)P\tilde{F}_2 - 2\tilde{F}_1^T\Lambda_5^T\tilde{F}_1$$
$$+ \theta_2^2\tilde{F}_1^T\Lambda_6\Lambda_6^T\tilde{F}_1 + \theta_2^2\tilde{F}_2^T\Lambda_8\Lambda_8^T\tilde{F}_2 - 2\tilde{F}_2^T\Lambda_7^T\tilde{F}_2 + (\theta_1^{-2} + 2\theta_2^{-2})\Delta^T(t)\Delta(t)$$
$$- 2\tilde{F}_1^T\Lambda_6\Gamma_1 e(t) - 2\tilde{F}_2^T\Lambda_8\Gamma_1 e(t) + \theta_3^2\tilde{F}_1^T\Lambda_6\Gamma_2\Gamma_2^T\Lambda_6^T\tilde{F}_1 + \theta_3^2\tilde{F}_2^T\Lambda_8\Gamma_2\Gamma_2^T\Lambda_8^T\tilde{F}_2$$
$$+ 2F_1^T\Lambda_5^T\tilde{F}_1 + 2F_2^T\Lambda_7^T\tilde{F}_2$$
$$= [e^T(t)\ \tilde{F}_1^T\ \tilde{F}_2^T]\Psi\begin{bmatrix}e(t)\\ \tilde{F}_1\\ \tilde{F}_2\end{bmatrix} + (\theta_1^{-2} + 2\theta_2^{-2})\Delta^T(t)\Delta(t) + 2F_1^T\Lambda_5^T\tilde{F}_1 + 2F_2^T\Lambda_7^T\tilde{F}_2$$

where
$$\Psi_{22} = -2\Lambda_5^T + \theta_2^2\Lambda_6\Lambda_6^T + \theta_3^2\Lambda_6\Gamma_2\Gamma_2^T\Lambda_6^T$$
$$\Psi_{33} = -2\Lambda_7^T + \theta_2^2\Lambda_8\Lambda_8^T + \theta_3^2\Lambda_8\Gamma_2\Gamma_2^T\Lambda_8^T$$
$$\Psi = \begin{bmatrix} \Psi_1 + 2\theta_3^{-2}D^T U_1^T U_1 D & P - \Gamma_1^T\Lambda_6^T & P - \Gamma_1^T\Lambda_8^T \\ P - \Lambda_6\Gamma_1 & \Psi_{22} & 0 \\ P - \Lambda_8\Gamma_1 & 0 & \Psi_{33} \end{bmatrix}$$

Using the Schur complement lemma, we can obtain that (25) is equivalent to $\bar{\Psi} \leq diag\{-\kappa I, 0\}$, from which we can obtain:

$$\dot{\Pi} < -\kappa\|e(t)\|^2 + \left(\theta_1^{-2} + 2\theta_2^{-2}\right)\tilde{\delta}^2 + 2F_1^T\Lambda_5^T\tilde{F}_1 + 2F_2^T\Lambda_7^T\tilde{F}$$
$$\leq -\kappa\|e(t)\|^2 + \left(\theta_1^{-2} + 2\theta_2^{-2}\right)\tilde{\delta}^2 + \|\Lambda_5\|M_1^2 + \|\Lambda_7\|M_2^2$$

When $\kappa\|e(t)\|^2 > \left(\theta_1^{-2} + 2\theta_2^{-2}\right)\tilde{\delta}^2 + \|\Lambda_5\|M_1^2 + \|\Lambda_7\|M_2^2$, $\Pi > 0$, $\dot{\Pi} < 0$, so (22) holds. □

5. Simulation

In the optical fiber vibration source detection system [22] shown in Figure 1, the optical fiber is buried underground in the same ditch with oil or gas pipelines. The PDFs of the output light intensity are affected by the input light intensity $u(t)$, false alarms (environmental interferences, such as a vehicle passing), as well as various destructive vibration sources (theft, geological disasters, etc.). Our goal is to detect whether these vibration sources are false alarms or real alarms. It is supposed that the PDFs of the output light intensity can be approximately expressed by the square root B-spline basis function described by $\sqrt{\gamma(z, u(t), F_1, F_2)} = \sum_1^3 v_i(z, u(t), F_1, F_2) b_i(z)$, where F_1 represents pickaxe digging and F_2 represents machine excavation. Suppose

$$b_i(z) = \begin{cases} |\sin 2\pi z|, z \in [0.5(i-1), 0.5i] \\ 0, z \in [0.5(j-1), 0.5j] \end{cases} \quad i \neq j \tag{30}$$

for $i = 1, 2, 3$. Recalling (2)–(4), it can be calculated that

$$\Lambda_1 = \begin{bmatrix} 0.25 & 0 \\ 0 & 0.25 \end{bmatrix}, \Lambda_2 = [\ 0\ \ 0\ ], \Lambda_3 = 0.25.$$

In this simulation, the parameters were selected as follows:

$$A = \begin{bmatrix} -0.5 & 0 \\ 0 & -1.3 \end{bmatrix}, G = \begin{bmatrix} 0 & 0 \\ 0 & 0.1 \end{bmatrix}, H = \begin{bmatrix} 0.2 & 0 \\ 0 & -0.3 \end{bmatrix}$$
$$G(V(t)) = \begin{bmatrix} 0 \\ 0.25\sqrt{v_1^2(t) + v_2^2(t)} \end{bmatrix}, D = \begin{bmatrix} 1 & 0 \\ 0 & 1 \end{bmatrix}$$

Consequently, it can be calculated that $U_1 = \begin{bmatrix} 1 & 1 \end{bmatrix}$ and $U_2 = \begin{bmatrix} 0 & 0 \\ 0 & 0.5 \end{bmatrix}$. According to (16), a nonlinear detection filter can be constructed. Select $\sigma = 1$; it can be verified that (A, Γ_1) is observable and

$$\Gamma_1 = \begin{bmatrix} \frac{1}{\pi} & \frac{1}{\pi} \end{bmatrix}, \Gamma_1 = \frac{1}{\pi}, \Delta(t) \leq 0.15.$$

The initial values are supposed to be $x(0) = \begin{bmatrix} 0.5 & 0.25 \end{bmatrix}$, $\hat{x}(0) = \begin{bmatrix} 0 & 0 \end{bmatrix}$. For $\lambda_1 = \lambda_2 = 1$, $\theta_1 = \theta_2 = 2$, $\theta_3 = -2$, $\eta = 2$, and $\kappa = 0.1$. From (22), the thresholds are $\alpha_0 = 0.4719$ and $\alpha = 0.5751$. By solving (25) with the LMI toolbox, we obtain:

$$P = \begin{bmatrix} 3.9269 & -4.5402 \\ -4.5402 & 6.4692 \end{bmatrix} R = \begin{bmatrix} 0.1106 \\ 0.1104 \end{bmatrix} L = \begin{bmatrix} 0.0527 \\ 0.0212 \end{bmatrix}$$
$$\Lambda_5 = \begin{bmatrix} 7.1833 & -8.5760 \\ -4.3862 & 9.5318 \end{bmatrix} \Lambda_6 = \begin{bmatrix} 0.4681 \\ -0.2479 \end{bmatrix}$$
$$\Lambda_7 = 10^6 \times \begin{bmatrix} 30.330 & -0.1912 \\ -0.1912 & 3.7291 \end{bmatrix} \Lambda_8 = \begin{bmatrix} 6.6378 \\ -2.0262 \end{bmatrix}$$

Figure 2 shows the PDFs of the output light intensity when there is no destructive vibration source (i.e., $F_1 = F_2 = 0$), and Figure 3 shows the PDFs of the output light intensity when some destructive vibration source occurs (i.e., $F_1 \neq 0$ and $F_2 \neq 0$). Comparing Figures 2 and 3, it can be seen that the PDFs of the output light intensity have changed significantly. In the simulation, it was assumed that the first destructive vibration source (pickaxe digging) starts from the 10th second and the second destructive vibration source (machine excavation) starts from the 30th second. Based on the fault detection filter (16) in this paper, the response of the residual $\varepsilon(t)$ is shown in Figure 4. It can be seen from Figure 4 that, when these faults occur, the value of the residual $\varepsilon(t)$ will change, but it always satisfies $\varepsilon(t) > 0.5751$. When $\varepsilon(t) > 0.5751$, an alarm should be sounded in the optical fiber vibration source detection system.

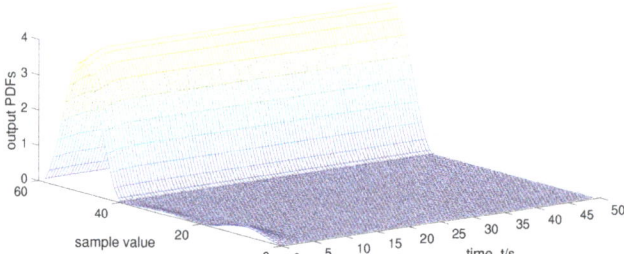

Figure 2. The 3D mesh of output PDFs when $F_1 = F_2 = 0$.

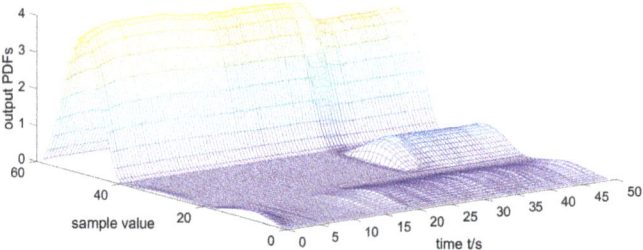

Figure 3. The 3D measure of output PDFs with faults.

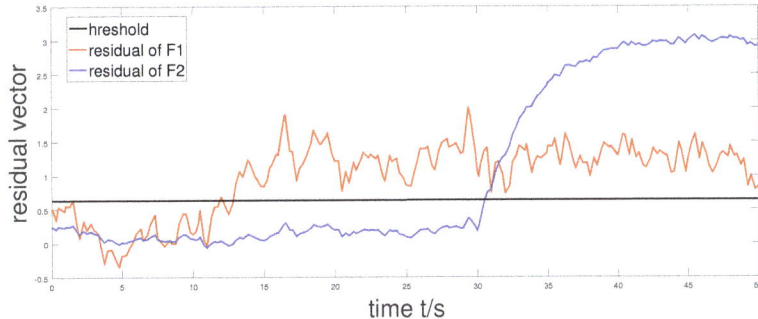

Figure 4. Response of residual vector $\varepsilon(t)$.

After the fault diagnosis filter is designed based on Theorem 1, we can obtain Figures 5–7. Figure 5 is the estimation of F_1 when pickaxe digging occurs. It can be seen from Figure 5 that the fault diagnosis filter can quickly track the change of the fault 10 s after the first destructive vibration source F_1 appears. Figure 6 is the response of the fault diagnosis observer when machine excavation F_2 exists. It can be seen from Figure 6 that, after the second vibration source appears, the fault diagnosis filter can quickly track fault F_2. Figure 7 is the response of the fault diagnosis observer with multiple faults F_1 (pickaxe digging) and F_2 (machine excavation), which can be detected, respectively, based on the methods in this paper. It can be seen from Figure 7 that, when faults F_1 and F_2 exist at the same time, the diagnostic filter can clearly diagnose F_1 and F_2. The corresponding vibration source strength can thus be estimated and helps to identify which type of damage.

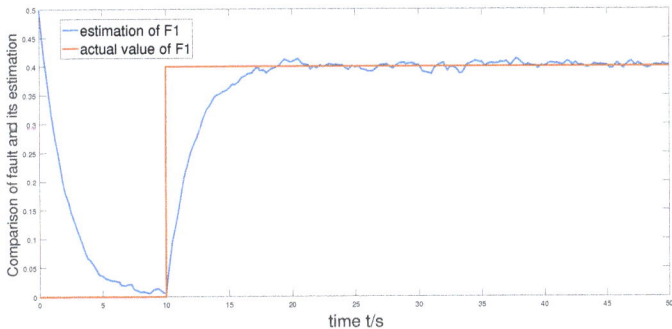

Figure 5. Comparison of fault F_1 and its estimation $\hat{F}_1$.

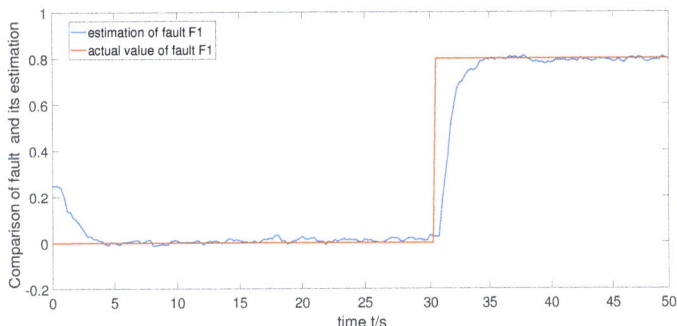

Figure 6. Comparison of fault F_2 and its estimation $\hat{F}_2$.

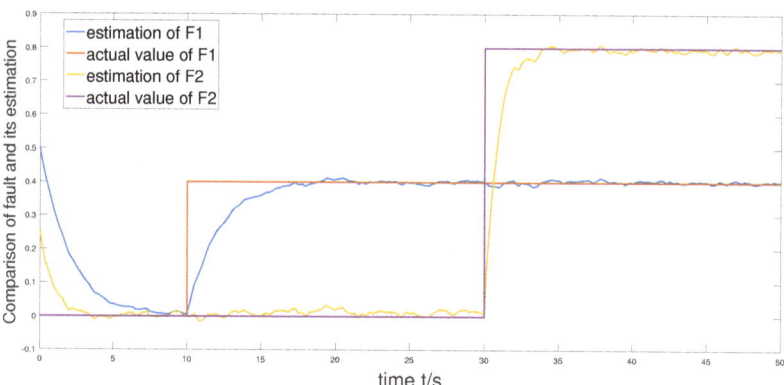

Figure 7. Composite graph of F_1, F_2, and their estimations $\hat{F}_1$, $\hat{F}_2$.

In the man–machine interface designed for the optical fiber vibration source detection and early warning system, we carried out a comparative experiment. We used the same set of data to compare the PDF thresholds. The experiment showed that, before adjusting the threshold value, the detection effect of the optical fiber signal under the influence of vibration is as shown in Figure 8. The platform detects that three columns have vibration alarm signals, and this section flashes to remind the user. The effect after using the method in this paper is shown in Figure 9, which proves that the method of fault isolation can reduce the false alarm rate and make the detection effect of the optical fiber vibration source more stable and accurate.

Figure 8. Vibration source alarm before using the isolation method.

Figure 9. Vibration source alarm after using the isolation method.

6. Conclusions

In this paper, in order to reduce the false alarm rate in oil or gas pipeline monitoring, we regarded the different vibrations in the system as faults and considered faults' isolation to identify different types of vibrations for a non-Gaussian stochastic distribution control model because of inevitable non-stationary interferences from the environment. The fault isolation started by using square root B-spline expansion and a nonlinear weighted dynamic model. The faults in the system were estimated separately to achieve the purpose of fault isolation. The output value of the system in this paper is not measurable, but the output PDFs can be measured by optical instruments. Firstly, the PDFs of the output signal were approximated by square root B-spline expansion. Secondly, the nonlinear dynamic model between the control input and the weights of PDFs was established by a dynamic neural network. Thirdly, based on the measured output PDFs and the input of the system, a filter-based residual generator was constructed to detect and diagnose the faults. Through LMIs, the feasibility criterion for the detection and isolation system faults was given, as well as the steady error ranges. Finally, the effectiveness of this method was verified for the optical fiber vibration source detection system.

7. Future Work

In the optical fiber vibration source detection system, there will be more types of faults, such as time-varying faults, multiplicative faults, etc. This paper only focused on the detection and isolation of constant faults in optical systems. In the future work, we will continue to study the detection and isolation of multiplicative faults and time-varying faults in stochastic distributed systems.

Author Contributions: L.Y., J.L. and T.L. conceived the project. L.Y., J.L. searched relevant literatures. L.Y., J.L. carried out the theoretical derivation. L.Y., J.L., T.L. and H.Q. provided the simulation results. L.Y., J.L. and T.L. analysed the simulation results and wrote the paper. Correspondence and requests for materials should be addressed to L.Y. All authors have read and approved the final manuscript.

Funding: The work in this paper is jointly funded by National Science Foundation of China under Grant Nos. 61573190, 61973168. They are gratefully acknowledged.

Institutional Review Board Statement: Not applicable.

Informed Consent Statement: Not applicable.

Data Availability Statement: Not applicable.

Conflicts of Interest: The authors declare no conflict of interest.

Nomenclature

$\gamma(z, u(t), F_1, F_2)$	output PDFs
$\hat{\gamma}(z, u(t))$	estimated output PDFs
$x(t)$	state vector
$\hat{x}(t)$	estimated value of the state vector
F_1	Fault 1
$\hat{F}_1$	estimates of fault F_1
F_2	Fault 2
$\hat{F}_2$	estimates of fault F_2
$v_i(u(t), F_1, F_2)$	the corresponding weights of B-spline expansion
$\omega_0(z, u(t), F_1, F_2)$	model error term
$b_i(z)$	the pre-specified basis functions
$y(t)$	system output
$e(t)$	state error vector
$u(t)$	input of nonlinear stochastic optical fiber vibration detection system
$\epsilon(t)$	fault detection residual vector
P	positive definite matrix to be solved
L	gain of fault diagnosis filter
$g(x(t))$	nonlinear function
$PDFs$	probability density functions
$LMIs$	linear matrix inequalities
FDI	fault detection and isolation

References

1. Yu, X.; Jiang, B.; Ke, Z. Observer-Based Fault Detection of Broken Rotor Bars in Traction Motors. In Proceedings of the 2017 29th IEEE Chinese Control and Decision Conference (CCDC), Chongqing, China, 28–30 May 2017; pp. 309–314.
2. Venghi, L.E.; Aguilera, F.; de la Barrera, P.M.; De Angelo, C.H. Detection and isolation of current-sensor and open-switch faults in electric traction drives. *IEEE Lat. Am. Trans.* **2021**, *19*, 1335–1346. [CrossRef]
3. Qiang, X.; Xue, R.; Zhu, Y. Multi-sensor Fusion Approach with Fault Detection and Isolation Based on two-state Probability Ratio. In Proceedings of the 2021 Sixth International Conference on Wireless Communications, Signal Processing and Networking, Chennai, India, 25–27 March 2021; pp. 325–329.
4. Yin, L.; Wang, H.; Guo, L.; Zhang, H. Data-driven Pareto-DE-based intelligent optimal operational control for stochastic processes. *IEEE Trans. Syst. Man Cybern. Syst.* **2019**, *51*, 4443–4452. [CrossRef]
5. Yan, B.; Tian, Z.; Shi, S. A Novel Distributed Approach to Robust Fault Detection and Identification. *Int. J. Electr. Power Energy Syst.* **2008**, *30*, 343–360. [CrossRef]
6. Wang, H.; Yao, L.N. Sensor Fault Diagnosis and Fault-Tolerant Control for Non-Gaussian Stochastic Distribution Systems. *Math. Probl. Eng.* **2019**, *50*, 1–13. [CrossRef]
7. Yao, L.; Xu, J.; Xu, F. Minimum Entropy Fault-Tolerant Control of the Non-Gaussian Stochastic Distribution System. *IET Control Theory Appl.* **2016**, *10*, 1194–1201. [CrossRef]
8. Guo, L.; Wang, H. Fault Detection and Diagnosis for General Stochastic Systems Using B-Spline Expansions and Nonlinear Filters. *IEEE Trans. Circuits Syst. I Regul. Pap.* **2005**, *52*, 1644–1652.
9. Cao, S.Y.; Guo, L. Fault Diagnosis with Disturbance Rejection Performance Based on Disturbance Observer. In Proceedings of the Proceedings of the 48h IEEE Conference on Decision and Control (CDC) held jointly with 2009 28th Chinese Control Conference, Shanghai, China, 16–18 December 2009; pp. 6947–6951.
10. Zhang, J.; Gao, Q.; Yuan, C.; Zeng, W.; Dai, S.L.; Wang, C. Similar Fault Isolation of Discrete-Time Nonlinear Uncertain Systems: An Adaptive Threshold Based Approach. *IEEE Access* **2020**, *8*, 80755–80770. [CrossRef]
11. Wang, H.; Kang, Y.; Yao, L.; Wang, H.; Gao, Z. Fault Diagnosis and Fault Tolerant Control for T–S Fuzzy Stochastic Distribution Systems Subject to Sensor and Actuator Faults. *IEEE Trans. Fuzzy Syst.* **2021**, *29*, 3561–3569. [CrossRef]
12. Zhang, Y.W. *Data Based Fault Isolation*; Northeast University Press: Shenyang, China, 2016.
13. Wang, Y.Q.; Hao, Y.E.; Ding, X.S.; Wang, G.Z. Fault Detection of Networked Control Systems Based on Optimal Robust Fault Detection Filter. *Acta Autom. Sin.* **2008**, *34*, 1534–1539. [CrossRef]
14. Yang, L.; Wang, Z.; Xiao, H.; Zhou, D. Least Square Fault Estimation for a Class of Sensor Networks. In Proceedings of the 2013 25th Chinese Control and Decision Conference (CCDC), Guiyang, China, 25–27 May 2013; pp. 4984–4988.
15. Biswas, S.; Nayak, P.K. A Fault Detection and Classification Scheme for Unified Power Flow Controller Compensated Transmission Lines Connecting Wind Farms. *IEEE Syst. J.* **2021**, *15*, 297–306. [CrossRef]
16. Tran, M.Q.; Elsisi, M.; Liu, M.K. Effective Feature Selection with Fuzzy Entropy and Similarity Classifier for Chatter Vibration Diagnosis. *Measurement* **2021**, *184*, 109962. [CrossRef]
17. Tran, M.Q.; Liu, M.K.; Elsisi, M. Effective Multi-sensor Data Dusion for Chatter Detection in Milling Process. *ISA Trans.* **2022**, *125*, 514–527. [CrossRef]
18. Ren, M.F.; Zhang, J.H.; Wang, H. *Control and Filtering for Non-Gaussian Systems*; Science Press: Beijing, China, 2016.
19. Cheng, Y.; Chen, B.; Zhang, W. Adaptive Multipoint Optimal Minimum Entropy Deconvolution Adjusted and Application to Fault Diagnosis of Rolling Element Bearings. *IEEE Sens. J.* **2019**, *19*, 12153–12164. [CrossRef]
20. Guo, L.; Yin, L.; Wang, H.; Chai, T. Entropy Optimization Filtering for Fault Isolation of Nonlinear Non-Gaussian Stochastic Systems. *IEEE Trans. Autom. Control* **2009**, *54*, 804–810.
21. Yin, L.; Lai, L.; Zhu, Z.; Li, T. Maximum Power Point Tracking Control for Non-Gaussian Wind Energy Conversion System by Using Survival Information Potential. *Entropy* **2022**, *24*, 818. [CrossRef]
22. Shu, M.X. Research on False Alarm Control Algorithm for Fiber Vibration Source Detection under Non-Stationary Disturbances. Master's Thesis, Nanjing University of Information Science & Technology, Nanjing, China, 2019.
23. Han, D. Alarm Control and Simulation Platform Construction for Disturbed Optical Fiber Vibration Detection. Master's Thesis, Nanjing University of Information Science & Technology, Nanjing, China, 2020.
24. Cai, Y. Research Progress on Safety State Monitoring Technology of Oil and Gas Pipeline System. *Pet. New Energy* **2022**, *34*, 65–70.
25. Wang, H. *Bounded Dynamic Stochastic Systems, Modelling and Control*; Springer Group: Berlin, Germany, 1999.
26. Guo, L.; Yi, Y.; Yin, L.P.; Wang, H. *Modeling, Analysis and Control Theory of Non-Gaussian Stochastic Distribution System*; Science Press: Beijing, China, 2019.

Article

Finite-Control-Set Model Predictive Control for Low-Voltage-Ride-Through Enhancement of PMSG Based Wind Energy Grid Connection Systems

Syed Wajahat Ali [1], Anant Kumar Verma [2], Yacine Terriche [3], Muhammad Sadiq [1], Chun-Lien Su [1,*], Chung-Hong Lee [1] and Mahmoud Elsisi [1,4]

1 Electrical Engineering Department, National Kaohsiung University of Science and Technology, Kaohsiung City 807618, Taiwan
2 Electric Power Conversion Systems Laboratory (SCoPE Lab), Universidad de O'Higgins, 611, Av. Libertador Bernardo O'Higgins, Rancagua 2820000, Chile
3 Center for Research on Microgrids, Department of Energy Technology, Aalborg University, 9220 Aalborg, Denmark
4 Department of Electrical Engineering, Faculty of Engineering at Shoubra, Benha University, Cairo 11629, Egypt
* Correspondence: cls@nkust.edu.tw

Citation: Ali, S.W.; Verma, A.K.; Terriche, Y.; Sadiq, M.; Su, C.-L.; Lee, C.-H.; Elsisi, M. Finite-Control-Set Model Predictive Control for Low-Voltage-Ride-Through Enhancement of PMSG Based Wind Energy Grid Connection Systems. *Mathematics* 2022, 10, 4266. https://doi.org/10.3390/math10224266

Academic Editor: António Lopes

Received: 15 October 2022
Accepted: 10 November 2022
Published: 15 November 2022

Publisher's Note: MDPI stays neutral with regard to jurisdictional claims in published maps and institutional affiliations.

Copyright: © 2022 by the authors. Licensee MDPI, Basel, Switzerland. This article is an open access article distributed under the terms and conditions of the Creative Commons Attribution (CC BY) license (https:// creativecommons.org/licenses/by/ 4.0/).

Abstract: Grid faults are found to be one of the major issues in renewable energy systems, particularly in wind energy conversion systems (WECS) connected to the grid via back-to-back (BTB) converters. Under such faulty grid conditions, the system requires an effective regulation of the active (P) and reactive (Q) power to accomplish low voltage ride through (LVRT) operation in accordance with the grid codes. In this paper, an improved finite-control-set model predictive control (FCS-MPC) scheme is proposed for a PMSG based WECS to achieve LVRT ability under symmetrical and asymmetrical grid faults, including mitigation of DC-link voltage fluctuation. With proposed predictive control, optimized switching states for cost function minimization with weighing factor (WF) selection guidelines are established for robust BTB converter control and reduced cross-coupling amid P and Q during transient conditions. Besides, grid voltage support is provided by grid side inverter control to inject reactive power during voltage dips. The effectiveness of the FCS-MPC method is compared with the conventional proportional-integral (PI) controller in case of symmetrical and asymmetrical grid faults. The simulation and experimental results endorse the superiority of the developed FCS-MPC scheme to diminish the fault effect quickly with lower overshoot and better damping performance than the traditional controller.

Keywords: model predictive control; PI control; wind energy; PMSG; reactive power; LVRT capability; grid faults

MSC: 93-08; 93B17; 93B35; 93B45; 93B51; 93B52; 93B70

1. Introduction

Recently, renewable energy sources like wind power farms are witnessing rapid incorporation into the electric power market, primarily because of reduced carbon footprint with less dependence on fossil fuels [1]. On the flip side, these sources are attributed to a weak dynamic system performance that yields power quality and stability issues [2,3]. Fast-paced research has been conducted to mitigate issues related to power control and grid faults by modifying the integration strategies in grid-connected wind turbines (GCWT) systems [4]. LVRT standards obligate a wind generation system to be linked to the power system during uncertain grid conditions and faults [5,6]. According to E.ON-Netz, Germany, LVRT condition requires an RES to retain grid connection and inject reactive power during grid irregularities [7]. Moreover, these issues motivate network authorities to revise the grid codes to enforce LVRT as a key capability for stable and robust GCWT systems operation [8,9].

Control problems in GCWT systems are usually dealt with using vector control [10]. In such schemes, active and reactive power components are generated by decoupling the system current into rotating reference frame (dq-frame) currents. Conventionally, PI-based controllers regulate rotor current vectors through the machine side converter (MSC) as well as grid current vectors through the grid side converter (GSC) [11,12]. Due to intrinsic restrictions of the PI controllers, particularly with nonlinear systems and for better grid fault mitigation, various advanced control techniques as well as hardware solutions are presented in the literature [13–22].

A compound method having repetitive control and fuzzy based PI control is proposed in [13] for power smoothening in a PMSG based GCWT system. Likewise, better THD with enhanced LVRT ability is achieved in a grid connected WECS using adaptive parameter for a neural-fuzzy hybrid control [15]. Using a feedback linearizing scheme, a sliding mode control is exploited in [16] to mitigate the sub synchronous oscillations under various grid disturbances in the connected wind energy system. In [17], authors applied virtual synchronous machine (VSM) on a PMSG-based WT network to analyze the small signal stability of the proposed controllers. Nevertheless, most of these control schemes fall short when it comes to requirements such as abundant memory, model accuracy, computation time, and big data for an effective learning process.

Some hardware modifications approaches are used to enhance LVRT functionality in GCWT systems. To protect the BTB converter of GCWT against high rotor current in case of grid faults, a crowbar circuit is generally applied [17,18]. Likewise, more viable hardware option for enhanced LVRT capability is to link the energy storage systems (ESSs) with GSC of the GCWT system [20]. The ESS based system helps to store energy, while in the crowbar option, power dissipation is the only way out. An alternative method used for reactive power compensation and grid support at the PCC is to install flexible AC transmission systems (FACTS) devices, such as a dynamic voltage restorer (DVR) [21], the static synchronous compensator (STATCOM) [22], and static var compensator (SVC) [14]. Although these devices help to maintain constant voltage levels, nevertheless, the majority of such devices are not cost-effective and make the system more expensive and multifarious.

Underlying research on enhancing the LVRT capability of PMSG-based GCWT systems is subject to achieving objectives such as regulating the rotor overcurrent and DC-link overvoltage as well as controlling the active and reactive power under and during grid faults/voltage dips [23]. In such constrained problems, MPC proved to be a prime framework due to its recurrent optimization of control objectives over a receding horizon [24]. The prediction procedure occurs at each sample time to achieve cost function minimization. Error is generated by comparing the reference value with the measured output from the system, which acts as future information for the subsequent sample period for every variable. There are two broad categories of MPC discussed in the literature, namely continuous control set [25] and finite control set (FCS) [26]. When compared to continuous MPC, FSC-MPC has the advantage of processing the switching signals directly as control inputs, thus avoiding the need for a modulation stage. FCS-MPC is more appropriate for the applications relating to the control of power inverters [27].

On the other hand, there are some obstacles while using FCS-MPC for the GCWT systems. One major issue is the time-consuming computations while searching for the optimal or minimal values from all the possible switching state vectors. This exhaustive search limits controller computation ability as well as decreases the step length of the prediction horizon [28]. Another challenge is selecting the right weighting factors (WFs) for the cost function. Generally, high WF is assigned to the cost function term with higher error values. Typically, algorithms related to evolutionary search are used for WF determination. Several other schemes make use of dynamic WF gain as the error function to tune WF online [29,30]. Nonetheless, unsuitable WF selection may complicate the cost function, worsening the overall control effort. Consequently, there is a trade-off amid accuracy and simplicity.

Keeping in mind the shortcomings mentioned in the literature above, this study proposes an improved FSC-MPC scheme to boost the de-coupled control of the injected real and reactive power into the power grid. With the suggested FCS-MPC scheme, both the machine side converter (MSC) and GSC of the GCWT system are controlled to suppress dc-link overvoltage and to meet LVRT demand using cost function minimization during transient conditions. The proposed scheme helps adjust the WFs only during transient or fault conditions while keeping a uniform value under steady-state condition for each coefficient of the cost function. Besides, Lyapunove's stability criteria as well as parameter sensitivity analysis are carried out to inspect the stability and robustness of the proposed control scheme. To summarize, the key aspects and contributions of this study are:

- An FCS-MPC scheme is utilized to enhance the LVRT operation of a PMSG-based grid connected wind generation system.
- Optimized switching states are selected by proposed predictive model to achieve reduced cross-coupling errors of active and reactive power predictions.
- Priority-based weighting factors are tuned for faster performance of the controller for P and Q power injection under various grid scenarios.
- DC-link overvoltage oscillation mitigation with better reference tracking.
- Lyapunove's stability criterion and parameter robustness analysis have been performed.
- Improved implementation of proposed scheme under both symmetrical and asymmetrical grid faults in accordance with recommended grid codes.
- Dynamic performance analysis and comparison of the proposed FCS-MPC method with classical PI controller.
- Experimental verification of the simulated results.

The remaining parts of the article are organized as follows. In Section 2, detailed time domain modelling of GCWT system is provided. The proposed FCS-MPC approach and its application on MSC and GSC is described in Section 3. Finally, Sections 4 and 5 present simulation as well as experimental results and conclusions, respectively.

2. Grid Connected Wind Turbine System

The design and modelling of PMSG based GCWT system is established in this section. Firstly, the mechanical specifics of the wind turbine are discussed, followed by the modeling of the B2B converter system, which entails MSC, GSC, DC-link, and the converter output filter, as shown in Figure 1.

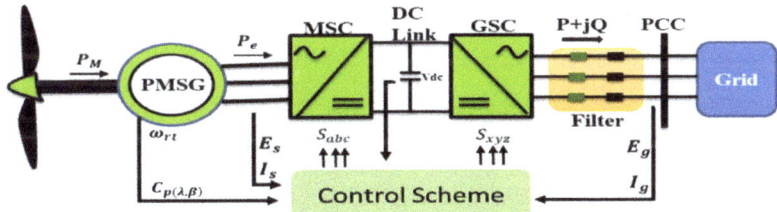

Figure 1. PMSG based GCWT System.

2.1. Wind-Turbine Modeling

The energy harnessed by the wind turbine is related to the wind speed and the turbine characteristics that can be expressed as [31]:

$$P_M = 0.5 \left[\rho A C_{p(\lambda,\beta)} v^3 \right] \quad (1)$$

where ρ is the density of the air, A is the swept area by the turbine blades, v is the speed of the wind, and C_p denotes the power coefficient, which is contingent upon tip speed ratio λ as well as pitch angle β. The value of λ is equated as

$$\lambda = \frac{\omega_{rt} \vartheta_{wb}}{v} \tag{2}$$

where ω_{rt} is the rotational speed of the turbine and ϑ_{wb} is the blade length of the wind turbine. Through the adjustment of λ, the maximum power can be extracted in case of varying the wind velocities with a maximum $C_{p(\lambda,\beta)}$ of 0.48 (Betz limit) at zero pitch angle as [31]:

$$C_{p(\lambda,\beta)} = 0.5175\left(-0.4\beta + \frac{116}{\lambda_a}\right)e^{\left(\frac{21}{\lambda_a}\right)} + \left(6.8e^{-3}\right)\lambda_a \tag{3}$$

where λ_a represents the constructional constraint constant.

2.2. Multiphase PMSG Modeling

The mathematical modeling of PMSG is mostly performed in space vector form by using park transformation. This transformation makes use of dq-frame or synchronous reference frame (SRF) to represent machine side variables such as voltages, power, and torque of the PMSG, as presented in Equations (4)–(8) [32]:

$$V_{ds} = -\omega_r L_s I_{qs} + R I_{ds} + L_s \frac{dI_{ds}}{dt} \tag{4}$$

$$V_{qs} = \omega_r L_s I_{ds} + \omega_r \Psi_r + R I_{qs} + L_s \frac{dI_{qs}}{dt} \tag{5}$$

$$T_{e.m} = \frac{3}{2}P[I_{qs}\Psi_r] \tag{6}$$

$$P_{stator} = \frac{3}{2}(V_{ds}I_{ds} + V_{qs}I_{qs}) \tag{7}$$

$$Q_{stator} = \frac{3}{2}(V_{qs}I_{ds} - V_{ds}I_{qs}) \tag{8}$$

where V_{ds}, V_{qs} are the stator voltages, I_{ds}, I_{qs} are the stator currents, L_s is the inductance of the stator, R is stator resistance, ω_r is the speed of the electric field, Ψ_r is the rotor flux linkage, $T_{e.m}$ is the electromagnetic torque, and P is the number of poles.

The mechanical and electrical torques can be related as follows:

$$P_m = \omega_r T_m; \quad \frac{d\omega_r}{dt} = \frac{1}{D}(T_e - T_m) - \frac{B}{D}\omega_r \tag{9}$$

where P_m is the mechanical power of the wind turbine, D is the inertia of the system and B is the friction-coefficient. Similarly, the mathematical model of GSC in dq-frame can be represented as follows [33]:

$$E_{dg} = V_{gd} - \omega_g L_g I_{qg} + R_g I_{dg} + L_g \frac{dI_{dg}}{dt} \tag{10}$$

$$E_{qg} = V_{gq} + \omega_g L_g I_{dg} + R_g I_{qg} + L_g \frac{dI_{qg}}{dt} \tag{11}$$

where E_{dg}, E_{qg} are the output inverter voltages, V_{gd}, V_{gq} are the grid voltages, I_{dg}, I_{qg} are the grid currents, L_s is the inductance of the filter, R_g is the filter resistance, and ω_g denotes the grid angular frequency.

3. FCS-MPC Scheme in Grid Connected Inverters

The FCS-MPC has become increasingly popular for the control and optimization of the grid-tied inverters [34]. The FCS-MPC is inherently a recurrent process at every sampling instant in order to determine the optimum future voltage vector of the inverter, which is close to the reference signal. In this way, those switching states, which minimize the cost function, are selected to be applied to the converter for the next sampling instant. The schematic of a grid-tied inverter is shown in Figure 2.

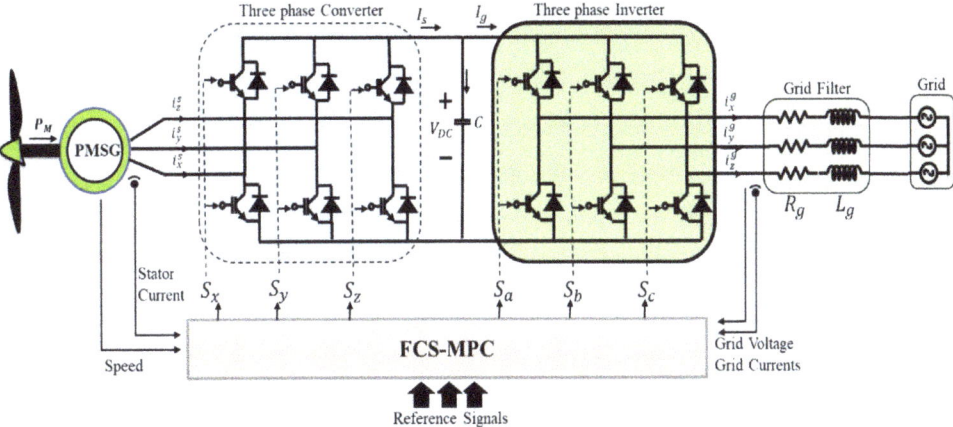

Figure 2. PMSG-based Grid-connected Inverter with FCS-MPC.

The switching states (Sx, Sy, Sz, Sa, Sb, Sc) have the following conditions:

$$S = \begin{cases} 0, & \text{switch in upper leg open, lower one closed} \\ 1, & \text{switch in upper leg close, lower one open} \end{cases} \quad (12)$$

The system dynamics at both sides of the DC-link capacitor can be written as follows:

$$\frac{d}{dt}v_{dc} = \frac{1}{C}(I_s - I_g) \quad (13)$$

$$I_s = \left(i^s_{xyz}\right)^T S_{xyz}; \; i^s_{xyz} = \begin{pmatrix} i^s_x & i^s_y & i^s_z \end{pmatrix}^T \quad (14)$$

$$I_g = \left(i^g_{xyz}\right)^T S_{abc}; \; i^g_{xyz} = \begin{pmatrix} i^g_x & i^g_y & i^g_z \end{pmatrix}^T \quad (15)$$

where v_{dc} is the DC-link voltage, I_s is stator current attained by the product of measured MSC currents (i^s_x, i^s_y, i^s_z) and switching states S_{abc}. Similarly, I_g is the grid current obtained by the product of measured GSC currents (i^g_x, i^g_y, i^g_z) and switching states S_{xyz}. Here, eight sequences of the switching state vectors are possible, either for MSC (S_{xyz}) or GSC (S_{abc}) sides. The finite switching states and corresponding voltage vector outputs on GSC are listed in Table 1.

Conventionally, the selection of switching states for the voltage vectors in a given cost function is subject to the lowest value by that particular state. However, this method is time-consuming, as all eight switching states need to be assessed through the cost function. In this study, we deal with the PMSG-based grid with faults, where control scheme is required to make quick decisions to comply with LVRT conditions. Therefore, to avoid the evaluation of each switching state in every cycle, evaluation is done when one of the switches changes its state as compared to the previous state. Hence, four out of eight possible states are checked in this case to reduce calculation complexity, as shown in Table 2.

Table 1. Operating and switching states.

State	Sa	Sb	Sc	Vector
0	0	0	0	0
1	1	0	0	V_{DC}
2	1	1	0	V_{DC}
3	0	1	0	V_{DC}
4	0	1	1	V_{DC}
5	0	0	1	V_{DC}
6	1	0	1	V_{DC}
7	1	1	1	0

Table 2. Subsequent probable states for the proposed controller scheme.

States	Existing States	Subsequent States $(S_x\ S_y\ S_z)$
0	(000)	(000) (001) (100) (010)
1	(100)	(000) (100) (101) (110)
2	(110)	(100) (010) (110) (111)
3	(010)	(000) (010) (011) (110)
4	(011)	(001) (010) (011) (111)
5	(001)	(000) (001) (011) (101)
6	(101)	(001) (100) (101) (111)
7	(111)	(101) (011) (110) (111)

For a non-zero voltage vector from the previous cycle, it will either maintain its state or switch to an adjacent vector. On the other hand, if the switching voltage vector from the previous cycle has a zero state, the resultant switching could be any nonzero vector. Figure 3 displays the switching sequence of the optimized voltage vectors.

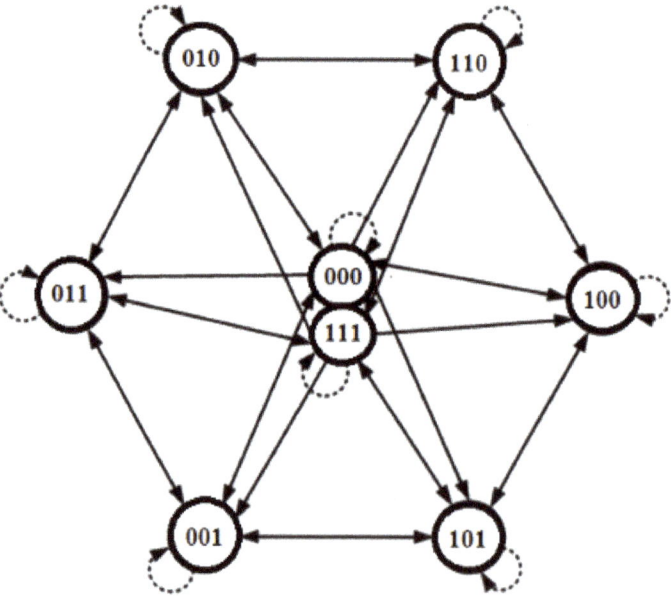

Figure 3. Selection of optimum switching vectors.

Under grid fault conditions, grid voltage drops instantly. As a result, the grid current rises to maintain the active power. When the grid voltage drops significantly, the current injection will reach a maximum allowed value, which may eventually decrease active power transfer to the load. This imbalance between input and output power causes an upsurge in the DC-link voltage magnitude. To keep the magnitude of DC-link voltage stable and to achieve better LVRT ability, the proposed FCS-MPC scheme suggests the use of controlling dq-frame currents on both sides of the DC link capacitor. Note that an increased rotor speed happens as grid power demand reduces during fault. Thus, the increase in speed will be compensated with rotor inertia by retaining a constant DC link voltage. Eventually, to meet LVRT requirements, reactive power is provided to the grid, and the active power is reduced under faulty conditions.

3.1. Machine Side Converter (MSC) Control

The FCS-MPC control scheme for MSC is a discrete-time technique applied in sampled time intervals. There are eight possible switching states for inverter voltage vectors. As stated, out of the total eight voltage vectors, two are null vectors. Using Euler approximation, Equations (4) and (5) can be transformed into equivalent discrete-time predicted forms as follows:

$$I_{ds(k+1)} = \left(1 - \frac{t_{int}R}{L_s}\right)I_{ds(k)} + \frac{t_{int}}{L_s}V_{ds(k)} + \omega_r I_{qs(k)} t_{int} \quad (16)$$

$$I_{qs(k+1)} = \left(1 - \frac{t_{int}R}{L_s}\right)I_{qs(k)} + \frac{t_{int}}{L_s}V_{qs(k)} - \omega_r I_{ds(k)} t_{int} - \frac{t_{int}}{L_s}E_{s(k)} \quad (17)$$

where k is the sampling interval. Equations (16) and (17) represent future values of the stator current $I_{s(k+1)}$ in dq-frame while taking into consideration all possible voltage vectors $V_{s(k)}$ generated by MCS, the measured stator current $I_{s(k)}$, and the stator voltage, i.e., E_s.

In this work, the Euclidean norm is selected for cost function due to its better traceability property. The cost function takes into account the stator currents all in dq-frame as follows:

$$C_a = (I_{ds(k+1)} - I^*_{ds(k+1)})^2 + (I_{qs(k+1)} - I^*_{qs(k+1)})^2 + F_{MSC} \quad (18)$$

The first two terms in (18) are devoted to tracking the references, i.e., calculating the error between the reference and forecasted stator currents in the dq-frame, and F_{MSC} is a bounded non-linear function for stator current magnitude, which can be represented as follows:

$$F_{MSC} = \begin{cases} 0 \text{ for } i_d < i_{s,M} \text{ and } i_q < i_{s,M} \\ \infty \text{ for } i_d > i_{s,M} \text{ or } i_q > i_{s,M} \end{cases} \quad (19)$$

Equation (19) shows that the maximum allowed value of the stator current i.e., $i_{s,M}$, that corresponds to the voltage vector, chosen for cost function minimization. Conversely, the cost function C_a will become infinity for any voltage vector, which corresponds to a value of stator current greater than $i_{s,M}$. Using (6), the value of the q-axis stator current reference is expressed as (20), where the optimum torque is obtained from the MPPT speed control. Figure 4 illustrates the proposed FCS-MPC approach with an internal PI loop and external current feedback loop.

$$I^*_{qs} = \frac{2T_{e.ref}}{3P\Psi_r} \quad (20)$$

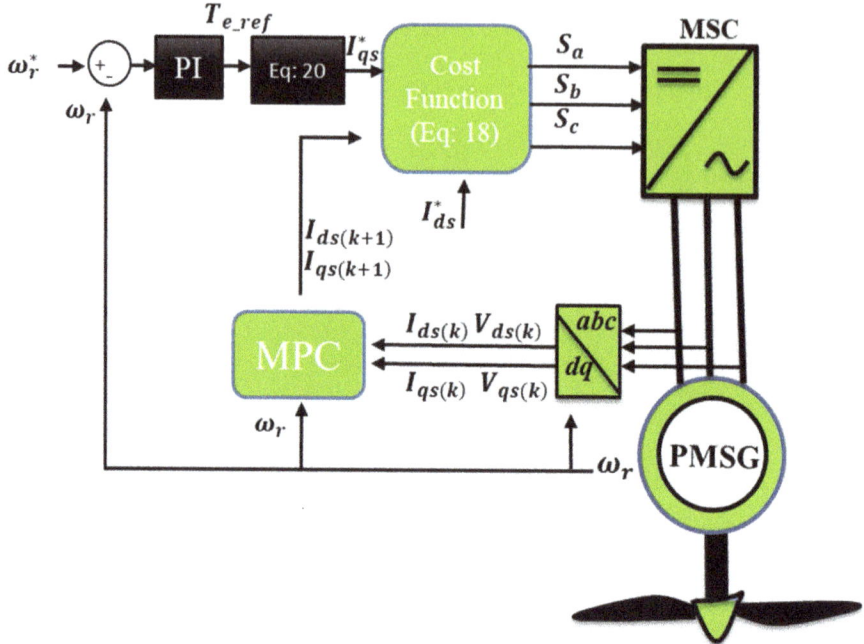

Figure 4. MSC with proposed FCS-MPC scheme.

3.2. Grid Side Converter (GSC) Control with FCS-MPC

Usually, GSC serves the purpose of stabilizing the DC-link voltage v_{dc} in case of faults or load variations on the grid side. The FCS-MPC controller in this study regulates the active and reactive power as well as DC link voltage by controlling d-axis and q-axis grid currents. Using (10) and (11), the discrete-time conversion of the dq-frame grid current is specified as follows [35].

$$\begin{bmatrix} I_{dg(k+1)} \\ I_{qg(k+1)} \end{bmatrix} = \Phi \begin{bmatrix} I_{dg(k)} \\ I_{qg(k)} \end{bmatrix} + \Gamma_i \begin{bmatrix} E_{dg(k+1)} \\ E_{qg(k+1)} \end{bmatrix} + \Gamma_g \begin{bmatrix} V_{gd(k)} \\ V_{gq(k)} \end{bmatrix} \qquad (21)$$

where Φ, Γ_i, and Γ_g are the state matrices parameters in discrete time.

Using Langrage's extrapolation approach, k^{th} to $(k+1)^{th}$ instant generation of reference grid current is equated as follows:

$$\begin{cases} I^*_{dg(k+1)} = 4I^*_{dg(k)} - 6I^*_{dg(k-1)} + 4I^*_{dg(k-2)} - 4I^*_{dg(k-3)} \\ I^*_{qg(k+1)} = 4I^*_{qg(k)} - 6I^*_{qg(k-1)} + 4I^*_{qg(k-2)} - 4I^*_{qg(k-3)} \end{cases} \qquad (22)$$

From the GSC predictive controller, the future values of the grid currents $I_{g(k+1)}$ are predicted for the given switching states using (23). Finally, from the cost function in (24), the error between the predicted and reference values of the grid currents becomes:

$$C_b = \gamma_d (I^*_{dg(k+1)} - I_{dg(k+1)})^2 + \gamma_q (I^*_{qg(k+1)} - I_{qg(k+1)})^2 \qquad (23)$$

where γ_d and γ_q are dq-frame weighting elements of grid currents for frequency regulation. Active power minimization is achieved through the first term of (24), while reactive power transfer to the grid is tracked by the second term. Active and reactive power to the grid is equated as follows:

$$\begin{cases} P_{g(k+1)} = 1.5\left(v_{dg(k+1)}I_{dg(k+1)}\right) \\ Q_{g(k+1)} = -1.5\left(v_{qg(k+1)}I_{qg(k+1)}\right) \end{cases} \quad (24)$$

As depicted in Figure 5, through the internal DC-link voltage control loop, the d-axis reference grid current $I^*_{dg(k+1)}$ is generated, which controls the active power transfer to the grid, while the reactive power is regulated by the q-axis grid current $I_{qg(k+1)}$, for which the reference can be obtained as:

$$I^*_{qg(k+1)} = \frac{Q_{g.ref(k)}}{-1.5V_{gd(k+1)}} \quad (25)$$

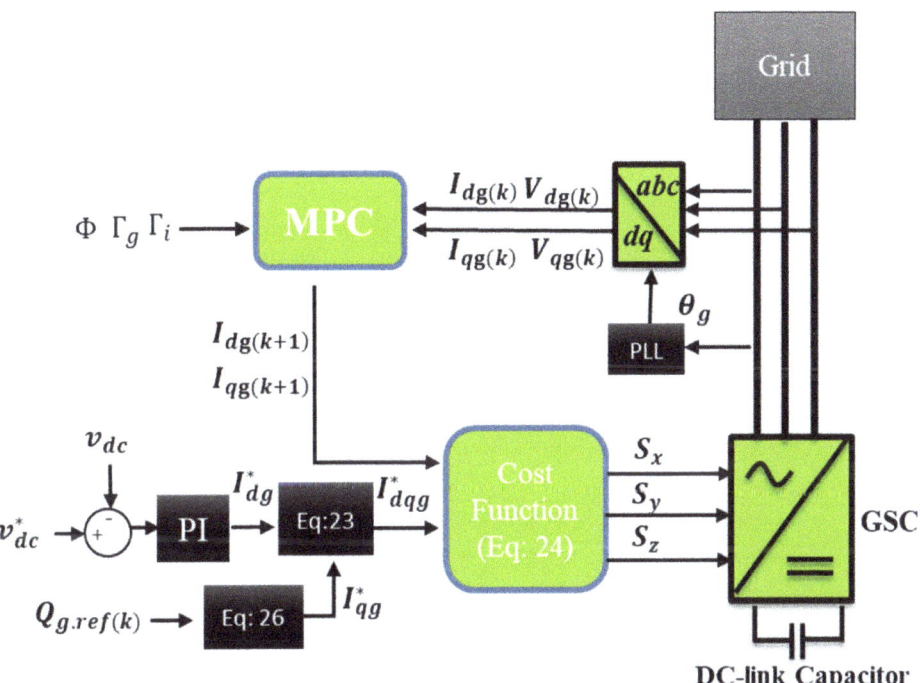

Figure 5. GSC with proposed FCS-MPC scheme.

3.3. Dynamic Weight Factors (γ_d, γ_q) Modification

The WFs in the cost function adjust the control objective to achieve an optimal output value. During steady state condition, a unity value is assigned to both the weights, as there is no change being detected. It is during the transient state when lower priority is granted to the term by dropping its weight factor, which is negatively affecting the cost function. This is further described in the flowchart in Figure 6, where a cross-coupling term is diminished by weight factor reduction.

Weight factors in the cost function are adjusted experimentally by iterative analysis and within the specified ranges in Table 3. For a sudden change in the active current with the constant reactive current (Sp < Sq), Yd is reduced to rectify the disturbance in the active power control, while Yq remains constant. Similarly, for an abrupt reactive power change (Sp > Sq), the penalty is now applied on Yq to reduce the cross-coupling effect and smoother operation.

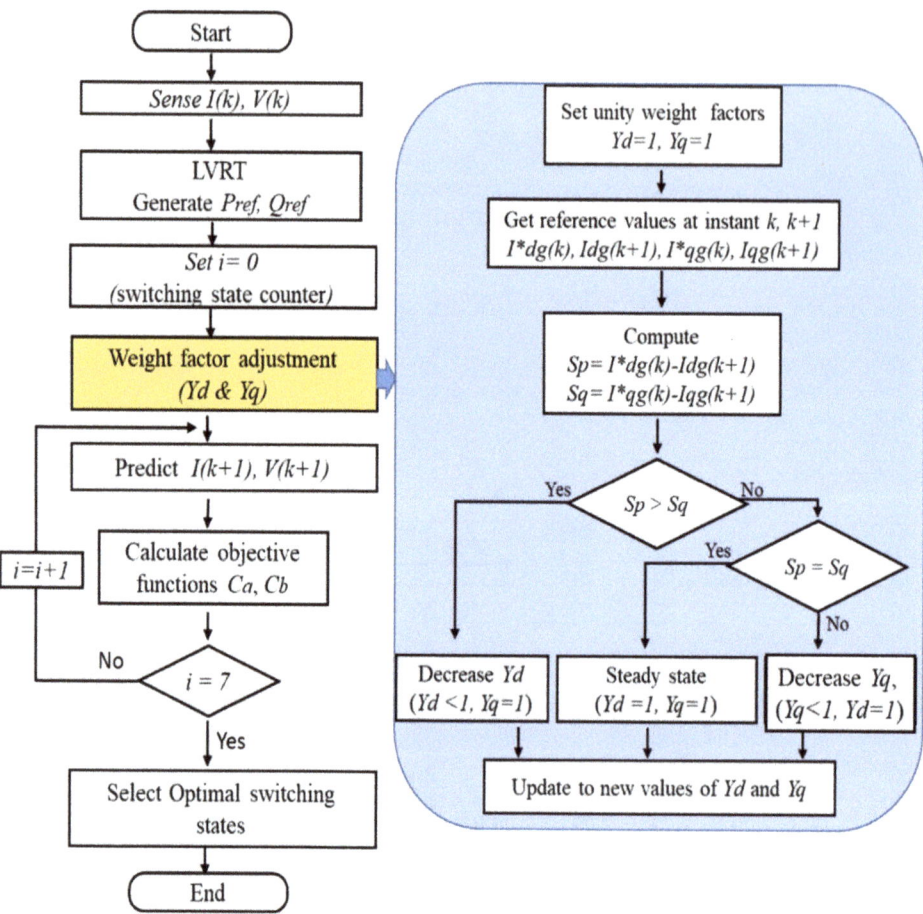

Figure 6. Flowchart of FCS-MPC with weight factor adjustment.

Table 3. WFs assortment criteria.

Parameter	Abrupt Active Power Change Sp < Sq	Steady-State Sp = Sq	Abrupt Reactive Power Change Sp > Sq
γ_d	(0.4–1)	1	1
γ_q	1	1	(0.2–0.8)

3.4. LVRT Requirements

One of the objectives of this study is to design the control scheme, which makes the GCWT system robust under symmetrical and asymmetrical voltage sags. To achieve this, the system needs to regulate the delivered active and reactive current injected into/absorbed from the power grid in accordance with grid integration standards and regulations [36]. The E.ON proposes that RES should supply 100% rated reactive current if a drop of 50% or more occurs in grid voltage for a predefined time duration [7].

With the occurrence of voltage sags, reactive power consumption/absorption by the grid is defined according to LVRT conditions as mentioned in grid codes [37]. In most cases, for a 50–90% drop in grid voltage magnitude, 2% reactive current of the total rated current is needed for every 1% drop of the grid voltage. The overall reactive support in case of voltage dip on the grid is equated using Equation (26) as under [38]:

$$\begin{cases} Q_{g.ref} = 0 & \forall\ v_{grid} > 0.9 v_n \\ Q_{g.ref} = (\frac{v_n - v_{grid}}{v_n})k & \forall\ 0.9 v_n > v_{grid} > 0.5 v_n \\ Q_{g.ref} = 1 & \forall\ v_{grid} < 0.5 v_n \end{cases} \quad (26)$$

where v_n is nominal grid voltage, v_{grid} shows grid voltage in case of voltage dip, and k is the droop constant with its value not more than 2 [39]. The flow chart for the LVRT process is presented in Figure 7.

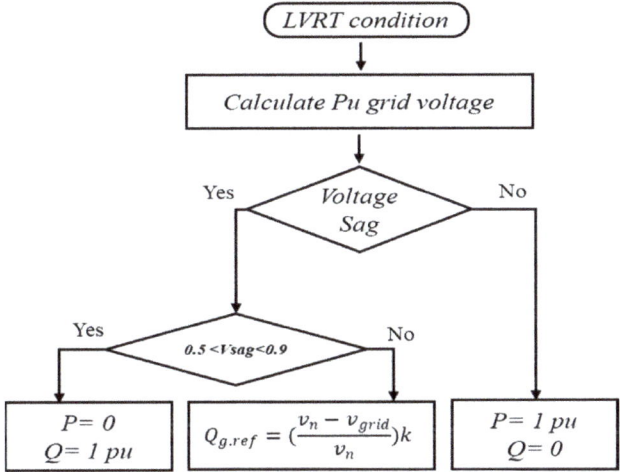

Figure 7. Flowchart of LVRT Scheme.

3.5. Stability Analysis

Lyapunav stability criterion is used to inspect the stability of the GCWT system in this study. Using (18), the error in the stator current can be collectively written as:

$$I_{s,err} = I_{S(k+1)} - I^*_{S(k+1)} \quad (27)$$

Using (16) and (17)

$$I_{s,err} = \left(1 - \frac{t_{int}R}{L_s}\right)I_{s(k)} + \frac{t_{int}}{L_s}V_{s(k)} - \omega_r I_{s(k)} t_{int} - \frac{t_{int}}{L_s}E_{s(k)} - I^*_{S(k+1)} \quad (28)$$

Here the control objective is to asymptotically minimize error $I_{s,err}$. The Lyapunove error function is written as

$$L(I_{s,err}) = \frac{1}{2}(I_{s,err})^2 \quad (29)$$

For a stable system, the derivative of Lyapunove function i.e., $\Delta L(I_{s,err})$, should be negative while $I_{s,err}$ converges to zero. Therefore, $I_{s,err}$ will lead to zero only if $\Delta L(I_{s,err}) < 0$. From (27), the time derivative of the Lyapunove function becomes:

$$\Delta L(I_{s,err}) = \frac{1}{2}\left[\left(1 - \frac{t_{int}R}{L_s}\right)I_{s(k)} + \frac{t_{int}}{L_s}V_{s(k)} - \omega_r I_{s(k)} t_{int} - \frac{t_{int}}{L_s}E_{s(k)}\right]^2 - \frac{1}{2}\left(I_{s,err(k)}\right)^2 \quad (30)$$

To ensure negative derivative of $\Delta L(I_{s,err})$, (4) in discrete form will be the future value of the voltage vector and can be written as:

$$V_s = -\omega_r \frac{L_s}{t_{int}} I_{s(k+1)} + E_{s(k)} + \frac{L_s}{t_{int}} L_{s(k)} \tag{31}$$

The criteria to be met by the system for Lyapunove stability is:

$$L(I_{s,err(k)}) \geq D_1 |I_{s,err(k)}|^2, \forall I_{s,err(k)} \in Y$$

$$L(I_{s,err(k)}) \geq D_2 |I_{s,err(k)}|^\delta, \forall I_{s,err(k)} \in \Gamma$$

$$L(I_{s,err(k+1)}) - L(I_{s,err(k)}) < -D_3 |I_{s,err(k)}|^\delta + D_4$$

$$D_1, D_2, D_3, D_4 \in \mathbb{R}^+, \delta \geq 1, Y \in \mathbb{R}^+, \Gamma \subset Y \tag{32}$$

Substituting (31) into (30), we get

$$\frac{1}{2}\left(\frac{t_{int}}{L_s}\right)^2 l^2 - \frac{1}{2}\left(I_{s(k)}\right)^2 \geq \Delta L_{(k)} \tag{33}$$

where $l \in \mathbb{R}^+$ is the quantization error. Using (32),

$$D_1 = D_2 = 1, D_3 = 0.5, D_4 = \frac{1}{2}\left(\frac{t_{int}}{L_s}\right)^2 l^2$$

Consequently, controlled parameters are limited within the bounded region, which is in accordance with Lyapunove stability criteria.

4. Simulation Results and Discussions

To monitor and evaluate the performance of the suggested FCS-MPC strategy, the following two scenarios are considered and performed in MATLAB/Simulink environment.

(a) P and Q transient performance with fixed and variable WFs.
(b) LVRT performance under symmetrical and asymmetrical faults on the grid.

In addition, comparisons are drawn between the proposed controller strategy and the PI controller to assess the operational performance during LVRT operations for the WECS [40]. The aforementioned control scheme is implemented by decoupling the d- and q-axes currents by using two PI controllers with feed-forward paths. In both loops, the PI controllers are tuned by plotting Bode plots of the open-loop transfer functions. To achieve critical damping behavior, the proportional gain has been set to get the frequency crossover in safe a margin, while integral gain has been set to get the highest gain without overshoots. The specification of the GCWT system is given in Table 4.

Table 4. Parameters of the GCWT system.

Parameter	Value
Rated Power	1.50 MW
Grid Voltage	576 V
DC link voltage	1150 V
Stator Resistor	3.2 mΩ
Stator Resistor	3.05 mH
Switching Frequency	20 KHz
DC-Link Capacitor	0.025 F
Filter Resistor	3.154 mΩ
Filter Inductor	0.44 mH

4.1. Analysis of Step-Change in Power (Active/Reactive)

The transient response of the FCS-MPC scheme is explored for different WFs operating conditions.

(a) Step-change in Active Power (P_{ref})

In this scenario, the decoupling ability is investigated with WFs fixed at unity, with a step change of 0 to 1 MW in reference active power P_{ref}, whereas the reactive power reference Q_{ref} is fixed at zero. During the transient period, the Q component experienced an unwanted cross-coupling in the case of fixed WFs. The cross-coupling on Q sustains for around 2.3 s, as shown in Figure 8a.

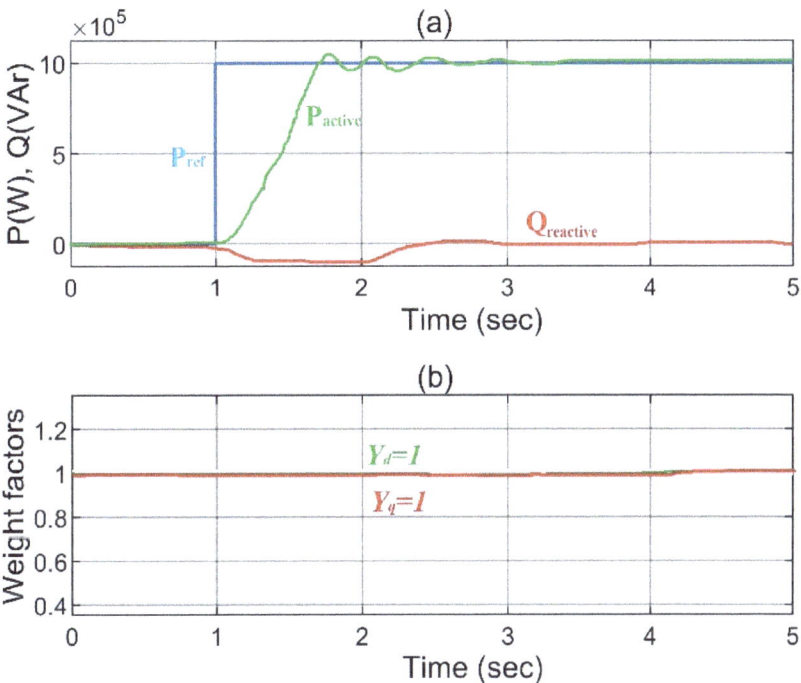

Figure 8. Step-response of FCS-MPC during fixed WFs. (**a**) Active power and Reactive power (**b**) Dynamics of WFs.

With variable WFs applied, the proposed FCS-MPC scheme successfully eliminates cross-couplings and reduces disturbances to insignificant values throughout the transient phase, as depicted in Figure 9a. Figure 8b illustrates the case of fixed WFs with unity value, while in the case of variable WFs, the Y_d (as shown in Figure 9b) is adjusted, agreeing with the adjustment rule described in Table 3.

(b) Step-change in Reactive Power (Q_{ref})

In this section, the FCS-MPC transient performance is examined in an alternative operating scenario, where Q_{ref} is suddenly changed from 0–1 MVAr, while keeping P_{ref} at zero. Transient responses were examined with fixed and variable WFs, and the results are presented in Figures 10 and 11, respectively. FCS-MPC systems with variable WFs experienced a settling time of around 0.4 s, which is less than the case of fixed WFs systems, where it is around 0.9 s.

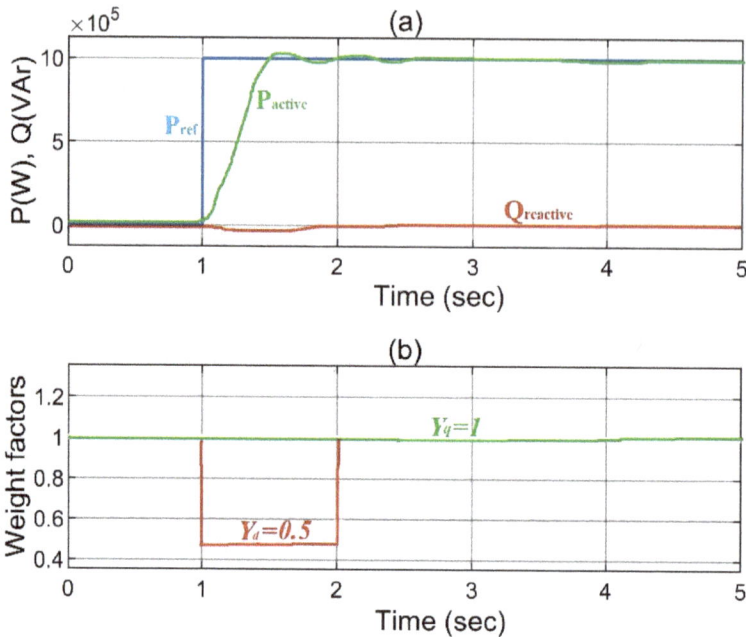

Figure 9. Step-response of FCS-MPC during Variable WFs. (**a**) Active power and Reactive power (**b**) Dynamics of WFs.

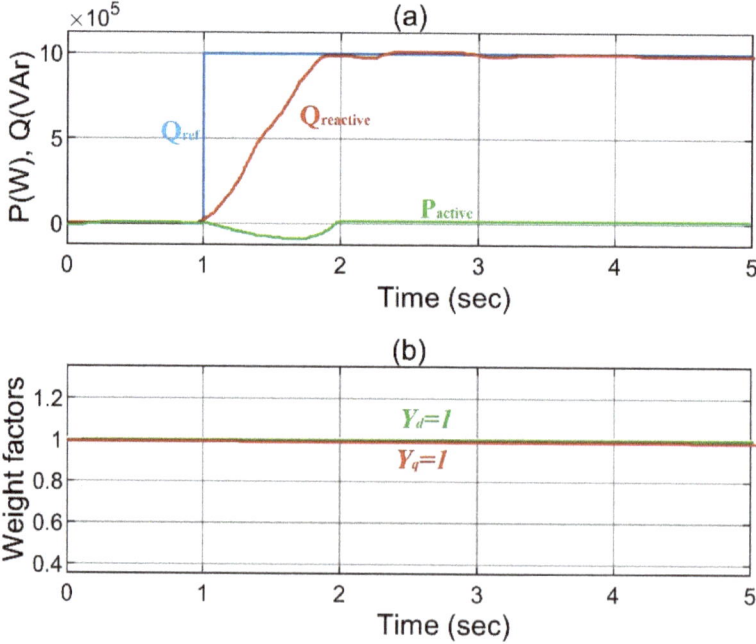

Figure 10. Step-response of FCS-MPC during fixed WFs. (**a**) Active power and Reactive power (**b**) Dynamics of WFs.

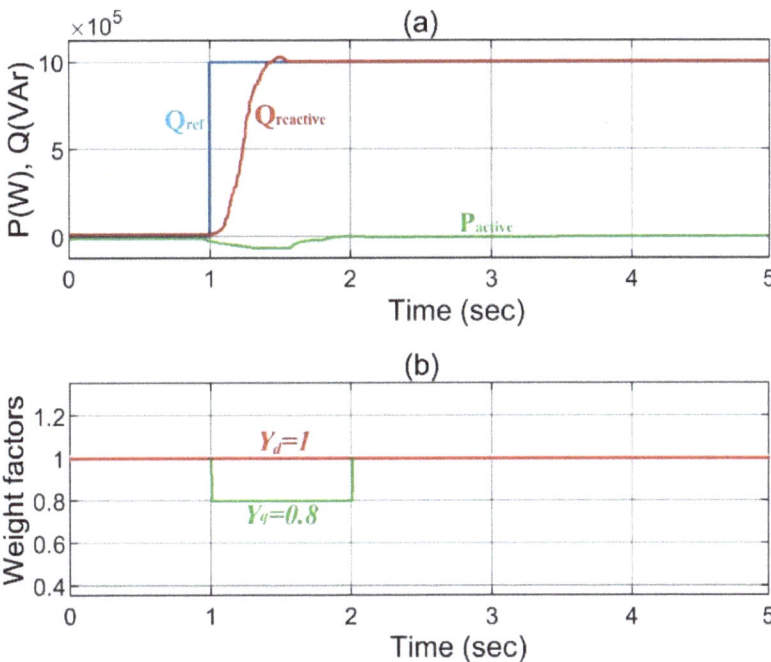

Figure 11. Step response of FCS-MPC during variable WFs. (**a**) Active and Reactive power (**b**) Dynamics of WFs.

In the findings illustrated in Figure 11a, the proposed FCS-MPC scheme with variable WFs, the cross-coupling is alleviated to a negligible level, and the disturbance is effectively mitigated during the transient phase. In this case, the value of Y_q is regulated at 0.8.

4.2. Fault Analysis on the Grid Side

(a) Symmetrical Fault Analysis

Symmetrical voltage fault of 30% (0.3 p.u.) of grid voltage is introduced for 0.5 seconds i.e., from t = 2.5 s to t = 3 s, as presented in Figure 12. The three-phase grid voltage and resulting grid current waveforms during grid voltage sag are depicted in Figure 12a. During nominal grid conditions before the 3-phase fault, the active power is generated at 1 p.u., while no reactive power injection is done from the PMSG by keeping $i_{qg,ref}$ at zero. As the voltage dip occurs at the PCC, Figure 12b shows that the DC-link voltage is regulated at the reference value of 1150 V by virtue of the proposed MPC scheme. During the voltage dip on the grid, the active power reduces in relation to the voltage drop, as a mismatch of mechanical generated power and electrical supplied power happens. Figure 12d depicts the reactive power injection to support the grid in accordance with (27), as active power decreases during fault. Execution of this limitation scheme provides the supplementary capacity to GSC for reactive power injection for grid code compliance. The proposed MSC controller in this case regulates the generator speed so that it keeps the value of DC-link voltage near the reference value. Moreover, the system inertia takes care of the power mismatch with increased mechanical speed as shown in Figure 13.

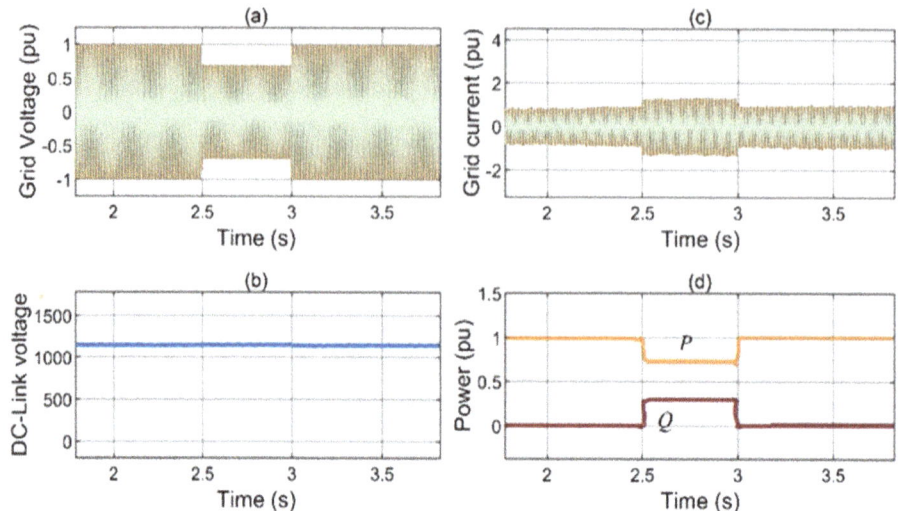

Figure 12. LVRT Performance of proposed scheme during symmetrical grid fault. (**a**) Grid voltage (**b**) Inverter current (**c**) DC-link voltage (**d**) Active and Reactive power.

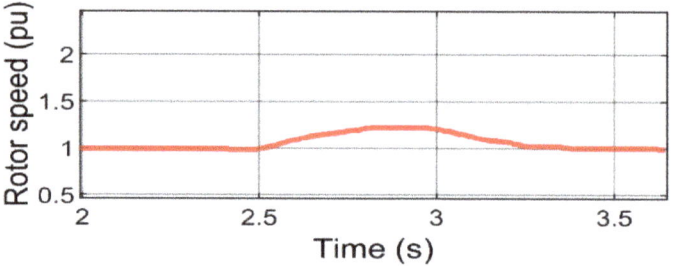

Figure 13. Increased rotor speed during fault.

In comparison to FCS-MPC, the conventional PI control method does not exhibit a satisfactory transient response, with the DC-link voltage ripple reaching 1490 V, as depicted in Figure 14b. Moreover, the PI controller fails to ensure optimum reactive compensation, with added delay to reach the steady-state value after the fault clears (Figure 14d).

(b) *Asymmetrical Fault Analysis*

The time and severity of the asymmetrical fault remained similar to the previous case. In the case of asymmetrical faults on the grid, a performance comparison of the proposed MPC controller is examined, as shown in Figure 15. Note that DC-link voltage remained stable with reduced fluctuations as shown in Figure 15b. The proposed controller is faster than the PI scheme in providing reactive power compensation is supplied to the grid as active power decreases with increased grid current due to the faulty condition.

With the PI methodology, in addition to DC-link voltage overshoot, the active power fluctuation with almost double the grid frequency is apparent in Figure 16d. Although GSC regulates the active and reactive power, the second-order DC-link oscillations adversely affect the converter operation. The settling time of the PI regulator is inferior, as it takes more time to achieve steady state as compared to the proposed predictive control scheme. This shows that the PI controller cannot deliver reasonable performance, indicating that the proposed MPC approach offers better LVRT performance.

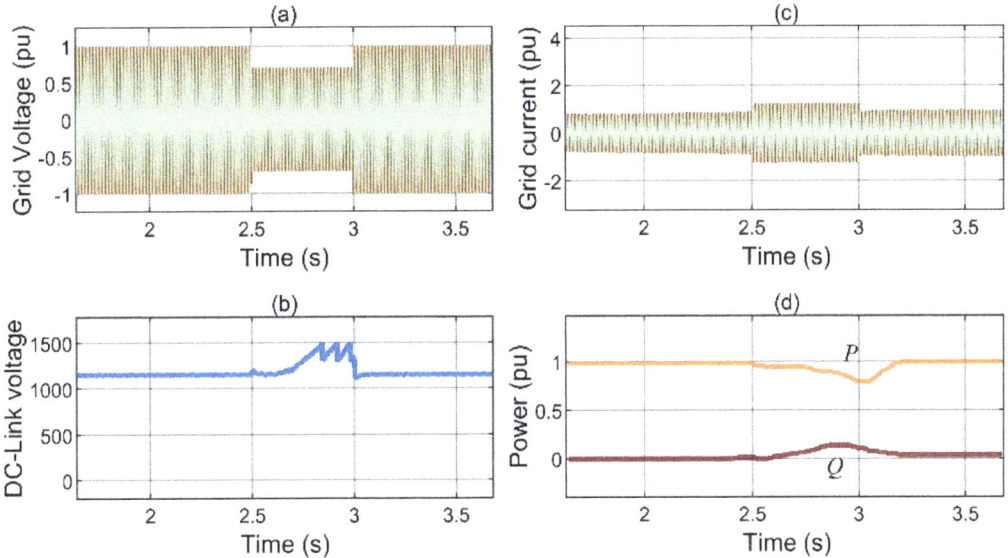

Figure 14. LVRT Performance of PI controller during symmetrical grid fault. (**a**) Grid voltage (**b**) Inverter current (**c**) DC-link voltage (**d**) Active and Reactive power.

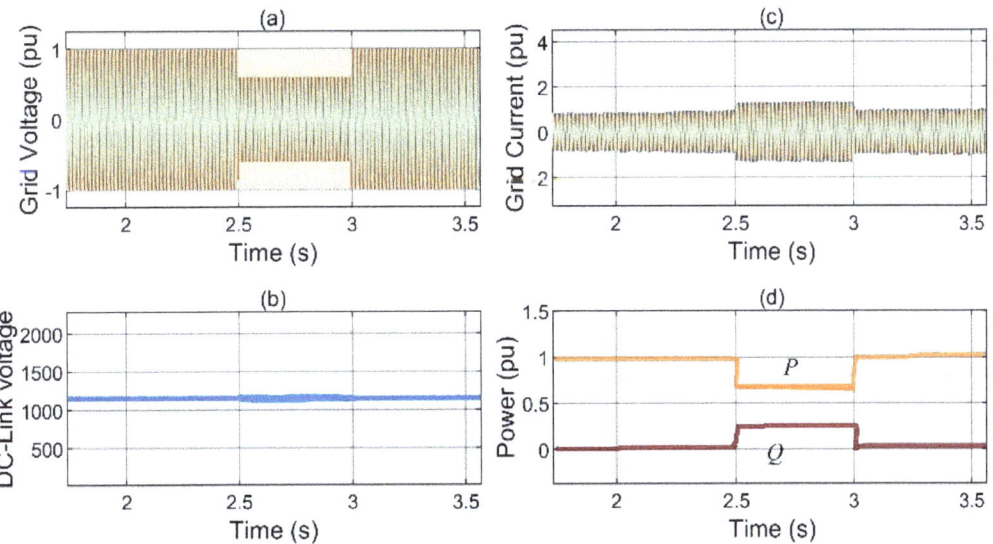

Figure 15. Enhanced LVRT capability of the proposed MPC scheme during asymmetrical grid faults. (**a**) Grid voltage (**b**) Inverter current (**c**) DC-link voltage (**d**) Active and Reactive power.

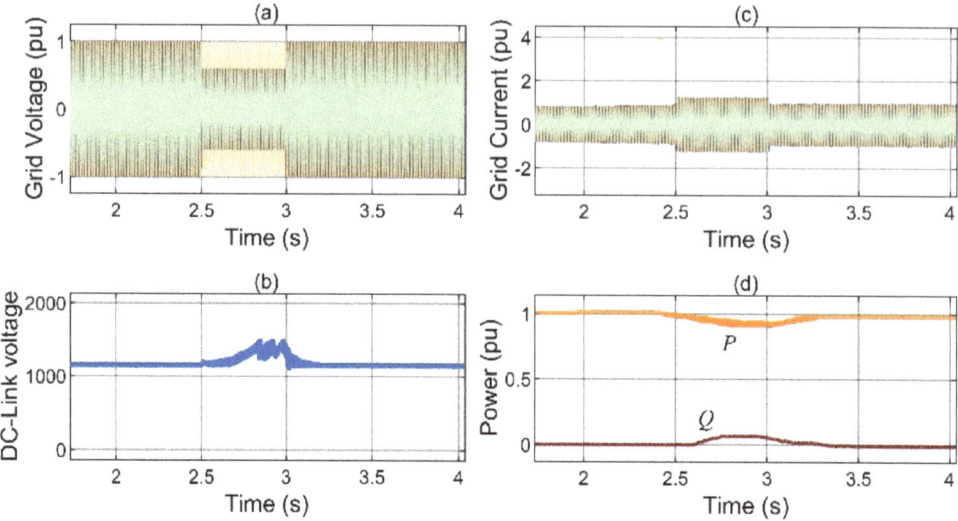

Figure 16. LVRT Performance of PI controller during asymmetrical grid fault. (**a**) Grid voltage (**b**) Inverter current (**c**) DC-link voltage (**d**) Active and Reactive power.

4.3. Experimental Results

In order to validate the performance of the proposed controller, an experimental setup is used as shown in Figure 17. The experimental verification is realized by OPAL-RT (OP5700) platform. The parameters of experimental tests are similar to those of simulation results. The sampling frequency of the FCS-MPC algorithm is 20 kHz, while the data sampling frequency is either 16 or 20 kHz, contingent upon the data logging duration as well as memory constraints.

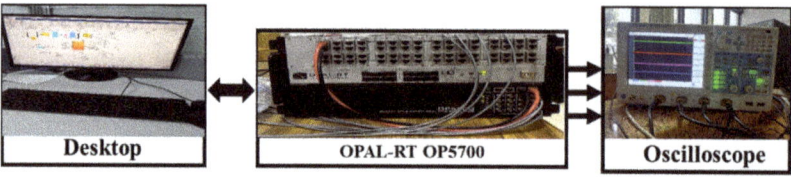

Figure 17. Experimental Steup.

Similar to simulation results, a symmetrical voltage sag of 30% is introduced at the grid side. As a result, dip in the grid voltage is evident, along with rise in inverter current in Figure 18. Furthermore, net DC-link voltage is upheld within at the reference value with very low ripple oscillations under sag conditions, as depicted in Figure 19.

The active and the reactive power are being regulated, corresponding to LVRT operation conditions. The dynamic response of the proposed predictive control is efficient in providing grid support by increasing in the reactive power injection along with active power reduction as the grid fault occurs. Thus, the results of the experimental setup presented here approve that the enhanced LVRT compliance can be achieved robustly by using the proposed FSC-MPC scheme.

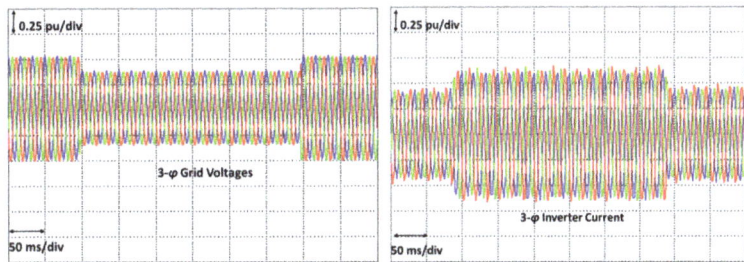

Figure 18. Grid Voltages and Inverter current under Symmetrical grid fault.

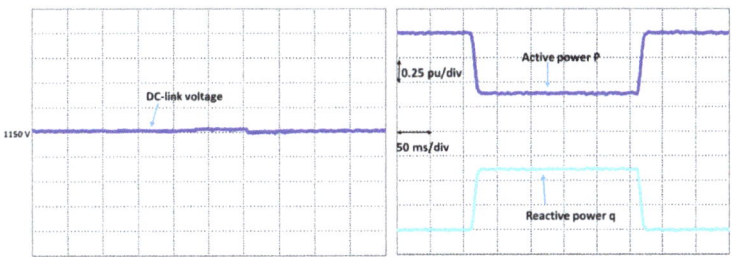

Figure 19. DC-link voLtage and Power regulation.

4.4. Parameter Robustness Analysis

With FCS-MPC being a model-based method, adequate system parameter values are pivotal for an overall robust control. Thus, the variation in the values of PMSG's resistance and inductance (L_s) do have a direct or indirect effect on the system performance, as can be seen from (16) and (17). The detuned PMSG model is used to examine the parameter robustness and sensitivity by variation in the values of L_s. The sensitivity of the proposed strategy is investigated by changing the L_s from 50% to 150% of its measured value. From Figure 20, it can be seen that dq-frame stator currents have higher oscillations in case of detuned parameter conditions as compared to real values. Nevertheless, the proposed FCS-MPC applied on the MSC side still manages to track the reference value under varying L_s conditions. The value of the stator current THDs in case of generator inductance variations of 50% and 150% are 7.35% and 8.81% respectively. Finally, a comparison of the proposed FCS-MPC and PI control with respect to parameter tuning, complexity, response, and computation cost/burden is summarized in Table 5. The computation burden here is the measure of execution time for the two control schemes. The execution time for the proposed scheme is longer than the simulation time, as FCS-MPC is required to execute at least three cycles to compute the predicted voltage vector values.

Table 5. Comparison of FCS-MPC and classical PI controller.

Features	PI Controller	FCS MPC
Parameter Decoupling	External	Internal
Tuning	Retuning required	Easy, no retuning needed
Secondary axis current control	Additional PI regulators required	Single cost function for error mitigation
Dynamic response	Slow	Fast
Computation burden	Medium	High

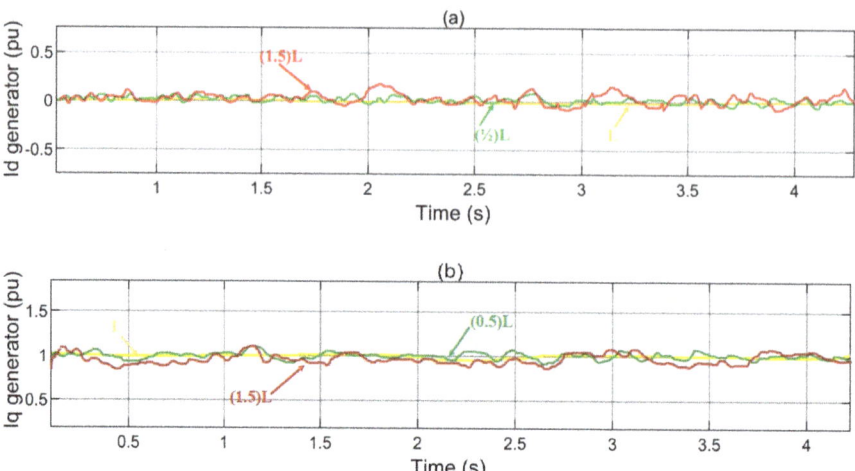

Figure 20. Parameter robustness analysis under inductance variation (**a**) d-axis stator current (**b**) q-axis stator current.

5. Conclusions

In this paper, time domain modeling and analysis of a direct-drive PMSG-based wind turbine along with FCS-MPC scheme with improved LVRT performances have been presented. In GCWT systems, the issues of cross-coupling of the active and reactive power during transient states have been addressed by efficiently incorporating variable WFs with the FCS-MPC scheme. The performance of the proposed controller is analyzed by fast selection and application of switching states on the MSC and GSC inverters during symmetrical and asymmetrical grid faults. Moreover, the abrupt increase in DC-link voltage in case of voltage dips is regulated using excess active power in rotor inertia of PMSG-based wind turbine during the faulty condition. The suggested FCS-MPC scheme shows better LVRT capability in comparison with the conventional PI control approach with enhanced DC-link voltage stability and reactive power compensation during various fault conditions.

Author Contributions: S.W.A.: investigation, conceptualization, methodology, software, writing—original draft; A.K.V.: conceptualization, methodology, validation; Y.T.: writing—review and editing; M.S.: data curation, conceptualization; C.-L.S.: supervision, writing—review and editing; M.E.: methodology, writing—review and editing; C.-H.L.: writing—review and editing. All authors have read and agreed to the published version of the manuscript.

Funding: The works of Chun-Lien Su and Mahmoud Elsisi were funded by the Ministry of Science and Technology of Taiwan under grant MOST 110-2221-E- 992-044-MY3 and MOST 110-2222-E-011-013.

Institutional Review Board Statement: Not applicable.

Informed Consent Statement: Not applicable.

Data Availability Statement: Not applicable.

Conflicts of Interest: The authors declare no conflict of interest.

References

1. Noman, F.M.; Alkawsi, G.A.; Abbas, D.; Alkahtani, A.A.; Tiong, S.K.; Ekanayake, J. Comprehensive Review of Wind Energy in Malaysia: Past, Present, and Future Research Trends. *IEEE Access* **2020**, *8*, 124526–124543. [CrossRef]
2. Bajaj, M.; Singh, A.K. Grid Integrated Renewable DG Systems: A Review of Power Quality Challenges and State-of-the-Art Mitigation Techniques. *Int. J. Energy Res.* **2020**, *44*, 26–69. [CrossRef]

3. Ali, S.W.; Sadiq, M.; Terriche, Y.; Naqvi, S.A.R.; Hoang, L.Q.N.; Mutarraf, M.U.; Hassan, M.A.; Yang, G.; Su, C.L.; Guerrero, J.M. Offshore Wind Farm-Grid Integration: A Review on Infrastructure, Challenges, and Grid Solutions. *IEEE Access* 2021, *9*, 102811–102827. [CrossRef]
4. Xie, Q.; Zheng, Z.; Huang, C.; Dai, T. Coordinated Fault Ride Through Method for PMSG-Based Wind Turbine Using SFCL and Modified Control Strategy. *IEEE Trans. Appl. Supercond.* 2021, *31*, 1–5. [CrossRef]
5. Mahela, O.P.; Gupta, N.; Khosravy, M.; Patel, N. Comprehensive Overview of Low Voltage Ride through Methods of Grid Integrated Wind Generator. *IEEE Access* 2019, *7*, 99299–99326. [CrossRef]
6. Shi, K.; Song, W.; Xu, P.; Liu, R.; Fang, Z.; Ji, Y. Low-Voltage Ride-Through Control Strategy for a Virtual Synchronous Generator Based on Smooth Switching. *IEEE Access* 2017, *6*, 2703–2711. [CrossRef]
7. E.ON2006-Netz-Grid Code-High and Extra High Voltage. Available online: https://wenku.baidu.com/view/6289c22bcfc789eb172dc88e.html (accessed on 6 October 2022).
8. Cardenas, R.; Pena, R.; Alepuz, S.; Asher, G. Overview of Control Systems for the Operation of DFIGs in Wind Energy Applications. *IEEE Trans. Ind. Electron.* 2013, *60*, 2776–2798. [CrossRef]
9. Yujun, L.; Yuan, X.; Li, J.; Xu, Z. Novel Grid-Forming Control of Permanent Magnet Synchronous Generator-Based Wind Turbine for Integrating Weak AC Grid without Sacrificing Maximum Power Point Tracking Demand as Frequency Controlled Reserve View Project Stability Analysis and Control Scheme. *IET Gener. Transm. Distrib.* 2021, *15*, 1613–1625. [CrossRef]
10. Benbouhenni, H.; Bizon, N. Advanced Direct Vector Control Method for Optimizing the Operation of a Double-Powered Induction Generator-Based Dual-Rotor Wind Turbine System. *Mathematics* 2021, *9*, 2403. [CrossRef]
11. Qais, M.H.; Hasanien, H.M.; Alghuwainem, S. Optimal Transient Search Algorithm-Based PI Controllers for Enhancing Low Voltage Ride-Through Ability of Grid-Linked PMSG-Based Wind Turbine. *Electronics* 2020, *9*, 1807. [CrossRef]
12. Yuan, L.; Meng, K.; Huang, J.; Dong, Z.Y. Investigating Subsynchronous Oscillations Caused by Interactions between PMSG-Based Wind Farms and Weak AC Systems. *Int. J. Electr. Power Energy Syst.* 2020, *115*, 105477. [CrossRef]
13. Pan, L.; Wang, X. Variable Pitch Control on Direct-Driven PMSG for Offshore Wind Turbine Using Repetitive-TS Fuzzy PID Control. *Renew. Energy* 2020, *159*, 221–237. [CrossRef]
14. Kapetanaki, A.; Levi, V.; Buhari, M.; Schachter, J.A. Maximization of Wind Energy Utilization Through Corrective Scheduling and FACTS Deployment. *IEEE Trans. Power Syst.* 2017, *32*, 4764–4773. [CrossRef]
15. Manohar, G.; Venkateshwarlu, S.; JayaLaxmi, A. An Elite Approach for Enhancement of LVRT in Doubly Fed Induction Generator (DFIG)-Based Wind Energy Conversion System (WECS): A FAMSANFIS Approach. *Soft Comput.* 2022, *26*, 11315–11337. [CrossRef]
16. Li, P.; Xiong, L.; Wu, F.; Ma, M.; Wang, J. Sliding Mode Controller Based on Feedback Linearization for Damping of Sub-Synchronous Control Interaction in DFIG-Based Wind Power Plants. *Int. J. Electr. Power Energy Syst.* 2019, *107*, 239–250. [CrossRef]
17. Muftau, B.; Fazeli, M.; Egwebe, A. Stability Analysis of a PMSG Based Virtual Synchronous Machine. *Electr. Power Syst. Res.* 2020, *180*, 106170. [CrossRef]
18. Haidar, A.M.A.; Muttaqi, K.M.; Hagh, M.T. A Coordinated Control Approach for DC Link and Rotor Crowbars to Improve Fault Ride-through of Dfig-Based Wind Turbine. *IEEE Trans. Ind. Appl.* 2017, *53*, 4073–4086. [CrossRef]
19. Gebru, F.M.; Khan, B.; Alhelou, H.H. Analyzing Low Voltage Ride through Capability of Doubly Fed Induction Generator Based Wind Turbine. *Comput. Electr. Eng.* 2020, *86*, 106727. [CrossRef]
20. Yan, L.; Chen, X.; Zhou, X.; Sun, H.; Jiang, L. Perturbation Compensation-Based Non-Linear Adaptive Control of ESS-DVR for the LVRT Capability Improvement of Wind Farms. *IET Renew. Power Gener.* 2018, *12*, 1500–1507. [CrossRef]
21. Chawda, G.S.; Shaik, A.G.; Mahela, O.P.; Padmanaban, S.; Holm-Nielsen, J.B. Comprehensive Review of Distributed FACTS Control Algorithms for Power Quality Enhancement in Utility Grid with Renewable Energy Penetration. *IEEE Access* 2020, *8*, 107614–107634. [CrossRef]
22. Sayahi, K.; Kadri, A.; Bacha, F.; Marzougui, H. Implementation of a D-STATCOM Control Strategy Based on Direct Power Control Method for Grid Connected Wind Turbine. *Int. J. Electr. Power Energy Syst.* 2020, *121*, 106105. [CrossRef]
23. Nasiri, M.; Mohammadi, R. Peak Current Limitation for Grid Side Inverter by Limited Active Power in PMSG-Based Wind Turbines During Different Grid Faults. *IEEE Trans. Sustain. Energy* 2017, *8*, 3–12. [CrossRef]
24. Yaramasu, V.; Wu, B. *Model Predictive Control of Wind Energy Conversion Systems*; Wiley: New York, NY, USA, 2017; ISBN 9781118988589.
25. Sadiq, M.; Aragon, C.A.; Terriche, Y.; Ali, S.W.; Su, C.-L.; Buzna, L'.; Elsisi, M.; Lee, C.-H. Continuous-Control-Set Model Predictive Control for Three-Level DC–DC Converter with Unbalanced Loads in Bipolar Electric Vehicle Charging Stations. *Mathematics* 2022, *10*, 3444. [CrossRef]
26. Azab, M. A Finite Control Set Model Predictive Control Scheme for Single-Phase Grid-Connected Inverters. *Renew. Sustain. Energy Rev.* 2021, *135*, 110131. [CrossRef]
27. Babaghorbani, B.; Beheshti, M.T.; Talebi, H.A. A Lyapunov-Based Model Predictive Control Strategy in a Permanent Magnet Synchronous Generator Wind Turbine. *Int. J. Electr. Power Energy Syst.* 2021, *130*, 106972. [CrossRef]
28. Kou, P.; Liang, D.; Li, J.; Gao, L.; Ze, Q. Finite-Control-Set Model Predictive Control for DFIG Wind Turbines. *IEEE Trans. Autom. Sci. Eng.* 2018, *15*, 1004–1013. [CrossRef]
29. Caseiro, L.M.A.; Mendes, A.M.S.; Cruz, S.M.A. Dynamically Weighted Optimal Switching Vector Model Predictive Control of Power Converters. *IEEE Trans. Ind. Electron.* 2019, *66*, 1235–1245. [CrossRef]

30. Li, X.; Zhang, H.; Shadmand, M.B.; Balog, R.S. Model Predictive Control of a Voltage-Source Inverter with Seamless Transition between Islanded and Grid-Connected Operations. *IEEE Trans. Ind. Electron.* **2017**, *64*, 7906–7918. [CrossRef]
31. Thapa, K.B.; Jayasawal, K. Pitch Control Scheme for Rapid Active Power Control of a PMSG-Based Wind Power Plant. *IEEE Trans. Ind. Appl.* **2020**, *56*, 6756–6766. [CrossRef]
32. Rahimi, M. Mathematical Modeling, Dynamic Response Analysis, and Control of PMSG-Based Wind Turbines Operating with an Alternative Control Structure in Power Control Mode. *Int. Trans. Electr. Energy Syst.* **2017**, *27*, e2423. [CrossRef]
33. Prior, G.; Krstic, M. A Control Lyapunov Approach to Finite Control Set Model Predictive Control for Permanent Magnet Synchronous Motors. *J. Dyn. Syst. Meas. Control. Trans. ASME* **2015**, *137*, 011001. [CrossRef]
34. Xia, C.; Liu, T.; Shi, T.; Song, Z. A Simplified Finite-Control-Set Model-Predictive Control for Power Converters. *IEEE Trans. Ind. Inform.* **2014**, *10*, 991–1002. [CrossRef]
35. Grid Converters for Photovoltaic and Wind Power Systems | IEEE EBooks | IEEE Xplore. Available online: https://ieeexplore.ieee.org/book/5732788 (accessed on 19 December 2021).
36. Alepuz, S.; Calle, A.; Busquets-Monge, S.; Kouro, S.; Wu, B. Use of Stored Energy in PMSG Rotor Inertia for Low-Voltage Ride-through in Back-to-Back NPC Converter-Based Wind Power Systems. *IEEE Trans. Ind. Electron.* **2013**, *60*, 1787–1796. [CrossRef]
37. Amer Saeed, M.; Mehroz Khan, H.; Ashraf, A.; Aftab Qureshi, S. Analyzing Effectiveness of LVRT Techniques for DFIG Wind Turbine System and Implementation of Hybrid Combination with Control Schemes. *Renew. Sustain. Energy Rev.* **2018**, *81*, 2487–2501. [CrossRef]
38. Talha, M.; Raihan, S.R.S.; Rahim, N.A. PV Inverter with Decoupled Active and Reactive Power Control to Mitigate Grid Faults. *Renew. Energy* **2020**, *162*, 877–892. [CrossRef]
39. Dai, J.; Xu, D.; Wu, B.; Zargari, N.R. Unified DC-Link Current Control for Low-Voltage Ride-through in Current-Source-Converter-Based Wind Energy Conversion Systems. *IEEE Trans. Power Electron.* **2010**, *26*, 288–297.
40. Barros, L.S.; Barros, C.M.V. An Internal Model Control for Enhanced Grid-Connection of Direct-Driven PMSG-Based Wind Generators. *Electr. Power Syst. Res.* **2017**, *151*, 440–450. [CrossRef]

Article

Design and Motion Characteristics of Active–Passive Composite Suspension Actuator

Hao Chen [1,2], Mingde Gong [1,2,*], Dingxuan Zhao [1,2], Wei Zhang [1,2], Wenbin Liu [1,2] and Yue Zhang [1,2]

[1] School of Mechanical Engineering, Yanshan University, Qinhuangdao 066004, China
[2] Key Laboratory of Special Transport Equipment of Hebei Province, Yanshan University, Qinhuangdao 066004, China
* Correspondence: gmd@ysu.edu.cn

Abstract: The suspension system needs both an active mode and passive mode when the emergency rescue vehicle is running on a complex road. Therefore, an active–passive composite suspension actuator (APCSA) is designed in this paper. Firstly, combined with computational fluid dynamics theory and dynamic mesh technology, the complete fluid domain of the original passive suspension actuator (PSA) is simulated. Secondly, in accordance with the simulation results and in consideration of the working conditions of the active suspension of the emergency rescue vehicle, the APCSA is designed, and its flow field characteristics are studied. Finally, test results show that the maximum recovery damping force/compression damping force of the APCSA is 2428.98 N/−1470.29 N, which is 53.5%/50.4% lower than that of the original PSA. Hence, the dynamic response capability of the actuator is effectively improved, which lays a foundation for improving the ride comfort and handling stability of emergency rescue vehicles on complex roads.

Keywords: emergency rescue vehicle; active–passive composite suspension; actuator; compound working mode; computational fluid dynamics; dynamic mesh

MSC: 76-04

1. Introduction

Emergency rescue vehicles are mainly used for rescues on land, which has a large load capacity and complex road conditions [1–4]. The suspension system can cushion the impact transmitted from the road to the vehicle body and ensure the driving smoothness and handling stability of the vehicle [5–7]. The commonly used suspension types include passive suspension, semiactive suspension and active suspension [8,9]. Compared with passive suspension and semiactive suspension, active suspension can actively adjust the suspension stiffness and damping parameters in accordance with the driving road conditions to improve the driving smoothness and stability of the vehicle [10–12]. In the case of ensuring the vibration suppression effect when driving on different roads, a single suspension mode cannot maintain low power consumption. Therefore, the suspension adopts an active mode under off-road conditions and a passive mode under good road conditions. This can effectively improve the environmental adaptability of the emergency rescue vehicle, reduce the power consumption and improve the operational life. A schematic of active and passive mode switching is shown in Figure 1. When the suspension is in the passive mode, the rod and rodless cavities of the actuator are connected with the accumulators to form a hydro-pneumatic spring. When the suspension is in the active mode, the rod and rodless cavities of the actuator are connected with a servo valve, and the servo valve controls the actuator to realize various control algorithms. The accumulator in front of the servo valve is used to stabilize the pressure pulsation, and the pump is driven by the engine. Furthermore, an overflow valve is set at the pump port to regulate the system pressure.

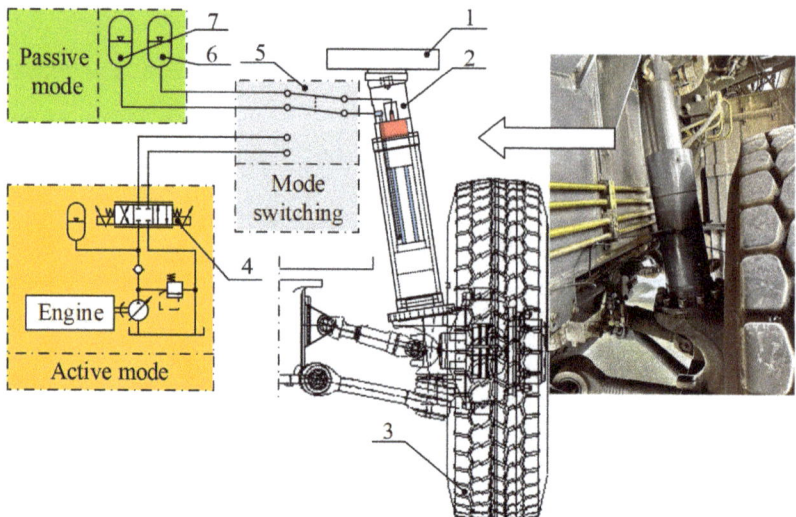

Figure 1. Schematic diagram of mode switching. 1. Body connecting plate. 2. Actuator. 3. Tyre. 4. Servo valve. 5. Mode switching valve block. 6. Accumulator of rodless cavity. 7. Accumulator of rod cavity.

Mode switching is realized by a mode switching valve block.

A suspension actuator is a key component of active suspension. The performance of the actuator directly affects the performance of the active suspension, further affecting the ride comfort and handling stability of the whole vehicle [13–15]. The suspension actuator of existing emergency rescue vehicles is designed for passive suspension, which cannot satisfy the requirements of active mode and passive mode at the same time. Therefore, it is necessary to design an active–passive composite suspension actuator (APCSA) to meet the needs of switching between active mode and passive mode. The channel parameters of the rod and rodless cavities in the suspension actuator will affect the actuator movement. If a channel's diameter is too small, it will increase the accumulation of pressure loss, reduce the circuit efficiency and cause noise and vibration [16,17]. Therefore, the design of the channels is particularly important.

Computational fluid dynamics (CFD) combines numerical calculation methods with data visualization to simulate the flow of liquid. It is a new technical method to solve the flow problem, in addition to theoretical analysis and experimental measurement [18–20]. Dynamic mesh technology can be used to simulate the problem wherein the flow field shape changes with time [21–25].

Abdalla et al. [26] used the Fluent software to study the influence of the actuator outlet size on flow and piston speed, and the simulation results showed that increasing the outlet area can increase the actuator flow and piston speed. Behrens et al. [27] used dynamic mesh technology to simulate the dynamic characteristics of a high-frequency actuator under the influences of inertia and oil compressibility. Lai et al. [28] used the CFD model to study the pressure characteristics of a hydraulic cylinder and found that the CFD model showed a better pattern of cushion processing compared with other models. Li et al. [29] analyzed the interior flow field in different clearance conditions and at different rotation rates in a rotary hydraulic cylinder with Fluent. The existing literature has simplified the fluid domain of an actuator, neglected the structure of the flow channel and reduced the accuracy of the simulation.

In this study, in consideration of the complex road conditions of emergency rescue vehicles, two suspension working modes are designed. Combined with CFD theory and dynamic mesh technology, the complete fluid domain of a passive suspension actuator

(PSA) is simulated. Then, the actuator structure is redesigned to improve the motion characteristics of the actuator, making it an APCSA that considers the needs of active and passive modes. Lastly, the performance of the APCSA is tested by experiments.

2. Numerical Simulation of Flow Field

2.1. Actuator Structure and Geometric Modelling

The PSA of an emergency rescue vehicle is taken as the research object. The structural model is shown in Figure 2. The diameter of the rodless cavity is 80 mm, the diameter of the rodless cavity channel is 10 mm, the diameter of the piston rod is 70 mm, the diameter of the rod cavity channel is 8 mm, and the stroke is 200 mm. The fluid domain is composed of four parts: the rod cavity, the rodless cavity, the rod cavity channel and the rodless cavity channel. The dynamic mesh technology is used to simulate the movement process of the piston rod, which lays the foundation for the structural design of the APCSA.

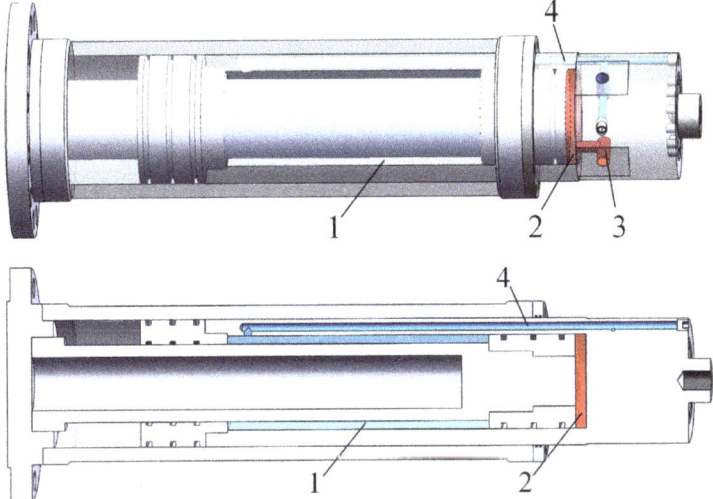

Figure 2. Actuator structure model. 1. Rod cavity. 2. Rodless cavity. 3. Rodless cavity channel. 4. Rod cavity channel.

The diameter of the hoses connecting the actuator and other components is 20 mm, which is much larger than the diameter of the internal flow channel of the actuator. Therefore, the flow resistance of the hoses can be ignored.

2.2. Flow Field Simulation

2.2.1. Meshing

To improve the mesh quality, the fluid domain model is imported into ICEM CFD for mesh generation. Since the shape of the piston motion area is regular, it is divided into hexahedral meshes. Furthermore, since the shapes of the channels are irregular, they are divided into tetrahedral meshes. Given the small size of the channel, a boundary layer effect exists in the flow, so the boundary layer grid is denser to ensure the effectiveness of the simulation results. Before the final determination of the mesh model, the mesh independence is verified to ensure that the final calculation results are the least sensitive to the change in mesh density. Taking the mass flow at the outlet as an indicator, the calculation result is as shown in Figure 3.

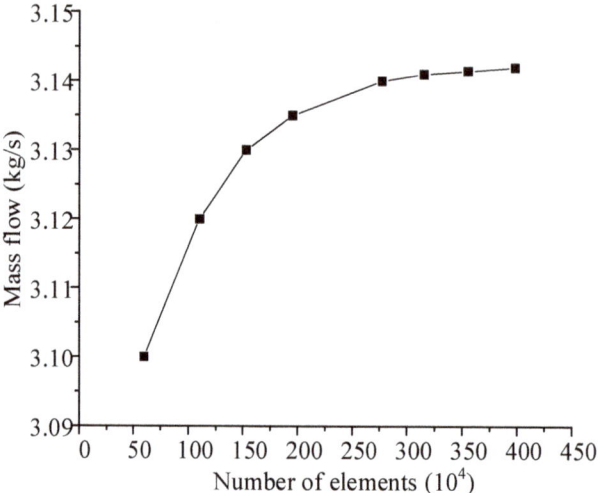

Figure 3. Mesh sensitivity check.

It can be seen from Figure 3 that when the number of elements exceeds 2.7 million, the mass flow at the outlet tends to be stable. In order to reduce the amount of computation and obtain reliable results, the total number of grids is determined to be approximately 2.7 million.

The fluid domain mesh model is shown in Figure 4. This study completely retains the real model of the actuator fluid domain and does not simplify it, such as via the intersection of flow channels, to ensure the correctness of the simulation results.

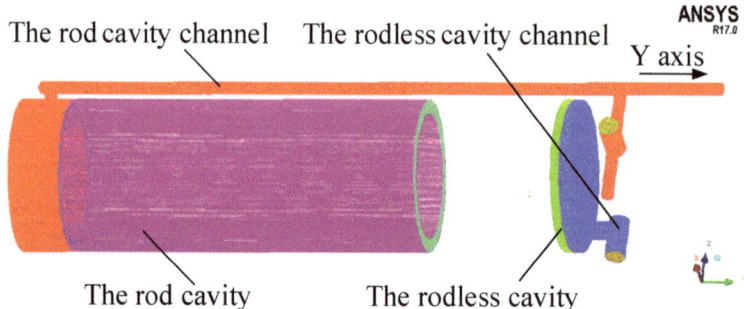

Figure 4. Fluid domain mesh model.

2.2.2. Fluid Mechanical Governing Equation

The following equations are applied.
The continuity equation is

$$\frac{\partial \rho}{\partial t} + \text{div}(\vec{u}) = \frac{\partial \rho}{\partial t} + \frac{\partial(\rho u_1)}{\partial x} + \frac{\partial(\rho u_2)}{\partial y} + \frac{\partial(\rho u_3)}{\partial z} = 0. \qquad (1)$$

The momentum equation is

$$\begin{cases} \frac{\partial(\rho u_1)}{\partial t} + \text{div}(\rho \vec{u} u_1) = \text{div}(\mu \text{grad} u_1) - \frac{\partial p}{\partial x} + S_1 \\ \frac{\partial(\rho u_2)}{\partial t} + \text{div}(\rho \vec{u} u_2) = \text{div}(\mu \text{grad} u_2) - \frac{\partial p}{\partial y} + S_2 \\ \frac{\partial(\rho u_3)}{\partial t} + \text{div}(\rho \vec{u} u_3) = \text{div}(\mu \text{grad} u_3) - \frac{\partial p}{\partial z} + S_3 \end{cases} \qquad (2)$$

The energy conservation equation is

$$\frac{\partial(\rho T)}{\partial t} + \frac{\partial(\rho u_1 T)}{\partial x} + \frac{\partial(\rho u_2 T)}{\partial y} + \frac{\partial(\rho u_3 T)}{\partial z} = \frac{\partial}{\partial x}\left(\frac{k_p}{c_p}\frac{\partial T}{\partial x}\right) + \frac{\partial}{\partial y}\left(\frac{k_p}{c_p}\frac{\partial T}{\partial y}\right) + \frac{\partial}{\partial z}\left(\frac{k_p}{c_p}\frac{\partial T}{\partial z}\right) + S_T \tag{3}$$

The transport equations of turbulent kinetic energy k and dissipation rate ε are

$$\frac{\partial(\rho k)}{\partial t} + \frac{\partial(\rho k u_i)}{\partial x_i} = \frac{\partial}{\partial x_j}\left[\left(\mu + \frac{\mu_t}{\sigma_k}\right)\frac{\partial k}{\partial x_j}\right] + G_k - \rho\varepsilon + S_k, \tag{4}$$

$$\frac{\partial(\rho\varepsilon)}{\partial t} + \frac{\partial(\rho\varepsilon u_i)}{\partial x_i} = \frac{\partial}{\partial x_j}\left[\left(\mu + \frac{\mu_t}{\sigma_k}\right)\frac{\partial \varepsilon}{\partial x_j}\right] + C_{1\varepsilon}\frac{\varepsilon}{k}G_k - C_{2\varepsilon}\rho\frac{\varepsilon^2}{k} + S_\varepsilon. \tag{5}$$

where ρ is the density of fluid. u_i and u_j are the velocity components of fluid in three directions (i = 1, 2, 3; j = 1, 2, 3); that is, u_1, u_2 and u_3 are the velocity components of fluid in the x, y and z directions, respectively. S_i is the generalized source term, (I = 1, 2, 3). p is the pressure on the fluid element. k_p is the heat transfer coefficient of the fluid. c_p is the specific heat capacity. T is the temperature. S_T is the part of the fluid mechanical energy converted into heat energy. μ is the dynamic viscosity. μ_t is the turbulent viscosity. k is the turbulence kinetic energy. G_k is the turbulent kinetic energy generation term caused by the average velocity gradient. σ_k and σ_ε are the Prandtl numbers corresponding to k and ε, respectively. S_k and S_ε are user-defined source terms. $C_{1\varepsilon}$ and $C_{2\varepsilon}$ are empirical constants; that is, $C_{1\varepsilon}$ = 1.44, $C_{2\varepsilon}$ = 1.92, σ_k = 1.0, and σ_ε = 1.3.

2.2.3. Parameter Setting

ANSYS Fluent is used for the numerical simulation of the model. The turbulence model is set as standard k–ε. The hydraulic oil is ISO-L-HM46 with a density of 889 kg/m³ and a dynamic viscosity of 0.04048 Pa·s. The inlet of the rodless cavity is set as the 'Pressure Inlet', and the pressure is 1.5 MPa. The outlet of the rod cavity is set as the 'Pressure Outlet', and the pressure is 0.05 MPa. The solver is set as 'Pressure-Based', and the calculation method is 'SIMPLE'.

The strategy of dynamic mesh updating adopts the 'Layering' updating method. The movement of the piston in the dynamic domain is defined by 'DEFINE_CG_MOTION', and the piston movement speed is set to 0.3 m/s. As the stroke of the actuator is relatively short, which is ±0.1 m, when the speed is 0.3 m/s, it only takes 0.33 s for the actuator to reach the maximum stroke. Therefore, the speed is reasonable for the practical operation of suspension in off-road conditions.

3. Simulation Results and Analysis

The flow speed and pressure loss of oil can be determined by analyzing the flow field inside the suspension actuator, which can provide a theoretical reference for the structural design of the actuator. Given that the motion speed of the actuator is 0.3 m/s, four simulation time points within 0.67 s are selected to analyze the dynamic flow field characteristics of the suspension actuator during its extension movement.

3.1. Actuator Flow Field Pressure Contour

The pressure contour of the actuator flow field is shown in Figure 5.

Figure 5 illustrates that during the extension movement of the actuator, a large pressure drop occurs from point A to point B in the rod cavity channel. When t = 0.67 s, the pressure from point A to point B at 10 positions is taken. The pressure curve is shown in Figure 6. The pressure of point A is 0.938 MPa and that of point B is 0.366 MPa, and the pressure loss is 0.572 MPa. Because the small diameter of the rod cavity channel causes a large pressure loss, the rod cavity channel needs to be redesigned.

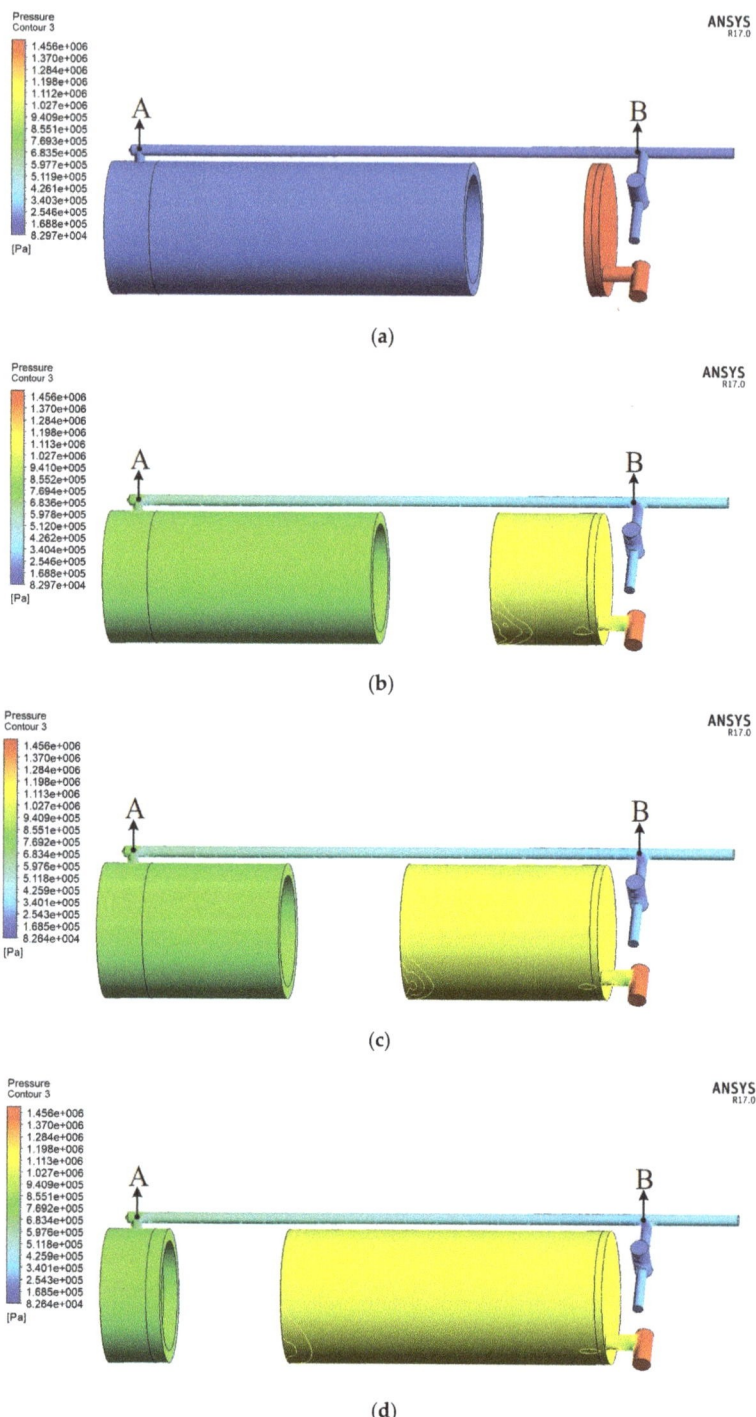

Figure 5. Pressure contour: (**a**) $t = 0$ s; (**b**) $t = 0.2$ s; (**c**) $t = 0.4$ s; (**d**) $t = 0.67$ s.

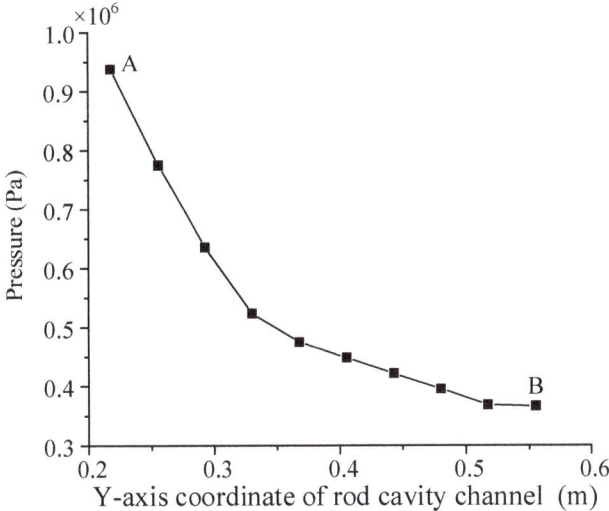

Figure 6. Pressure curve of the rod cavity channel.

3.2. Actuator Flow Field Velocity Contour

The velocity contour of the actuator flow field is shown in Figure 7.

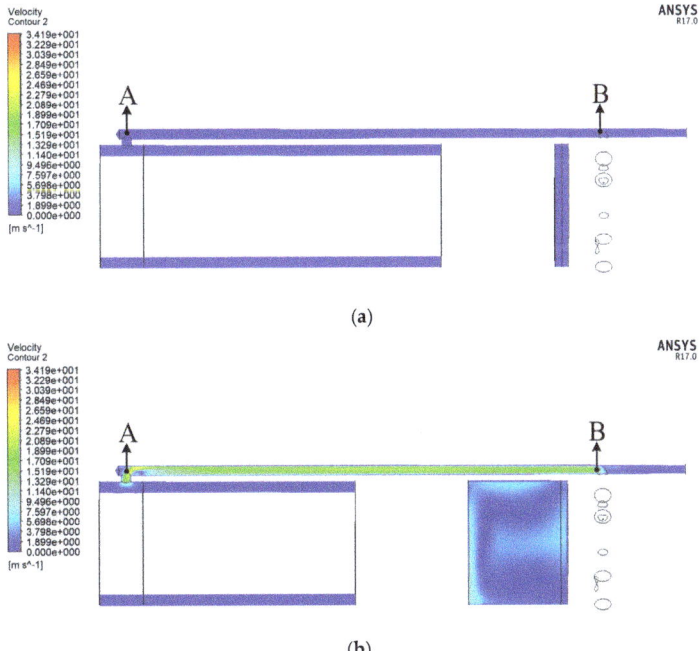

(a)

(b)

Figure 7. Cont.

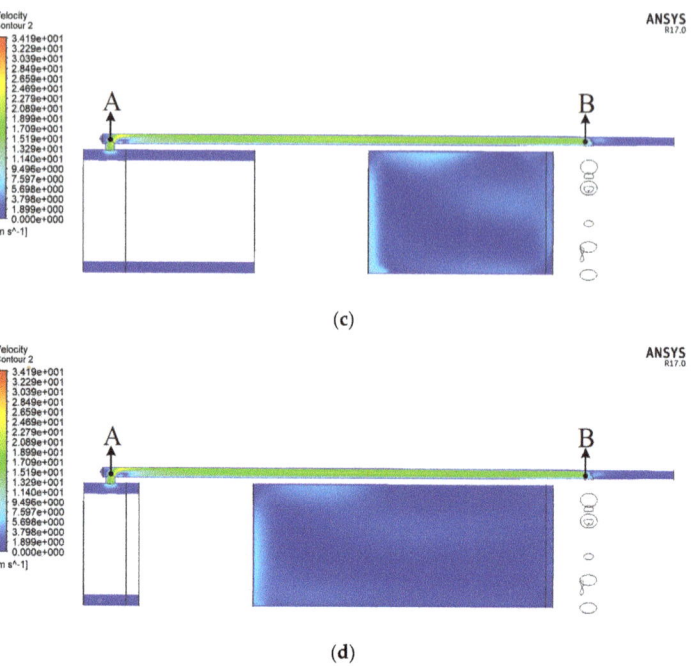

(c)

(d)

Figure 7. Velocity contour: (**a**) $t = 0$ s; (**b**) $t = 0.2$ s; (**c**) $t = 0.4$ s; (**d**) $t = 0.67$ s.

As seen in Figure 7, during the extension movement of the actuator, the flow speed of the oil increases after it enters the rod cavity channel from the rod cavity, whilst the speed of other parts, such as the rodless cavity, does not change significantly. The flow speed from point A to point B at 10 positions at $t = 0.67$ s is determined. The velocity curve is shown in Figure 8. The maximum flow speed from point A to point B is 18.63 m/s, and the flow speed at most locations is stable near this velocity. Therefore, during the extension movement of the actuator, the flow speed of the rod cavity channel is too fast to be achieved in the experiment, so the rod cavity channel should be redesigned to reduce the flow speed.

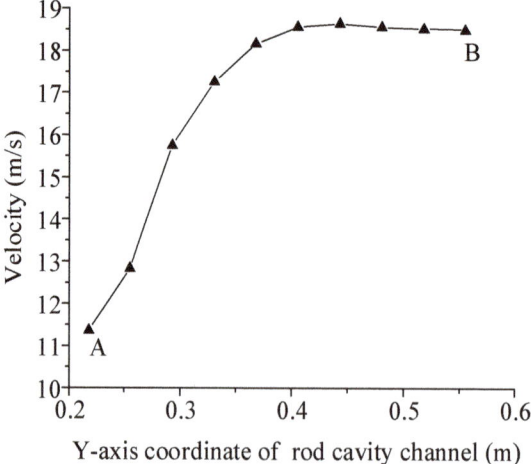

Figure 8. Velocity curve of rod cavity channel.

4. Structure Design and Flow Field Simulation of the APCSA
4.1. Structural Design of the APCSA

Given that the installation position of the suspension actuator on an emergency rescue vehicle is difficult to change, the external dimensions of the APCSA should be the same as before. To improve the motion characteristics and responsiveness of the actuator in active mode, a rod cavity channel 4-2 (Figure 9) is added, which enlarges the equivalent flow area of the rod cavity channel. During the movement of the actuator, the two rod cavity channels work together to improve the flow capacity of the rod cavity. On the premise of guaranteeing the structural strength and not changing the installation size, the diameter d of flow channel 4-2 is set to 5 mm, 6 mm, 7 mm and 8 mm. The smaller flow passage diameter can allow the actuator to obtain better structural strength. Therefore, if the smaller channel diameter can meet the requirements of flow speed and pressure drop, the smaller diameter will be selected. Therefore, the selection of the channel diameter is the result of considering the structural strength, pressure drop and flow rate.

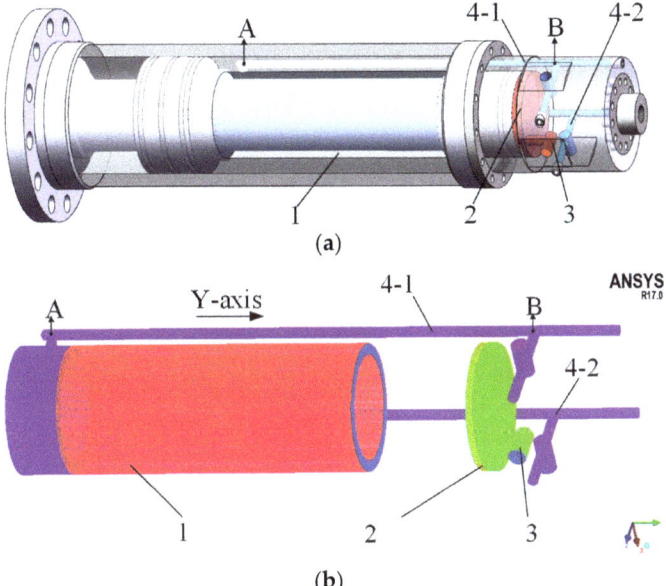

Figure 9. Structural model and fluid domain mesh model: (**a**) structure model; (**b**) mesh model. 1. Rod cavity. 2. Rodless cavity. 3. Rodless cavity channel. 4-1. Rod cavity channel. 4-2. Rod cavity channel (d = 5, 6, 7, 8 mm).

The simulation parameters are consistent with those presented in Section 2.2.3. Dynamic mesh simulation is carried out in Fluent.

When t = 0.67 s, the pressure and flow velocity at 10 positions from point A to point B in rod cavity channel 4-1 are taken, and the comparison curves are as shown in Figures 10 and 11.

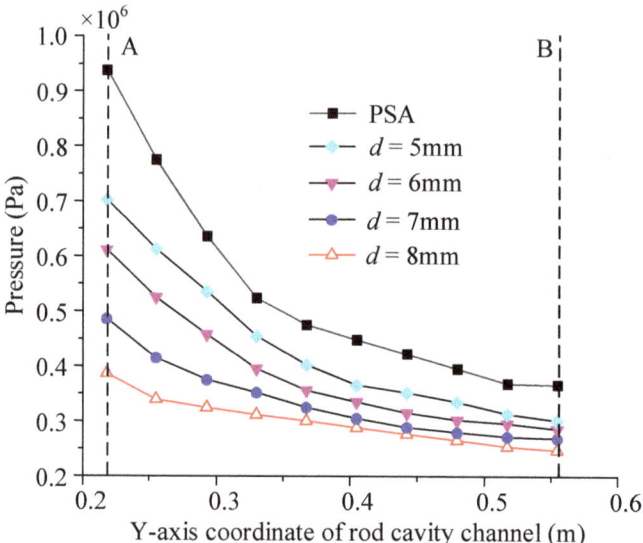

Figure 10. Pressure curve at different diameters.

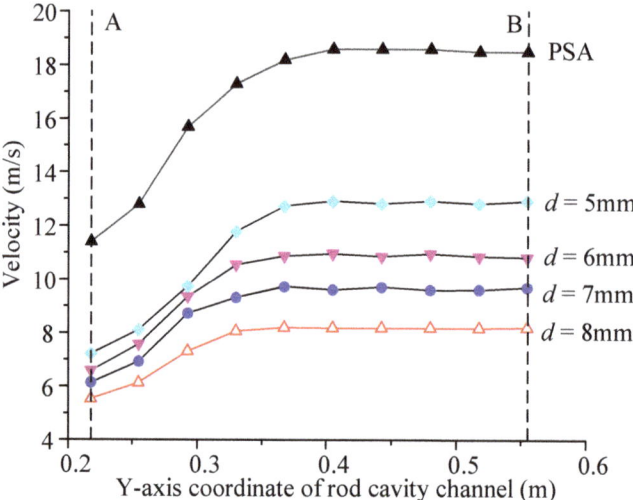

Figure 11. Velocity curve at different diameters.

As seen in Figures 10 and 11, the larger the diameter of rod cavity channel 4-2, the smaller the pressure and pressure drop from point A to point B, and the lower the steady flow speed between points A and B. A comparison of the pressure drops from point A to point B with different diameters is shown in Figure 12, and a comparison of the steady flow speeds is displayed in Figure 13.

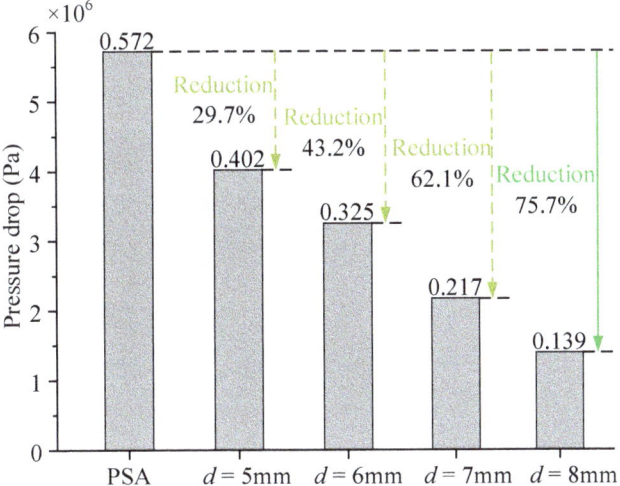

Figure 12. Comparison of pressure drop at different diameters.

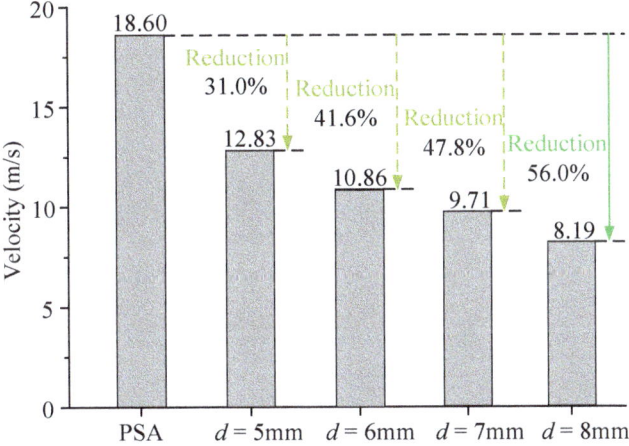

Figure 13. Comparison of flow speed at different diameters.

Figures 12 and 13 demonstrate that when the diameter d of rod cavity 4-2 is 5 mm, 6 mm, 7 mm and 8 mm, respectively, the pressure drop from point A to point B decreases by 29.7%, 43.2%, 62.1% and 75.7%, respectively, compared with PSA, and the steady flow speed between points A and B decreases by 31.0%, 41.6%, 47.8% and 56.0%, respectively. Therefore, on the premise of ensuring the structural strength and not changing the installation size, the diameter d of rod cavity channel 4-2 should preferably be 8 mm.

4.2. Simulation Results (d = 8 mm)

The flow field pressure contour of the APCSA when the diameter of rod cavity channel 4-2 is 8 mm is shown in Figure 14. Given the symmetrical structure of the two rod cavity channels, taking rod cavity channel 4-1 as an example, the flow field velocity contour diagram of its profile is as shown in Figure 15.

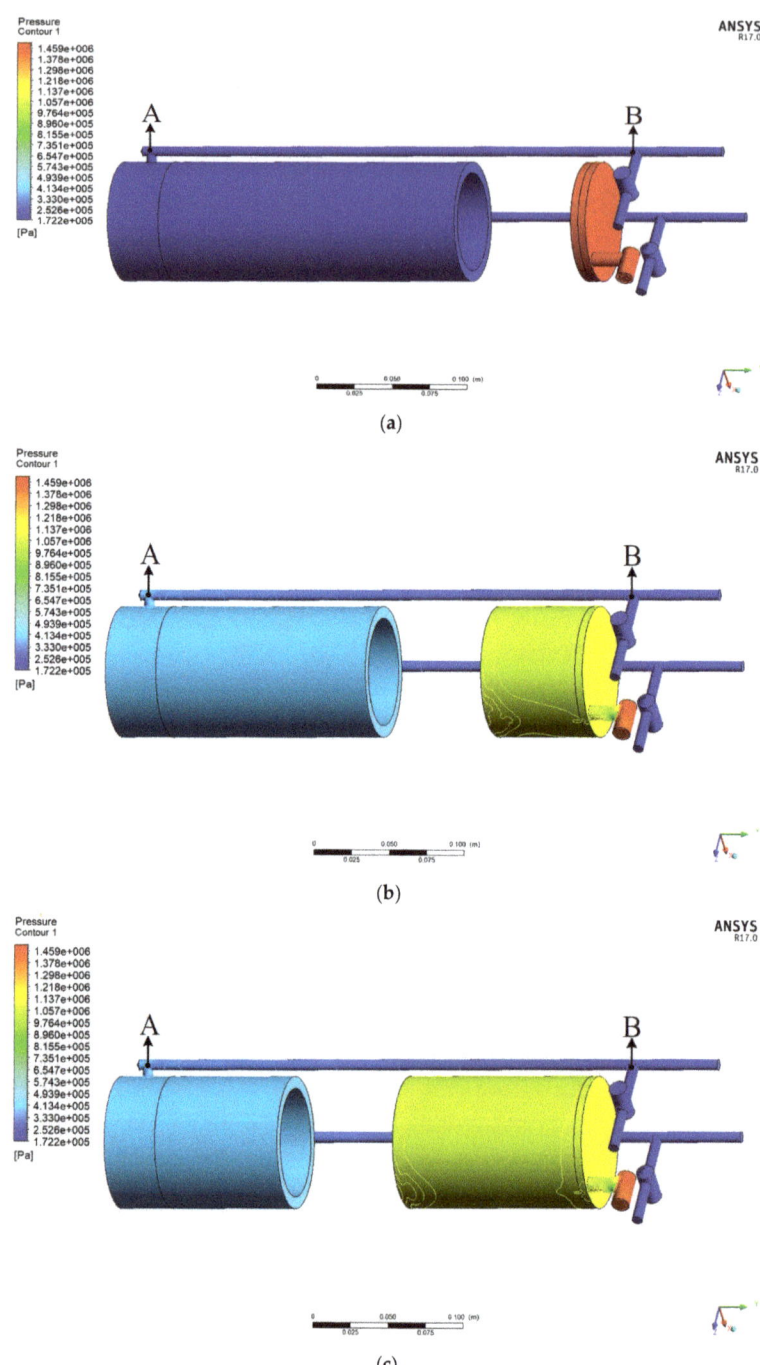

Figure 14. *Cont.*

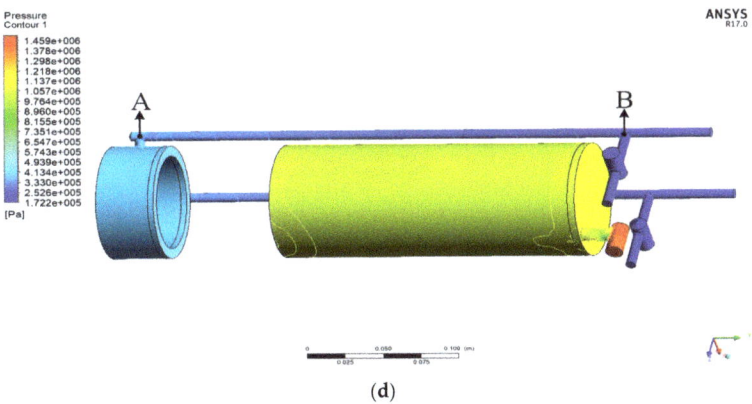

(**d**)

Figure 14. Pressure contour: (**a**) $t = 0$ s; (**b**) $t = 0.2$ s; (**c**) $t = 0.4$ s; (**d**) $t = 0.67$ s.

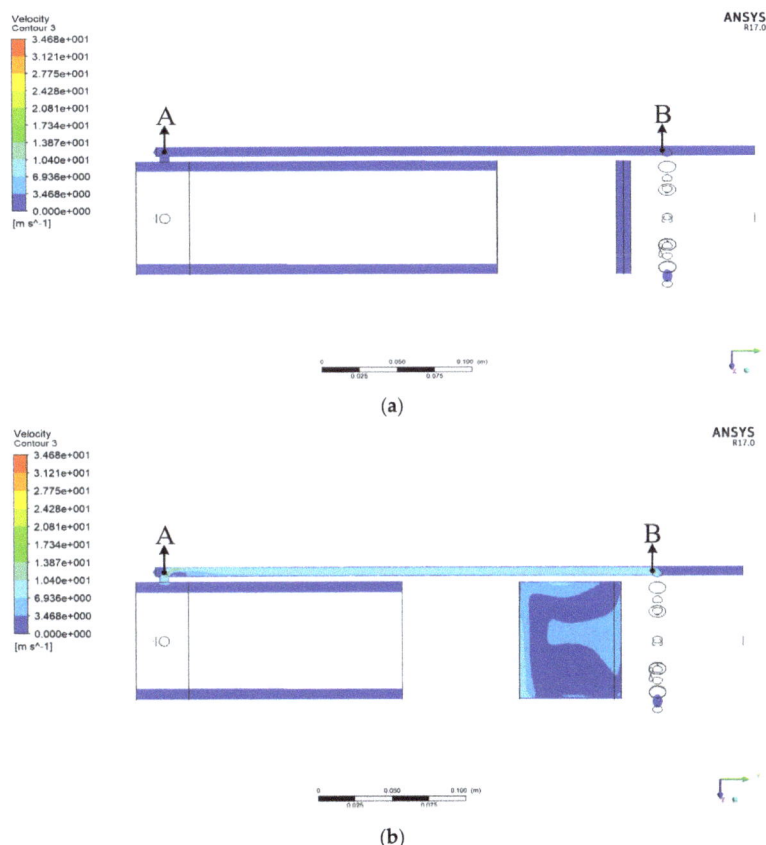

Figure 15. *Cont.*

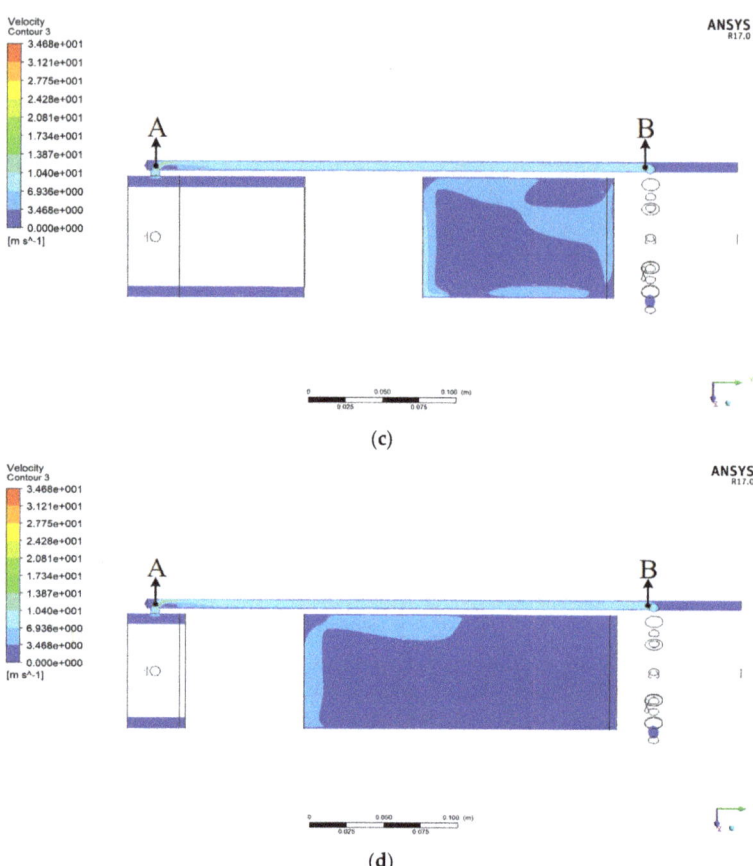

Figure 15. Velocity contour: (**a**) $t = 0$ s; (**b**) $t = 0.2$ s; (**c**) $t = 0.4$ s; (**d**) $t = 0.67$ s.

Figure 14 demonstrates that during the extension movement of the actuator—that is, when $t = 0.2$ s, $t = 0.4$ s and $t = 0.67$ s—the pressure drop from point A to point B in the rod cavity channel is small. As seen in Figure 10, when $t = 0.67$ s, the pressure at point A is 0.387 MPa, and the pressure at point B is 0.248 MPa, so the pressure drop is 0.139 MPa. Compared with PSA, the APCSA effectively reduces the pressure loss in the rod cavity channel.

As seen in Figure 15, during the extension movement of the actuator, the flow speed of the oil increases after it enters the rod cavity channel from the rod cavity, whilst the speed of other parts, such as the rodless cavity, does not change significantly. Figure 11 illustrates that the maximum flow velocity from point A to point B is 8.19 m/s, and the flow velocity at most positions is stable around this velocity. Compared with PSA, the APCSA effectively reduces the flow velocity in the rod cavity channel and meets the requirements of the actuator movement speed.

5. Experiment

To further compare the performance of the PSA and APCSA, a suspension actuator test bench is established, as shown in Figure 16. The APCSA test bench is divided into an actuating bench and a pumping station. The actuating bench includes a counterweight, a force sensor, a suspension actuator and a frame, etc. The pumping station includes an electro-hydraulic servo valve, an oil pressure sensor, a hydraulic pump, a hydraulic oil tank and an accumulator, etc. The PSA is shown in Figure 17a, and the APCSA is shown in

Figure 17b. In the experiment, the diameter of rod cavity channel 4-2 is 8 mm, and the mass of the counterweight is 1000 kg. In addition, the pressure at the pump outlet is 9 MPa.

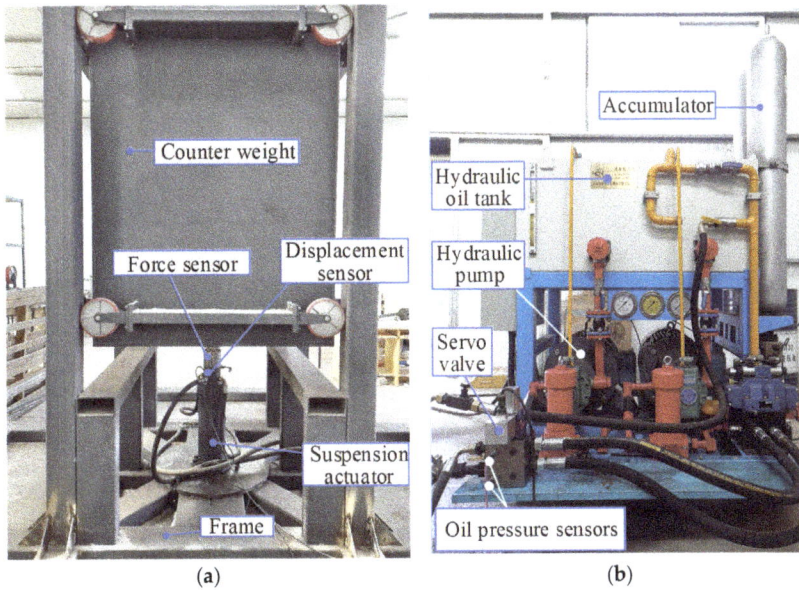

Figure 16. Suspension actuator test bench: (**a**) actuating bench; (**b**) pump station.

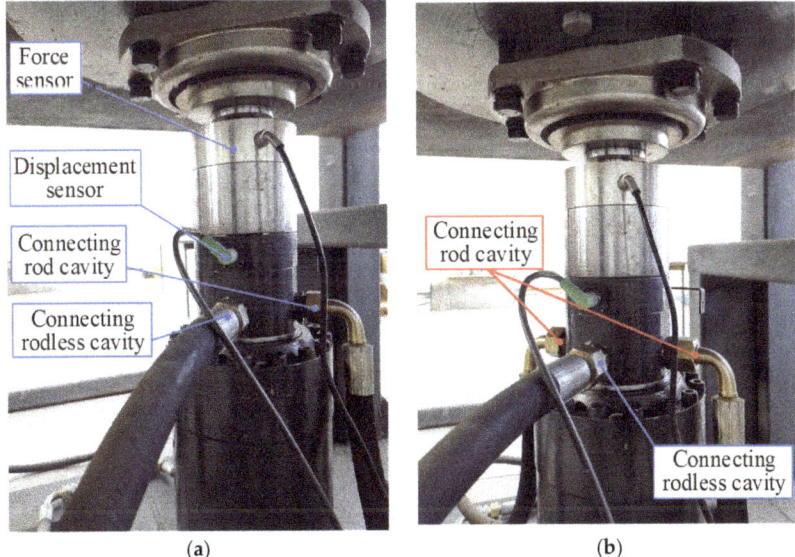

Figure 17. Actuator structure comparison diagram: (**a**) PSA; (**b**) APCSA.

A displacement step and square wave response tests are carried out for the PSA and APCSA, respectively. The actuator structure is the only variable, and other conditions, such as system pressure and counterweight weight, remain the same. The experimental response curves are shown in Figures 18 and 19.

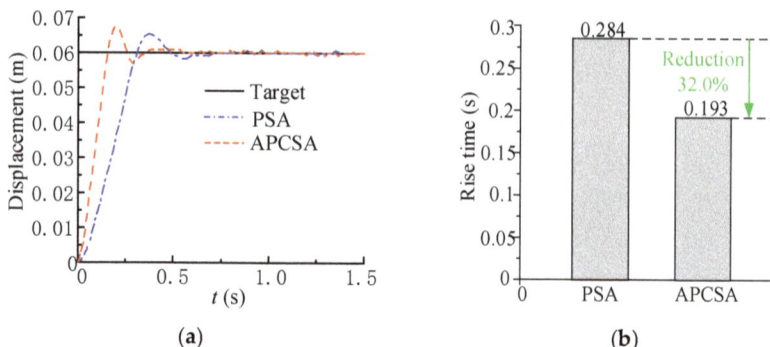

Figure 18. Displacement step response: (**a**) response comparison curve; (**b**) rise time comparison chart.

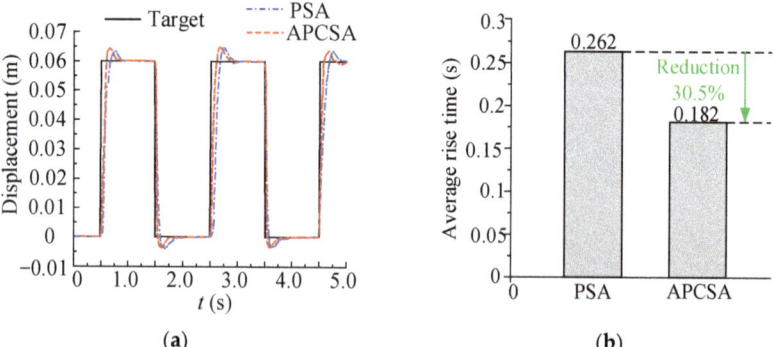

Figure 19. Displacement square wave response: (**a**) response comparison curve; (**b**) rise time comparison chart.

Figure 18 shows that under the step signal, the time required for the PSA to rise to 0.06 m is 0.284 s, and the time required for the APCSA is 0.193 s, which is 32% less than the rising time of the PSA; in other words, the response speed of the APCSA is significantly improved.

As seen in Figure 19, under the square wave signal, the response time of the APCSA during rising and falling decreases. A comparison diagram of the mean values for rising to 0.06 m three times is shown in Figure 19b. The mean time of the PSA rising to 0.06 m is 0.262 s, and the mean time of the APCSA rising is 0.182 s, which is 30.5% lower than that of the PSA. Therefore, the response speed of the APCSA is proven to be significantly improved once again.

Sinusoidal signals with an amplitude of 0.06 m and frequencies of 0.5 and 1 Hz are used to test the following effect of the two actuators. The displacement curves of the experimental results are shown in Figures 20 and 21.

The time delay and amplitude attenuation ratio are used as performance indexes, and a comparison is shown in Table 1. Figure 20 and Table 1 indicate that under the sinusoidal signal with a frequency of 0.5 Hz, the time delay of the displacement curve of the PSA is 0.10 s, and the amplitude attenuation ratio is 5.5%. The time delay of the APCSA is 0.04 s, and the amplitude attenuation ratio is 0.3%, which improves the displacement following effect.

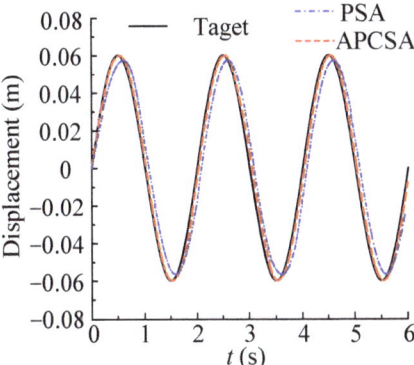

Figure 20. The 0.5 Hz sinusoidal response.

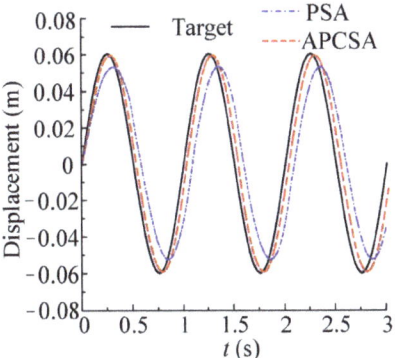

Figure 21. The 1 Hz sinusoidal response.

Table 1. Performance index comparison.

Comparison	Time Delay (s)		Amplitude Attenuation Ratio (%)	
	0.5 Hz	1 Hz	0.5 Hz	1 Hz
PSA	0.10	0.13	5.5	10.8
APCSA	0.04	0.05	0.3	0.5
Performance improvement	60.0%	61.5%	94.5%	95.4%

Figure 21 and Table 1 show that under the sinusoidal signal with a frequency of 1 Hz, the displacement curve of the PSA lags behind obviously, the time delay is 0.13 s, and the amplitude attenuation ratio is obvious, with a rate of 10.8%. The APCSA has a good displacement following effect, with a time delay of 0.05 s and an amplitude attenuation ratio of 0.5%. To summarize, the higher the target frequency, the more obvious the performance improvement achieved.

In the sinusoidal test with a frequency of 1 Hz, the theoretical output force F of the actuator was calculated as follows:

$$F = P_1 A_1 - P_2 A_2 \tag{6}$$

where P_1 is the rodless cavity pressure, P_2 is the rod cavity pressure, A_1 is the force area of the rodless cavity, and A_2 is the force area of the rod cavity. P_1 and P_2 are obtained using oil pressure sensors. The pressure sensors are installed on the pipelines connected with the rod cavity and the rodless cavity of the actuator to detect the pressures at the inlet and outlet of the flow channel.

The actual output force N of the actuator can be obtained using the force sensor. The theoretical output force of the PSA is F_1, and the actual output force is N_1. The theoretical output force of the APCSA is F_2, and the actual output force is N_2. The output force curves are shown in Figure 22.

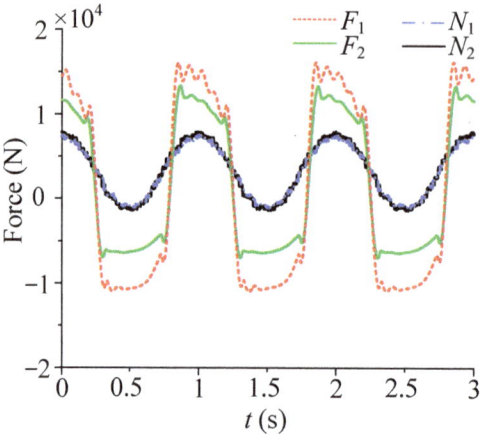

Figure 22. Different output force curves: F_1 is the theoretical output force of the PSA; N_1 is the actual output force; F_2 is the theoretical output force of the APCSA; N_2 is the actual output force.

According to the force analysis of the piston rod,

$$F = N + C + G, \qquad (7)$$

where C is the equivalent damping force of the hydraulic cylinder and G is the inertia force. Taking one cycle as an example, the equivalent damping force C can be obtained by removing the inertia force G, as shown in Figure 23. The equivalent damping force–displacement curve is shown in Figure 24, and the equivalent damping force–velocity curve is shown in Figure 25.

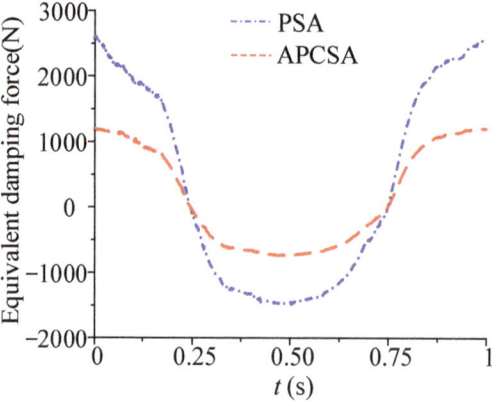

Figure 23. Equivalent damping force.

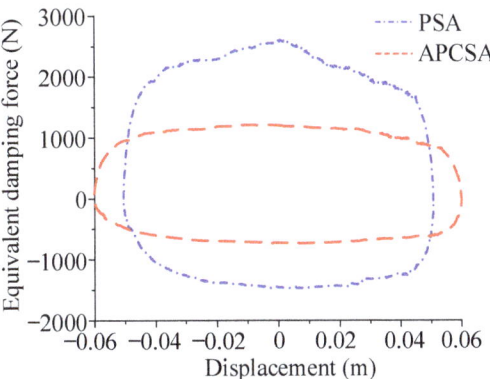

Figure 24. Equivalent damping force–displacement curve.

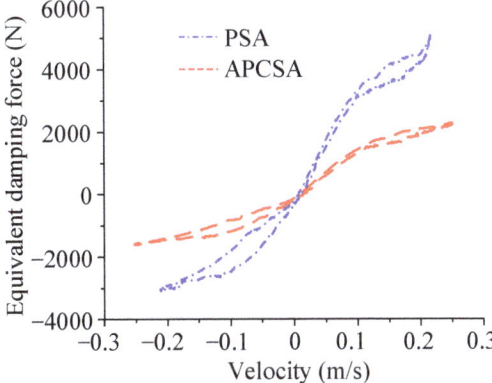

Figure 25. Equivalent damping force–velocity curve.

The maximum restoring damping force/compression damping force can be obtained from Figures 24 and 25. As shown in Table 2, the maximum restoring damping force/compression damping force of the PSA reaches 2608.16 N/−1472.51 N, indicating that substantial energy is consumed in the actuator, which presents a disadvantage for the control of electro-hydraulic active suspension. The maximum restoring damping force/compression damping force of the APCSA is 1209.88 N/−735.35 N, which is 53.6%/50.1% lower than that of the PSA, thus improving the dynamic response capability of the actuator. The driving road surface of emergency rescue vehicles is complex and diverse, and when the suspension is in active mode, the suspension actuator should have a fast response rate and high control accuracy. The maximum resilience damping force/compression damping force of the actuator is reduced by the redesign, so that it satisfies the requirements of active suspension for the actuator. Such a redesign lays the foundation for improving the driving smoothness and handling stability of emergency rescue vehicles on complex road surfaces.

Table 2. Comparison of damping force.

Maximum Damping Force	PSA	APCSA	Reduction
Restoring	2608.16 N	1209.88 N	53.6%
Compression	−1472.51 N	−735.35 N	50.1%

6. Conclusions

(1) Combined with CFD theory and the dynamic mesh technique, a simulation study on a typical PSA is carried out to redesign the actuator structure and overcome the structural barriers between passive and active suspension actuators. Hence, a type of APCSA can be obtained to meet the needs of switching between active mode and passive mode.

(2) The flow field simulation results indicate that after diameter selection, the pressure loss of the rod cavity channel of the PSA is 0.572 MPa, and the maximum flow speed is 18.63 m/s. Meanwhile, the pressure loss of the rod cavity channel of the APCSA is 0.139 MPa, and the maximum flow speed is 8.19 m/s. Thus, the pressure loss is reduced by 75.7%, and the maximum flow speed is reduced by 56.0%. The effect of the structural redesign is obvious.

(3) In the step and sinusoidal response experiments, the response velocity and displacement following performance of the APCSA are significantly improved compared with the PSA. The maximum restoring damping force/compression damping force of the APCSA is 2428.98 N/−1470.29 N, which is 53.5%/50.4% lower than that of the PSA. The dynamic response ability of the actuator is improved. The APCSA will assist the active suspension system of the whole vehicle to realize various advanced control algorithms.

Author Contributions: Conceptualization, M.G. and H.C.; methodology, H.C.; software, H.C.; validation, H.C., W.L. and Y.Z.; formal analysis, M.G. and H.C.; investigation, H.C.; resources, M.G.; data curation, H.C.; writing—original draft preparation, H.C.; writing—review and editing, M.G.; visualization, H.C. and W.Z.; supervision, D.Z. All authors have read and agreed to the published version of the manuscript.

Funding: This work was supported by the National Natural Science Foundation of China (No. 52175063), the Natural Science Foundation of Hebei Province (E2021203145) and the Joint Fund for Regional Innovation and Development of the National Natural Science Foundation of China (U20A20332).

Data Availability Statement: Not applicable.

Conflicts of Interest: The authors declare no conflict of interest.

References

1. Zhou, C.; Liu, X.H.; Xu, F.X. Intervention criterion and control strategy of active front steering system for emergency rescue vehicle. *Mech. Syst. Signal Process.* **2021**, *148*, 107160. [CrossRef]
2. Xue, J.; Tu, Q.; Pan, M.; Lai, X.; Zhou, C. An improved energy management strategy for 24t heavy-duty hybrid emergency rescue vehicle with dual-motor torque increasing. *IEEE Access* **2020**, *9*, 5920–5932. [CrossRef]
3. Li, P.; Yan, J.; Tu, Q.; Pan, M.; Xue, J. A novel energy management strategy for series hybrid electric rescue vehicle. *Math. Probl. Eng.* **2018**, *2018*, 1–15. [CrossRef]
4. Xu, F.; Liu, X.; Chen, W.; Zhou, C. Dynamic switch control of steering modes for four wheel independent steering rescue vehicle. *IEEE Access* **2019**, *7*, 135595–135605. [CrossRef]
5. Jeong, K.; Choi, S.B.; Choi, H. Sensor fault detection and isolation using a support vector machine for vehicle suspension systems. *IEEE T. Veh. Technol.* **2020**, *69*, 3852–3863. [CrossRef]
6. Abdi, B.; Mirzaei, M.; Gharamaleki, R.M. A new approach to optimal control of nonlinear vehicle suspension system with input constraint. *J. Vib. Control* **2018**, *24*, 3307–3320. [CrossRef]
7. Jing, X.J.; Pan, H.H.; Sun, W.C. Robust finite-time tracking control for nonlinear suspension systems via disturbance compensation. *Mech. Syst. Signal Process.* **2017**, *88*, 49–61.
8. Shah, D.; Santos, M.M.D.; Chaoui, H.; Justo, J.F. Event-triggered non-switching networked sliding mode control for active suspension system with random actuation network delay. *IEEE T. Intell. Transp. early access.* **2021**. [CrossRef]
9. Bai, R.; Guo, D. Sliding-mode control of the active suspension system with the dynamics of a hydraulic actuator. *Complexity* **2018**, *2018*, 5907208. [CrossRef]
10. Liu, Y.J.; Zeng, Q.; Tong, S.; Chen, C.; Liu, L. Actuator failure compensation-based adaptive control of active suspension systems with prescribed performance. *IEEE T. Ind. Electron.* **2020**, *67*, 7044–7053. [CrossRef]
11. Attia, T.; Vamvoudakis, K.G.; Kochersberger, K.; Bird, J.; Furukawa, T. Simultaneous dynamic system estimation and optimal control of vehicle active suspension. *Vehicle Syst. Dyn.* **2019**, *57*, 1467–1493. [CrossRef]

12. Ramalingam, M.; Thirumurugan, M.A.; Kumar, T.A.; Jebaseelan, D.D.; Jebaraj, C. Response characteristics of car seat suspension using intelligent control policies under small and large bump excitations. *Int. J. Dyn. Control* **2020**, *8*, 545–557. [CrossRef]
13. Enders, E.; Burkhard, G.; Munzinger, N. Analysis of the influence of suspension actuator limitations on ride comfort in passenger cars using model predictive control. *Actuators* **2020**, *9*, 77. [CrossRef]
14. Han, S.Y.; Zhang, C.H.; Tang, G.Y. Approximation optimal vibration for networked nonlinear vehicle active suspension with actuator time delay. *Asian J. Control* **2017**, *19*, 983–995. [CrossRef]
15. Li, H.; Gao, H.; Liu, H.; Liu, M. Fault-tolerant h control for active suspension vehicle systems with actuator faults. *Part I J. Syst. Control. Eng.* **2011**, *226*, 348–363. [CrossRef]
16. Tang, X.; Duan, X.; Gao, H.; Li, X.; Shi, X. CFD investigations of transient cavitation flows in pipeline based on weakly-compressible model. *Water* **2020**, *12*, 448. [CrossRef]
17. Liu, C.; Li, X.; Li, A.; Cui, Z.; Li, Y. Cavitation onset caused by a dynamic pressure wave in liquid pipelines. *Ultrason. Sonochem.* **2020**, *68*, 105225. [CrossRef]
18. Abdulkarim, A.H.; Ates, A.; Altinisik, K.; Canli, E. Internal flow analysis of a porous burner via CFD. *Int. J. Numer. Method Heat* **2019**, *29*, 2666–2683. [CrossRef]
19. Hsu, C.H.; Chen, J.L.; Yuan, S.C.; Kung, K.Y. CFD simulations on the rotor dynamics of a horizontal axis wind turbine activated from stationary. *Appl. Mech.* **2021**, *2*, 147–158. [CrossRef]
20. Rezaeiha, A.; Montazeri, H.; Blocken, B. CFD analysis of dynamic stall on vertical axis wind turbines using Scale-Adaptive Simulation (SAS): Comparison against URANS and hybrid RANS/LES. *Energ. Convers. Manag.* **2019**, *196*, 1282–1298. [CrossRef]
21. Yang, X.; Zhou, H.; Wu, H. CFD modelling of biomass ash deposition under multiple operation conditions using a 2D mass-conserving dynamic mesh approach. *Fuel* **2022**, *316*, 123250. [CrossRef]
22. Mlakar, D.; Winter, M.; Stadlbauer, P.; Seidel, H. Subdivision-specialized linear algebra kernels for static and dynamic mesh connectivity on the GPU. *Comput. Graph. Forum* **2020**, *39*, 335–349. [CrossRef]
23. Zhu, Q.; Zhang, Y.; Zhu, D. Study on dynamic characteristics of the bladder fluid pulsation attenuator based on dynamic mesh technology. *J. Mech. Sci. Technol.* **2019**, *33*, 1159–1168. [CrossRef]
24. Salinas, P.; Regnier, G.; Jacquemyn, C.; Pain, C.C.; Jackson, M.D. Dynamic mesh optimisation for geothermal reservoir modelling. *Geothermics* **2021**, *94*, 102089. [CrossRef]
25. Zheng, Z.; Yang, W.; Yu, P.; Cai, Y.; Zhou, H.; Boon, S.K. Simulating growth of ash deposit in boiler heat exchanger tube based on CFD dynamic mesh technique. *Fuel* **2020**, *259*, 1–16. [CrossRef]
26. Abdalla, M.O.; Nagarajan, T. A computational study of the actuation speed of the hydraulic cylinder under different ports' sizes and configurations. *J. Eng. Sci. Technol.* **2015**, *10*, 160–173.
27. Behrens, B.A.; Hübner, S.; Krimm, R.; Wager, C.; Vucetic, M.; Cahyono, T. Development of a hydraulic actuator to superimpose oscillation in metal-forming presses. *Key Eng. Mater.* **2011**, *473*, 217–222. [CrossRef]
28. Lai, Q.; Liang, L.; Li, J.; Wu, S.; Liu, J. Modeling and analysis on cushion characteristics of fast and high-flow-rate hydraulic cylinder. *Math. Probl. Eng.* **2016**, *2016*, 1–17. [CrossRef]
29. Li, S.B.; Liu, Y.L. Numerical simulation on flow field of the rotary cylinder's spiral flow. *Appl. Mech. Mater.* **2011**, *63*, 365–368. [CrossRef]

Article

Adaptive Sensorless PI+Passivity-Based Control of a Boost Converter Supplying an Unknown CPL

Sebastián Riffo [1,*], Walter Gil-González [2], Oscar Danilo Montoya [3,4], Carlos Restrepo [1,5,*] and Javier Muñoz [4,*]

1. Department of Electrical Engineering, Universidad de Talca, Curicó 3340000, Chile
2. Department of Electrical Engineering, Universidad Tecnológica de Pereira, Pereira 660003, Colombia
3. Grupo de Compatibilidad e Interferencia Electromagnética, Facultad de Ingeniería, Universidad Distrital Francisco José de Caldas, Bogotá 110231, Colombia
4. Laboratorio Inteligente de Energía, Facultad de Ingeniería, Universidad Tecnológica de Bolívar, Cartagena 131001, Colombia
5. Principal Investigator Millenium Institute on Green Ammonia as Energy Vector (MIGA), Santiago de Chile 7820436, Chile
* Correspondence: sebastian.riffo@utalca.cl (S.R.); crestrepo@utalca.cl (C.R.); jamunoz@utalca.cl (J.M.)

Abstract: This paper presents an adaptive control to stabilize the output voltage of a DC–DC boost converter that feeds an unknown constant power load (CPL). The proposed controller employs passivity-based control (PBC), which assigns a desired system energy to compensate for the negative impedance that may be generated by a CPL. A proportional-integral (PI) action that maintains a passive output is added to the PBC to impose the desired damping and enhance disturbance rejection behavior, thus forming a PI+PBC control. In addition, the proposed controller includes two estimators, i.e., immersion and invariance (I&I), and disturbance observer (DO), in order to estimate CPL and supply voltage for the converter, respectively. These observers become the proposed controller for an adaptive, sensorless PI+PBC control. Phase portrait analysis and experimental results have validated the robustness and effectiveness of the adaptive proposed control approach. These results show that the proposed controller adequately regulates the output voltage of the DC–DC boost converter under variations of the input voltage and CPL simultaneously.

Keywords: passivity based control; Hamiltonian function; asymptotic stability convergence; sensorless control design; adaptive control design; unknown constant power load

MSC: 93-02

1. Introduction

1.1. General Context

Recent advances in electrical distribution networks with DC technologies for medium and low-voltage applications have boosted the massive integration of multiple distributed energy resources, such as renewable generation [1], energy storage systems [2], and controllable loads [3], among others. The main characteristic of integrating these devices in DC networks is the need to use power electronic converters to manage their behavior and take each one of them to an optimal operating point [4]. Figure 1 presents most of the typical DC–DC converters used to interface distributed energy resources and controllable loads to a DC bus.

Note that the technology of the converter will depend exclusively on the distributed energy resource it interfaces. In the case of solar and wind sources, the converter is unidirectional, and it may be a buck or boost converter [5]. Battery energy storage systems must be bidirectional in nature, as the battery behaves as a load in some periods and as a power supply in others [6]. For this reason, bidirectional boost converters constitute an alternative to manage energy behavior in batteries. In the case of controllable loads (linear or nonlinear), the energy flow goes from the DC bus to the load, which implies that a buck or boost converter can be used to integrate them into the DC network.

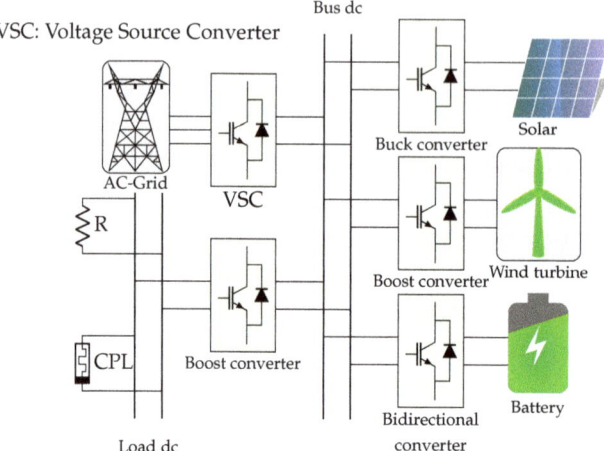

Figure 1. Some classical converters employed to interface distributed energy resources and loads in DC networks.

In Figure 1, it is evident that power electronic converters play the most important role in the massive integration of distributed energy resources and loads into DC networks. This implies that advanced control techniques are required to manage energy requirements effectively.

1.2. Motivation

The power electronic converters presented in Figure 1 pose important challenges to the operation of entire DC grids, given that efficient methodologies are needed to control the DC system at primary, secondary, and tertiary levels. The primary control design is the first layer that associates the system's behavior with its physical devices, i.e., this control stage is entrusted with operating each converter. It is necessary to consider the system's physical requirements regarding its response speed while ensuring a stable behavior under normal operating conditions [7]. The secondary control is also known as restorative control, which aims to stabilize the operation of the DC network under abnormal conditions, i.e., temporary short-circuit or load disconnections, with the main purpose of preserving all the state variables within a secure range of operation [8]. On the other hand, the tertiary control stage, also known as the optimization stage, is entrusted with defining the operative conditions of the network (signal references) in order to minimize or maximize some performance indicators [9].

The main interest of this research corresponds to the primary control design for a converter that interfaces the DC network with an energy user. Specifically, it focuses on designing a controller for a boost converter to support the voltage profile of a constant power load at the terminals while assuming that the voltage of the DC network and the value of the constant power consumption are unknown. This is a critical problem in microgrid energy management systems, as it is necessary to design an efficient controller that ensures the stable operation of the load and grid under normal operating conditions [10]. However, this is a challenging control task, given the nonlinearities introduced by the load (negative impedance) and that the boost converter has a nonlinear model [11,12]. Due to the above, it is important to study nonlinear controls that include estimators for the external inputs to the system, guaranteeing its stability [13–15].

1.3. Literature Review

Multiple studies on control methods implemented in boost converters have been presented in the specialized literature. Stability analysis for a boost converter supplied a constant power load (CPL) was proposed by [16]. A robust sliding mode control based on pulse-width modulation was described in [17] in order to remove possible instabilities provided by the CPL in DC microgrids. An adaptive backstepping sliding mode control to regulate the output voltage of a boost converter connected to a CPL was proposed in [18]. A sliding mode control to manage the output voltage of a boost converter feeding a CPL was presented in [19], where the authors employed a switching surface that relieves the inrush current in the boost converter and external disturbances by maintaining its output voltage at the desired value. Incremental passivity-based control (PBC) was presented in [20,21] to stabilize the output voltage of a DC–DC converter under time-varying disturbances, which were addressed by implementing a proportional-integral (PI) observer. In [22], a robust type-II fuzzy technique based on pulse-width modulation was presented to control a DC–DC boost converter with a CPL. The authors of [23] designed a controller to regulate the output voltage of a DC–DC boost converter feeding a CPL. This controller was based on a sliding mode control method and included a finite-time parameter observer. An adaptive output feedback control to maintain the output voltage of a DC–DC boost converter was shown in [24]. This control added an estimate for the converter's inductor current and load conductance based on a reduced-order state observer. The study by [25] designed a PI-PBC method to ensure that the output voltage of a DC–DC boost converter remained at the desired value. This method included a parameter estimation-based observer for the converter inductor current. Finally, the authors of [26] presented a nonlinear control based on the interconnection and damping assignment (IDA) PBC strategy to regulate the output voltage of a boost-type DC–DC converter.

1.4. Contribution and Scope

Considering the aforementioned literature review, this research article makes the following contributions:

i. The formulation of a general nonlinear control design based on PBC theory, which regulates the voltage at the terminals of an unknown constant power load fed by a boost converter.
ii. The addition of a PI design that maintains passive output to improve the convergence of the proposed control and remove the oscillations generated by the disturbance.
iii. The combination of the immersion and invariance (I&I) and disturbance observer techniques to estimate the CPL and input voltage of the converter with the proposed controller, thus making it an adaptive, sensorless PI+PBC control, as verified by the simulation and experiment results.

The main advantage of the proposed PBC design, which includes PI action, is that it ensures the asymptotic stable operation of the boost converter, taking into account that its input voltage, as well as the CPL values, are estimated in real-time (online). This is particularly important because the control law in closed-loop operation is independent of physical measures, namely the voltage input and load current. This approach reduces the number of sensors required.

1.5. Document Organization

The remainder of this document is structured as follows: the mathematical modeling of the DC–DC boost converter using averaging modeling theory and control problem formulations is presented in Section 2. The design of the proposed adaptive controller with the inclusion of the estimator is described in Section 3. Section 4 presents the phase portrait analysis and experimental results used to validate the proposed controller. Finally, Section 5 lists the main conclusions of this research.

2. Mathematical Modeling and Problem Formulation

This section uses averaging modeling theory to describe the general mathematical modeling of the boost converter feeding a constant power load. It also presents the equilibrium point for this system, which is essential in designing any control approach. In addition, the control problem formulation and the requirements for the voltage regulation of the studied converter are defined.

2.1. DC–DC Boost Converter Modeling

A boost converter is a DC–DC converter whose voltage output has a higher DC value than its input voltage, which makes it a step-up converter. A boost converter is composed of two semiconductor switches (diode and IGBT) and two elements for energy storage, namely the capacitor and the inductor [27]. Figure 2 illustrates a boost converter supplying a CPL. Its dynamic model is achieved using two of Kirchhoff's laws. The second law is applied at node, which connects the capacitor, inductor, and IGBT. In contrast, Kirchhoff's first law is applied to the closed-loop trajectory that contains the inductor, thus generating its dynamic model:

$$L\dot{i} = -(1-u)v + E,$$
$$C\dot{v} = (1-u)i - \frac{P}{v}, \tag{1}$$

where $i, v, E \in R_{>0}$ are the inductor current, output voltage, and input voltage, respectively. $P \in R_{>0}$ is the CPL, $u \in [0,1]$ is the control input, and $L, C \in R_{>0}$ are inductance and capacitance values, respectively.

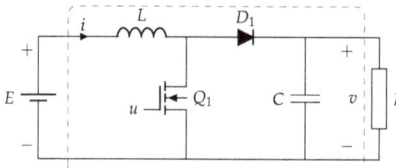

Figure 2. Scheme of a DC–DC boost converter supplying a CPL.

The determination of the equilibrium point for the boost converter (1) is straightforward:

$$\varepsilon := \left\{ (i, v) \in R_{>0}^2 \mid iE - P = 0 \right\}. \tag{2}$$

2.2. Control Problem Formulation

The control challenges for the dynamic model (1) lie in the extracted power load P and input voltage E, which are assumed to be unknown. Hence, the aims of the proposed controller are:

i. To design a control law in order to regulate the output voltage v at the desired equilibrium point $v^\star$;
ii. To develop an observer to estimate the value of the CPL which achieves an adaptive control;
iii. To propose an estimator for the input voltage E in order to obtain a sensorless control scheme.

For the sake of simplicity, defining $x_1 := i$, $x_2 := v$ yields the following:

$$L\dot{x}_1 = -(1-u)x_2 + E,$$
$$C\dot{x}_2 = (1-u)x_1 - \frac{P}{x_2}. \tag{3}$$

The assignable equilibrium set for the dynamic model (3) can be expressed as

$$\varepsilon_x := \left\{ (x_1, x_2) \in R_{>0}^2 \mid x_1 E - P = 0 \right\}. \tag{4}$$

Hence, for a given $x_{2\star}$ in (4), the desired equilibrium point for $x_{1\star}$ is

$$x_{1\star} = \frac{P}{E}. \tag{5}$$

Remark 1. *The main challenges in designing a controller to regulate the voltage output for a boost converter feeding a constant power terminal are the nonlinearities caused by the product between control inputs and state variables—which generates a bilinear system—and the presence of the CPL. This generates a negative impedance in the normal operation of the converter, which may lead to instabilities if it is not considered in the control design [28].*

3. Adaptive PI+PBC Design

PBC is a well-founded theory that is supported by Lyapunov analysis and exploits the advantages of the port-Hamiltonian modeling of physical systems to design closed-loop controllers that maintain the pH structure of the system by modifying their internal energy behavior [29]. There are multiple approaches based on PBC theory, such as standard PBC design [30], interconnection and damping assignment (IDA-PBC) [26], the energy shaping PBC approach [31], and PBC with PI gains for purely bilinear systems [27]. The nature of the open-loop pH model determines the selection of a particular PBC theory to design a controller for a physical system.

In this research, the proposed controller is designed under the following considerations:

i. The design of a PI-PBC control that guarantees locally asymptotically stability at desired equilibrium point $(x_{1\star}, x_{2\star})$ is described while assuming P and E as known parameters;
ii. The immersion and invariance (I&I) technique is implemented to estimate the unknown CPL;
iii. The proposed controller includes a nonlinear disturbance observer (DO) to observe the input voltage E;
iv. By incorporating the I&I and DO techniques into the proposed controller, an adaptive sensorless PI+PBC control scheme is reached.

The dynamic system (3) can be presented as an Euler–Lagrange (EL) structure [29]:

$$M\dot{x} + (J(1-u) + R(x))x = \zeta, \tag{6}$$

where $x = [x_1, x_2]^\top$ is the state variable; and $M > 0 \in R^{2\times 2}$, $R \geq 0 \in R^{2\times 2}$, and $J = -J^\top \in R^{2\times 2}$ are the generalized inertia (matrix associated with the energy storage devices in the converter), damping, and interconnection matrices, respectively. These matrices are represented as

$$M = \begin{bmatrix} L & 0 \\ 0 & C \end{bmatrix}, \quad R = \begin{bmatrix} 0 & 0 \\ 0 & \frac{P}{x_2^2} \end{bmatrix}, \quad J = \begin{bmatrix} 0 & 1-u \\ -(1-u) & 0 \end{bmatrix}, \quad \zeta = \begin{bmatrix} E \\ 0 \end{bmatrix}.$$

The energy function $H(x)$ of the dynamic system (6) is

$$H(x) = \frac{1}{2} x^\top M x, \tag{7}$$

which is a positive definite function.

Remark 2. Note that the differentiation with respect to time in (7) accomplishes the following power balance equation:

$$\dot{H}(x) = \underbrace{Ex_1}_{\text{Input power}} - \underbrace{P}_{\text{Output power}}, \tag{8}$$

which shows that the difference regarding the change in stored energy is equal to the difference between the input and output power.

3.1. PI+PBC Design

This subsection presents the general passivity-based control design for the converter model using a general Hamiltonian function that moves the equilibrium point to the desired operating point by ensuring asymptotic stability in closed-loop operation. The addition of the integral action of the PBC feedback control law is also described in detail.

3.1.1. PBC Design

The proposed controller is based on a PBC methodology [29] that stabilizes the dynamic model (6).

Theorem 1. *Let us assume that the dynamic model (6) is controlled with the control input*

$$u_{PBC} = \frac{x_1\left(x_{1\star} - \dfrac{P}{x_2} + P\dfrac{x_2 - x_{2\star}}{x_2^2}\right) - x_2(E - x_{2\star})}{x_1^2 + x_2^2}. \tag{9}$$

Therefore, the dynamic model (6) is locally stable in closed-loop.

Proof. First, the error is defined as $e : x - x_\star$, and the dynamic model (6) is proposed as follows in closed loop:

$$M\dot{e} + (J + R(x))e = 0, \tag{10}$$

where $x_\star$ is constant, so $\dot{e} = \dot{x}$.

By proposing the desired stored energy function in closed loop, the dynamic model (6) is expressed as

$$H(e) = \frac{1}{2}e^\top M e. \tag{11}$$

Taking its derivative with respect to the time along the trajectory (10) yields (6) as

$$\begin{aligned}
\dot{H}(e) &= -e^\top (J + R(x))e, \\
&= -e^\top J e - e^\top R(x) e \\
&= -e^\top R(x) e, \\
&\leq 0
\end{aligned} \tag{12}$$

which implies that the system is passive.

Now, by subtracting (10) in (6), the following equation is achieved:

$$(J(1-u) + R(x))x - (J + R(x))e = \zeta. \tag{13}$$

Alternatively, Equation (13) can be expressed as

$$G(x)u + (J + R(x))x - (J + R(x))e = \zeta, \tag{14}$$

with $G(x) = [-x_2, x_1]^\top$, and its full-rank left annihilator $G(x)^\perp = [x_1, x_2]$, which meets $G(x)^\perp G(x) = 0$. Multiplying $G(x)^\perp$ in (14) yields

$$x_{1\star} = \frac{Px_{2\star} + x_1x_2(x_{2\star} - E)}{x_2^2}. \tag{15}$$

The proposed PBC is obtained by solving (14) as

$$u_{PBC} = [G(x)^\top G(x)]^{-1} G(x)^\top (J + R(x))e - (J + R(x))x + \zeta)$$

$$= \frac{x_1\left(x_{1\star} - \dfrac{P}{x_2} + P\dfrac{x_2 - x_{2\star}}{x_2^2}\right) - x_2(E - x_{2\star})}{x_1^2 + x_2^2}, \tag{16}$$

which completes the proof. □

3.1.2. PI Design

A PI controller was added to the proposed control law (16) in order to ensure that the closed-loop system is locally asymptotically stable.

Theorem 2. *A PI controller is introduced into the dynamic system* (6) *as*

$$\begin{aligned} u_{PI} &= -K_p G(x)^\top e - K_i G(x)^\top z \\ \dot{z} &= e, \end{aligned} \tag{17}$$

where $K_p, K_i \in R^{2\times 2} > 0$ *are proportional and integral diagonal matrices, respectively.*

Now, the closed-loop system takes the following form:

$$M\dot{e} + (J + R(x))e = u_{PI}. \tag{18}$$

Analyzing the derivative with respect to the time of the desired stored energy function (11) along the trajectory (18) yields

$$\begin{aligned} \dot{H}(e) &= -e^\top (J + R(x))e + e^\top u_{PI} \\ &= -e^\top J(u)e - e^\top R(x)e + e^\top u_{PI} \\ &= e^\top R(x)e + e^\top u_{PI} \\ &< e^\top u_{PI}, \end{aligned} \tag{19}$$

which implies that the map $u_{PI} \to e$ is passive according to $H(e)$ (for more details, see [32]). Therefore, the closed-loop system (18) is locally asymptotically stable with the Lyapunov function

$$W(e,z) = H(e) + \frac{1}{2}K_i z^\top z. \tag{20}$$

Proof. By defining $\chi = [x, z]^\top$, the closed-loop system (18), represented as an EU structure, can be expressed as

$$\begin{bmatrix} M & 0 \\ 0 & K_i \end{bmatrix}\dot{\chi} + \begin{bmatrix} J + R(x) + G(x)K_p G(x)^\top & G(x)K_i G(x)^\top \\ -G(x)K_i G(x)^\top & 0 \end{bmatrix}\chi = 0. \tag{21}$$

By using the candidate Lyapunov function (20) and taking its deviate with respect to time along the trajectory (21), the following is obtained:

$$\dot{W}(e,z) = \dot{H}(e) + k_i \dot{\chi} \chi$$
$$< e^\top u_{PI} + k_i \dot{\chi} \chi$$
$$= -K_p e^\top e - K_i e^\top \chi + K_i e^\top \chi \quad (22)$$
$$= -K_p e^\top e < 0.$$

Invoking the LaSalle–Yoshizawa theorem [33], the closed-loop system (21) is locally asymptotically stable as long as

$$\lim_{t \to \infty} \chi(t) = 0. \quad (23)$$

$e \to 0$ is fixed, hence $e = 0$ in (21), which implies that $z \to 0$. □

3.2. CPL Estimator

The proposed PI+PBC control requires knowing the CPL to compute the control law, and the CPL is usually unknown. This study employs an immersion and invariance (I&I) technique for estimating said load.

Theorem 3. *The load P in the dynamic system (3) is estimated with*

$$\hat{P} = \alpha + \gamma \beta(x_2)$$
$$\dot{\alpha} = -\gamma \beta'(x_2) \left(\frac{1-u}{C} x_1 - \frac{\hat{P}}{C x_2} \right), \quad (24)$$

where $\gamma > 0$ is the gain of the I&I technique.
By denoting the estimation error as

$$\tilde{P} = \hat{P} - P, \quad (25)$$

where $\tilde{P}$ is the estimation error of CPL and $\hat{P}$ is its estimation, the following is obtained:

$$\lim_{t \to \infty} \tilde{P}(t) = 0. \quad (26)$$

Proof. Taking the derivative of the estimation error (25) with respect to time yields the following result:

$$\dot{\tilde{P}} = \dot{\hat{P}} = \dot{\alpha} + \gamma \beta'(x_2) \dot{x}_2$$
$$= \dot{\alpha} + \gamma \beta'(x_2) \left(\frac{1-u}{C} x_1 - \frac{P}{C x_2} \right) \quad (27)$$
$$= \dot{\alpha} + \gamma \beta'(x_2) \left(\frac{1-u}{C} x_1 - \frac{\hat{P} - \tilde{P}}{C x_2} \right).$$

Now, by substituting $\dot{\alpha}$ in (28), the following result is achieved

$$\dot{\tilde{P}} = \gamma \beta'(x_2) \frac{\tilde{P}}{C x_2}. \quad (28)$$

Now, it is necessary to define $\beta(x_2)$ in order to ensure that the convergence of $\hat{P}$ will be exponential, which is defined as

$$\beta(x_2) = -\frac{1}{2} C x_2^2, \quad (29)$$

and its time derivative is

$$\beta'(x_2) = -Cx_2. \tag{30}$$

By replacing (30) in (28), the following expression is obtained:

$$\dot{\tilde{P}} = -\gamma \tilde{P} \Rightarrow \tilde{P}(t) = \tilde{P}(0)e^{-\gamma t}. \tag{31}$$

In (31), it can be noted that $\tilde{P}(t)$ will exponentially tend to zero for all initial conditions. □

3.3. Input Voltage Estimator

Theorem 4. *For the system (3), a DO technique to estimate input voltage is designed as follows:*

$$\begin{aligned} \hat{E} &= \zeta + \rho x_1 \\ \dot{\zeta} &= -\frac{\rho}{L}(\zeta + \rho x_1 - (1-u)x_2), \end{aligned} \tag{32}$$

where $\rho > 0$ is the gain of the DO technique. Defining the estimate error as $\tilde{E} = \hat{E} - E$ yields

$$\lim_{t \to \infty} \tilde{E}(t) = 0. \tag{33}$$

Proof. By taking the derivative $\tilde{E}$ concerning time along the trajectories (3) and (32), the following is obtained:

$$\begin{aligned} \dot{\tilde{E}} &= \dot{\hat{E}} = \dot{\zeta} + \rho \dot{x}_1 \\ &= -\frac{\rho}{L}\tilde{E} \Rightarrow \tilde{E}(t) = \tilde{E}(0)e^{-\frac{\rho}{L}t}, \end{aligned} \tag{34}$$

which satisfies the convergence property in (33). □

3.4. Adaptive Sensorless Control Design

By replacing the estimates $\hat{P}$ of (24) and $\hat{E}$ of (32) into (16), (15), and (17), the proposed adaptive sensorless control takes the following form:

$$\begin{aligned} u &= \hat{u}_{PBC} + \hat{u}_{PI} = \frac{x_1\left(\hat{x}_{1\star} - \frac{\hat{P}}{x_2} + \hat{P}\frac{x_2 - x_{2\star}}{x_2^2}\right) - x_2(\hat{E} - x_{2\star})}{x_1^2 + x_2^2} + \hat{u}_{PI}, \\ \hat{u}_{PI} &= -K_p G(x)^\top \hat{e} - K_i G(x)^\top \hat{z}, \\ \hat{e} &= [x_1 - \hat{x}_{1\star},\ x_2 - x_{2\star}]^\top, \\ \dot{\hat{z}} &= \hat{e}, \\ \hat{x}_{1\star} &= \frac{\hat{P}x_{2\star} + x_1 x_2 (x_{2\star} - \hat{E})}{x_2^2}. \end{aligned} \tag{35}$$

4. Results

This section presents the performance of the controller described in Section 3. The adaptive sensorless PI+PBC has been designed to stabilize the output voltage in a boost converter supplying an unknown CPL. Phase portrait analysis and experimental results are employed to evaluate the dynamic behavior of the proposed controller. The boost converter prototype's list of components and values is presented in Table 1.

Table 1. Description of the boost converter's components.

Component	Description	Type/Value
Q_1	Power MOSFET	IRFB4110
D_1	Schottky Power Diode	RURG8060
L	Inductor	Wurth Elektronik 74435584700, 47 µH
C	Multilayer Ceramic Capacitor	TDK C5750X7S2A106M230KB, 10×10 µF

The RT-Box of Plexim was used to implement the proposed controller with a time sample of 10 µS. Figure 3 depicts the implemented prototype system. The gains of the adaptive controller were tuned online via of the RT-box of Plexim. These gains are: $k_{p1} = 0.2$, $k_{p2} = 0.05$, $k_{i1} = 0.4$, $k_{i2} = 5$, $\gamma = 0.1$ and $\rho = 2$.

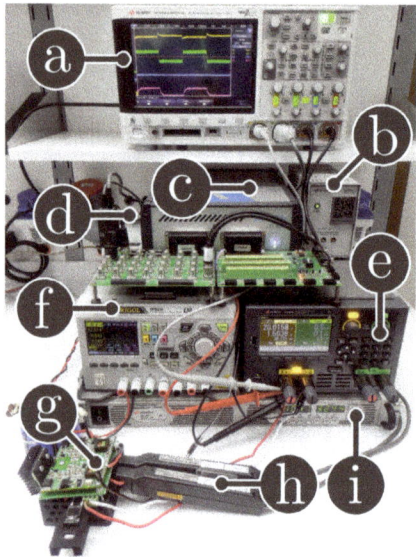

Figure 3. Experimental setup: (a) oscilloscope, (b) DC electronic device in CPL mode, (c) RT-Box with analog and digital breakout boards, (d) current probe power supply, (e) MOSFET driver power supply, (f) DC–DC boost converter, (g) current probes, (h) input voltage power supply, and (i) differential voltage probe.

The phase portrait for the boost converter implemented with the proposed controller is shown in Figure 4. The desired equilibrium point ($\star$) for the boost converter is calculated with $E = 10$ V, $P = 20$ W, $x_{1\star} = 2$ A, and $x_{2\star} = 15$ V. Figure 4 also shows five trajectories for different initial points. It can be observed that the state variables move in ranges $1.5 \text{ A} \leq x_1(0) \leq 4 \text{ A}$ and $6.5 \text{ V} \leq x_2(0) \leq 17 \text{ V}$. According to the figure, if $x_2(0) < x_{2\star}$, x_1 initially increases above its equilibrium point, while $x_2(0)$ goes near the desired equilibrium point; meanwhile, if $x_2(0) > x_2^\star$, x_1 and x_2 converge directly to their equilibrium points.

Figure 5 illustrates the estimation of the input voltage when the CPL has a constant value ($P = 20$ W). Figure 5a presents the dynamic response of the estimate $\hat{E}$ (blue line) when the input voltage (yellow line) increases from 10 to 8 V. In contrast, Figure 5b reveals the estimate $\hat{E}$ (blue line) when the input voltage (yellow line) decreases from 10 to 12 V. These figures show that the estimation of the input voltage $\hat{E}$ can be validated and that its convergence rate is very fast.

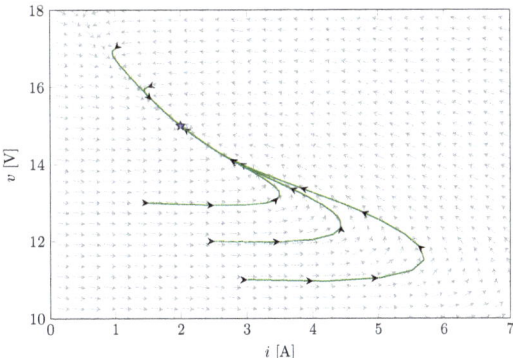

Figure 4. Phase portrait for the PI+PBC method implemented in the boost converter.

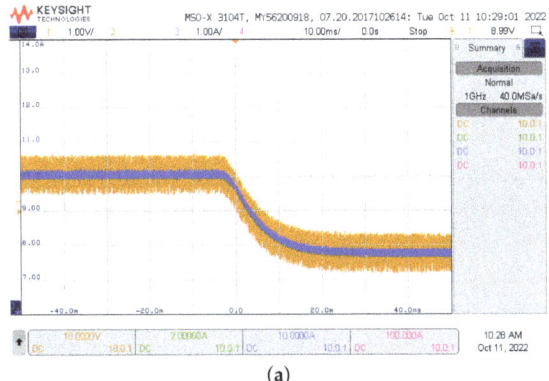

(a)

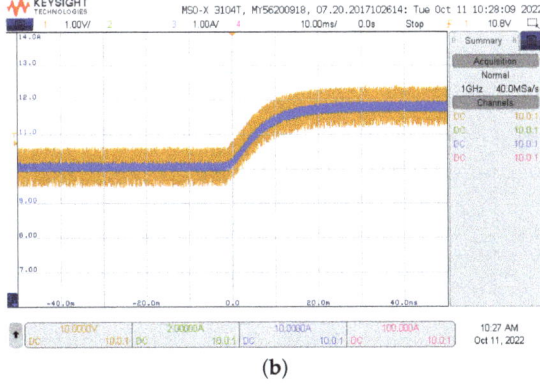

(b)

Figure 5. Dynamic response of the estimate $\hat{E}$: (**a**) input voltage changes between 10 to 8 V; and (**b**) input voltage changes between 10 to 12 V. CH1: (1 V/div), CH3: (1 V/div).

Figure 6 depicts the experimental response of the boost converter while considering that the CPL varies between 20 and 40 W like a 100 Hz square waveform. In this case, it is also considered that the desired output voltage is $x_{2*} = 15$ V, and the input voltage for the boost converter varies from 10 and 8 V at the same time. Figure 6a shows the output voltage x_2 (yellow line), the inductor current x_1 (green line), the control signal u (blue line), and the estimate $\hat{P}$ (purple line). Figure 6b depicts the input voltage E (yellow line) and the estimate $\hat{E}$ (blue line).

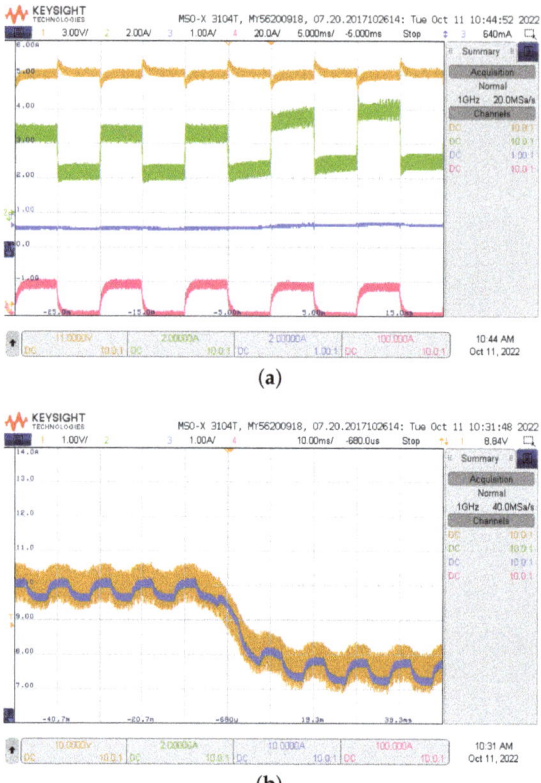

(a)

(b)

Figure 6. Dynamic response of the proposed controller: (a) Experimental results for the boost converter when the CPL is a 100 Hz square waveform between 20 and 40 W, with a duty cycle of 0.5. CH1: x_2 (3 V/div), CH2: x_1 (2 A/div), CH3: u (1/div), CH4: $\hat{P}$ (20 W/div), and time base of 5 ms. (b) Input voltage changes from 10 V to 8 V. CH1: (1 V/div), CH2: (1 V/div), and time base of 10 ms.

In Figure 6a, it can be observed that the adaptive sensorless PI+PBC control can instantly stabilize the output voltage of the boost converter. The settling time for the output voltage is 1.53 ms, and its average overshoot is 5.1%, while the inductor current has a settling time of around 0.171 ms and no overshoot. This demonstrates the adequate performance of the proposed controller under simultaneous CPL and input voltage variations. Additionally, it is observed that the inductor current x_1 (green line in Figure 7a) increases when the input voltage E decreases. This behavior is expected, given that the balance point for the inductor current depends inversely on the input voltage, as presented in (5) (hyperbolic relation between voltage and current in the presence of a CPL).

Figure 7 presents the experimental response of the boost converter when its input voltage changes from 10 V to 12 V, and the CPL varies between 20 and 40 W like a 100 Hz square waveform simultaneously. The desired output voltage remains the same $x_{2\star} = 15$ V. Figure 7a illustrates the output voltage x_2 (yellow line), the inductor current x_1 (green line), the control signal u (blue line), and the estimate $\hat{P}$ (purple line). Figure 7b shows the input voltage E (yellow line) and its estimation $\hat{E}$ (blue line).

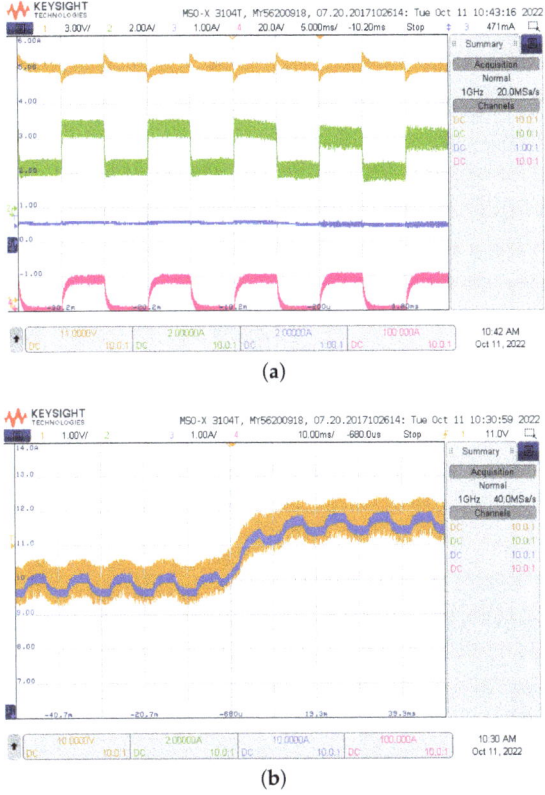

(a)

(b)

Figure 7. Dynamic response of the estimate $\hat{E}$: (**a**) input voltage changes from 10 to 8 V. CH1: x_2 (3 V/div), CH2: x_1 (2 A/div), CH3: u (1/div), CH4: $\hat{P}$ (20 W/div), and time base of 5 ms; (**b**) input voltage changes from 10 to 12 V. CH1: (1 V/div), CH2: (1 V/div), and time base of 10 ms.

It can be seen in Figure 7a that the adaptive sensorless PI+PBC control instantly continues to regulate the output voltage of the boost converter under the changes considered. This is supported by the fact that the settling time for the proposed controller is 1.53 ms, and its average overshoot is 5.1%. It is worth mentioning that, as expected, when the voltage input increases, the total current flowing through the inductor decreases since its movement is required to ensure constant power transference from the source to the load.

General Remarks

From the experimental validation presented for a boost converter feeding an unknown CPL while using the proposed controller, it is possible to observe that:

i. The presented estimator to determine the behavior of the voltage input has an exponential convergence to the exact value when the behavior of the constant power load remains constant (see Figure 5), regardless of whether the voltage input increases or decreases from an initial value. Notwithstanding, when the load varies with a square form and the voltage input also increases or decreases, the behavior of the voltage input estimator follows the average behavior of the input, albeit with square-form oscillations (see Figures 6b and 7b), which is expected because the DO estimator presented in Section 3.3 is dependent on the current measured at the inductor, which is also a function of the current provided to the load.

ii. The load estimator presented in Figures 6a and 7a converges exponentially to the exact value, as predicted by the I&I method presented in Section 3.2. This is also expected since the estimator depends only on the voltage measured at terminals of the load, which is the control variable that remains constant, with small variations each time the load changes.

iii. In general, the proposed PI+PBC approach demonstrated easy tuning characteristics (two control gains), and fast asymptotic convergence to the desired voltage reference, regardless of whether the load current and the voltage input are measured or estimated. These characteristics make the proposed PI+PBC structure a robust control approach that deals with voltage control in the face of unknown CPLs, thus reducing the number of sensors required in the physical implementation layer.

5. Conclusions

This paper presented the design of an adaptive control to regulate the output voltage of a DC–DC boost converter supplying an unknown CPL. The proposed controller used PBC theory to stabilize the output voltage at its desired value, and a PI action was added to accelerate its convergence. The PI action maintained a passive output, essential for PBC theory, and injected the desired damping, thus enhancing disturbance rejection. Additionally, the proposed controller added two observers, which allowed it not to depend on some parameters that, in general, can be difficult to measure. The I&I and DO techniques turned the controller into an adaptive sensorless PI+PBC control, whose robustness and effectiveness were evaluated by employing phase portrait analysis and experimental results. The whole set of these tests showed its ability to regulate and maintain the output voltage of the DC–DC boost converter at its desired values.

Some possible future works derived from this research may include: (i) extending the proposed control design and observers to classical second-order DC–DC converters (buck, buck-boost, and non-inverting buck-boost topologies) feeding CPLs, (ii) implementing inverse optimal control with integral action for controlling DC–DC converters in microgrid applications, Developing a sliding mode control with the I&I and DO techniques makes it more robust and allows the system to have a faster convergence.

Author Contributions: Conceptualization, methodology, software, and writing (review and editing): W.G.-G., O.D.M., S.R., C.R. and J.M. All authors have read and agreed to the published version of the manuscript.

Funding: This work was partially supported by the Chilean Government under projects ANID/-FONDECYT/1191028, ANID/FONDECYT/1191680, SERC Chile (Anid/Fondap/15110019), and Millennium Institute on Green Ammonia as Energy Vector MIGA (ANID/Millennium Science Initiative Program/ICN2021 023).

Data Availability Statement: No new data were created or analyzed in this study. Data sharing is not applicable to this article.

Conflicts of Interest: The authors declare no conflict of interest.

References

1. Mathew, E.C.; Das, A. Integration of renewable energy sources with MVDC network. In Proceedings of the 2020 IEEE International Conference on Power Electronics, Drives and Energy Systems (PEDES), Jaipur, India, 16–19 December 2020. [CrossRef]
2. Bharatee, A.; Ray, P.K.; Subudhi, B.; Ghosh, A. Power Management Strategies in a Hybrid Energy Storage System Integrated AC/DC Microgrid: A Review. *Energies* **2022**, *15*, 7176. [CrossRef]
3. Silani, A.; Cucuzzella, M.; Scherpen, J.M.; Yazdanpanah, M.J. Robust output regulation for voltage control in DC networks with time-varying loads. *Automatica* **2022**, *135*, 109997. [CrossRef]
4. Iskender, I.; Genc, N. Power Electronic Converters in DC Microgrid. In *Power Systems*; Springer International Publishing: Berlin/Heidelberg, Germany, 2019; pp. 115–137. [CrossRef]
5. Ramos-Paja, C.A.; Montoya, O.D.; Grisales-Noreña, L.F. Photovoltaic System for Microinverter Applications Based on a Non-Electrolytic-Capacitor Boost Converter and a Sliding-Mode Controller. *Electronics* **2022**, *11*, 2923. [CrossRef]
6. Xie, D.; Wang, L.; Zhang, Z.; Wang, S.; Kang, L.; Yao, J. Photovoltaic Energy Storage System Based on Bidirectional LLC Resonant Converter Control Technology. *Energies* **2022**, *15*, 6436. [CrossRef]

7. Prieto-Araujo, E.; Bolboceanu, D.B.; Sanchez-Sanchez, E.; Gomis-Bellmunt, O. Design methodology of the primary droop voltage control for DC microgrids. In Proceedings of the 2017 IEEE Second International Conference on DC Microgrids (ICDCM), Nuremburg, Germany, 27–29 June 2017. [CrossRef]
8. Gao, F.; Kang, R.; Cao, J.; Yang, T. Primary and secondary control in DC microgrids: A review. *J. Mod. Power Syst. Clean Energy* **2018**, *7*, 227–242. [CrossRef]
9. Moayedi, S.; Davoudi, A. Distributed Tertiary Control of DC Microgrid Clusters. *IEEE Trans. Power Electron.* **2016**, *31*, 1717–1733. [CrossRef]
10. Oucheriah, S. Nonlinear control of the boost converter subject to unknown constant power load and parasitics. *Int. J. Electron. Lett.* **2022**, *0*, 1–11. [CrossRef]
11. Emadi, A.; Khaligh, A.; Rivetta, C.; Williamson, G. Constant Power Loads and Negative Impedance Instability in Automotive Systems: Definition, Modeling, Stability, and Control of Power Electronic Converters and Motor Drives. *IEEE Trans. Veh. Technol.* **2006**, *55*, 1112–1125. [CrossRef]
12. Shi, L.; Lei, W.; Li, Z.; Huang, J.; Cui, Y.; Wang, Y. Bilinear Discrete-Time Modeling and Stability Analysis of the Digitally Controlled Dual Active Bridge Converter. *IEEE Trans. Power Electron.* **2017**, *32*, 8787–8799. [CrossRef]
13. Chang, Y.; Zhou, P.; Niu, B.; Wang, H.; Xu, N.; Alassafi, M.O.; Ahmad, A.M. Switched-observer-based adaptive output-feedback control design with unknown gain for pure-feedback switched nonlinear systems via average dwell time. *Int. J. Syst. Sci.* **2021**, *52*, 1731–1745. [CrossRef]
14. Zhang, H.; Wang, H.; Niu, B.; Zhang, L.; Ahmad, A.M. Sliding-mode surface-based adaptive actor-critic optimal control for switched nonlinear systems with average dwell time. *Inf. Sci.* **2021**, *580*, 756–774. [CrossRef]
15. Chen, Q.X.; Chang, X.H. Resilient filter of nonlinear network systems with dynamic event-triggered mechanism and hybrid cyber attack. *Appl. Math. Comput.* **2022**, *434*, 127419. [CrossRef]
16. Hamidi, S.A.; Nasiri, A. Stability analysis of a DC–DC converter for battery energy storage system feeding CPL. In Proceedings of the 2015 IEEE International Telecommunications Energy Conference (INTELEC), Osaka, Japan, 18–22 October 2015; pp. 1–5.
17. Singh, S.; Fulwani, D.; Kumar, V. Robust sliding-mode control of dc/dc boost converter feeding a constant power load. *IET Power Electron.* **2015**, *8*, 1230–1237. [CrossRef]
18. Wu, J.; Lu, Y. Adaptive backstepping sliding mode control for boost converter with constant power load. *IEEE Access* **2019**, *7*, 50797–50807. [CrossRef]
19. Martinez-Treviño, B.A.; El Aroudi, A.; Vidal-Idiarte, E.; Cid-Pastor, A.; Martinez-Salamero, L. Sliding-mode control of a boost converter under constant power loading conditions. *IET Power Electron.* **2019**, *12*, 521–529. [CrossRef]
20. He, W.; Li, S.; Yang, J.; Wang, Z. Incremental passivity based control for DC–DC boost converter with circuit parameter perturbations using nonlinear disturbance observer. In Proceedings of the IECON 2016-42nd Annual Conference of the IEEE Industrial Electronics Society, Florence, Italy, 23–26 October 2016; pp. 1353–1358.
21. He, W.; Li, S.; Yang, J.; Wang, Z. Incremental passivity based control for DC–DC boost converters under time-varying disturbances via a generalized proportional integral observer. *J. Power Electron.* **2018**, *18*, 147–159.
22. Farsizadeh, H.; Gheisarnejad, M.; Mosayebi, M.; Rahei, M.; Khooban, M.H. An intelligent and fast controller for DC/DC converter feeding CPL in a DC microgrid. *IEEE Trans. Circuits Syst. II Express Briefs* **2019**, *67*, 1104–1108. [CrossRef]
23. He, W.; Shang, Y. Finite-Time Parameter Observer-Based Sliding Mode Control for a DC/DC Boost Converter with Constant Power Loads. *Electronics* **2022**, *11*, 819. [CrossRef]
24. Zhang, X.; He, W.; Zhang, Y. An Adaptive Output Feedback Controller for Boost Converter. *Electronics* **2022**, *11*, 905. [CrossRef]
25. Zhang, X.; Martinez-Lopez, M.; He, W.; Shang, Y.; Jiang, C.; Moreno-Valenzuela, J. Sensorless Control for DC–DC Boost Converter via Generalized Parameter Estimation-Based Observer. *Appl. Sci.* **2021**, *11*, 7761. [CrossRef]
26. Serra, F.M.; Magaldi, G.L.; Fernandez, L.M.; Larregay, G.O.; CH, D.A. IDA-PBC controller of a DC–DC boost converter for continuous and discontinuous conduction mode. *IEEE Lat. Am. Trans.* **2018**, *16*, 52–58. [CrossRef]
27. Gil-González, W.; Montoya, O.D.; Espinosa-Perez, G. Adaptive control for second-order DC–DC converters: PBC approach. In *Modeling, Operation, and Analysis of DC Grids*; Elsevier: Amsterdam, The Netherlands, 2021; pp. 289–310.
28. AL-Nussairi, M.K.; Bayindir, R.; Padmanaban, S.; Mihet-Popa, L.; Siano, P. Constant Power Loads (CPL) with Microgrids: Problem Definition, Stability Analysis and Compensation Techniques. *Energies* **2017**, *10*, 1656. [CrossRef]
29. Ortega, R.; Perez, J.A.L.; Nicklasson, P.J.; Sira-Ramirez, H.J. *Passivity-Based Control of Euler-Lagrange Systems: Mechanical, Electrical and Electromechanical Applications*; Springer Science & Business Media: Berlin/Heidelberg, Germany, 2013.
30. Ortega, R.; Van Der Schaft, A.; Castanos, F.; Astolfi, A. Control by interconnection and standard passivity-based control of port-Hamiltonian systems. *IEEE Trans. Autom. Control* **2008**, *53*, 2527–2542. [CrossRef]
31. Harandi, M.R.J.; Taghirad, H.D. On the matching equations of kinetic energy shaping in ida-pbc. *J. Frankl. Inst.* **2021**, *358*, 8639–8655. [CrossRef]
32. Cisneros, R.; Gao, R.; Ortega, R.; Husain, I. A PI+ passivity-based control of a wind energy conversion system enabled with a solid-state transformer. *Int. J. Control* **2021**, *94*, 2453–2463. [CrossRef]
33. Krstic, M.; Kokotovic, P.V.; Kanellakopoulos, I. *Nonlinear and Adaptive Control Design*; John Wiley & Sons Inc.: Hoboken, NJ, USA, 1995.

Article

Mathematical Chemistry Approaches for Computer-Aid Design of Free-Shaped Structures in Architecture and Construction Engineering

Viorel Chihaia [1,*], Mihalache Ghinea [2,*], Stefan Chihaia [3] and Andreea Neacsu [1]

[1] Institute of Physical Chemistry Ilie Murgulescu, Romanian Academy, Splaiul Independentei 202, Sector 6, 060021 Bucharest, Romania

[2] Department of Machines and Manufacturing Systems, University Politehnica of Bucharest, Sector 6, 060042 Bucharest, Romania

[3] Faculty for Architecture and Planning, Vienna University of Technology, Karlsplatz 13, 1040 Vienna, Austria

* Correspondence: vchihaia@icf.ro (V.C.); mihalache.ghinea@upb.ro (M.G.)

Abstract: The use of computers in architecture and construction engineering simplifies and automatize many manual operations, especially in the case of curved surfaces such as shell structures. Moreover, it allows fast screening and characterization of many technical solutions through computer-solving equations and the verification of buildings and metallic structures stabilities in different weather and seismic conditions. In parallel, significant efforts have been made to characterize and explore carbon-based nanosystems. Important mathematical concepts and methods were developed for the description of such structures in the frame of mathematical chemistry. Because the lattice topology of shell structures in architecture and nanosystems in chemistry are similar, it is possible to transfer well-established theoretical concepts and knowledge of using nanosystems to the design of shell structures. The topologies of the nanosystems are characterized by lower densities of edges per node offering better solutions for curved surfaces than the typical grids used in architecture. As far as we know, no such connections between the topologies of nanosystems and shell structures have been established before. This transfer would be helpful for increased accuracy and speed in finding the best technical solutions for the building's design. In this paper, we identify and propose for the design of the shell structures several mathematical approaches developed for atomistic systems.

Keywords: computer-aid design 1; shell structures 2; grids 3; nanocarbons 4; finite element Method 5

MSC: 74K25; 52B22; 52B10; 52C25; 52-08; 70B05; 05C10; 05C30; 05C38

Citation: Chihaia, V.; Ghinea, M.; Chihaia, S.; Neacsu, A. Mathematical Chemistry Approaches for Computer-Aid Design of Free-Shaped Structures in Architecture and Construction Engineering. *Mathematics* **2022**, *10*, 4415. https://doi.org/10.3390/math10234415

Academic Editor: Junseok Kim

Received: 12 October 2022
Accepted: 21 November 2022
Published: 23 November 2022

Publisher's Note: MDPI stays neutral with regard to jurisdictional claims in published maps and institutional affiliations.

Copyright: © 2022 by the authors. Licensee MDPI, Basel, Switzerland. This article is an open access article distributed under the terms and conditions of the Creative Commons Attribution (CC BY) license (https://creativecommons.org/licenses/by/4.0/).

1. Introduction

Modern architecture uses more and more polyhedral platonic geometric forms and curved surfaces together with traditional orthogonal shapes. The curved surfaces, characterized by bended, curled and twisted curves, can be designed as more interesting and pleasantly shapes, with a high degree of continuity. The most representative curved surface is the geodesic dome, which is a hemispherical shell structure based on supported and self-supported triangular, quadrilateral, or hexagonal lattices. In 1919, Walther Wilhelm Johannes Bauersfeld designed the first building with an icosahedron shape, a planetarium for the company Carl Zeiss, in Berlin, Germany (see Figure 1). Richard Buckminster Fuller, a prolific architect and engineer, continued to popularize this technology as a building design. He introduced the term of the geodesic dome.

Figure 1. The Zeiss planetarium observatory, Berlin, Germany [1]. A hexagonal grid was used in order to create the spherical structure, called geodesic dome.

The three-dimensional curved surfaces, called shell structures, have one dimension much smaller than the other two and are constructed from panels of various shapes. Some beams along the edges of the panels give resistance to the structure against the external loads. The panel shapes and the size of the beams are designed in such a way as to reduce the bending moments and structure compression. The connected beams that form a shell structure define a grid or mesh. The beams are arranged along the edges of the grids. The alternative way to describe a grid is to define the connection points of beams, called nodes of the grid.

The 3D curved surface is discretized on a 3D grid with simple predefined mesh topologies, such as triangular, quadrahedral, pentagonal and hexagonal lattices [2]. The structured meshes with implicit connectivity are the most familiar and simple. In the most general form, the triangular grids are unstructured. The triangular grids can be easily automated and have important benefits for numerical treatments. However, they encompass a high density of edges and high connectivity of the grid nodes (of the order of six edges connected to a node). The implementations of non-triangular grids are numerically more efficient and provide less density, superior transparency and greater design freedom. They can be obtained by merging of few triangular rings of the grids. The exterior edges of the triangles that share a node (called the central node) can be considered as a larger ring of a new grid. The size of the new ring is equal to the connectivity of the corresponding central node. Thus, for planar grids four- and six-member rings are formed, but for non-planar grids, other ring sizes are also determined.

The quadrilateral mesh has four coordinating nodes. Quadrilateral grids are compatible with planar or regular shapes (cylinders, cones). The hexagonal grids involve less coordination of the node to 3. However, it is more appropriate for the planar or cylindrical meshes and requires to be deformed for the spheroidal or ellipsoid shapes. Pentagonal grids give the sphericity and concave shapes, and the heptagonal and octagonal grids generate objects with a convex shape.

For the mechanical (structural stability and deformation) characterization of the shell structure under external forces, a further discretization (or meshing) of the beams and nodes is required for the Finite Elements Model (*FEM*) simulations, which make calculations for a limited number of points and interpolate the results for the entire surface or volume.

Several mathematical tools were developed in the field of architecture. Geometry computing is the field of mathematics that has been developed and applied to freeform architecture, by computer design, surface discretization on grids with the help of the Bezier curves, and calculation at points extra grid nodes by Non-uniform rational basis spline (*NURBS*). Building Information Modelling (*BIM*) is the digital integrated technique that integrates and simplifies the collaboration and data management of the architecture, engineering and construction industries. BIM identifies the technical solutions that have to balance the constraints of the engineering (material properties, technological solutions) and financial (cost, sustainability, maintenance) aspects. Several computer graphics and computer-aided design applications—*CAD* software (*ArchiCAD* [3], *Blender* [4], *Grasshopper* [5], *Rhino 3D* [6] and *SketchUp* [7], just to enumerate a few of them) are available for the design of free-form surfaces and the characterization of the shell structures for architectural and interior modeling and industrial design. *FEM* can further use the designed shell structures by meshing free-form surfaces and characterize the stability of the shell structures under various external factors (wind, rain, snow, ice, shocks and vibrations) based on the static and dynamic linear-elastic stress analysis (*Ansys* [8], *Autodesck* [9], *AutoFEM* [10], *Catia* [11], *Dlubal* [12], *FreeCAD* [13], *KiCAD* [14], *OpenFOAM* [15], *PyCAD* [16] and *SolidWORKS* [17]). Thus, the overuse of construction materials and disasters can be avoided by predicting the minimal size of the beams and nodes in order to control the stress below the values of the breaking thresholds, in order to avoid construction collapse.

Mathematical chemistry is a subfield of mathematics, which provides the theoretical framework and methodology for the various fields of chemistry [18–21]. In particular, different fields of mathematical chemistry (chemistry graph theory, algorithms of structure enumeration and generation, molecular static and dynamic methods) were developed, parameterized and applied to the investigation of various structures formed by carbons atoms. At the nanoscale the carbon atoms form two-dimensional lattices, which are characterized by five- and six-member rings, where carbon atoms are connected to another three neighbor carbons atoms by strong covalent bonds. The topologies of these nanosystems are very similar to those of the macroscopic shell structures but have fewer edges per node and implicitly more reduced self-weight.

In the present paper, we transfer some knowledge to architecture and construction engineering and mathematical tools developed by materials science researchers in their approaches to the nanostructures formed by atoms. Section 2 is dedicated to the description of the problematics of the nanostructures, especially those formed by the carbon atoms (tube like, cones, junctions and fullerenes) and to some mathematical tools developed for their characterization (graphs, topologies, Schlegel diagram, Hamilton and spiral paths, enumeration and building algorithms). Various carbon-based nanosystems are presented and their topology is discussed from the perspective of building algorithms. In Section 3 we suggest the transfer of some mathematical tools developed for nanosystems to the shell structures based on five- and six-member rings. The design of five- and six-ring shell structures to an imposed ground contour is presented. A calculation scheme is suggested. A modified Elastic Network Model is proposed as a particle-based dynamic simulation method. The possibilities of using various software for the transferring of the nanosystem models to the macroscale and discretization for the Finite Element Method simulations are suggested.

2. Carbon Nanoscale Structures

Carbon presents many allotropes, with the most known natural structures as crystals, diamond (the carbon atoms form a three-dimensional 3D crystalline lattice) and graphite (the carbon atoms are stacked on hexagonal lattices on two-dimensional sheets), or amorphous materials (the carbon atoms fill the three-dimensional, without regular arrangements) [22–24]. These systems are compact and extended and are built by carbon atoms that are mostly connected in a hybridization sp^3, sp^2 or mixed, respectively. Many other 3D compact carbon structures are predicted to be stable by molecular simulations [25,26].

The carbon atoms might also form limited-size allotropes, where each atom is arranged in a two-dimensional hexagonal-type lattice, similar to the graphite layer, called graphene [27,28]. The graphene sheets can be folded in such a way to form differently shaped nano-objects [29] as tubes [30], tori and foams.

A single-wall carbon nanotube can be built by rolling up a hexagonal lattice (graphene or a layer of graphite) [31], along the chiral vector

$$\vec{C}_h = n\vec{e}_1 + m\vec{e}_2 \equiv (n,m), \; n,m \in \mathbb{Z} \tag{1}$$

where $\vec{e}_1 = \frac{a}{2}(\sqrt{3},1)$, and $\vec{e}_2 = \frac{a}{2}(\sqrt{3},-1)$ (see Figure 2a) are the vectors that describe the hexagonal lattice, of length $a = |\vec{e}_1| = |\vec{e}_2| = l\sqrt{3}$, with l as the internode distance. n and m are any integer numbers. A nanotube of diameter $d = \frac{a}{\pi}\sqrt{n^2 + nm + m^2}$ is obtained by rolling the planar hexagonal sheet along the vector

$$\vec{T} = h\vec{a}_1 + k\vec{a}_2 \equiv (h,k), \; h,k \in \mathbb{Z} \tag{2}$$

where $h = (2m+n)/\delta$ and $k = -(2n+m)/\delta$ are integer numbers determined by n and m in such a way that $\vec{T}$ is orthogonal to $\vec{C}_h$. δ is the greatest common integer divisor of integers $2n + m$ and $n + 2m$. The number of hexagonal rings in the nanotube is $N = 2(n^2 + nm + m^2)/\delta$.

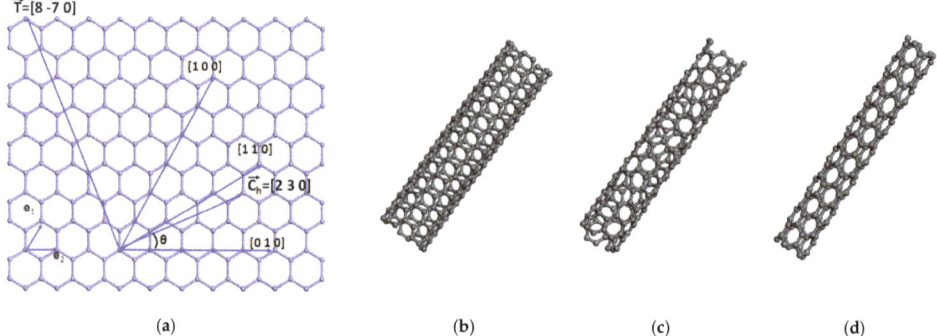

Figure 2. The definition of the parameters of a nanotube-based on the hexagonal lattice (**a**), the zigzag $\vec{C}_h \| [100])$ (**b**), the chiral $\vec{C}_h \| [530]$ (**c**) and the armchair $\vec{C}_h \| [110]$ (**d**) nanotubes are built for the chiral parameters (5,0), (5,3) and (5,5), respectively.

The hexagonal lattice is a 2D planar lattice of hexagonal rings, sharing a common edge with their neighboring rings. The existence of five and/or seven-member rings such as in some carbon flakes makes the system nonplanar (see Figure 3a–d).

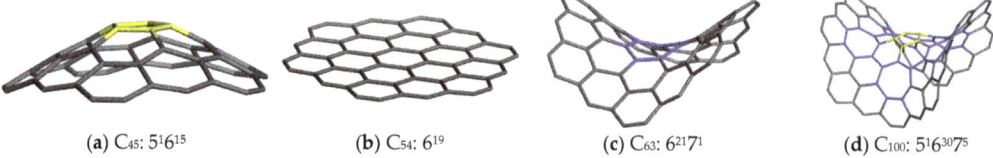

(**a**) C_{45}: $5^1 6^{15}$ (**b**) C_{54}: 6^{19} (**c**) C_{63}: $6^{21} 7^1$ (**d**) C_{100}: $5^1 6^{30} 7^5$

Figure 3. The effects of five- and seven-rings on a six-ring flake. The first three flakes consist of two layers of hexagonal rings around a central ring, which is a pentagon (**a**), hexagon (**b**) or heptagon (**c**). The fourth flake (**d**) has combined defects and consists of a central pentagonal ring, five neighbor heptagonal rings and hexagonal rings. The pentagonal and heptagonal rings are colored yellow and blue, respectively. The index n of the carbon structure C_n indicates the number of carbon atoms, and $5^h 6^k 7^l$ indicates the number of pentagons—h, hexagons—k and heptagons—l in the structure C_n.

Nanocones are formed when one or a few pentagonal rings are inserted in the middle of a graphene piece [32,33]. Topologically, such cones can be derived from a hexagonal lattice (see Figure 4a), where a sixth region is removed and the non-three-coordinated atoms are bond-connected (dash lines in Figure 4a) [34]. The central ring becomes a five-member ring (see Figure 4b).

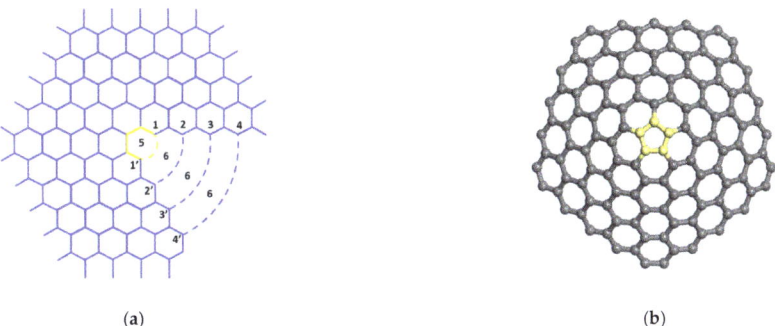

Figure 4. The topology of the hexagonal lattice used for the nanocone construction (**a**) and the cone structure after the connection of the numbered nodes (**b**). The pentagonal ring is yellow colored.

The nanotubes obtained from rolled graphite sheets (see, for example, Figure 5a) are monodimensional systems, but they can be transformed into three-dimensional systems by introducing several non-hexagonal rings. Thus, two nanotubes of different chirality types can be joined by introducing pentagonal and hexagonal rings. In Figure 5b, a heterojunction between two nanotubes (9,0) and (9,9) is shown; there is a heptagonal ring at the boundary between the (9,0) nanotube and the heterojunction, and a pentagonal ring at the boundary between (9,9) and the heterojunction. When several successive pentagonal rings are inserted into a nanotube, it transforms into a nano-spiral system (see Figure 5c), or into a closed torus (see Figure 5d), when several heptagonal rings are also considered.

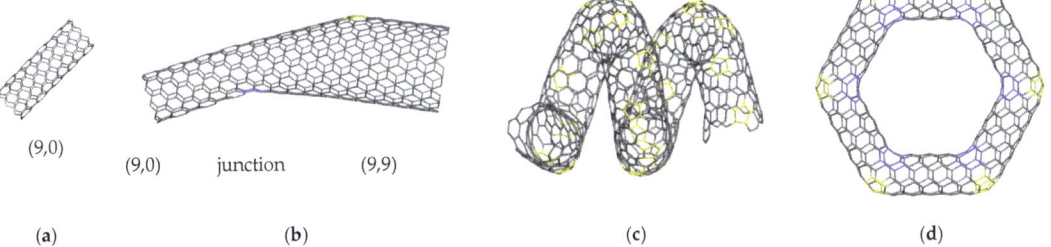

Figure 5. The (9,0) nanotube (**a**), a hetero-junction between two nanotubes (9,0) (the left end) and (9,9) (the right end) (**b**) [35], a (9,0)-based spiral [36] (**c**) and a closed torus (**d**). The pentagonal and heptagonal rings are colored yellow and blue, respectively; the other rings are hexagonal.

When the carbon atoms form 12 pentagons that share their edges with none or additional hexagonal rings cage-type structures C_n, named fullerenes, are formed. The first discovered fullerene is C_{60} [37], formed by $n = 60$ carbon atoms arranged on a sphere and called Buckminsterfullerene after the name of Richard Buckminster Fuller. Except for $n = 22$, a fullerene can be formed by any number of carbon atoms $n \geq 20$. The C_{22} contains four-member rings or even seven-member rings depending on how the pentagons are arranged [38]. The fullerenes with only five- and six-member rings are called classical fullerenes, or just fullerenes. The fullerenes that also contain other types of rings are called extended or non-classical fullerenes. In Figure 6, two spherical fullerenes C_{20} and C_{60}, are shown.

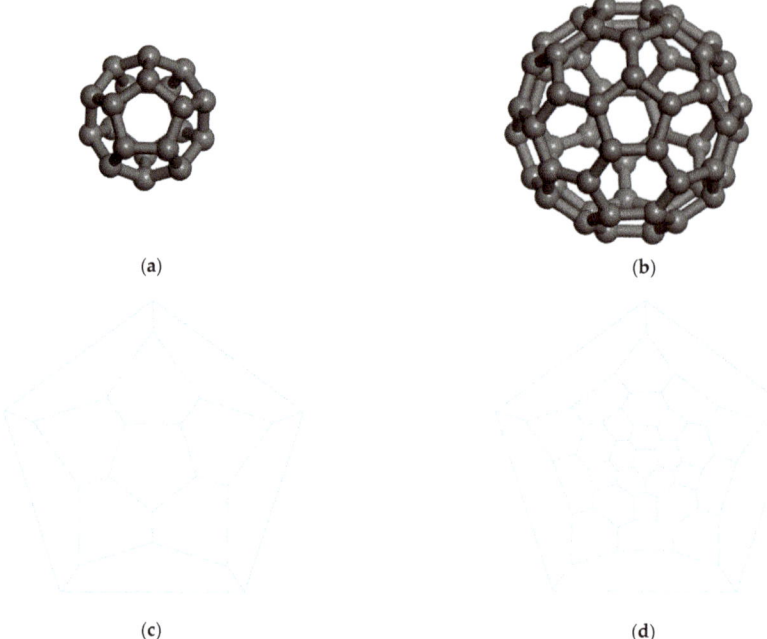

Figure 6. The structures with icosahedron symmetry I_h of the C_{20} (**a**) and C_{60} (**b**) fullerenes, and their corresponding 2D Schlegel diagrams (**c**,**d**).

The topology of the polyhedrons is analyzed by graph theory (a subfield of discrete mathematics) that analyses the pairwise connectivity of the connected structures. Thus, a graph is a set $G = (V, E)$, where V are the vertices (occupied by atoms or molecules) and E are the edges (pairs of atoms or molecules) [39]. A fullerene is a three-regular graph (each node is connected to the other three nodes) with faces that are five or six in size. From each vertex (the carbon atoms) three edges start (the bond between two carbon atoms), and each edge is shared by two rings. Therefore, a fullerene C_n made by n carbon atoms has $n_E = 3/2n$ edges. Since every edge is determined by the intersection of two faces, the number of edges is $n_E = (5n_P + 6n_H)/2$, where n_P and n_H are the number of pentagonal and hexagonal rings, respectively. Based on the Euler theorem for the convex polyhedrons $n_F + n = n_E + 2$, where $n_F = n_P + n_H$ is the total number of faces. Thus, the number of pentagonal and hexagonal faces can be determined as $n_P = 12$ and $n_H = n/2 - 10$. There is a huge number of possible arrangements for the pentagonal and hexagonal rings, estimated at n^9, each case corresponding to an isomer of C_n [40].

The connectivity of the nodes in the graph is described by a matrix called the connection matrix. The elements have a value of 1 when the rows and columns correspond to connected nodes, and a value of 0 when the respective nodes are not connected. The dual graph, defined by the central points of the rings, is a triangular graph. The number of vertices, edges, and faces of the dual graph is equal to the number of rings, edges, and vertices of the initial graph, respectively [41].

The distinction between two isomers of C_n can be made by their symmetry or by the determinant of the connectivity matrix that describes the topology of the fullerenes [42]. Another tool provided by graph theory is the Schlegel diagrams [43], a method for reducing the representation of fullerene to a two-dimensional graph that describes the connectivity of the nodes on the graph and the arrangement of the rings (see Figure 6c,d).

The smallest fullerene, C_{20}, has a spherical shape and consists only of 12 pentagons, no hexagons, and has 30 edges (see Figure 5a). The arrangement of the $n_P = 12$ pentagonal and $n_H = 20$ hexagonal rings of C_{60} is the same as in the case of the standard soccer-ball polyhedron and has 90 edges (see Figure 5b). The pentagonal and hexagonal rings can also be arranged in various orders, yielding a variety of 1812 isomers but being less stable than buckminsterfullerene. The most stable fullerene satisfies the so-called isolated pentagonal rule (IPR), which states that two pentagonal rings must not share an edge [44]. The explanation of IPR is that a pentagonal ring is surrounded by five hexagonal rings, reducing the strain energy. Any other isomer of C_{60} has at least a pair of pentagonal rings that share one edge. It is shown that the complementary units (CU), which are the pieces of the carbon network remaining after the removal of the pentagonal rings from the structure [45], stabilize the isomers of C_{84}. The CUs lead the planar area and the adjacent pentagons induce the sphericity of the fullerenes and increase the strain energy.

Considering the centers of the pentagonal rings and connecting them, we obtain the dual graph of the dodecahedron, which is the icosahedron, a polyhedron with 20 triangle faces (see Figure 7a) [46]. The vertices of the icosahedron have a degree of 5. After coloring each of the three neighboring faces of an icosahedron with the same color (Figure 7b), the unfolded icosahedron looks like Figure 7c.

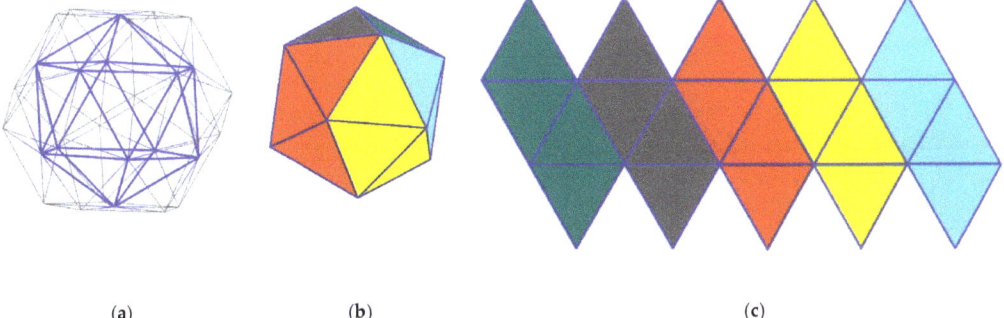

(a)   (b)   (c)

Figure 7. The icosahedron dual polyhedron of the dodecahedron (**a**,**b**) and the neighborhood of its faces, unfolded to a plan (**c**). The gray lines indicate the edges of the dodecahedron and blue lines specify the edges of the triangular faces of the icosahedron.

By decorating the equilateral triangle faces with an equilateral triangle cut from the carbon hexagonal lattice (see Figure 8), we can produce the Schlegel diagrams for the fullerenes of different sizes with the highest symmetry, the icosahedral one. These isomers are among the most stable fullerenes, as the pentagons are at the largest distances.

The pentagons are formed at the sites of the 12 sets of crossing tree triangles, and the other rings are hexagons, with a number of fullerene vertices of $(m^2 + mn + n^2)$, where m and n are integer numbers that determine the orientation of the equilateral triangle.

$$\vec{f}_1 = m\vec{e}_1 + n\vec{e}_2, \vec{f}_2 = -n\vec{e}_1 + (m+n)\vec{e}_2, n, m \in \mathbb{Z} \qquad (3)$$

and $\vec{e}_1$ and $\vec{e}_2$ are the vectors of the hexagonal lattice (see Figure 8).

Depending on how the five- and six-membered rings are arranged, different isomers can be constructed for a given order n. In Figure 9, three isomers of C_{90} are presented as examples. The first two isomers (see Figure 9a,b), with an oblong shape and a symmetry of C_{5h}, are actually capped nanotubes of type (5,0) and (5,5) with two halves of C_{20} and C_{60} at the ends, respectively. A round-shaped fullerene with the symmetry C_{2v} is presented in Figure 9c. Any nanotube can be capped with half of a fullerene. Therefore, such nanotubes are also called cylindrical fullerenes. The capped nanotubes are less stable because of the high curvature at the ends of the nanotubes. A nanotube decorated by dispersed pentagons may have a spiral shape, depending on the distribution of the pentagonal rings.

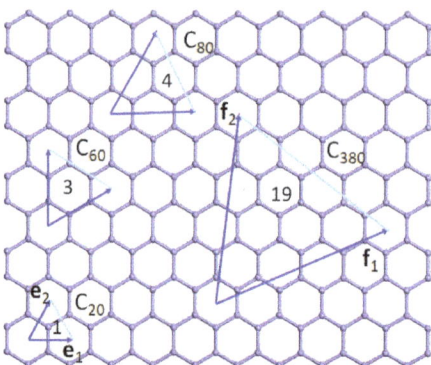

Figure 8. The equilateral cuts of a carbon hexagonal lattice, which can be used for decoration of the equilateral triangle faces of the icosahedron in a Goldberg–Coxeter construction of the icosahedral fullerenes. The vertices of the triangles are the points where the pentagons are formed. The details of the triangle decoration for C_{20}, C_{60}, C_{80} and C_{380} with 1, 3, 4 and 19 carbon atoms per triangle, respectively are presented. The $(\vec{e}_1, \vec{e}_2)$ and $(\vec{f}_1, \vec{f}_2)$ are the vectors for the unit cell and for a supercell of the hexagonal lattice, respectively. For example, the equilateral triangle defined for $m = 3$ and $n = 2$ by the vectors $\vec{f}_1 = 3\vec{e}_1 + 2\vec{e}_2$, $\vec{f}_2 = -2\vec{e}_1 + 5\vec{e}_2$ contains $m^2 + mn + n^2 = 19$ carbon atoms per triangular face; 20 such triangles can be used for the construction of the fullerene C_{380}.

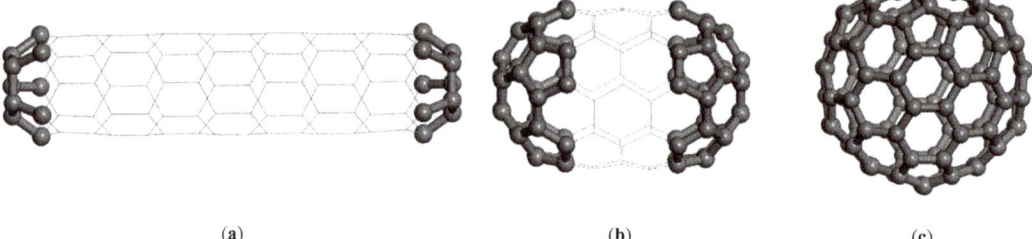

(a)   (b)   (c)

Figure 9. Depending on the pentagonal ring arrangement, different C_{90} fullerene isomers are formed: a closed nanotube with half of the buckyball C_{20} (**a**) and half of the buckyball C_{60} (**b**), respectively, at each end, and a complete buckyball (**c**).

How can the arrangement of the rings be described? The solution is provided by graph theory, which defines the Hamilton path as a path that begins at one face (usually a pentagonal one) and proceeds in a spiral order through each face that is visited exactly once [47,48]. A similar path can be determined by using the vertices as references instead of the faces. When the path ends at the same initial face or vertex, the Hamiltonian path is called the Hamiltonian cycle. In the first row of Figure 10 are presented the Hamiltonian paths for C_{20} and C_{60} fullerenes, the smallest fullerenes with the icosahedral symmetry Ih. The numbering of the nodes is along the Hamilton path. Thus, based on the ordering of the types of rings, the different isomers can be distinguished and the unique isomers are identified.

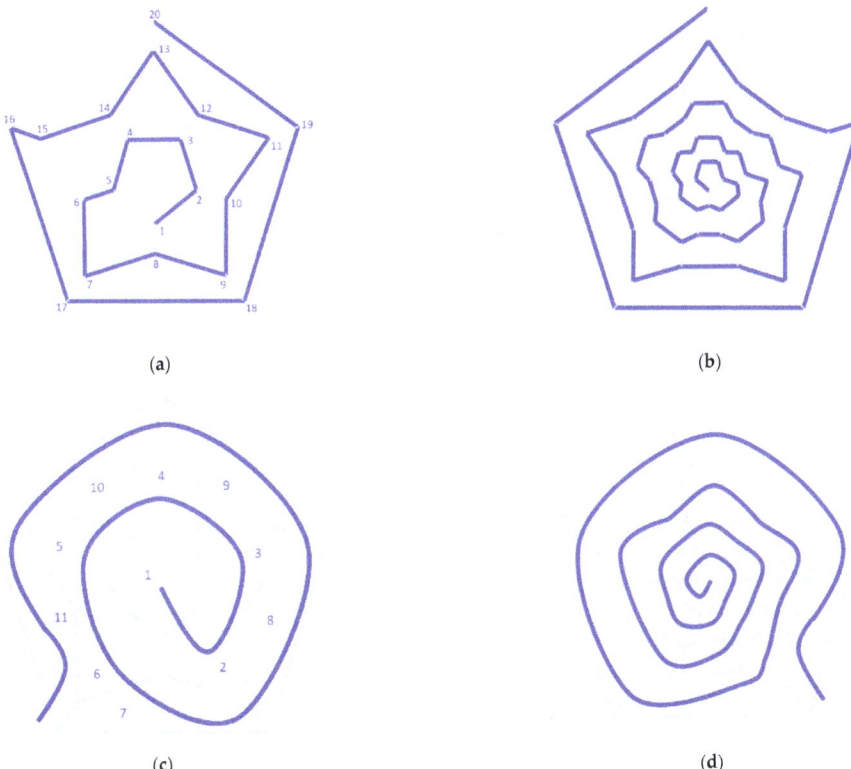

Figure 10. The Hamilton path (**a**,**b**) and the spiral path (**c**,**d**), constructed by successively crossing the vertices and faces, respectively for C20 (**a**,**c**) and C60 (**b**,**d**) are marked by the thick blue curves.

The spiral path can be used for the generation of all the isomers of C_n in the so-called spiral algorithm [49], which specifies the positions of the pentagons along the spiral path. For fullerenes larger than $n = 380$, there are a few cases of isomers that cannot be generated by this algorithm [50]. Software can generate the 3D isomers of fullerenes: *Buckygen* [51], *AME* [52], *CaGe* [53], *Fullgen* [54], *Fui-GUI* [55] and *Fullerene* [56]. These codes differ by implementation, performance and completeness of the sets of isomers, and some of them generate both the 3D structure and the Schlegel diagram.

The isomers can be transformed from one to another by the Stone–Wales rearrangements [57], which consist of the rotation of a common edge of two pentagonal rings by 90° (see Figure 11a). Some rings different from five and six-member rings, which are considered defects, are produced for other situations. Larger fullerenes can be constructed from a given fullerene by insertion of a dimer C_2 into a hexagonal ring connected to two pentagonal rings (the Endo–Kroto procedure [58], see Figure 11b) or insertion of pentagonal and hexagonal rings (see Figure 11c,d). Thus, the connectivity of the respective rings with the environmental atoms is preserved. Fullerene coalescence [59] is another growth mechanism that can be described at the atomic scale [60].

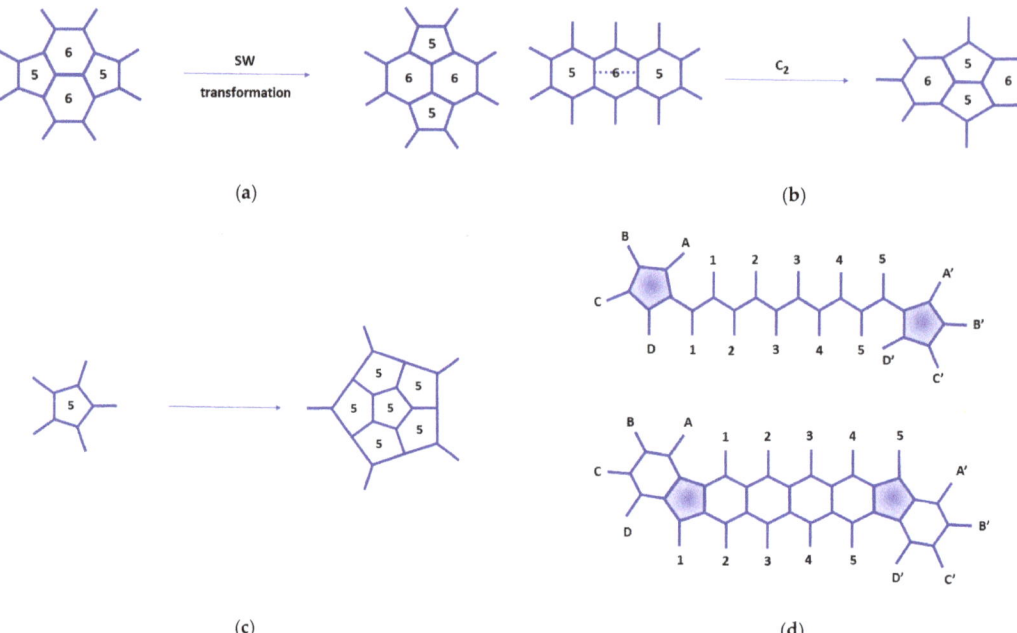

Figure 11. The Stone-Wale transformation of the isomers (**a**) and the growth of the fullerenes by insertion of a C_2 dimer (**b**), of pentagonal (**c**) or hexagonal (**d**) rings.

For a given Schlegel diagram or connectivity matrix, with specified internode distances, the coordinates of the nodes can be determined by the distance geometry algorithms [61–63]. The procedure is capable to give the Cartesian coordinates of the fourth vertex (denoted by the index 0 in Figure 12) with desired distances from the other three neighbor vertices 1–3 which for the Cartesian coordinates are already determined. In order to satisfy all the internode demanded distances the algorithm can be iteratively applied for all the nodes. An alternative procedure for a known Schlegel diagram consists of successive assembling of the rings, which have edges of lengths corresponding to the desired internode distances. The procedure starts with three assembled rings that share one node and continue by adding rings of appropriate size along the spiral path.

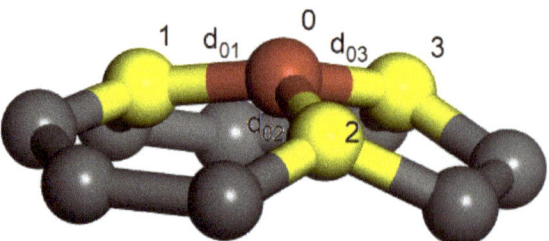

Figure 12. The definition of the interatomic distances d_{oi}, between a three-coordinated node (index, $I = 0$) and its neighboring nodes ($I = 1$–3).

3. Applications to Architecture and Construction Engineering

The concepts and mathematical methods presented in the previous section are very useful for the design of shell structures with topologies characterized by three-coordinated nodes, as in the case of the carbon nanosystems. The linear, spiral, and junction tube-like substructures can be used as connection elements and supporting poles for shell structures. The fullerene and cone curved-type structures can be used as components of the shell structures. The transformation procedures presented in Figure 11 can be used for the redesign of shell structures in order to control the shape of the shell and the uniform distribution of the mechanical tension along the shell, for structure stabilization.

For a fixed contour of the grid shell on the ground, a patch of compatible fullerene can be chosen. A procedure for the completion of the fullerene piece with the given contour, as for the filling curve, can be applied by inserting new vertices and flipping edges to obtain a triangulation [64]. Depending on the density of these triangles near the contour and their topology, the triangular patches are merged into a coarse-grained grid of pentagons and hexagons, and occasionally other types of cycles. To control stress within the grid vertices network, nodes are displaced in space to ensure specific inter-vertices distances. The beams that are oriented along the edges of the fullerene-type structure form the shell structure.

The fullerene-type shell structures can be treated in terms of a very simple particle-based model such as the *Elastic Network Model* (*ENM*), where the nodes of the structure are represented by particles that interact through elastic forces [65,66] along the grid edges (see Figure 13). ENM was developed as a simulation tool for the study of protein flexibility by coarse-graining the vibrational normal modes. It reduces the computational effort by replacing the interatomic force calculation with a simple elastic interaction [67,68]. Thus, the elastic energy of the shell structure is

$$E_{elast} = \sum_{i<j=1}^{N} \gamma_{ij} \left(\left| \vec{r}_{ij} \right| - d_{ij} \right)^2 \tag{4}$$

where N is the total number of nodes, γ_{ij} and d_{ij} are the elastic constants and the length of the beam that connect the nodes i and j, $\left|\vec{r}_{ij}\right|$ is the current distance between the nodes i and j. The parameter $\left|\vec{r}_{ij}\right| - d_{ij}$ represents the deviation from the length of the beam. The deformation strain or longitudinal strain of the edge i–j is defined as $\varepsilon_{ij} = \frac{\left|\vec{r}_{ij}\right| - d_{ij}}{d_{ij}}$ and it has negative and positive values indicating the beam contraction and elongation, respectively. In our model, we consider only the elastic deformation of the beams. For the case of plastic deformation, the Finite Element Method has to be applied.

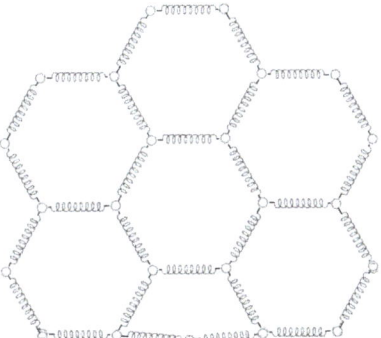

Figure 13. The equivalence of a shell structure to an elastic network of springs with the same connectivity matrix as the original structure.

The *ENM* has to be modified by applying some external forces (gravitation, mass of the deposited ice or dust on the shell, waves induced by wind, rain or earthquakes) on nodes. The ground-supported particles are considered solidly fixed to the support and follow its motion due to the waves generated by earthquakes or soil motion such as sliding by the interaction energy

$$E(|\vec{r}_i - \vec{r}_{i\perp}|) = \begin{cases} \infty, & |\vec{r}_i - \vec{r}_{i\perp}| \geq 2d_{i0} \\ \sum_{i<j=1}^{N} \gamma_{i0}(|\vec{r}_{i0}| - d_{i0})^2, & |\vec{r}_i - \vec{r}_{i\perp}| < 2d_{i0} \end{cases} \quad (5)$$

where γ_{i0} is the elastic constant of the beam connected to the ground and d_{i0} is the maximum allowed distance between the ground-supported nodes and the support.

The static gravitational forces are considered through the mass of the beams and their connection nodes and the additional mass of the deposited materials on the shell. It is expressed as $\vec{F}_i^g = m_i \vec{g}$, where m_i is the mass of node i and $\vec{g} = g\vec{k}$ is the gravitational acceleration, with g—the gravitational constant and $\vec{k} = (0\ 0\ 1)^T$—the direction of the gravity, which is chosen to be vertical. The corresponding gravitation energy of the node at the high h_i is $E_i^g = m_i g h_i$. The mass of a node is given by its own mass m_{0i}, plus half of the mass m_{ij} of the beams that are connected by the nodes i and j, and the eventual mass of the deposited material as ice on the i–j beam. The mass m_{ij} is equally distributed to the two nodes i and j. Thus, the mass of each node i is $m_i = m_{0i} + \frac{1}{2} \sum_{j}^{i-neighb} m_{ij}$, where the summation is over the nodes j that are neighbor nodes of i. The nodes are treated as virtual particles.

The temperature effects, due to the external environment or sunlight, can be considered through the thermal linear expansion coefficient α, with an additional contribution to the deformation of each beam $\Delta\varepsilon_{ij} = |\vec{r}_{ij}|\alpha T$, where T is the temperature. In this simplified model, the effects of the beam's profile are ignored, and the beams are subjected only to axial load. The effects of the beam's bending can be considered by discretizing the beam into additional particles that interact through the elastic forces. In order to also treat the bending and twisting of the beams, the model can be improved by considering the contributions to the potential energy of the bonding and dihedral angles formed by the neighboring nodes, respectively:

$$E_{bend} = \sum_{j=1}^{N} \sum_{j<k}^{i-neighb} \gamma_{ijk}\left(\theta_{ijk} - \theta_{ijk}^o\right)^2 \quad (6)$$

$$E_{torsion} = \sum_{j<k}^{neighbours\ j-neighb} \sum_{i}^{k-neighb} \sum_{l} \gamma_{ijkl}\left(\phi_{ijkl} - \phi_{ijkl}^o\right)^2 \quad (7)$$

The bending and torsion angles θ_{ijk}^o and ϕ_{ijkl}^o correspond to the equilibrium configuration of the beams, and the parameters γ_{ijk} and γ_{ijkl} characterize the elastic contribution of the bending and torsional distortions.

Usually, the beams are made from the same material, and the elastic, bending and torsion constants are related to Young's modulus E and shear modulus G as $\gamma_{ij} = \frac{EA}{L}$, $\gamma_{ijk} = \frac{EI}{L}$ and $\gamma_{ijkl} = \frac{GJ}{L}$ [69], where L and A are the length and cross-section of the beam, and I and J are the cross-section and polar moment of inertia, respectively. If the beams have very similar geometries, then L, A, I and J can be considered the same for any beam. Therefore, the elastic, bending and torsion energies of the shell structure are directly related to the connectivity matrix, which reflects the shell topology.

The potential energy of the shell structure is given by the summation of all the components that act on each virtual particle $E(\{\vec{r}_j\}_{j=1..N})$. The force that acts on the nodes $i = 1, N$ is:

$$\vec{F}_i = -\frac{d}{d\vec{r}_i} E(\{\vec{r}_j\}_{j=1..N}) \quad (8)$$

The virial stress of particle i with the Cartesian components $\alpha, \beta = x, y, z$ is defined as [70,71]

$$\sigma_i^{\alpha\beta} = -\left\langle \frac{1}{V_i}\left(m_i v_i^\alpha v_i^\beta + \sum_{j<i} f_{ij}^\alpha r_{ij}^\beta\right)\right\rangle \quad (9)$$

where V_i and m_i are the characteristic volume and the mass of the particle i, $v_i^\alpha, f_{ij}^\alpha$ and r_{ij}^α are the components along the direction $\alpha = x, y, z$ of the velocity of i, of the force and distance vector between the i and j particles, respectively. Due to the local nature of the interactions, the considered particles j are the neighbor particles of i. The $\alpha, \beta = x, y, z$ components of the total virial stress are $\sigma^{\alpha\beta} = \frac{1}{V}\sum_{i=1}^N V_i \sigma_i^{\alpha\beta}$, where $V = \sum_{i=1}^N V_i$ is the total volume of the particles. The stiffness tensor $C_{\gamma\delta}^{\alpha\beta}$ describes the stress tensor in terms of the strain tensor

$$\sigma^{\alpha\beta} = C_{\gamma\delta}^{\alpha\beta} \varepsilon^{\gamma\delta} \quad (10)$$

which is the generalized Hooke's law.

On each node of the beam mesh the local macroscopic normal and tangential components, P_i^N and P_i^T can be calculated as the projections along the normal and in-plane components of the plane determined by the three neighbor particles of the considered particle located on node i [72]

$$\gamma_i = h_{i\perp}\left[P_i^N - P_i^T\right] \quad (11)$$

where $h_{i\perp}$ is the distance from the particle located on node i to the plane determined by the three neighbor nodes.

The static calculations are essential for the design of the equilibrium configurations through the determination of the node positions [73], in the absence of the external forces exerted by wind, rain and earthquakes. The internode distances are the lengths of beams that assure tension in the structure with a value below the breaking value specified in material properties databases [74]. Thus, the length of each individual beam element is determined in order to uniformly distribute the tension over the shell structure. The equilibrium configurations can be used to determine the stresses and strains in the shell structures when external forces are applied to the structures.

For the equilibrium configuration $\{\vec{r}_i^0\}_{i=1..N}$ of the shell system, determined by the geometry equilibration, the forces on each node of the system are negligible $\vec{F}_i = 0, i = 1, N$. Considering some small displacements about the equilibrium positions $\{\vec{r}_i^0\}_{i=1..N}$, the potential energy of the system can be expanded in a Taylor series

$$E(\{\vec{r}_i\}_{i=1..N}) = E(\{\vec{r}_i^0\}_{i=1..N}) + \frac{1}{2}\sum_{i<j}\vec{r}_i^T H_{ij} \vec{r}_j \quad (12)$$

where $H_{ij} = \frac{\partial^2 E}{\partial \vec{r}_i \partial \vec{r}_j}$ is the second-derivative or Hessian matrix of the potential energy. The full spectra of vibration frequencies of the shell structures can be determined by applying the lattice vibrations harmonic theory. The low-frequency vibration motions describe the shell structure deformation as a hole and it can be used for identification of the areas with a high amplitude deformation. The high vibration modes are localized vibrations on some nodes and are related to the high deformation of the beams that connect those nodes. The vibration spectra depend on the topology of the shell structure. Thus, some dangerous vibration modes that are responsible for the large structural deformation can be attenuated or even annihilated by modification of the shell topology. The investigation of the propagation of waves caused by wind, rain and earthquakes can be regarded as perturbations of vibration modes specific to the investigated shell structure.

The numeric dynamic simulations of the particles under the influence of the external forces can be performed by time integration of Newton's second law using similar algorithms as in Molecular Dynamics methods. The time propagation of the particles can be conducted by time discretization with the timestep Δt of Newton's equation of motion, using the Verlet algorithm [75]

$$\vec{r}_i(t + \Delta t) = 2\vec{r}_i(t) - \vec{r}_i(t - \Delta t) + \vec{a}_i(t)\Delta t^2 \quad (13)$$

or using a derived algorithm that allows the velocities calculation at the next time step, called the velocity Verlet algorithm

$$\vec{r}_i(t + \Delta t) = \vec{r}_i(t) + \vec{v}_i(t)\Delta t + \vec{a}_i(t)\Delta t^2 \quad (14)$$

$$\vec{v}_i(t + \Delta t) = \vec{v}_{ii}(t) + \frac{1}{2}(\vec{a}_i(t) + \vec{a}_i(t + \Delta t))\Delta t \quad (15)$$

where $\vec{r}_i(t)$, $\vec{v}_i(t)$ and $\vec{a}_i(t) = \vec{F}_i(t)/m_i$ are the vectors of positions, velocities and accelerations at time t. The timestep Δt is chosen large enough in order to simulate longer evolution of the system, but not too large, in order to conserve the total energy of the system. The initial structure must be obtained by a static equilibration, and the initial velocities are obtained under the influence of external forces.

Knowing the coordinates of the nodes or the node's connectivity in the fullerene-type shell structure, the length and thickness of the beams that form the shell, the elastic parameters of the beams, and the applied forces on the shell, the simulation based on the Finite Strip Method allows the cross-section elastic buckling analysis [76]. The software CUFSM [77] has an interface to generate the input files with cross-sectional imperfections based on CUFSM buckling modes for the code ABAQUS [78].

Various computational chemistry software can be used to produce the nanostructures and save the atoms' coordinates in files of type pdb (Protein Date Base) or xyz (Cartesian coordinates). Such files can be imported into CAD codes as Blender [4] allows, together with the add-ons molblend [79] or atomic [80], the conversion of the nanostructures to a macroscopic object by size rescaling and automatic meshing of the edges of the fullerene- or tube-like objects (see Figure 14). Blender is a free program, oriented towards 3D design, rendering, meshing, sculpting and artistic modeling. It is able to perform some simulations and animations, considering various forces.

In FEM, the deformation of each finite element of the discretized beams determines stress within the grid [81,82]. By its scripting capabilities, Blender can be involved in FEM, but for more advanced simulations, the Blender data can be exported to more specialized software. Thus, the code Blender can be used to create 3D objects and meshes and then export them as .iges or .stp files to Salome-Mecha [83], which is a platform for numerical simulation and has more advanced FEM capabilities. Blender meshes can be exported to Rhino 3D [6] in a variety of formats, as .ply (stanford), .stl, .fbx or .obj (wavefront). Alternatively, an add-on [84] developed for Blender can be used for such conversions. The meshes can be exported to slicer applications such as Cura [85], which can prepare the 3D models for printing with a 3D printer. The UV Blender function can be used for mapping the 3D coordinates into 2D coordinates and unwrapping the 3D objects into planar objects.

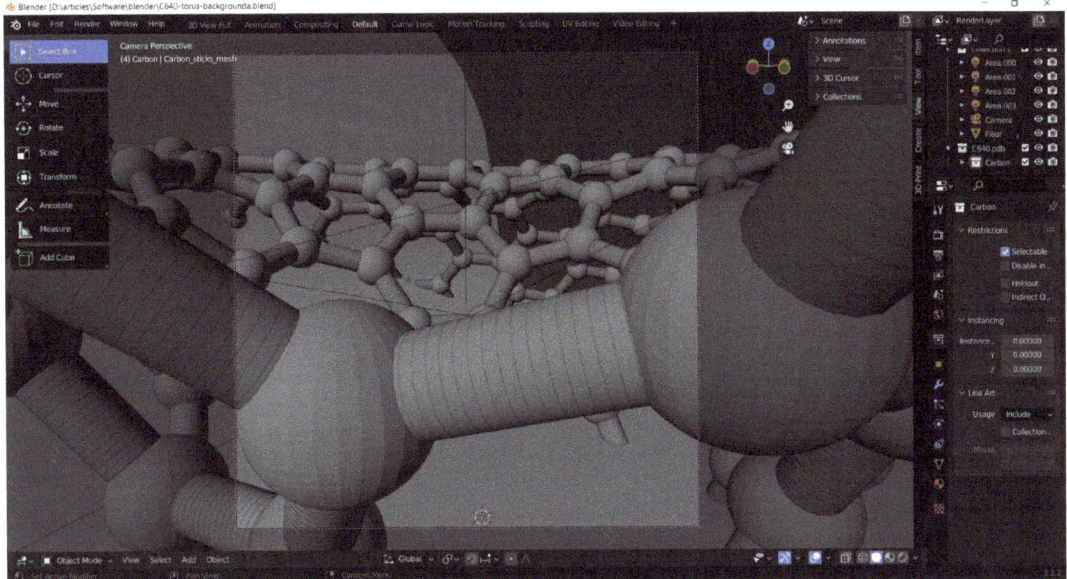

Figure 14. The meshing produced by the *Blender* program for the nodes and edges of a torus that are imported from a pdb-format file.

4. Conclusions

In the present paper, we attempt to connect two distinct human activity fields, nanochemistry and architecture, which have different aims and address different space and time scales, but they approach similar lattice systems with 2D topologies. The topologies of the carbon-based nanosystems are characterized by nodes that are three-coordinated and lower compared with those of the shell structures. Thus, the nanostructures are characterized by a lower density of edges per node, which means fewer complex grids to cover the same curved surface.

The various mathematical tools developed in the framework of the graph theory and the computing geometry for the description of carbon-type nanosystems and their stability characterization are presented, which might be of use for the design of free-shaped structures in architecture and construction engineering. The enumeration and building methods for the various nanostructures and their use for the design of the shell structures are presented. A particle-based simulation method is proposed for the investigation of the shell systems by the modification of the Elastic Network Model. The simulation method can be applied for the determination of the equilibrium configuration and the dynamics of the shell structures under the influence of external factors such as wind, rain or earthquakes. Thus, the possible scenarios for the shell structures collapsing can be investigated.

Various software products used in computing chemistry, computer graphics, and computer-aided design as well as the conversion data between such software are discussed. Thus, a framework for software from the fields of nanochemistry, architecture, and construction is established, which opens up the opportunity for knowledge transfer from nanochemistry to architecture and construction.

Author Contributions: V.C. and M.G. have conceived of the presented idea. A.N. designed the nanostructures and performed their geometrical optimizations. S.C. contributed knowledge about architecture problematics and the current mathematical methods used by architects. All authors wrote the manuscript, discussed the results and contributed to the final manuscript. All authors have read and agreed to the published version of the manuscript.

Funding: Politehnica University of Bucharest assured financial support for the publication of the present article.

Institutional Review Board Statement: Not applicable.

Informed Consent Statement: Not applicable.

Data Availability Statement: Not applicable.

Acknowledgments: The authors gratefully acknowledge the computing time granted by the Institute of Physical Chemistry "Ilie Murgulescu" on the *HPC-ICF* infrastructure that was developed in the frame of the Capacities Project 84 CpI/13.09.2007—National Authority for Scientific Research, Bucharest, Romania.

Conflicts of Interest: There are no conflicts of interest.

References

1. Zeiss Planetarium. Berlin. Available online: https://www.freeimageslive.co.uk/free_stock_image/zeiss-planetarium-jpg (accessed on 7 October 2022).
2. Neuhaeuser, S.; Mielert, F.; Rippmann, M.; Sobek, W. Architectural and structural investigation of complex grid systems. In *Spatial Structures–Permanent and Temporary*; IASS Symposium: Shanghai, China, 2010.
3. Available online: https://graphisoft.com/solutions/archicad (accessed on 7 October 2022).
4. Available online: https://www.blender.org (accessed on 7 October 2022).
5. Available online: https://www.grasshopper3d.com (accessed on 7 October 2022).
6. Available online: https://www.rhino3d.com (accessed on 7 October 2022).
7. Available online: https://www.sketchup.com (accessed on 7 October 2022).
8. Available online: https://www.ansys.com (accessed on 7 October 2022).
9. Available online: https://www.autodesk.com (accessed on 7 October 2022).
10. Available online: https://autofem.com (accessed on 7 October 2022).
11. Available online: https://www.3ds.com/fr/produits-et-services/catia (accessed on 7 October 2022).
12. Available online: https://www.dlubal.com (accessed on 7 October 2022).
13. Available online: https://www.freecadweb.org (accessed on 7 October 2022).
14. Available online: https://www.kicad.org (accessed on 7 October 2022).
15. Available online: https://www.openfoam.com (accessed on 7 October 2022).
16. Available online: http://pyacad.sourceforge.net (accessed on 7 October 2022).
17. Available online: http://www.solidworks.com (accessed on 7 October 2022).
18. Klein, D. Mathematical Chemistry! Is It? And if so, What Is It? *Hyle Int. J. Philos. Chem.* **2013**, *19*, 35–85.
19. Sintunavarat, W.; Turab, A. A unified fixed point approach to study the existence of solutions for a class of fractional boundary value problems arising in a chemical graph theory. *PLoS ONE* **2022**, *17*, e0270148. [CrossRef] [PubMed]
20. Baldonedo, J.; Fernández, J.R.; Segade, A.; Suárez, S. CMMSE: Numerical analysis of a chemical targeting model. *J. Mathem. Chem.* **2022**, *60*, 2125–2138. [CrossRef]
21. Rajpoot, A.; Selvaganesh, L. Study of Bounds and Extremal Graphs of Symmetric Division Degree Index for Bicyclic Graphs with Perfect Matching. *Iranian J. Math. Chem.* **2022**, *13*, 145–165.
22. Falcao, E.H.L.; Wudl, F. Carbon allotropes: Beyond graphite and diamond. *J. Chem. Technol. Biotechnol.* **2007**, *82*, 524–531. [CrossRef]
23. Tiwari, S.K.; Kumar, V.; Huczko, A.; Oraon, R.; De Adhikari, A.; Nayak, G.C. Magical Allotropes of Carbon: Prospects and Applications. *Crit. Rev. Solid State Mat. Sci.* **2016**, *41*, 257–317. [CrossRef]
24. Burian, A.; Dore, J.C.; Jurkiewicz, K. Structural studies of carbons by neutron and x-ray scattering. *Rep. Prog. Phys.* **2019**, *82*, 016501. [CrossRef]
25. Rao, C.N.R.; Seshadri, R.; Govindaraj, A.; Sen, R. Fullerenes, nanotubes, onions and related carbon structures. *Mat. Sci. Eng.* **1995**, *R15*, 209–262. [CrossRef]
26. Matar, S.F.; Solozhenko, V.L. Ultra-hard rhombohedral carbon by crystal chemistry and ab initio investigations. *J. Solid State Chem.* **2021**, *302*, 122354. [CrossRef]
27. Boehm, H.P.; Clauss, A.; Fischer, G.O.; Hofmann, U. Das Adsorptionsverhalten sehr dünner Kohlenstoff-Folien. *Z. Anorg. Allg. Chem.* **1962**, *316*, 119–127. [CrossRef]
28. Novoselov, K.S.; Geim, A.K.; Morozov, S.V.; Jiang, D.; Zhang, Y.; Dubonos, S.V.; Grigorieva, I.V.; Firsov, A.A. Electric Field Effect in Atomically Thin Carbon Films. *Science* **2004**, *306*, 666–669. [CrossRef] [PubMed]
29. Schultz, H.P. Topological organic chemistry. polyhedranes and prismanes. *J. Org. Chem.* **1965**, *30*, 1361–1364. [CrossRef]
30. Iijima, S. Synthesis of carbon nanotubes. *Nature* **1991**, *354*, 56–58. [CrossRef]
31. Lee, R.K.F.; Cox, B.J.; Hill, J.M. The geometric structure of single-walled nanotubes. *Nanoscale* **2010**, *2*, 859–872. [CrossRef] [PubMed]

32. Balaban, A.; Klein, D.; Liu, X. Graphitic cones. *Carbon* **1994**, *32*, 357–359. [CrossRef]
33. Naess, S.N.; Elgsaeter, A.; Geir, H.; Knudsen, K.D. Carbon nanocones: Wall structure and morphology. *Sci. Technol. Adv. Mat.* **2009**, *10*, 065002. [CrossRef]
34. Klein, D.J.; Balaban, T. The Eight Classes of Positive-Curvature Graphitic Nanocones. *J. Chem. Inf. Model* **2006**, *46*, 307–320. [CrossRef]
35. Available online: http://www.jcrystal.com/products/wincnt/index.htm (accessed on 7 October 2022).
36. Available online: https://www.ch.ic.ac.uk/motm/spirala.html (accessed on 7 October 2022).
37. Kroto, H.W.; Heath, J.R.; O'Brien, S.C.; Curl, R.F.; Smalley, R.E. C60: Buckminsterfullerene. *Nature* **1985**, *318*, 162–163. [CrossRef]
38. Killblane, C.; Gao, Y.; Shao, N.; Zeng, X.C. Search for Lowest-Energy Nonclassical Fullerenes III: C22. *J. Phys. Chem.* **2009**, *113*, 8839–8844. [CrossRef]
39. Fournier-Viger, P.; He, G.; Cheng, C.; Li, J.; Zhou, M.; Lin, C.-H.J.; Yun, U. A survey of pattern mining in dynamic graphs. *WIREs Data Min. Knowl. Discov.* **2020**, *10*, e1372-30. [CrossRef]
40. Brinkmann, G.; Goedgebeur, J.; Mélot, H.; Coolsaet, K. House of Graphs: A database of interesting graphs. *Discret. Appl. Math.* **2013**, *161*, 311–314. [CrossRef]
41. Cioslowski, J. Note on the asymptotic isomer count of large fullerenes. *J. Math. Chem.* **2014**, *52*, 1–5. [CrossRef]
42. Xue, W.; Wang, H.; Liu, G.; Meng, L.; Xiang, S.; Ma, G.; Li, W. Matrix description of the complete topology of three-dimensional cells. *Sci. Rep.* **2016**, *6*, 25877. [CrossRef]
43. Ziegler, G.M. Schlegel diagrams for 4-polytopes. In *Lectures on Polytopes*, 1st ed.; Axler, S., Gehring, F.W., Ribet, K.A., Eds.; Springer: New York, NY, USA, 1995; Volume 152, pp. 127–148.
44. Kroto, H.W. The stability of the fullerenes Cn, with n = 24; 28; 32; 36; 50; 60 and 70. *Nature* **1987**, *329*, 529–531. [CrossRef]
45. Suh, S.H.; Bae, J.Y.; Jeong, S.W.; Park, K.K.; Bakó, I.; Chihaia, V. The effect of complementary units on the stability of higher fullerenes C84. *J. Optoelectron. Adv. Mat.* **2010**, *12*, 1139–1146.
46. 't Hart, M. The projection point geodesic grid algorithm for meshing the sphere. *J. Comput. Phys.* **2022**, *454*, 110993. [CrossRef]
47. Marusic, D. Hamilton Cycles and Paths in Fullerenes. *J. Chem. Inf. Model.* **2007**, *47*, 732–736. [CrossRef] [PubMed]
48. Ilić, A.; Stevanović, D. Constructions of hamiltonian graphs with bounded degree and diameter O(logn). *Appl. Mathem. Lett.* **2009**, *22*, 1715–1720. [CrossRef]
49. Manolopulos, D.E.; May, J.C.; Down, S.E. Theoretical studies of the fullerenes: C34 to C70. *Chem. Phys. Lett.* **1991**, *181*, 105. [CrossRef]
50. Manolopulos, D.E.; Fowler, P.W. A fullerene without a spiral. *Chem. Phys. Lett.* **1993**, *204*, 1–7. [CrossRef]
51. Brinkmann, G.; Goedgebeur, J.; McKay, B.D. The smallest fullerene without a spiral. *Chem. Phys. Lett.* **2012**, *522*, 54. [CrossRef]
52. Cvetković, D.; Fowler, P.; Rowlinson, P.; Stevanović, D. Constructing fullerene graphs from their eigenvalues and angles. *Lin. Alg. Appl.* **2002**, *356*, 37–56. [CrossRef]
53. Brinkmann, G.; McKay, B.D. Construction of planar triangulations with minimum degree 5. *Discret. Math.* **2005**, *301*, 147–163. [CrossRef]
54. Available online: http://cs.anu.edu.au/~{}bdm/plantri (accessed on 1 April 2022).
55. Myrvold, W.; Bultena, B.; Daugherty, S.; Debroni, B.; Girn, S.; Minchenko, M.; Woodcock, J.; Fowler, P.W. FuiGui: A graphical user interface for investigating conjectures about fullerenes. *MATCH Commun. Math. Comput. Chem.* **2007**, *58*, 403–422.
56. Schwerdtfeger, P.; Wirz, L.; Avery, J. Program Fullerene: A Software Package for Constructing and Analyzing Structures of Regular Fullerenes. *J. Comput. Chem.* **2013**, *34*, 1508–1526. [CrossRef]
57. Stone, A.J.; Wales, D.J. Theoretical studies of icosahedral C60 and some related species. *Chem. Phys. Lett.* **1986**, *128*, 501–503. [CrossRef]
58. Endo, M.; Kroto, H.W. Formation of carbon nanofibers. *J. Phys. Chem.* **1992**, *96*, 6941–6944. [CrossRef]
59. Xie, Z.-X.; Liu, Z.-Y.; Wang, C.-R.; Huang, R.-B.; Lin, F.-C.; Zheng, L.-S. Formation and Coalescence of Fullerene Ions from Direct Laser Vaporization. *J. Chem. Soc. Faraday Trans.* **1995**, *91*, 987–990. [CrossRef]
60. Zhao, Y.; Smalley, R.E.; Yakobson, B.I. Coalescence of fullerene cages: Topology, energetics, and molecular dynamics simulation. *Phys. Rev.* **2002**, *66*, 195409. [CrossRef]
61. Dong, Q.; Wu, Z. A linear-time algorithm for solving the molecular distance geometry problem with exact inter-atomic distances. *J. Global Optimiz.* **2002**, *22*, 365–375. [CrossRef]
62. Liberti, L.; Lavor, C.; Maculan, N.A. Branch-and-Prune algorithm for the Molecular Distance Geometry Problem. *Int. Trans. Oper. Res.* **2008**, *15*, 1–17. [CrossRef]
63. Lavor, C.; Alves, R. Recent Advances on Oriented Conformal Geometric Algebra Applied to Molecular Distance Geometry. *Syst. Patterns Data Eng. Geom. Calc.* **2021**, *13*, 19–30.
64. Liepa, P. Filling Holes in Meshes. In *Eurographics Symposium on Geometry Processing, Proceedings of the 2003 Eurographics Association/ACM SIGGRAPH Symposium on Geometry Processing*; Kobbelt, L., Schroeder, P., Hoppe, H., Eds.; ACM Digital Library: New York, NY, USA, 2003; pp. 200–206.
65. Caliskan, E.; Kirca, M. Tensile characteristics of boron nanotubes by using reactive molecular dynamics simulations. *Comput. Mat. Sci.* **2022**, *209*, 111368. [CrossRef]
66. Le, M.Q.; Mortazavi, B.; Rabczuk, T. Mechanical properties of borophene films: A reactive molecular dynamics investigation. *Nanotechnology* **2016**, *27*, 445709. [CrossRef]

67. Tirion, M.M. Large Amplitude Elastic Motions in Proteins from a Single-Parameter. Atomic Analysis. *Phys. Rev. Lett.* **1996**, *77*, 1905–1908. [CrossRef]
68. Sinitskiy, A.V.; Voth, G.A. Coarse-graining of proteins based on elastic network models. *Chem. Phys.* **2013**, *422*, 165–174. [CrossRef]
69. Li, C.; Chou, T.-W. A structural mechanics approach for the analysis of carbon nanotubes. *Int. J. Solids Struct.* **2003**, *40*, 2487–2499. [CrossRef]
70. Tsai, D.H. The virial theorem and stress calculation in molecular dynamics. *J. Chem. Phys.* **1979**, *70*, 1375–1382. [CrossRef]
71. Liu, B.; Qiu, X. How to Compute the Atomic Stress Objectively? *J. Comput. Theor. Nanosci.* **2009**, *6*, 1081–1089. [CrossRef]
72. De Miguel, E.; Jackson, G. The nature of the calculation of the pressure in molecular simulations of continuous models from volume perturbations. *J. Chem. Phys.* **2006**, *125*, 164109. [CrossRef]
73. Pisanski, T.; Plestenjak, B.; Graovac, A. NiceGraph Program and its applications in chemistry. *Croat. Chem. Acta.* **1995**, *68*, 283–289.
74. MatWeb—Online Materials Information Resource. Available online: https://matweb.com (accessed on 7 October 2022).
75. Verlet, L. Computer "Experiments" on Classical Fluids. I. Thermodynamical Properties of Lennard-Jones Molecules. *Phys. Rev.* **1967**, *159*, 98–103. [CrossRef]
76. Zveryayev, Y.M. A consistent theory of thin elastic shells. *J. Appl. Mathem. Mech.* **2016**, *80*, 409–420. [CrossRef]
77. Available online: www.ce.jhu.edu/bschafer/cufsm (accessed on 7 October 2022).
78. Available online: https://www.3ds.com/products-services/simulia/products/abaqus (accessed on 7 October 2022).
79. Available online: https://remington.pro/software/blender/atomic (accessed on 7 October 2022).
80. Available online: https://github.com/floaltvater/molblend (accessed on 7 October 2022).
81. Jones, R.F., Jr. A Curved Finite Element for General Thin Shell Structures. *Nucl. Eng. Design* **1978**, *48*, 415–425. [CrossRef]
82. Rikards, R.B.; Goldmanis, M.V. A Curved Finite Element of Revolution Shells after Timoshenko's Shear Model. *ZAMM—J. Appl. Mathem. Mech.* **1985**, *65*, 427–435. [CrossRef]
83. Available online: https://www.salome-platform.org (accessed on 7 October 2022).
84. Available online: https://github.com/ALanMAttano/Blender_4_Rhino (accessed on 7 October 2022).
85. Available online: https://github.com/Ultimaker/Cura (accessed on 7 October 2022).

MDPI
St. Alban-Anlage 66
4052 Basel
Switzerland
Tel. +41 61 683 77 34
Fax +41 61 302 89 18
www.mdpi.com

Mathematics Editorial Office
E-mail: mathematics@mdpi.com
www.mdpi.com/journal/mathematics

www.ingramcontent.com/pod-product-compliance
Lightning Source LLC
LaVergne TN
LVHW070430100526
838202LV00014B/1570